DAVID A. H

UNVEILING

THE

MYSTERIES

OF THE

LAST DAYS

Systematic Prophecy from Genesis to Revelation

Tate Publishing & Enterprises

Published by Tate Publishing & Enterprises, LLC
127 E. Trade Center Terrace | Mustang, Oklahoma 73064 USA
1.888.361.9473 | www.tatepublishing.com

Tate Publishing is committed to excellence in the publishing industry. The company reflects the philosophy established by the founders, based on Psalm 68:11, *"The Lord gave the word and great was the company of those who published it."*

Book design copyright © 2010 by Tate Publishing, LLC. All rights reserved.
Cover design by Amber Gulilat
Interior design by Stefanie Rooney

Published in the United States of America

ISBN: 978-1-61566-876-2
Religion, Christian Theology, Eschatology
10.03.10

UNVEILING

THE

MYSTERIES

OF THE

LAST DAYS

Dedication

This book is dedicated to my wife, Susan, whose support, love, and encouragement made this manuscript possible. This book is also dedicated to my sons, Michael and Stephen, who have been blessings to their parents, sounding boards for much of this material, and sources of encouragement.

Table of Contents

Preface

Almost daily, humanity's fears fill the news. Speculations abound about super tsunamis, mega earthquakes, wars, terrorism, weapons of mass destruction, meteorites, global warming and cooling, overpopulation, localized and global famine, new potent forms of pestilence, water shortages, pollution, endangered species, ecological disasters, the consumption of all fossil fuels and other "limited" natural resources, destruction of forests, and so many more. The bleakest of these (e.g., nuclear holocaust) are so terrifyingly catastrophic that, for most people, it is simply impossible to imagine life continuing beyond them. It is not unusual for people to compare these often-sensationalized doomsday or "end of the world" scenarios to biblical events or even give them biblical references. Unfortunately, these references do not convey the Bible's promise of a thousand years of unbridled peace and prosperity but instead focus on the hopelessness of the end of the earth and all humanity.

Incredibly, the Bible addresses many of these fears in often surprising ways. For example, there is apparently at least a thousand years' supply of fossil fuel still available, and the earth will provide the necessities of life (food, raiment, and water) for orders of magnitudes more people than it currently does. On the other hand, many doomsday scenarios appear to play out during the seven-year tribulation (the transition period just prior to the thousand years of prosperity) but without the earth's or humanity's predicted total destruction. Amazingly, the Bible's descriptions seem to exceed even the most pessimistic projections; but even then, half the world's population still survives this horrible period.

These are just a few of the insights resulting from researching this manuscript, which was borne out of a simple desire to help Bible students discover and correlate the Bible's many disparate prophetic clues. The basic goals were not particularly ambitious: layout a basic framework to help casual prophecy students understand how different prophetic events relate to each other and gather references from throughout the Bible to gain fuller, richer pictures of each event than is possible from relying on a single passage.

The first research step was classifying every biblical passage in a database according to its possible prophetic timeframes. From there, timeframe passages were sorted and classified by specific prophetic events, the reference's strength, and possible event sequences. Next, prophetic event passages were searched for inconsistencies with current interpretations. Interpretation issues were resolved through additional research; interpretation refinements; or when necessary, new interpretations based on all available information from these passages. Surprisingly, this process led to the discovery of many unexpected prophetic events (e.g., Jesus' coronation), the rejection of several previously accepted interpretations (e.g., the Jews' place of refuge following the abomination of desolation), and many interpretation refinements (e.g., the timing of the abomination of desolation).

This process often presents many challenges as clear, straightforward readings of the text produce apparent paradoxes or force symbolic versus literal discussions. For example, the doctrine of the Holy Trinity is a well-known paradox that sparks much debate. How can it be that there is only one God while at the same time he has three personages: Father, Son, and Holy Spirit? While inconceivable and unexplainable, there it is throughout both Old and New Testaments, and many prophetic events are virtually incomprehensible without acknowledging this paradox.

The sheer volume of Scripture referenced made directly quoting it impractical; however, I encourage you to have a Bible handy to look up and read the referenced scriptures. Additionally, Bible prophecy is a dynamic field. To get additional information, updates, a companion poster, and additional study material, please see my Web site at www.revelationroadmap.com. Finally, it is my personal belief that we have barely tapped into the prophetic details that God has so freely made plainly visible in his Word. For this reason, this work generally avoids considering any hidden meanings in the Bible (e.g., hidden Bible codes) or the work of extra-biblical prognosticators such as Nostradamus in favor of detailed biblical analysis. It is my sincere hope that you will enjoy discovering the secrets of prophecy as much as I have and that this will trigger a deeper love of Scripture.

A Prophetic Primer

From their inception, the prophecies of the Bible have both fascinated and mystified people. Their authority, accuracy, and longevity set them apart from fortunetellers, mystics, and any other prognosticators. While their visions span thousands of years, from antiquity to beyond the end of the world, people's greatest prophetic interest focuses on the tantalizing clues of the much-anticipated—and dreaded—"end times." Often raising more questions than they answer, end-time prophecies frequently shroud their true meanings within complex symbols, leaving their interpretation to only the most diligent Bible students. They confuse many by simultaneously warning of cataclysmic wars while promising everlasting peace and prosperity. End-time images permeate modern culture, as many key end-time events, people, and symbols have integrated themselves into popular entertainment and language. For example, who has not heard of Armageddon or the number of the beast (666)? After all, popular movies have often featured fictionalized versions of these and other prophetic events and images. The Omen movies drew upon prophesies of the antichrist, the four horsemen of the apocalypse, the whore of Babylon, and Jesus' return. The movie Armageddon conveys the possible end of the world by drawing on the name of the assembly place for the last and greatest battle of humanity. These and many other references to end-time prophecies in movies, news reports, and documentaries heighten awareness while simultaneously blurring the actual referenced events. These media confuse Armageddon with the end of the world, distort the antichrist into a number of strange and hideous egomaniacs, and paint Jesus' glorious return as heroic humans leading hopelessly outmanned armies in desperate struggles against wicked empires or impending disasters. Careful examination of both Old and New Testament texts reveals Armageddon is actually a watershed ushering in a thousand years of peace and prosperity; Jesus Christ personally returns from heaven and single-handedly subdues all armies fighting in this battle; and the antichrist is a disarmingly charming man with great persuasive power.

These are just a few pieces of the end-time puzzle, which, like any puzzle, yields clearer pictures with each piece's discovery and proper placement. The process of slowly unveiling end-time prophecy's rich tapestry starts by piecing together the clues found in the writings of the prophets (Isaiah through Malachi), the four gospels, and Revelation, which together contain most key end-time prophecies. The clues in these works tend to be easy to unearth but difficult to comprehend, as symbolism often obfuscates the underlying events they are describing. This obfuscation thwarts most casual observers, leaving prophetic puzzle solving in the hands of only the most diligent Bible detectives. These detectives forage throughout the Bible for the critical clues that unlock the symbol's mysteries. Sometimes the clues are in the symbol's passages, but more often, they lay hidden in sundry locations throughout the Bible's sixty-six books. While the nuances of prophetic studies seem to magnify the discovery process, Isaiah 28:9-10 indicates it is actually no different from any other form of biblical research, as even basic doctrine must be learned precept by precept.

Throughout this book, these clues will be explored to search out the details of not only the aforementioned events but the entire timeline of prophetic events, starting with the church's advent and continuing through to the new creations: new heaven, new earth, and new Jerusalem. In between lies a host of history-altering events awaiting discovery:

- the church's rapture
- a seven-year tribulation period
- the opening of earth's title deed
- the issuance of a royal coronation decree
- the new king's coronation
- wars in heaven and on earth
- the abomination of desolation
- the mark of the beast
- the harvest of wheat and tares
- the war in the valley of Megiddo
- the fall of Mystery, Babylon The Great (Mystery Babylon)
- the wedding feast
- Jesus' return with his armies
- the judgments of the saints
- Jesus' transition period, including the judgments of the earth's inhabitants
- Jesus' millennial reign with the construction of a new temple
- the final rebellion
- the end of the heavens and the earth
- the great white throne judgments
- the indescribably beautiful new heaven, new earth, and new Jerusalem

First, this chapter lays basic groundwork by covering some key principles of prophetic study: the rationale for its study, what differentiates biblical prophecies from other forms of predictions, basic rules of interpretation, and a series of keys to unlocking prophetic secrets. Next, chapter two provides a general, high-level introduction of the end-time timeline divided into smaller prophetic periods. Finally, the remaining chapters fill in the details of each prophetic period.

Prophecy Study Justification

Many Christian mentors have discouraged countless Bible students from studying prophecy. This is primarily out of fear these studies will distract the students, keeping them from their important daily duties of serving God and other people. While it is true some eschatology (prophecy studies, especially future events) students have gone overboard and lost focus on other aspects of their Christian duties when they immerse themselves in exploring the mysteries of the "end times," there remain many solid reasons to study this difficult subject:

- Christians can receive comfort by understanding God's nature, the future of the world, God's protective work in their lives, and their final disposition.

- It motivates Christians to serve God ever more faithfully because they know that he observes people's works, judging and rewarding them accordingly (both evil and good).

- Variously estimated at anywhere between 25 to 100 percent of the Bible's overall content, prophecy occupies such a substantial portion of Scripture that it simply cannot be ignored by serious students of God's Word.

- Revelation 1:3 and Revelation 22:7 promise blessings on those who read, hear, and keep the words of that prophetic book.

- Prophecy can be a tremendous witnessing tool to reach both the unsaved and the backslidden Christian.

- Eschatology encourages the study of many other biblical fields, as they often inextricably intertwine themselves with prophetic images and references.

- False predictions and prophecies can easily mislead the prophecy novice (as evidenced throughout history in several well documented, false end dates and the number of people who sold property, quit jobs, left families, and made other "end of the world" preparations because of them).

Undoubtedly, God gave prophecy for people to study and understand, but he also warned its study should complement and not exclude or hinder other Christian responsibilities. For example, in 1 Corinthians 13:2-3, Paul warned mastering prophecy and its mysteries is not sufficient by itself to please God. In this passage, the Greek root word for charity is agape (Strong's G26), which is one of two forms of love found in the New Testament. The second, phileo, appears inferior since Peter responded with it when Jesus questioned Peter's love (agape) for him (John 21:15-17). Agape is the unconditional love of Jesus' two great commandments in Matthew 22:37-40: to love God and one another. Its presence in the lives of Christians compels them to serve God full heartedly, obeying all of his commandments. Its absence negates all their other good works and manifests itself through various ungodly activities, including a lack of compassion and willful disobedience to God's commandments. Christians fully in God's will strike balances in all aspects of their lives so they do not neglect agape-love growth while still fulfilling their duties to study all aspects of Scripture (2 Timothy 2:15), including prophecy.

Biblical Prophecy's High Standards

Once Christians start studying prophecy, they immediately confront the confusion introduced by the myriad predictions emanating from psychics and other self-proclaimed prognosticators. These often amusing, sometimes ludicrous predictions appear in virtually every type of media, print to video, and most commonly at each year's onset when people naturally wonder about the future. What separates the extra-biblical predictions of mystics, fortunetellers, and soothsayers from biblical eschatology? Predominately, it is the Bible's authority, its prophecies' accuracy, and the longevity of its predictions.

Starting with their authority, Amos 3:7 declares prophecy's purpose: to eliminate doubt and confusion about God's actions. Simply, God does not perform anything without first revealing it so people can authoritatively identify what is and is not God's work. Woven throughout the pages of the Bible, God's decrees foretell (foretold) the rise and fall of kings; the fall of cities and nations; long-term droughts; plagues God placed on humanity; the birth, life, and death of the Savior of the world; and the new covenant (the Bible's New Testament). They span thousands of years, with some decrees carried out almost immediately while others were fulfilled anywhere from a generation to thousands of years later. Others still await future fulfillment. Most of these occur during the last days and provide fascinating end-time insights.

Old Testament law lays out two fundamental criteria for determining a prophet's authority. The first is found in Deuteronomy 13:1-5 and focuses on the prophet's message. Anyone directing or encouraging people to worship or follow any other gods does not speak with God's authority and is, by definition, a false prophet. (God never sends prophets to contradict his word, tempt people, or lead people astray.) Deuteronomy 18:20-22 lays out the second criteria and extends its standard to prophecies made in the name of any god. It requires uncompromisingly high accuracy standards, as true prophets must be 100 percent accurate for each and every prophecy. Any error, no matter how minor, immediately marks the prophet as false. Compare this standard with the prediction success rates of modern psychics where unfulfilled or partially correct predictions and success rates of 10 percent or less are common. These accuracy rates disqualify these prognosticators as prophets of God, and Old Testament law declares all their works profane and condemns them to death.

When God reveals all mysteries (eliminating the need for prophets), a stricter law replaces the first two: anyone claiming to speak for God is, by definition, a false prophet and faces the death penalty. During Jesus' reign, people guard this standard so zealously that even parents execute this sentence on their own children (Zechariah 13:3). The end of mysteries, and by extension, prophecies, comes after the death of the two witnesses of

Revelation 11 (probably the last true prophets) and the blowing of the seventh trumpet in the middle of the seven-year tribulation (Revelation 11:15). Possibly, Revelation 13's infamous false prophet may be the first subjected to this last law's judgments. While not entirely clear, the point becomes moot by virtue of the false prophet's failure to meet the standards of the other two laws.

Commonly, people also measure prophets by their miracles since God often used miracles to establish a prophet's authority and credibility. Unfortunately, this is a poor measure, as demonstrated by the miracles of false prophets (e.g., Pharaoh's magicians in Exodus 7-9 and Revelation's false prophet who emulates some of Elijah's greatest miracles in Revelation 13:13-15). False prophets' abilities to emulate God's miracles means it is impossible to ascertain whether a prophet speaks God's words solely by the presence (or absence) of miracles. Therefore, only the Old Testament standards of Deuteronomy 13:1-5 and 18:20-22 are valid measures of a prophet's authority.

The third criterion separating God's prophecies are their longevity. Genesis' garden of Eden was the scene of the Bible's earliest recorded prophecy, roughly six thousand years ago. Other Old Testament prophecies have survived for over twenty-five hundred years while New Testament prophecies have survived for almost two thousand years. As a whole, these prophecies cover events spanning the time from the dawn of man to the glorious future new creations. Some prophecies are direct, unequivocal pronouncements while others are more obscure and hidden. For example, prophecies foretelling the Babylonian captivity and Israel's subsequent return generally fall into the first category while the majority of Daniel's prophecies fall into the second. Regardless, the Bible's prophecies have remained unchanged since they were recorded thousands of years ago. They are recorded where skeptic and believer alike can readily scrutinize them.

Basic Rules of Interpretation

Often, people are reluctant to explore prophecies (or any portions of Scripture for that matter) because they perceive the Bible as incomprehensible. The Bible's complexity and arguments over its inerrancy contribute to this. Part of this problem stems from the fact that the Bible is a unique book that serves as a textbook for spiritual elementary students but still reveals secrets to professors with many years of postgraduate study. Another part comes from its diverse subject matter, including basic law, world history, and the mysteries of God. These issues have led many to question the Bible's accuracy and claim its esoteric nature is beyond anyone's comprehension. However, the Bible's own testimony disputes these assertions: "All scripture is given by inspiration of God, and is profitable for doctrine, for reproof, for correction, for instruction in righteousness," (2 Timothy 3:16). Without equivocation, the Bible claims all Scripture comes directly from God and corrects, builds, and edifies people, regardless of their spiritual maturity or their mastery of its secrets.

Second Peter 1:20-21 continues these themes: "Knowing this first, that no prophecy of the scripture is of any private interpretation. For the prophecy came not in old time by the will of man: but holy men of God spake as they were moved by the Holy Ghost." Again, the Bible claims its Scripture originates from God but now expands this precept to include its method of delivery: the Holy Spirit's moving of selected righteous men. While men penned Scripture's words, the words they wrote were God's not theirs. This passage also adds the precept that Scripture's interpretation is not private or personal. Fundamentally, this controversial verse simply limits Scripture's meaning to that intended by its author, God, and he is its final arbiter. Further, it is each individual's responsibility to set aside all personal bias so they can diligently seek these truths (2 Timothy 2:15). As shown by example of the Bereans who faithfully tested the apostles' teachings (Acts 17:10-11), God bestows special praise on those delving into Scripture seeking the truth. Rather than be intimidated by

Scripture's complexities, faithful Christians embrace them, trusting God to illuminate them.

Over time, scholars have created various rules to aid in the discovery of God's truths through strict methods of scriptural interpretation. Known as hermeneutics, these rules define methodical, disciplined approaches for understanding any facet of Scripture, including prophecy. They form a common sense approach for searching the Bible for its treasures without deviating from its balanced doctrine. While small variations exist between different hermeneutic lists, a general list of rules includes:

- Grammatical interpretation: Words, phrases, and sentence construction can all alter meanings. Each needs careful inspection and exploration to avoid erroneous conclusions.[1]

- Local contextual interpretation: Verses immediately before and after a passage directly influence its meaning, and a passage's interpretation cannot occur in isolation from its local context.

- General contextual interpretation: Single scriptural passages do not stand alone and must be consistent with all other Scripture. Two corollaries to this rule are:

  - Less ambiguous passages should take interpretational precedence over more ambiguous ones.

  - Doctrinal "extremes" must be balanced against each other. Based on Deuteronomy 5:32 (do not depart from the law to go to the right or to the left), this corollary instructs people to search with equal fervor doctrine laying to the left and right so the balanced path lying somewhere in between is located.

- Historical connotation: Historical context influences passages and their interpretation.

- Author context: Exploration of the author's background and other works can provide insights into difficult texts. This time-honored technique for general literature is extended for the Bible to account for both its human writer and its heavenly originator, God. Of greatest importance are Scripture's originator and its spiritual conduit, the Holy Spirit.

- Progressive revelation: The Holy Spirit progressively reveals doctrinal revelations in more detail with the passage of time. As a corollary, detailed revelations build on earlier, less developed revelations.

- Symbolic interpretation: Wherever the Bible explains symbolic meanings, these symbolic interpretations take interpretational precedence. Consideration for alternative interpretations occurs only when the biblically suggested ones fail to fit the current context.

Still other hermeneutic rules exist, and many of these are far more mechanical than this list. These are especially prevalent among Jewish scholars with their rich traditions of Scripture study and include some focusing on the Hebrew language's various intricacies and their Old Testament usages. However, this section's rules present a solid foundation and are generally sufficient for scriptural studies.

These rules might lead one to conclude biblical studies are a simple rote process. Just read, apply the rules, turn the crank, and doctrinal insights are routinely manufactured. The truth is quite the opposite. Many discussions of hermeneutics include the process for discovery, hypothesizing, testing, and validating doctrinal theories. It is a process familiar to scientists, mathematicians, and researchers. Known facts and assumptions are the basis for postulating new theories. Each new theory goes through hermeneutic testing to purge its flaws. Testing is completed only when all hermeneutic rules are satisfied, especially the need for full scriptural consistency throughout the entire Bible. Passages contradicting or refuting the theory should cause the theory to be refined or abandoned. From personal experience, it often takes two or more full Bible searches before new theories are well tested. Diligent students always seek to validate all doctrinal beliefs by continuously challenging them throughout their lives. The freedom represented by this process of hypothesis, test, and discovery is troubling to some who fear it too easily allows erroneous doctrines. To prevent this, they sometimes add rules restricting new theories from ever contradicting certain fundamental pillars of the faith. Strong, consistent application of the rules of hermeneutics and the discovery process should be sufficient to prevent and correct false doctrines without resorting to these other somewhat arbitrary and redundant restrictions.

For prophetic studies, these rules remain unchanged; but prophetic interpretation generally requires far more foundational insights than other areas of biblical studies. They also require understanding of their fulfillment time horizons: near-term, mid-term, far-term, split horizon, or multiple occurrences. Near-term is any fulfillment within a person's typical life span (seventy years), mid-term is for up to the silent period between the two testaments (approximately five hundred years), and long-term is anything longer than this. Split horizon refers to passages containing prophecies fulfilled at different times while multiple occurrences refer to passages fulfilled more than once. These are best illustrated with examples:

- Short-term: Joseph's interpretations of the dreams of Pharaoh's butler and baker (Genesis 40)

- Mid-term: God's plan to bring the children of Israel out of Egypt (Genesis 46:1-4)

- Long-term: The promise of the new covenant (Jeremiah 31:31–40)

- Split horizon: Isaiah 61:1–2's acceptable year of the Lord (fulfilled in Luke 4:16–21) and day of God's vengeance (still waiting fulfillment)

- Multiple occurrences: The fall of Babylon first to the Medes and Persians and the future fall of Mystery Babylon.

Language and perspective are other barriers for prophetic interpretation. Ancient languages lack the capability to adequately describe today's technology (e.g., computers, space flight, automobiles, planes, missiles), often forcing prophecy's true meanings to be masked by symbolism. Additionally, the observer's perspective affects their descriptions of events. To reconstruct an event, investigators must interview multiple witnesses to get a complete picture. Likewise, it takes all of the Bible's multiple perspectives to create an accurate picture. Finally, it is important to recognize that often, prophecy only becomes understandable during the time immediately preceding or following its fulfillment. This is best illustrated by Daniel 12:4, which states the book would remain a mystery (sealed) until the end times. As foretold, Daniel was the last book to have a commentary. Ironically, as end-time prophecies shed their veils, 2 Peter 3:3-4 shows people becoming less receptive to their warnings and people's apostasy growing.

Keys to Unlocking End-time Prophetic Secrets

To unlock prophecy's secrets, prophetic keys are needed. Most are illustrations, or types, of specific prophecy concepts. For example, King Solomon is a type of Jesus. He was not Jesus, but as shown in Table 1, specific aspects of his life give useful insights into Jesus' life. Every type's symbolic representation has limitations beyond which it fails. For King Solomon, flaws like those in Table 2 are clearly not representative of Jesus; however, these flaws do not eliminate the symbolic application of King Solomon as a type of Jesus. They do serve as a warning to approach symbolic applications carefully. When applied properly, biblical types introduce powerful insights in biblical truths. When applied improperly, one can contort them into absurd and ridiculous conclusions. For example, a misapplication of Solomon's life might lead one to reach the ludicrous conclusion that Jesus would eventually worship other gods and have his kingdom removed from him. The rules of hermeneutics prevent serious prophecy students from accepting these conclusions since the rest of Scripture not only fails to support them but also directly contradicts them.

Table 1: King Solomon's Reflections of Jesus

King Solomon	Jesus
Man of Peace	Prince of Peace
A son of David	The Son of David
Crowned king while prior king, David, was alive	Crowned king while prior king, God the Father, is alive
Adonijah tries to steal his throne	The antichrist tries to steal His throne
Builds first temple	Builds last temple
Nations and people seek his wisdom	Nations and people seek His wisdom
Wisest man to live	Possesses the wisdom of God
Many nations bring their wealth to him	All nations bring their wealth to Him
Gold as available as rocks in Jerusalem	The wealth of the world flows from Jerusalem

Table 2: King Solomon's Differences Compared to Jesus

King Solomon	Jesus
King of Israel	King of kings, Lord of lords
Not worshiped	Worshiped as God
Marries many wives	Has one wife
Builds profane places to false gods	Destroys all profane places
Worships false gods	Destroys all false gods
Has kingdom taken from his children	Establishes an everlasting dominion
Rules 40 years	Rules 1000 years
Crowned in Jerusalem	Crowned in Heaven

The remainder of this chapter introduces several prophetic keys. Succeeding chapters freely draw on these to explain otherwise mysterious references. While crucial to unleashing the Bible's mysteries, they often challenge normal human sensibilities. For example, one of the keys addresses Israel's position as God's wife, but how is this possible? These images regularly raise many difficult questions without clear or easy answers. For now, it is best to explore the keys and ignore the paradoxes. The following discussions provide keys that:

- categorizes people into key groups
- inspects references to Jesus' marriage supper
- introduces the mysteries of the kingdoms of heaven and God
- explores the fall of Babylon the great
- looks at some intricacies of the Day of the Lord
- investigates the basis for God's redemption of the earth
- examines the most important preparatory last day prophecy: Israel's rebirth
- considers the greatness of Israel's last day armies
- observes the dangers of Israel's desire for peace
- recognizes the impacts of the book of Revelation

Jews, Gentiles, and Christians

The Bible divides the family of man into several fundamental genealogical and spiritual groups. While these influence end-time interpretation, many are troubling to Christians, who, based on interpretations of Galatians 3:28 and Colossians 3:11, question which, if any, of these divisions exist and whether they extend to Christians as a whole. However, understanding distinctions between Jewish and non-Jewish Christians is critical to deciphering some of Jesus' parables.

From a genealogical perspective, Genesis 9:18-29 divides the world's population into four broad groups:

- Shem: the descendents of quality
- Japheth: the descendents of quantity
- Ham: the cursed descendents of Canaan
- Ham: the unblessed descendents

Figure 1 shows these divisions, along with Genesis 10's division of nations. While their modern names are different, many of these nations play crucial roles in end-time prophecies.

Figure 1: Genesis' List of Nations

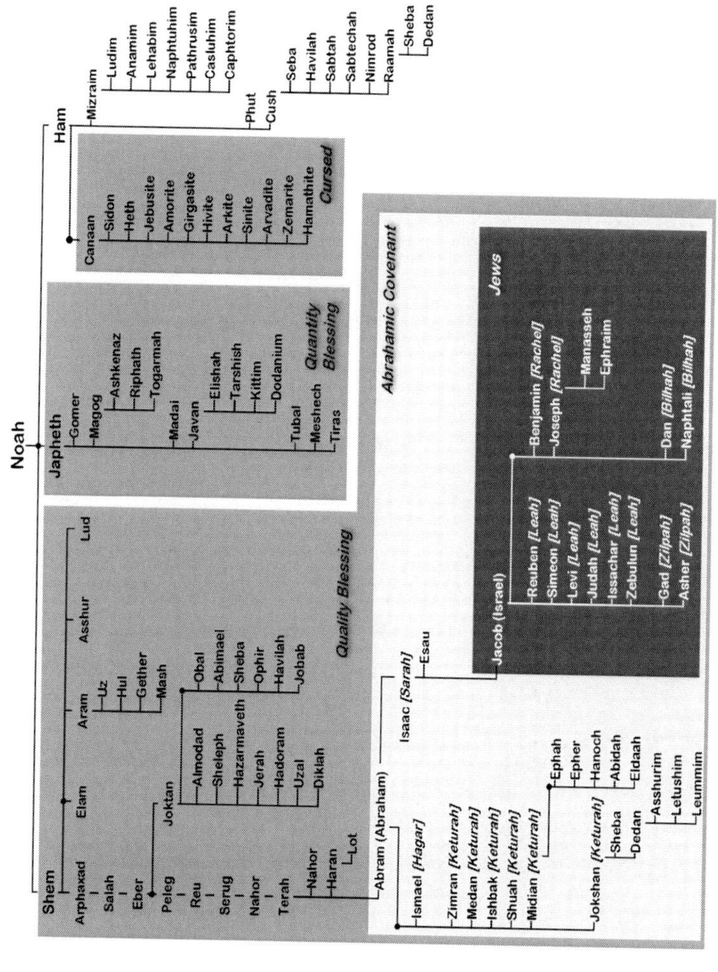

Next, Genesis turns its focus almost exclusively to Shem's descendents and specifically to Abraham (Abram), who receives unconditional blessings (Genesis 17:4-8). While all of Abraham's descendant's receive a portion of these blessings, the bulk of them, including the messianic promise, went to Israel (Genesis 35:10-12) and his twelve sons. From this point on, the world was divided into Jews (children of Israel) and Gentiles (everyone else). Genesis 48-49 details the individual blessings to each of Israel's children. Key among these blessings is the messianic promise given to Judah (Genesis 49:8-12) and the double-portion inheritance given to Joseph (Genesis 48), which made Joseph's two sons joint heirs with Israel's other children.

Spiritually, the Old Testament separates people into two groups: the righteous and the wicked. According to Ezekiel 18:20-32, a person's righteousness is determined at death, regardless of their prior life's works. Then the righteous enjoy the rewards of heaven while the wicked endure the torment of hell. A person's heritage, Jew or Gentile, neither guaranteed their destination nor helped at the time of their judgment. In reality, the Jews' status as God's chosen people has often proven a heavy burden since God's judgment always starts with his people (1 Peter 4:17), whom he holds to the higher standards.

Jesus' crucifixion added two new spiritual classifications: saved (Christians) and unsaved. One key difference, permanence, separates these from the Old Testament's righteous and wicked. Now people can repent, ask for Jesus' forgiveness, turn from sin, and have their name permanently written in the Lamb's (Jesus) Book of Life. The presence of one's name in Lamb's Book of Life "saves" them from the wicked's (unsaved) punishment in both hell and the lake of fire. In a manner reminiscent of Israel's marriage covenant, this salvation is a binding contract established between God and humanity. Unlike the marriage covenant, salvation is not established with a single race but all humanity (Romans 10:9-13) and is a gift freely given and received (John 3:16-21). It requires people to call on the only name that can save them: Jesus (Acts 4:12).

Since its inception, the covenant's simple provisions has

generated numerous critics, who often argue its lack of reliance on works (activities designed to "earn" one's way into heaven) encourages lazy believers. To a degree, this has proven true and leads to a third New Testament spiritual classification: carnality (1 Corinthians 3:1-4). Applying only to the saved, carnality speaks of both spiritual immaturity and sinful lives. Carnal Christians are saved and destined for heaven but choose to embrace sin and its pleasures. Spiritually mature Christians continually strive to overcome sin while carnal Christians lead lives virtually indistinguishable from the unsaved. Today, the majority of people are unsaved. Of the saved minority, most are carnal, and sadly, only a very small percentage of people ever grow into spiritually mature Christians.

The last of the Bible's divisions considered here is particularly critical for decoding a number of key prophecies: the church and the bride. The definition of the church is straightforward, as it references all saved believers: Jew, Gentile, spiritually mature, and carnal. The definition of the bride is far more subtle. Jesus' wedding parables contain the following participants:

- the groom (Matthew 22:1-14, Matthew 25:1-13)

- the groom's father (the king) (Matthew 22:1-14)

- the bride (John 3:29)

- the wedding party (represented by ten virgins of Matthew 25:1-13)

- the servants (Matthew 22:1-14)

- the invited guests who refuse to come (Matthew 22:1-14)

- the replacement guests (Matthew 22:1-14)

- the rejected replacement guests (Matthew 22:1-14)

Of these, the easiest to identify are the groom, Jesus, and his Father, God the Father. Identifying the rest of the participants is far more problematic. The difficulties arise immediately with the bride and the wedding party.

In the Bible, the wedding party consists of the bride's relatives while the guests are the couple's friends. According to most commentaries, the wedding party, the guests, and the bride allude to the church, and many use these terms virtually interchangeably. However, this view provides no explanation why some of Matthew 25's ten virgins would be taken and others left (Matthew 25:1-13) and fails to address the apparent difficulties of the Jews being part of the bride of Christ when they are already the wife of God the Father. The first issue challenges the doctrine of the Christian's eternal security. If the bride and the wedding party both represent the church, then how could some Christians remain on earth while others go to the wedding (heaven)? This infers some Christians have lost their salvation, a contradiction of the external security doctrine. With many clearer references supporting this doctrine, it is probably safe to assume the ten virgins do not represent the church.

The Jew's relationship to God the Father presents additional difficulties, as numerous references to the millennial reign show God's continuing recognition of the old covenant. Through this time, this marriage covenant remains in force, unbroken from its confirmation during the days of Joshua. While God not only punished his bride but also produced a bill of divorce against her for her unfaithfulness, it is clear he also has not released her from her covenant so she can marry another. Polygamy might be a possible solution to this issue; but even when practiced in the Old Testament, only men took multiple spouses. For practical reasons, the wife could not take multiple spouses due to paternal inheritance. If the paternal parentage was ever in doubt, then the rights of inheritance would be muddled. Fundamentally, Israel, as the wife of God the Father, cannot take God the Son as a spouse unless her first husband dies or releases her from her vows—neither a likely possibility.

An alternative interpretation is the ten virgins represent the wife of God the Father: the Jews. By heredity, each descendent of Israel is a Jew at birth, and this status is not affected by other events such as salvation. If Jews, saved and unsaved, are the wedding party, then the bride must consist of only Gentile Christianity. While this interpretation changes neither how either group is judged or receives salvation, it does differentiate the two.

While potentially troubling, this interpretation resolves the prior issues since, as the wife of God, the Jews are close relatives of the groom and thus qualified to be part of the wedding party; but since they are not the bride, the issues of polygamy are resolved. Also, since there have always been saved and unsaved Jews, the question of why some of the virgins are taken and others are left is resolved. The five virgins with their lamps (bodies) filled with the oil (the Holy Spirit's presence) represent saved Jews and the five with empty lamps and represent the unsaved. At the groom's return, the saved virgins enter the wedding hall with the groom and his bride while the others are left behind. Likewise, when Jesus returns, he will take the saved Jews to heaven and leave the unsaved Jews on earth to face the seven-year tribulation.

Now, the rest of the wedding participants become easier to identify. The Jews remaining on earth serve as the Father's servants (Matthew 22:1-14) and are responsible for inviting the wedding's guests. They first call the nobles and leaders on earth. Later, they go out to the highways and byways searching for replacement guests. Since the servants are Jews, the guests must be unsaved Gentiles. The rejected replacement guests are the most difficult to explain, and the great tribulation chapter covers them only after additional groundwork is laid.

Summarizing, the wedding ceremony participants are:

- the groom: Jesus Christ
- the groom's father, the king: God the Father
- the bride: Gentile Christianity
- the wedding party: saved Jews
- the servants: unsaved Jews
- the invited guests who refuse to come: unsaved noble Gentiles
- the replacement guests: other unsaved Gentiles

Considering the historically high levels of animosity between Jews and Christians, this interplay seems odd. Today, people view Christianity as principally a Gentile religion; but it should be noted that Jews played critical roles in the birth and spread of Christianity. The Gospel first went to the Jews, who preached it to the Gentiles only after much soul-searching debate. Even today, large numbers of Jews are Christians, and the parable of the ten virgins suggests this number may be as high as 50 percent at the rapture.

This section covered the Bible's genealogical and spiritual divisions. The genealogical division started with Noah's sons, continued to Genesis's list of nations, and concluded with Jews and Gentiles. Before Jesus, people were in one of two spiritual groups: righteous or wicked. Now, prior to the rapture, all people are either saved or unsaved. At the rapture, Jesus returns to get his bride (saved Gentiles) and her wedding party (saved Jews). Unsaved Jews remain on earth to serve God by searching for and inviting guests to Jesus' upcoming wedding.

Marriage Supper of the Lamb

The preparations for the Lamb's marriage are featured in several kingdom of heaven parables. The first of these is the parable of the ten virgins in Matthew 25:1-13. Here, the bridal party, composed of ten virgins, prepare and wait for the upcoming wedding. Unlike, today's preplanned weddings, where the date is known weeks or months in advance, it is clear by the groom's abrupt midnight arrival and the virgin's reaction that neither the bridal party nor the bride knew when the groom would return. Surprisingly, when the bridegroom does return, he does not enter the bride's city but announces his arrival with a shout from outside the city. Then, the bride and bridal party immediately meet the bridegroom outside the city and go with him to his father's land. Stragglers are left behind and are barred from the wedding hall.

Another kingdom parable, the wedding feast in Matthew 22:1-14, gives insights into the wedding's guests and subsequent wedding feast. The wedding's host is the king, the groom's father, and he sends his servants to gather the invited guests. The wedding's location is the king's land, and based on the

meal's readiness, both the wedding and the meal are imminent. These guests provoke the king's wrath by first refusing to
come and then killing the king's servants. The king responds
by destroying their city and sending his servants to find new
guests. Interestingly, the new guests wear the finest wedding
garments. Since they did not know they would be attending the
wedding, their host must provide this attire. Curiously, one of
the replacement guests provokes the king's wrath by refusing to
wear these special garments and the king responds by expelling
him from the wedding hall and throwing him into a place of
horrible punishment (hell).

When speaking of preparing a place for believers in John
14:2-3, Jesus invoked images of Old Testament laws where land
ownership transferred only through paternal inheritance. These
inheritance laws created interesting dilemmas for young men
wanting to date since all the local women were ineligible for
marriage because they were close relatives. This forced him
to leave home to find a bride. Once engaged, he would return
home to prepare a place to live with his future bride. By tradition, the groom's father was responsible for determining when
this place was ready, so neither the groom nor the bride knew
the wedding's date. During the preparation time, the bride and
her wedding party (the virgins) stayed behind, preparing to
leave with the groom at a moment's notice.

The search for a bride for Isaac in Genesis 24 fills in some
additional details of the engagement process. Here, the groom's
representative left the father's land searching for a suitable
mate. Once found, he entered negotiations with her father for
the right to propose. When these terms were met, the bride was
brought in and asked whether she accepted the proposal. Since
the groom's representative only paid for the right to propose
marriage, any payments were nonrefundable and the potential
bride was under no obligation.

Now a fascinating wedding ritual emerges. It starts with
the son leaving his father's land to find a bride. When he finds
a prospect, he negotiates the price for the right to propose; pays

the price; proposes; and if she accepts, he returns to his father's land to prepare a place for them to live following their marriage. Since they have no way of knowing when the groom will return for the wedding, the bride and her party must continually be ready to launch off on a possibly long and arduous journey. When he returns, the groom does not reenter the bride's city but shouts from outside and waits there for the bride and bridal party to meet him. They then return to the father's land, where the father prepares the marriage supper. When ready, the father sends his servants to call the wedding guests for the wedding and marriage feast. As soon as the guests arrive, the marriage occurs and the marriage feast is served.

Now consider the parallels to Jesus' life. Like the groom, Jesus left his Father's land (heaven) and came to earth to find his bride (the church). He also paid a price for the right to propose: his life. Before he returned home to his Father's land, he extended a marriage proposal that remains open until the day he returns to get his bride. While away, he labors in love, preparing a home for the bride and bridal party. Soon, he promises to return for them, but like the groom, even he does not know when this will occur (Matthew 24:36). When the promised time comes, Jesus will return to get his bride, but like the groom, he will stop just short of the earth and from the clouds, shout for his bride and her party to meet him. Then, all Christians, dead and alive, will instantly receive new bodies, meet Jesus in the air, and return with him to heaven. There, they will await the guests' arrival. Their arrival will be delayed since replacements must be found after the invited guests refuse to come and the Father destroys their city. When the new guests arrive, Jesus and his bride will finally be married, and all heaven will enjoy perhaps the grandest wedding feast ever.

The Mysterious Kingdoms of Heaven and God

The next prophetic key is the mysteries in the kingdom of God and heaven, which are mentioned over a hundred times throughout the New Testament. These descriptions reveal many aspects of God's spiritual kingdom, and the search for their underlying meanings often inspires impassioned debates. Understandably, most of the kingdom references occur within the four Gospels and most prominently in Jesus' parables. The significance of the two different kingdoms causes confusion and stirs debate among scholars. Some contend one represents heaven while the other represents Jesus' millennial reign.

Kingdom of heaven references are found only in the book of Matthew while kingdom of God references appear throughout the New Testament, including Matthew. Several of Matthew's kingdom of heaven parables appear elsewhere as kingdom of God parables. These overlapping parable references and the lack of kingdom of heaven references outside of Matthew suggest they are two names for the same thing.

The Bible's first references to the kingdoms appear in Matthew (Matthew 3:1-2, Matthew 4:17, Matthew 10:7, and Mark 1:14-15) when John the Baptist and Jesus preach the Gospel of the kingdom. They call people to repent and proclaim it is at hand (near). Interestingly, the only time the Bible clearly proclaims the kingdom of God has arrived (present tense) is halfway through the seven-year tribulation in Revelation 12:10. The coming kingdom of God was preached throughout the New Testament by John the Baptist, Jesus, and their disciples (Matthew 3:1-2, 4:17, 10:7; Mark 1:14-15; Luke 4:43, 8:1, 9:2, 9:11, 9:60-62, 10:9-11; Acts 1:3). Its importance continues to this day as Christians preach it throughout the world.

Twelve separate parables provide the primary insights to the kingdom's mysteries:

- the fig tree and the kingdom at hand (Luke 21:29–32)
- the harvest of wheat and tares (Matthew 13:24–30, Matthew 13:36–43)
- the net full of good and bad fish (Matthew 13:47–50)
- the treasure in the field (Matthew 13:44)
- the pearl of great price (Matthew 13:45–46)

- the mustard seed (Matthew 13:31–32, Mark 4:26–32, Luke 13:18–19)

- the leaven in the loaves (Matthew 13:33, Luke 13:20–21)

- the king and the unforgiving servant (Matthew 18:23–35)

- the man and the day laborers (Matthew 20:1–16)

- the king, the marriage feast, and the guests (Matthew 22:1–14, Luke 14:15–24)

- the ten virgins (Matthew 25:1–13)

- the nobleman and the three servants (Matthew 25:14–30, Luke 19:11–27)

Three additional parables support the first twelve but do not contain key phrases marking them as kingdom parables:

- the judgment of the sheep and goats (Matthew 25:31–46)

- the householder bringing out treasures (Matthew 13:52)

- the sower and the seed (Matthew 13:3–8, Matthew 3:11–23, Mark 4:3–8, Mark 4:11–20, Luke 8:5–8, Luke 8:10–18)

These parables cover a wide range of topics, including Jesus' marriage, the coming judgments, the last days' harvest of the good and wicked, the effects of sin, the kingdom's value, and the kingdom's power. Particularly crucial to understanding end-time prophecy are the parables of the fig tree, the harvest, the marriage feast, the ten virgins, the nobleman's three servants, and the judgment of the sheep and goats. As the prophetic timeline unfolds, each contributes valuable insights. For now, it is sufficient to understand the kingdom of God parables hold many key end-time secrets.

Babylon's Fall

Another prophetic key is Revelation 18's destruction of the previously mentioned city of the obstinate wedding guests. Their city is known by several names but probably the most famous is Mystery Babylon, which is a variant of the name found only in Revelation 17:5. Theories about this city's modern identity abound with speculation, including a modern revival of ancient Babylon (perhaps in modern Baghdad), Rome, and New York City. Alternative theories suggest Mystery Babylon is not a city but a system of religion, a system of commerce, a form of government, or a combination of any of these. However, various descriptions of her destruction suggest a physical location. For example, Revelation 18:8 shows her being quickly destroyed by fire with the normal aftereffects of war: death, mourning, and famine. Both the manner of its destruction and the destruction's aftermath point to a physical city and seem to rule out any of the alternative proposals. The great tribulation chapter explores clues to Mystery Babylon's identity while this section focuses on the city's destruction and its possible ties to ancient Babylon.

Clues to links between Mystery Babylon and ancient Babylon abound, including not only their names but also the pronouncements of angels at their destruction. Revelation 18:2 repeats the phrase "is fallen" for Mystery Babylon. Most commentators treat this as a device emphasizing the certainty and completeness of its destruction, but several other passages such as Revelation 14:8, Isaiah 14:4, Isaiah 21:9, and Jeremiah 51:8 show this same "emphasis" when speaking of Babylon's destruction. Rather than simple emphasis, these verses probably refer to two falls: ancient Babylon's fall to Media-Persia and Mystery Babylon's future fall. Although ancient Babylon remained inhabited for some time after its fall in Daniel 5, its national sovereignty was forever broken. After the Persians, Alexander the Great conquered it and briefly ruled from its palaces. Throughout this time, Babylon never regained its autonomy and was probably destroyed prior to 100 BC. It lay in ruins until Saddam Hussein started reconstruction in the twentieth century, and today it is an uninhabited archaeological site.

Unless their physical locations are the same, the relationship of Mystery Babylon to ancient Babylon is a mystery. Do their religious, governmental, or commercial systems tie them together? Perhaps it is simply people's desire to replace God's throne with a single, worldwide government. The best clue is found in Nebuchadnezzar's vision of a statue with a golden head (Daniel 2:28-45). In this vision, the head represents the first Babylon. Several other portions of the statue represent empires following it, with each lower portion representing a succeeding empire. Each successive portion of the statue is composed of materials of decreasing value. The first, Babylon, is made of gold, and the last is clay mixed with some iron. A stone cut without hands (Jesus) crushes the feet, destroying the entire statue. The feet of clay describe a future alliance of nations exploited by the antichrist in his quest to rule the world from this alliance's capital, Mystery Babylon. The statue links ancient Babylon (the head) to Mystery Babylon (the feet of clay) through several intervening world powers. God destroys the entire statue by crushing the feet of clay (Mystery Babylon and the alliance of nations).

Interestingly, Mystery Babylon may also be linked to Jericho through a veiled reference found in the instructions given to Joshua in Joshua 6:2-5. Table 3 summarizes the parallels between instructions to destroy Jericho and Mystery Babylon's future demise. While the great tribulation chapter explores Mystery Babylon's identity and destruction, salient Mystery Babylon facts seen in this section include:

- It is an actual city linked to ancient Babylon through Nebuchadnezzar's vision of the golden-headed statue
- It is the antichrist's seat of power
- It is destroyed before the Lamb's marriage supper

Table 3: Comparison of the Destruction of Jericho and Mystery Babylon

	Jericho	Mystery Babylon
Destroyed by	Joshua, a type of Jesus	Jesus
Destroyed on	Seventh day	Seventh millennia (seventh day)
Destroyed after	Priests blow seven trumpets	Angel blows the seventh trumpet
Destroyed after	People of Israel shout	Heaven's inhabitants shout at Jesus' coronation

The Day of the Lord

The Day of the Lord prophetic key appears prominently in both Old and New Testaments. This day is reserved for the wicked (Proverbs 16:4), and during it, God pours out unparalleled judgment. The Day of the Lord is always associated with God's judgment, with many passages showing both men's fear and God's anger. For example, Isaiah 13:6-9 speaks of men's hearts melting and God's cruel wrath and fierce anger. Zephaniah 1:14-15 speaks of men crying bitterly while Jeremiah 46:10 speaks of God avenging himself on his adversaries.

These descriptions make Amos's proclamation very intriguing: "Woe unto you that desire the Day of the Lord! To what end is it for you? The Day of the Lord is darkness, and not light" (Amos 5:18). Apparently, the Jews were confused about the Day of the Lord, with some believing it would be a time when Israel receives good things (light), including becoming the head and not the tail. Since Amos shows this is not the case, how is this confusion possible? Perhaps, the use of similar phrases in reference to both Jesus' reign and God's judgment is the problem. Often, "that day" refers to both the day of God's judgment and Jesus' millennial reign. For example, Isaiah 5:30 describes a day of darkness while Zephaniah 3:16-19 and Zechariah 13:1 describe a time of God's salvation, forgiveness, joy, and love.

How long are the Day of the Lord and "that day"? The seventieth week of Daniel in Daniel 9:24-27 provides a clue. The seventy weeks of God's judgment are broken into two parts: sixty-nine weeks (seven plus sixty-two) and a single week.[2] The first sixty-nine weeks predicted the year of Jesus' death and are past. The seventieth week points to an unspecified time in the future that immediately precedes Jesus' return. This week starts with the antichrist confirming a covenant with Israel and culminates in the greatest war ever fought. Revelation shows this is a seven-year period, with each of Daniel's days representing one year.

If, as Daniel's seventieth week implies, God's "that day" judgment lasts seven years, why does the Bible refer to it as a day? Clearly, this exceeds a twenty-four-hour day and the year represented by each day in Daniel's seventy weeks. Further exasperating this, "that day" also refers to Jesus' millennial reign. Fortunately, the Bible gives additional clues in 2 Peter 3:8 (see also Psalm 90:4), where a day is equated to a thousand years. This makes Jesus' millennial reign only a single day in God's eyes, and "that day" could refer to a specific, thousand-year period.

Potentially, the thousand-year day unlocks many prophetic Scriptures. Consider, for example, Mark 2:27-28, where Jesus proclaims his lordship of the Sabbath. Like "that day," Jesus claims lordship over a single day. Could he be referring to a thousand years? If he is, could he be referring to a specific time? Exodus 20:8-10 commands that the Sabbath, the seventh day, be kept holy. If Jesus is referring to a specific period, could it, like the Sabbath, be the seventh? According to the Bible, roughly six thousand years (six days) have transpired from Adam to the present:

- Approximately 1,500 years from Adam to Noah
- Approximately 2,500 years from Noah to Jesus
- Approximately 2,000 years from Jesus to the present

Could this mean the next thousand-year period is a Sabbatical day and this is Jesus' Sabbath? This seems likely considering that on the Sabbath, Jesus fed the hungry (Luke 6:1-5), healed the sick (Mark 3:1-5), and taught the wisdom of God (Luke 4:31), all distinguishing characteristics of his millennial reign. Probably, "that day" includes both Christ's thousand-year reign and Daniel's seven-year seventieth week immediately preceding it.

Does the application of thousand-year days apply to other prophetic passages? For example, Hosea 6:1-3 speaks of three days when it foretells the children of Israel's suffering. For the first two days, God smote the children of Israel, virtually to the point of death. God then revives the nearly lifeless Israel before raising her up on the third day. Her third day prosperity (raising) is tied to the Lord coming to them, suggesting that Hosea's third day is also "that day", Jesus' millennial reign. In the context of twenty-four days, it is difficult to understand how after only forty-eight hours the nation of Israel would be in need of revival. This is especially true in light of how long Israel has suffered persecution and the fact that Daniel's seventieth week portends at least seven years of suffering before "that day". However when the thousand-year day principle is applied to this passage, it suggests the Jews suffer for the two millennia prior to Jesus' reign. If Israel's national founding in 1948 is part of Hosea's prophesied revival, then her two thousand years of suffering since her dispersion in AD 72 corresponds to Hosea's two days of God's smiting. Remarkably, Israel's national rebirth occurred only after World War II put her very survival in doubt and Hosea's promised revival was desperately needed.

Another possible application of this prophetic key is Jesus' prophecies of his death and resurrection:

> Jesus answered and said unto them, "Destroy this temple, and in three days I will raise it up." Then said the Jews, "Forty and six years was this temple in building, and wilt thou rear it up in three days?" But he spake of the temple of his body.
>
> John 2:19-21

The primary application of this verse is Jesus' resurrection, where Jesus' rebuilt temple, his body, was resurrected on the third day. Intriguingly, by using the millennial day, this can be extended to include Jerusalem's physical temple. Two days ago (two thousand years), the second temple was destroyed, but on the third day, during his millennial reign, Jesus will rebuild the temple.

The millennial day theory may also give insights into the following fig tree parable.

> He spake also this parable; A certain man had a fig tree planted in his vineyard; and he came and sought fruit thereon, and found none. Then said he unto the dresser of his vineyard, "Behold, these three years I come seeking fruit on this fig tree, and find none: cut it down; why cumbereth it the ground?" And he answering said unto him, "Lord, let it alone this year also, till I shall dig about it, and dung it: And if it bear fruit, well: and if not, then after that thou shalt cut it down."
>
> Luke 13:6-9

God's fig tree (shown later to be Israel) has been unproductive for three years. The vineyard's dresser intercedes on behalf of the tree, and it receives one more year to become productive before the owner destroys it. Could each year represent a millennial day? God confirmed his marriage to Israel around 1400 BC. The addition of three millennial days sets the date of the dresser's intercession around AD 1600. During these three thousand years, Israel has been predominantly unproductive. God gives Israel a fourth period (until AD 2600) to start producing fruit. Is Jesus implying he returns during this fourth year after Israel has been unproductive for three? Likewise, could the three days Jonah spent in the belly of the whale represent the same three years the fig tree is unproductive?

A common objection to the millennial theory is its possible abuse by date setters wanting to set firm dates for Jesus' return. However, the time span's lack of precision does not lend itself to this. For example, does the day start at sunset, as the Jews observe, or at sunrise, as some cultures observe, or as is common today (midnight)? This alone introduces half a day of uncertainty (five hundred years). Combining this with rounding errors and calendar uncertainties introduced over the last 2,500 years, it becomes obvious the millennial day is essentially use-less for date setting, and other prophetic indicators are far more useful for narrowing the time of Jesus' return.

An interesting Old Testament story suggestive of "that day" involves Naaman, a Gentile afflicted with leprosy, and Elisha, a prophet of God (2 Kings 5:1-14). Naaman had long suffered from leprosy and its ravaging effects of permanent scarring and disfiguration. When he sought Elisha's help, Elisha instructed him to wash seven times in the Jordan River. After much trepi-dation, Naaman's servants finally persuaded him to follow the prophet's directions. Through six washings, both the leprosy and its effects were present, but when Naaman came out the seventh time, his skin was like a little child's. Not only was the disease gone but also all of its effects. Throughout the Bible, leprosy is a type of sin, and its rotting effects illustrate sin's impact on people. Here, Naaman could represent the world in general and the Gentiles in particular. Each washing in the Jor-dan River represents a thousand-year day. For six millennia, sin plagues humanity, and people suffer greatly. Finally, the seventh millennium brings relief, and sin, along with all of its past and present effects, disappears. What a beautiful picture of Jesus' millennium reign!

The Earth's Redemption

The next prophetic key focuses on the redemption, or reclaim-ing, of land by its absentee owner. An Old Testament story involving Jeremiah's purchase of land just prior to the Babylo-nian captivity illustrates this process. Though this land would remain dormant for the captivity's full seventy years, Jeremiah purchased it as a sign the Jews would once again reclaim their property. Jeremiah 32:7-15 shows the land's purchase. Under ownership restrictions imposed by Leviticus 25:23-26's laws, only certain close relatives may purchase a Jew's land. Here, Hanameel approaches a close relative possessing redemption rights, Jeremiah. When Jeremiah agrees to the transition, he takes witnesses and creates two documents: a book with the evidence of purchase and the book of purchase. The book of purchase remains unsealed while, to preserve its integrity, Jeremiah seals the evidence of purchase. Only the owner, or his rightful heir, can legally break the evidence of purchase's seals. Both documents are then stored in a safe place until Jeremiah (or his direct relative) returns to reclaim his rightful property. While squatters may occupy Jeremiah's land during his absence, these documents give him legal authority to reclaim it at any time.

In the future, another sealed book is seen in Revelation. This mysterious book is God's evidence of purchase proving his rightful claim to his land, the earth (Exodus 9:29). At the tribulation's beginning, the earth's owner in absentia (God) is ready to take back his rightful property. Jesus alluded to God's reclamation, or redemption, of his land in the parable of the vineyard's husbandmen in Matthew 21:33-41. Here, the vineyard's owner (God the Father) improved the property and left workers (the world) in charge of it as he traveled. When his servants (prophets) came to get the owner's annual proceeds, the workers beat some and killed others. Eventually, the owner sent his son (Jesus), whom they also killed. Eventually, the owner destroys the wicked husbandmen and gives the vineyards to others. To do so, he has to redeem his property, physically return, and take its possession. This occurs during the tribulation, when Jesus opens the earth's evidence of purchase, God the Father destroys the wicked husbandmen, and Jesus takes physical possession of the earth.

Israel's Rebirth

Of all prophetic keys, none is a greater indicator of the immanency of the end times than Israel's national rebirth. Jesus tied his future end-times return to the budding of a fig tree, an Old Testament symbol of Israel (Matthew 24:32-34). Ezekiel also foretold this when he compared Israel to a valley of dry, dead bones that will stand up, grow flesh, come back to life, and become a great army (Ezekiel 37:1-14). Today, Israel's twentieth-century rebirth is the single most important fulfilled end-time prophecy. An important part of Israel's rebirth is the gathering of Jews scattered throughout the world. Ezekiel 34:11-13 and Isaiah 11:11-12 (just a couple of the numerous passages covering the gathering of the Jews) show God personally recovering the Jews from numerous countries. Isaiah 43:3-6 shows some countries allowing the Jews' return only under God's heavy coercion.

Ezekiel 20:34-36 suggests the hurdles these countries present are similar to those God overcame with Pharaoh so long ago. The similarities include the treatment of the Jews prior to their release, the messengers sent to demand their release, and God's reaction to obstinate leaders. As the Jews were enslaved and abused by Egypt, so have they also been oppressed by many modern nations, including Nazi Germany, Stalin's Russia, several modern Muslim nations, and many terrorist organizations.

Just as God sent Moses to plead with Pharaoh (Exodus 3:10), in the future, he sends two witnesses to plead with the antichrist and the nations of the world (Revelation 11). These witnesses become even more interesting, as they are not named but perform miracles reminiscent of both Moses and Elijah, the same two men seen with Jesus at the mount of transfiguration (Matthew 17:1-5).

Finally, as God sent plagues upon the Egyptians when Pharaoh rebelled (Exodus 3:19-20), in the future, he sends a similar series of plagues on the world during the seven-year tribulation (see Table 4). Though Table 4's last entry is not one of the plagues, it does reflect God's final response to both Pharaoh and the antichrist. Though Revelation does not list all of the Egyptian's plagues, it also neglects to itemize all of the witnesses' plagues. It is possible these messengers will inflict the rest during the tribulation. Additionally, as God protected the Jews in the land of Goshen during Pharaoh's plagues, he again protects the Jews in a special place during Daniel's seventieth week. The special place is prepared in the wilderness and shelters them from the judgments of the great tribulation.

Table 4: Egyptian Plagues versus Seven-year Tribulation Plagues

Plague	Exodus	Revelation
Water into blood	Exodus 7:20	Revelation 8:10
Frogs	Exodus 8:3	Revelation 16:13 (implied)
Lice	Exodus 8:16	
Flies	Exodus 8:24	
Plagues on cattle	Exodus 9:3	
Boils	Exodus 9:9	Revelation 16:2
Hail	Exodus 9:18	Revelation 16:21
Locusts	Exodus 10:4	Revelation 9:3
Darkness	Exodus 10:21	Revelation 16:10
Firstborn	Exodus 11:4	
Armies destroyed	Exodus 14:26-28	Revelation 19:21

David, Goliath, and Israel

Israel's rebirth stirred regional and worldwide opposition, forcing her to fight for survival. In response, she created a strong national defense such as the exceedingly great army coming out of Ezekiel's valley of dry bones (Ezekiel 37:10). It is curious for Ezekiel to describe Israel's army as great since normally these adjectives are reserved for only the largest, best-equipped, and best-trained armies. In Israel's case, however, it seems unlikely this tiny nation will ever possess a large army or people will ever consider it the equal of the world's three superpowers: Russia, China, or the United States. Ezekiel must be referring to something else. Zechariah 12:8, set in the seventieth week of Daniel ("that day"), provides a clue. This verse not only shows God actively protecting Israel, but also Israel as a nation full of fierce warriors, as even the feeblest inhabitant of Jerusalem fights like the renowned fighter, David. David was so renowned as a warrior that women sang his praises for killing tens of thousands of enemies (1 Samuel 18:7). This suggests every Israeli warrior is able to defeat many enemy soldiers and Israeli armed forces win wars even when vastly outnumbered. This matches Israel's modern military exploits, where she has won several wars while fighting under significant personnel and weapons disadvantages. But even the victories of the 1948 war of independence, the 1967 six-day war, and the 1973 Yom Kippur war have not elevated Israel's army to the "great" level. They are fierce, resourceful, and dedicated warriors; but ultimately, an army's battlefield conquests prove its greatness. For example, it took Allied victories over Nazi Germany and Japan in World War II before America's armed forces achieved this status.

To explore Zechariah's reference more deeply, it is useful to look at David's most famous conquest. This came when he was a youth and defeated the nine-foot-tall giant, Goliath, who everyone else refused to fight. Prior to fighting Goliath, 1 Samuel 17:33-37 shows David first receiving King Saul's permission. David justified his confidence in his ability to defeat Goliath on his killing of a lion and a bear that attacked his father's sheep. After receiving the king's permission, David defeated Goliath, establishing his reputation as a fierce warrior. Do David's victories over the beasts and Goliath have any link to end-time events? Amos 5:18-19 provides a potential tie-in, as during the Day of the Lord, Israel flees from a lion just to run into a bear and is then attacked by a serpent when she stops to rest. Both Israel and David have three enemies, the first two being the same: a lion and a bear. The lion and the bear are also seen in another important portion of end-time prophecy: Daniel 7's four great beasts (a lion; a bear; a leopard; and a terrible, nondescript creature). Clearly, a leopard is not a man (Goliath) or a serpent, but could the last unnamed beast represent them? If it does, then, like David's past heroics, Israel will fight three enemies, one like a lion, one like a bear, and one resembling both Goliath and Daniel's fourth great beast. While exploration of the enemies' identities must wait until the great tribulation chapter, it is safe to assume that if Israel can survive these attacks, her army will have proven worthy of Ezekiel's description (exceedingly great).

Israel's Faux King

Naturally, these conflicts drive this tiny nation to thirst for peace, but their attempts to quench it only plunges them deeper into tribulation, as Israel once again foolishly chooses its leaders. For example, in the time of judges, Israel was to rely exclusively on God and have no form of centralized government. Instead, they first attempted to make Abimelech king and later, during the days of Samuel, sought yet another king. This last request resulted in the end of the time of judges and the coronation of Saul.

In both cases, Israel sought a king against God's will. These demands were made during the days of the judges. During this time, God sent judges to lead the nation, and Israel's disobedience would temporarily force God to remove his protection and blessings. This allowed other nations to abuse them and eventually caused Israel to plead for God's help. On one occasion, God sent the judge Gideon to deliver Israel from the hands of the Midianites and Amalekites (Judges 6-8). Following God's directions, Gideon first destroyed his father's altar to Baal, along with its accompanying grove, and then led a small group of men (three hundred total) in the destruction of a much larger army. In gratitude, Israel's leaders begged Gideon and his descendents to become their king. Motivated by their fear of God, Gideon and seventy of his sons refused. After Gideon's death, yet another of his descendents, Abimelech, sought and received the title rejected by the others. He then ordered the rest of his brothers executed. Only the youngest, Jotham, survived and eventually, in Judges 9:8-15, leveled a series of charges against Abimelech and the men of Israel. Jotham's indictment heavily drew on critical Bible symbols having deeper spiritual applications. The fig tree, olive tree, and vine asked by the trees to rule over them are symbolic of the nation of Israel and spiritual fruits, especially the Holy Spirit. Like Gideon and the rest of his sons, the fruitful plants refused to abandon their God-ordained roles by giving in to lust and pride. Only worthless bramble, such as Abimelech, rebel against God's will by seeking their own pleasure, power, wealth, and glory. To their hurt, the men of Israel made just such a man their king.

Prior to Saul's coronation in 1 Samuel 10:1, Samuel warned the Jews of the suffering the king they demanded would inflict on them (1 Samuel 8:11-20). Without compensation, they would lose much: property, possessions, sons, daughters, servants, livestock, and freedom. More ominously, God tells them when they cry out because of the king they chose he would not hear them. Even with these warnings, the people demanded their king and received Saul rather than God's chosen king, David. Again, these passages weave in the symbols of the olive trees and vines, demonstrating the king takes away the best of their physical possessions and spiritual fruits.

In the future, Israel repeats these mistakes. Instead of waiting for God's king, Jesus, they become impatient and demand a king. Once again, they turn to bramble, the antichrist, with whom they enter into an extremely ill-advised peace treaty. Until overthrown by Jesus, this cruel man rules as he pleases. As he did during Saul's reign, God ignores Israel's pleas for relief from their bramble king. Israel's relief does not come until they desire to see Jesus (Matthew 23:37-39), and sadly, this only occurs after two-thirds of Israel has perished (Zechariah 13:8-9) and Jerusalem has virtually fallen (Zechariah 14:2). Israel pays a horrific price for making this bramble their king, and to their shame, this is not the first time, nor the second, but at least it will be their last.

Revelation: The Last Days Road Map

This section's last, and perhaps most important, key is Revelation's sequential nature. Starting with its seven churches, the book of Revelation serves as an end-time road map, guiding its readers through the prophetic timeline turn by turn until it reaches its final destination with the eternal new creations. This enables it to serve as a "Rosetta stone" that assists in the correlation of a myriad of separate, unrelated prophecies dispersed throughout the rest of Scripture. Unique in this regard among the books of the Bible, Revelation is critical to understanding many aspects of the last days and forms the basis for the timeline discussions for the rest of this book. The rest of this section introduces more of Revelation's interesting elements.

Revelation's author is most likely John the apostle (though there is some debate on this point), who also authored the last of the four gospels, the book of John. Many see interesting parallels between the two books, especially in the descriptions of Judas in John and the antichrist in Revelation. John probably wrote the book of Revelation around AD 96, when he was a prisoner on the isle of Patmos. Its introductory verse provides the book's title: "The Revelation of Jesus Christ." The title sets the tone for the book, which focuses on revealing Jesus Christ both as redeemer and king. This verse also explains God gave the book of Revelation to John and this book's alternate title is "The Revelation to Saint John the Divine". Revelation 1:19 lays out Revelation's scope, covering the past (seen), the present (are), and the future (shall be). Although John is to record the past, precious little of Revelation deals with it. Even this verse restricts the past to just the things seen by John to this point in the vision, a very narrow window.

One of Revelation's most interesting aspects is its application of numbers, especially the Bible's "perfect" numbers. Four "perfect" numbers take prominent roles throughout its pages: three (divine perfection), seven (spiritual perfection), ten (ordinal perfection), and twelve (governmental perfection). Three represents the trinity of God (Father, Son, and Holy Spirit) and appears in Revelation as:

- the Holy Trinity
- the unholy trinity
- three woes

- three sets of judgments (seals, trumpets, and vials)
- three rewards for believers (crown and raiment, riches, and dominions)
- three falls of Satan (expelled from heaven, bound in bottomless pit, and thrown in lake of fire)

Seven, also known as the number of completion, is the length of a week and the number of millennial days in humanity's history. It is also the number of the Holy Spirit, and his stamp is all over the book of Revelation:

- seven letters, seven candlesticks, seven churches, seven stars, and seven spirits of God (Revelation 1–3)
- seven lamps and seven spirits of God (Revelation 4)
- seven seals (Revelation 5–8)
- Lamb of God: seven horns, seven eyes, and seven spirits of God (Revelation 5:6)
- seven angels and seven trumpets (Revelation 8–11)
- seven thunders (Revelation 10:4)
- seven angels, seven plagues, and seven vials (Revelation 16)
- Dragon: seven heads and seven crowns (Revelation 12:3)
- Beast: seven heads and sitting on seven hills (Revelation 13:1, Revelation 17)
- seven kings (Revelation 17)
- seven dooms (Revelation 17–20) (Babylon, beast, false prophet, kings, Gog and Magog, Satan, and the unbelieving)
- seven new things (Revelation 21–22) (new heaven, new earth, new peoples, new Jerusalem, new temple, new light, and new paradise with river of life)

Ten represents the perfection of divine order and appears elsewhere in the Ten Commandments, the tithe, and the ten virgins. In the book of Revelation, ten appears as:

- the dragon's ten horns (Revelation 12:3)

- the beast's ten horns and ten crowns
  (Revelation 13:1, Revelation 17)

- Smyrna's ten days of suffering (Revelation 2:10)

Twelve represents governmental perfection and appears in the Bible as the twelve tribes of Israel, twelve months per year, and twelve apostles. In the book of Revelation, twelve appears as:

- 12,000 sealed from each of twelve tribes (Revelation 7)

- a crown of twelve stars (Revelation 12:1)

- new Jerusalem: twelve gates, twelve foundations, and 12,000 furlongs long (Revelation 21)

- Tree of Life: twelve manners of fruit (Revelation 22:2)

While these other aspects of Revelation are both interesting and distinctive, its most important and compelling feature is its sequential, prophetic timeline. It forms the foundational structure for interpreting prophecies following Jesus' ascension. While Revelation's narrative does not include every biblical end-time event, it provides enough information that it greatly simplifies the process of deciphering the placement of other events.

Summary

The Bible's end-time prophecies comprise a significant portion of Scripture. Its high standards and strong credentials set it apart from all other forms of predictions and prognosticating. Their understanding serves several purposes, including evangelism, believer's edification, and protection from the enemy's lies. Its mastery requires proficient use of hermeneutics plus a good working knowledge of scriptural truths and doctrines. This chapter introduced a few of the keys to unlocking prophecy's secrets. The following chapters build on these basics to create the last days' detailed timeline, which is Revelation centric but freely draws additional narratives from the rest of Scripture.

Timeline Overview

End-time prophetic studies tend to become detail-oriented processes where it is often easy to lose sight of the big picture, a classic example of the cliché that one cannot see the forest due to the trees. Before looking at the timeline's details, this chapter surveys the big picture by briefly summarizing the entire prophetic timeline. The detailed descriptions in the succeeding chapters follow the flow of these high-level discussions to make it easier to cross-reference the two descriptions.

The prophetic timeline consists of four major chronological periods:

- the church age (approximately two thousand years)
- the tribulation (seven years, perhaps longer depending on transition times)
- Jesus' millennial reign (one thousand years)
- eternity: new heaven and new earth (immeasurable thousands of years)

The shortest of these four periods is the tribulation. It lasts only seven years but is so full of prophetic events that it contains four subdivisions:

- transition period starting with the rapture (uncertain duration)
- tribulation period (first three and a half years)
- midtribulation (a short transition period)
- great tribulation (last three and a half years)

The next shortest period, Jesus' millennial reign, also has short transition periods. The first starts at the end of the great tribulation and continues through several judgments until the normal operation of the millennial reign is established. A final transition occurs between the millennial reign and eternity as the present heaven and earth vanish and final judgments are pronounced.

Figure 2 shows the chronological layout of these four major periods and their subdivisions. Overlaying this chronology are Revelation's seven major themes (phases): preparation, redemption, coronation, decision, subjugation, dominion, and perfection. The first theme, preparation, includes the complete church age and is a time of preparation for Jesus' return. Its distinguishing characteristics are the propagation of the Gospel of Christ, a time of Jewish distress, the preparation of the world for the fulfillment of tribulation prophecies, Jesus' preparation for the arrival of his bride with her bridal party, and the bride's arrival in heaven. The earth's redemption theme is next and is the time when Jesus redeems the earth by breaking each of the seven seals on Revelation's mysterious book (Revelation 6-8). The coronation theme, with its seven trumpet judgments, follows (Revelation 8-11). Each trumpet leads up to Jesus' coronation as King of kings and Lord of lords, which occurs after all seven trumpets have sounded. His coronation ushers in the most tumultuous period the world ever endures: the periods covered by the decision and subjugation themes. The decision theme forces earth's remaining inhabitants to decide whether they will serve God while, in the subjugation theme, seven vial judgments subject all people and dominions under Jesus' ruling authority. Jesus' return starts the transition into the dominion theme, featuring

Jesus' thousand-year reign over the whole earth. A transition period consisting of the destruction of the existing creation and humanity's final judgments leads into Revelation's final theme: perfection. The perfection theme brings everlasting, perfect creations free from sin and its effects.

Figure 2: High-Level Prophetic Timeline

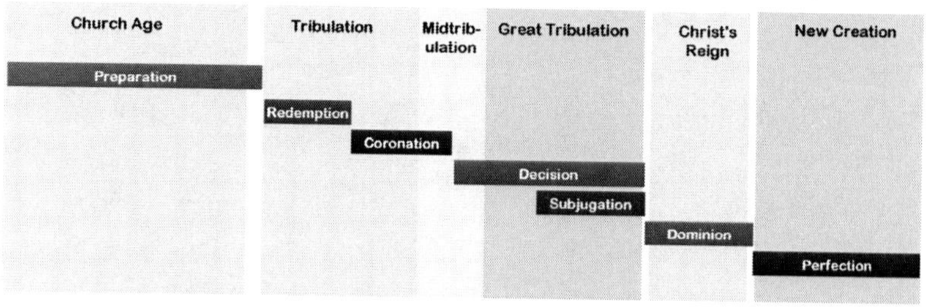

Together, figure 3 and figure 4 show all details of Revelation's timeline. These figures show the relative relationships of events in different periods. Figure 5 through figure 9 decompose the detailed timelines into smaller, easier to read pieces. Each covers a different portion of the timeline and shows the many prophetic details of each. In these figures, event spacing merely illustrates sequential relationships and does not imply timeframes. The following sections expand the descriptions of each Revelation theme.

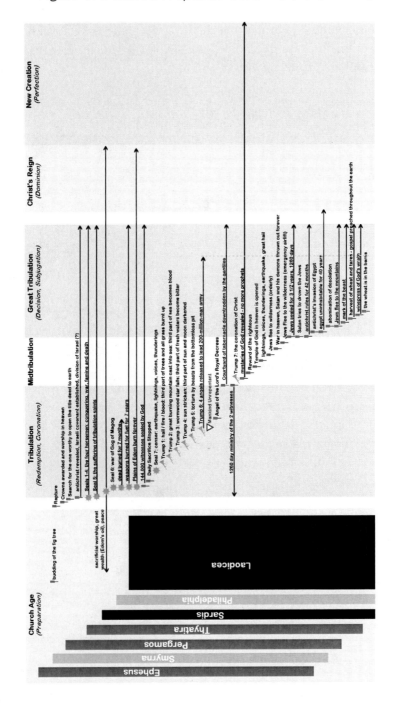

Figure 4: Detailed Prophetic Timeline (Part 2 of 2)

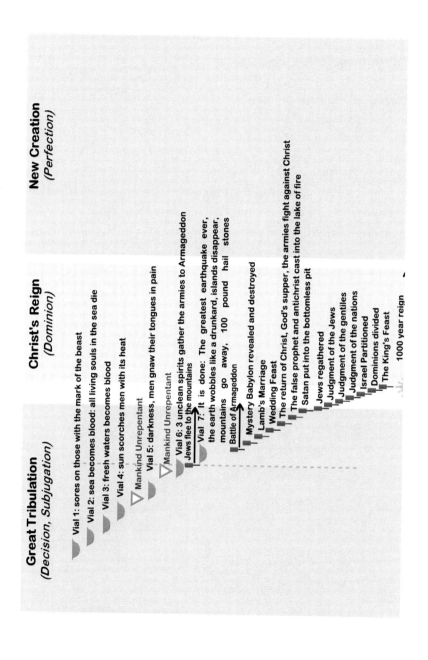

Preparation

During the preparation theme, Jesus prepares a place in his Father's land for the church; the Holy Spirit prepares the bride by calling, nurturing, and protecting church members; and the church prepares the world for Jesus' return through the proclamation of his Gospel. Also known as the church age, this period started in the first century when Jesus founded the church and ends with the rapture. Revelation 1-3 reveals the church age through a vision of Jesus Christ and letters written to seven first-century churches located in ancient Asia Minor (modern Turkey). Collectively, the seven letters foretell church history, with each successive letter foreshadowing the dominant characteristics of each successive period. Church periods are marked by the characteristics of the period's dominant church. Just as all seven churches existed when John received Revelation's vision, all seven church types exist during any church period. Figure 5 shows the seven churches in sequence, and Table 5 lists key characteristics of each of the seven churches, along with timeframes for their corresponding church period. The dates are only approximate, and differences are prevalent among various scholars.

Figure 5: Church Age Timeline

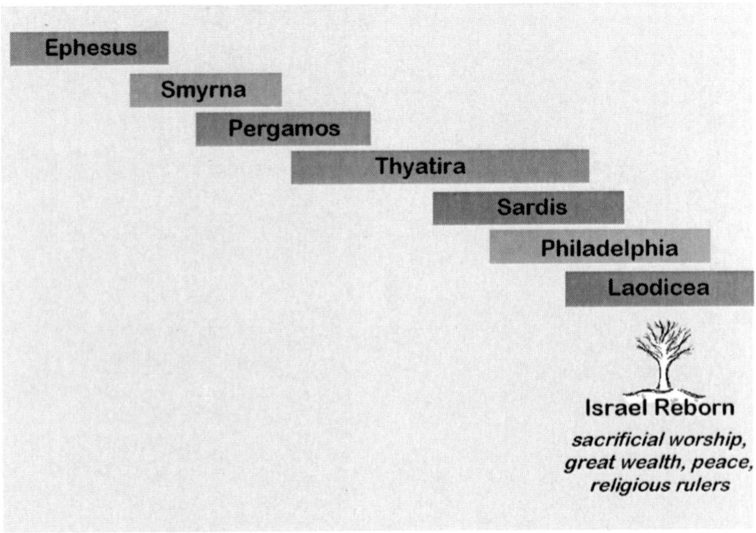

Ephesus

Smyrna

Pergamos

Thyatira

Sardis

Philadelphia

Laodicea

Israel Reborn

*sacrificial worship,
great wealth, peace,
religious rulers*

For Israel, the church age is a dark time. It starts with them being scattered to the four corners of the earth and only deteriorates from there. Throughout this time, they suffer greatly under numerous curses laid on them by their husband, God the Father. They are reluctant witnesses for the righteousness of God, as everywhere they go, people ask why God has forsaken them. Jeremiah 22:9 shows the answer: "Then they shall answer, Because they have forsaken the covenant of the Lord their God, and worshipped other gods, and served them." Their suffering is immense since God has laid the burden of all righteous blood, from Abel to Zachariah, on their account (Matthew 23:35). Not all is hopeless for Israel, as Scripture makes it clear God has not permanently rejected Israel, and this allows them to cling to the hope of a future national rebirth.

The last days bring the restoration of hope, as Jerusalem awakes one more time and the nation's dead and dry bones again come to life. Jews start returning to their homeland and continue to do so until Jesus finishes the task of gathering them on his return. The curses that were the exclusive purview of the Jews now start migrating to their enemies. The time of Jesus' return is now very close, and the generation witnessing these events does not pass away before he returns. Prior to his return, Israel must survive extremely perilous times where just their presence brings fear and conflict to the world. They struggle for their very survival as they become a cup of trembling, which eventually causes the whole world to drink God's fury. Their enemies are numerous and strong, but they will all be thwarted, as each citizen of Jerusalem fights with the strength of David. As Israel grows stronger, so do her enemies. Before Jesus' return, they fight many of Daniel 7's beasts as every nation seeks the final elimination of Israel: humanity's last desperate attempt for Satan's "final solution."

Table 5: The Seven Churches of the Church Age

Church	Approximate Dates	Church Characteristics
Ephesus	Up to AD 100	The zealous apostolic church that got so busy doing the work of God and defending the faith that they lost their love for God.
Smyrna	AD 100–312	The first of two faultless churches. This is the persecuted church marked by its physical poverty and spiritual wealth.
Pergamos	AD 312–600	A faithful church that tolerates false doctrine.
Thyatira	AD 600–1500	A church of love and works but permeated by the teaching of false doctrines.
Sardis	AD 1500–1750	The first of two churches without any praise. It is a church that on the outside appears alive but is actually dead. Even in this church there are some worthy members.
Philadelphia	AD 1750–1900	The second of two faultless churches. Also known as the "perfect" church of brotherly love. It has an open door, tremendous works, and great love.
Laodicea	AD 1900–present	The last church prior to the rapture. An indifferent church with tremendous material wealth and no praise. It is characterized by a lack of love, works, and spiritual poverty. Most of its members will stand before God naked and without rewards.

Before the church age concludes, it is likely Israel experiences several changes that set the stage for an early, devastating tribulation war. Some of Israel's changes include:

- tabernacle erected and sacrificial worship started
- Israel believes they finally have peace and safety
- Israel acquires great wealth

While not clear, it seems reasonable that most, if not all, are in place prior to the rapture. For example, sacrificial worship must be in place before Daniel's abomination of desolation in the middle of the seven-year tribulation and logically would be in place prior to this war. Israel's prewar confidence of safety and security might be the direct result of a covenant with death Ephraim makes with the antichrist at the start of the tribulation. Israel's great wealth triggers a major early tribulation war, and whatever its source, it must be discovered prior to the war's onset.

As the church age ends, moral conditions on the earth have deteriorated to match those seen prior to two other famous judgments of God: Noah's flood and the destruction of Sodom and Gomorrah. It is also a time of great pride, explosive knowledge growth, rapid worldwide travel, spiritual apostasy, scoffing, and mocking. People see, ignore, and ridicule the warnings of impending doom. Even in the church, rampant materialism displaces God's spiritual things. Consequently, sin abounds, and it continually occupies people's thoughts. People freely dedicate themselves and their bodies to fulfilling the desires of the flesh. Drunkenness, gluttony, sexual indulgences, and sexual deviancies abound.

Revelation's preparation theme ends with the rapture, the church's physical removal from the earth (1 Corinthians 15:51-52). Occurring at a time known only to God the Father, all church members instantly receive a new, immortal, sinless body as they rise to meet Jesus in the air. Jesus then leads them to heaven and the place prepared for them. Those remaining on earth after the rapture clearly know the righteous have disappeared. Their response is, for the most part, apathetic indifference that appears void of the panic one might expect. At no time do they consider that the removal of the righteous clears the path for God to pour out his wrath on all unbelievers (Isaiah 57:1).

A brief transition period of uncertain duration precedes the tribulation's start. Figure 6 displays the timeline of both the transition period and the first half of the seven-year tribulation. All known tribulation transition activities occur in heaven, and these start with God judging the believers brought to heaven in the rapture. At this judgment, the believers receive crowns and raiment reflective of their works on earth. Next, an incredible heavenly worship scene commences. As the worship fervor starts to subside, God the Father brings out the earth's title deed, and a search commences for someone worthy to open it. Only Jesus is found, and when he takes the book, the worship reaches a three-part climax consisting of all saints throughout history, over 100 million angels, and all creatures throughout God's creations.

Figure 6: Tribulation (first three and a half years) Timeline

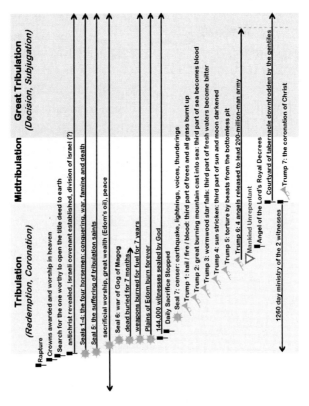

Redemption

Now begins the most horrific time in history: the seven-year tribulation. The Bible splits it into halves, with the first half simply called the tribulation and the second half called the great tribulation, emphasizing its greater severity of judgments.[1] It starts with Jesus opening earth's title deed. As Jesus breaks each of the book's first four seals, he reveals a different horse and rider of the infamous four horsemen of the apocalypse. Each rider traverses the earth from its principle cities to its extreme outposts. Starting in the tribulation's earliest moments, these horsemen continue riding and afflicting the world with their plagues, presumably until Jesus' return.

The first of these horsemen rides a white horse, has the implements of war without any visible ammunition, imitates the Son of God, and sets out to subdue the world. Known by many names, including the beast, the son of perdition, and the antichrist, his first act (and one of the few recorded in this period) is the confirmation, or strengthening, of a peace treaty with Israel (also called a treaty with death), and specifically with Israel's religious leaders and the children of Ephraim. Israel now believes peace and safety have finally arrived, but the Bible sounds its warning: sudden destruction is coming. At roughly the same time the first horseman starts riding, two men with the power of the Old Testament prophets Elijah and Moses start witnessing against him.

The second seal's horseman rides a red horse, carries a great sword, and brings war. The third seal's horseman rides a black horse, carries a set of balances, and brings famine. The fourth seal's horseman, the last of the apocalypse, rides a pale horse and kills the wicked. The combined efforts of these four horsemen take a tremendous toll on the earth's inhabitants. By the end of the great tribulation, they will have destroyed 25 percent of the world's population, or 1.6 billion people (based on current estimates of a 6.4 billion people world population).

The fifth seal introduces martyrs. These are not Christians (who are safely in heaven) but are new converts who reject the antichrist. Throughout the seven-year tribulation, the antichrist wages an escalating war against both God and his people. This seal reveals just the first of the martyred saints, and their deaths continue at least until the Lamb's marriage supper and probably until Jesus finishes appointing all millennial rulers (Revelation 20:5-6).

The sixth seal brings a series of catastrophes, including a great earthquake moving islands and mountains, a substantial reduction of the sun and moon's light, things falling to the earth, and the sky rippling like a scroll. The situation becomes so terrifying that people flee into mountains and rocks for safety from God's wrath. The likely reason for these catastrophes is an invasion of Israel by a northern and southern alliance. This war, propelled by the invader's greed, quickly turns bad for them as God intervenes and Israel uses all its available weaponry to fend off its own annihilation. Surprisingly, the war seems to end almost as quickly as it begins. The war immediately destroys five-sixths of the primary invading nation. Likely, the destruction extends to many other nations, but the scope and range of the destruction is not clear. After the war, Israel spends seven months burying the fallen that pollute their northern lands and seven years burning weapons seized in the battle for fuel. For over a thousand years, oil fields in the plains of Eden (southeast of Jerusalem) will be an environmental disaster, burning out of control.

Before Jesus breaks the last seal, angels protect 144,000 Jews from the remaining judgments by sealing them with the mark of God. When Jesus breaks the seventh and last seal, he exposes this book's contents for the first time in millennia. Before the next series of judgments starts, an angel thrusts a censer filled with the prayers of the saints down to the earth. Earthquakes, lightning, voices, and thunders afflict the earth and those on it. It is probably in this timeframe that the antichrist stops the Jews from performing daily sacrifices (Daniel 11:31).

Coronation

The coronation theme's seven trumpet judgments begin when a storm of hail and fire mixed with blood destroys a third of all plant life on the earth. A second trumpet causes a great burning mountain to fall into the sea, destroying a third of the saltwater creatures and shipping. The third trumpet brings a great star down from heaven, and it turns a third of the fresh waters bitter. Possibly a direct result of the first three trumpets, the fourth trumpet darkens a third of the stars, moon, and sun.

The last three trumpets bring the three great woes of Revelation, one for each trumpet. The first woe releases diabolical beasts from the bottomless pit. Day and night for five months, these beasts torment those without the seal of God. The sixth trumpet brings the second woe as four fallen angels are released from the confines of the Euphrates River. These angels lead and drive a 200-million-man army, which eventually destroys a third of humanity. Between the effects of the four horsemen of the apocalypse and six trumpet judgments, half the world's population dies (around 3.2 billion people at today's estimated population of 6.4 billion). After this, God checks for the first of three times to see if he can end the judgments but finds even these first two woe judgments have had no effect.

Prior to the last woe's trumpet judgment, a mighty angel comes to earth with a little book of royal decrees. With one foot on dry land and one on the waters, he cries out, and seven thunders speak. The mighty angel then swears an oath on the highest authority possible (God Almighty) and promises there will be no delay in finishing the mysteries of God.

As shown in figure 7, the coronation theme continues into the period traditionally known as the midtribulation. The first of these events is an apparent loss of Jewish autonomy, as they lose control of both the temple mount and Jerusalem. For forty-two months, they are unable to restrict and control the movement of Gentiles in these areas (most likely a byproduct of the antichrist's peace treaty). After this, the antichrist kills the two witnesses who have been an irritant to him since his arrival in the first seal. These witnesses have had the gall to boldly proclaim God's truth to the world's inhabitants, including who and what he is, God's call for repentance, Jesus' coming coronation, and the rightful king's return to the earth. For three and a half days, people celebrate and exchange gifts in gratitude for their deaths. This is abruptly interrupted when a heavenly voice calls and they ascend slowly to heaven. Within an hour, a major earthquake hits Jerusalem, destroying a tenth of the city and killing seven thousand people.

Figure 7: Midtribulation Timeline

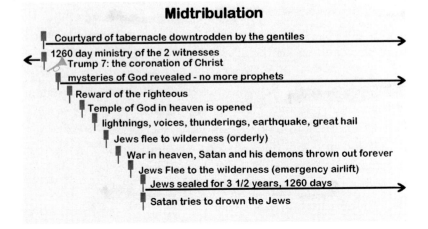

Now, gloriously, the seventh trumpet proclaims the arrival of the seven-year tribulation's seminal event: Jesus' coronation. Every prior event in heaven during the tribulation has led up to this moment. The seal judgments portrayed Jesus as the rightful heir, claiming his land, and the seven trumpet judgments proclaimed his royalty. The mighty angel promised it, and the two witnesses testified of it. Now, accompanied by the blaring of the seventh trumpet and shouts from the hosts of heaven, Jesus is crowned King of kings and Lord of lords. He is a king without peer, wielding absolute power in mercy, love, and with a rod of iron. The world is angry because:

- Jesus' wrath has come upon them (Revelation 11:18)

- their judgment has come (Revelation 11:18)

- the righteous of all ages are rewarded (Revelation 11:18)

- those who destroy the earth (sinners) will be destroyed (Revelation 11:18)

The next three and a half years produce the greatest turmoil and suffering ever experienced by humanity, as the antichrist struggles to consolidate, expand, and hold onto his power and the wicked rebel against their new king in heaven.

Jesus' coronation brings two judgments: one for the world's wicked and another for heaven's righteous. The former is a series of judgments involving God's wrath that continues to escalate until the end of the great tribulation. The second is the reward judgment of the righteous where the righteous' works are burned by fire. The fire destroys the wood, hay, and stubble of sin and leaves the precious jewels and metals of good works. This is the second of three reward judgments with the crown and raiment judgment, occurring just after the rapture and the dominion judgment coming after Jesus' return. Jesus' coronation also reveals the mysteries of God; opens God's heavenly temple; and brings earthquakes, lightning, thunders, and great hail. These events lead many Jews to flee to a place of safety in the wilderness of Edom.

Next, God the Father starts subjugating Jesus' enemies as Michael and his angels fight Satan and his demonic forces. As unbelievable as it may sound, Satan has maintained access to the throne of God even after his rebellion and fall.[2] As he did with Job, he has used this access to make false accusations and brazenly proclaim the sins and flaws of the righteous before God. Now, Michael's forces thoroughly rout Satan and his armies. He casts them down to the earth, where they are forced to remain until Jesus' return. Satan's arrival on earth is the third of the trumpet's three woes, and he aims his full wrath directly at the earth's inhabitants, particularly Jews and saints.

Satan's eviction brings urgency to the Jews' evacuation to

Edom's safe place, as they now fly to safety (Revelation 12:14). Those reaching this place in time are sealed in its protective cocoon for 1,260 days. Stragglers are left out, vulnerable to Satan's attacks.

Decision

The great tribulation has begun, and this hectic, chaotic time sees:

- the antichrist's ascension to power
- the revealing of the last member of the unholy trinity (the false prophet)
- the abomination of desolation
- the last great evangelistic crusade
- the last series of judgments
- the last and greatest war
- Mystery Babylon's destruction
- Jesus' return at the height of the great war

Figure 8 shows the flow for milestones of the great tribulation (for continuity, this figure overlaps figure 7). Since his defeat at the hands of Michael and his angels, Satan's anger is at an all-time high. In a short time, Michael has eliminated his access to the throne of God and God has thwarted his attempt to destroy the Jews in the wilderness. He seeks revenge by corrupting and destroying anything cherished by God. He finds a willing and equally angry partner in the antichrist.

Figure 8: Great Tribulation
(2nd three and a half years) Timeline

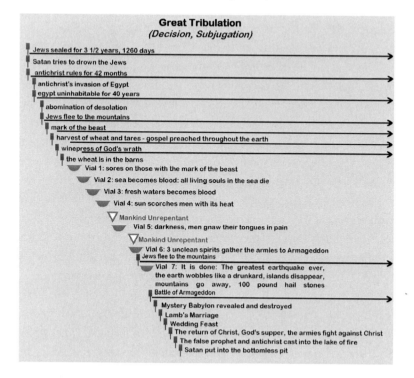

Great Tribulation
(Decision, Subjugation)

Jews sealed for 3 1/2 years, 1260 days
Satan tries to drown the Jews
antichrist rules for 42 months
antichrist's invasion of Egypt
egypt uninhabitable for 40 years
abomination of desolation
Jews flee to the mountains
mark of the beast
harvest of wheat and tares - gospel preached throughout the earth
winepress of God's wrath
the wheat is in the barns
Vial 1: sores on those with the mark of the beast
Vial 2: sea becomes blood: all living souls in the sea die
Vial 3: fresh waters becomes blood
Vial 4: sun scorches men with its heat
Mankind Unrepentant
Vial 5: darkness, men gnaw their tongues in pain
Mankind Unrepentant
Vial 6: 3 unclean spirits gather the armies to Armageddon
Jews flee to the mountains
Vial 7: It is done: The greatest earthquake ever, the earth wobbles like a drunkard, islands disappear, mountains go away, 100 pound hail stones
Battle of Armageddon
Mystery Babylon revealed and destroyed
Lamb's Marriage
Wedding Feast
The return of Christ, God's supper, the armies fight against Christ
The false prophet and antichrist cast into the lake of fire
Satan put into the bottomless pit

In order to enslave and destroy both God's creation and his people, Satan gives the antichrist his full power, authority, and seat (throne). His help fuels the antichrist's meteoric rise to power as he uses deceit, flatteries, cunning, and wit to manipulate people and circumstances to take power peacefully. Satan subjugates all national powers, including Daniel 7's first three beasts, under the antichrist's complete and arbitrary control. Though his power is far from absolute, the antichrist maintains control within a single international ruling authority until Jesus destroys him forty-two months later.

Under the antichrist's reign, the old nations still maintain their own political structures, leaders, and military forces. This includes an alliance of ten nations (Daniel 7) that form his primary base of power. Sometime after he comes to power, the antichrist solidifies his position by destroying three of the leaders who put him there. During his reign, he fights many wars designed to solidify his power, suppress opposition, enslave people, and acquire wealth. It is likely that he now invades Egypt and several of its neighboring nations on two separate occasions. The effects of these attacks are devastating, as he rapes the nations of their wealth and resources, completely wastes the land, makes the area uninhabitable for forty years, and scatters the people of Egypt throughout the earth. The Egyptians will remain dispersed throughout the earth until well into Jesus' reign, when the land is again becomes livable.

Neither Satan nor the antichrist are content with world domination. They also seek to steal the worship of men that rightfully and legally (the first and second commandments) belongs to God. They fight a spiritual war unparalleled in the annals of man, where their goals are simple: force everyone to worship them and kill anyone who does not. As people start worshipping them, the antichrist is emboldened and mocks God. He blasphemes God's name, God's tabernacle, and those dwelling in heaven (God, the angels, and the saints) as he fights against and kills many of the remaining great tribulation saints.

Satan and the antichrist expand the spiritual battle by adding a third, and final, partner to their team. This beast, the false prophet, imitates the prophets of God and completes the unholy trinity, a direct counterfeit of the Holy Trinity (Father, Son, and Holy Spirit). The false prophet appears to the have the authority of two major religions (perhaps Christianity and Judaism) while performing many miracles suggestive of Elijah. He carries out two signature works: the creation of the image of the beast and the introduction of a new monetary system, the mark of the beast. The first is most likely Daniel's abomination of desolation, and it appears to live and speak. Everyone is forced to worship it on pain of death. The second requires people to have a mark embedded, or possibly imprinted, in their right hand or forehead. This will be the world's only legal tender.

Now arrives a unique point in history; everyone, everywhere must decide between God and Satan. This is focal point of the Revelation's decision theme and reaches this point when God sends three angels to respond to the image and the mark of the beast. They preach God's ultimatum to everyone in every nation and in every language. Their messages are simple: give God his due, Mystery Babylon will be destroyed, and those following the unholy trinity will suffer eternal damnation in the lake of fire. Between the first and third angels' messages, people must decide whether to serve God or Satan. They can take care of their immediate, short-term needs by receiving the mark of the beast but spend eternity paying for it in the lake of fire; or they can reject the mark and struggle to survive the great tribulation while avoiding eternal damnation in the lake of fire.

From this point until Jesus' return, God's judgments slay enormous numbers of the earth's wicked while countless numbers of those rejecting the antichrist become martyrs at his hands. This is Jesus' harvest of the wheat and tares, where Jesus personally harvests the wheat (the great tribulation saints) and another angel harvests the tares (the wicked). God calls the wheat blessed, people who will rest from their labors and have their works follow them. The tares, also called wild grapes, face destruction in the winepress of God's wrath, another name for the battle of Armageddon. This winepress, located just outside Jerusalem, is eventually trod by Jesus, who stains his garments in its overflowing juices. Before Jesus concludes treading the grapes, its juice, the blood of his enemies, reaches the bridles of horses and flows for over two hundred miles. The angel's tare harvest continues through the rest of the great tribulation and includes all the vial judgments plus Jesus' obliteration of the world's armies on his return.

Subjugation

The last judgments, the seven vials of God's wrath, now start and are likely retribution for the suffering of the tribulation and great tribulation saints. Regardless of their motivation, their effect is the subjugation of all people on earth under Jesus' authority. These judgments start as angels bring the vials out of God's heavenly temple and smoke from the glory of God fills the temple. The seven vial judgments are:

1. noisome and grievous sores on those with the mark of the beast

2. salt waters become blood and every living soul dies

3. fresh waters become blood

4. the sun scorches men with its heat

5. the capital and kingdom of the beast are filled with darkness

6. the armies of all nations are gathered to Armageddon

7. the battle of Armageddon

As he did after the sixth seal, God looks to see if the people on earth are repentant. After both the fourth and fifth vials, God finds humanity is unrepentant. The angel's pouring of the sixth vial seals humanity's fate, dries up the Euphrates River, and causes three demonic spirits to call all the nations to Armageddon. Their arrival is a signal to Jews to flee to the mountains. Any remaining in Jerusalem after this face the brunt of the wrath of Armageddon's invaders.

The seventh vial is the last of God's seven-year tribulation judgments, and a great voice emphasizes this by proclaiming, "It is done!" This is a terrible time unlike anything before or after. It is so bad that if the events continued unchecked and unchanged, nothing would survive, man or beast. It would see the elimination of an additional 3 billion people and according to Zephaniah, all life including beast, fowl, and fish. Fortunately, God interrupts (shortens) these events with Jesus' return. This reprieves half of the earth's population and rescues God's chosen people: the Jews.

This time sees mammoth hailstones weighing seventy-five pounds and the greatest earthquake ever. The earthquake is so massive and widespread that it removes islands, levels mountains, destroys entire cities, and divides Jerusalem into three parts. It also ushers in the greatest war ever in the valley Megiddo, also known as Jezreel. This valley of decision is the same valley where the last king of Judah was defeated and the reign of David's lineage ended. Now this valley sees the reign of David's lineage resume with Jesus. Lastly, it brings Mystery Babylon's destruction at the hands of the same leaders who empowered the antichrist. God calls his people out of the city, and when they are safely gone, the city is utterly destroyed in less than an hour. This is Babylon's second fall, and this time God leaves her forever desolate and unoccupied. Only wild animals will occupy her hills from this day forward. For millennia, she seduced nations, destroyed saints, and killed the apostles; but now kings, merchants, and traders all mourn her destruction while in heaven all celebrate her demise and the end of her wicked reign, deeds, and seductive influence.

In heaven only the Lamb's wedding followed by its marriage supper remains. They do not take place until after God destroys the city of the guests who refused their wedding invitations (Mystery Babylon). These guests' refusal delayed the wedding while God sent his servants to find, invite, and bring in replacement guests: the tribulation and great tribulation martyrs. As the guests arrive, God gives them proper wedding attire and they prepare to witness the Lamb's marriage.

As the wedding celebrations die down, people on earth are dying in huge numbers, and without God's direct and immediate intervention, nothing on earth will survive. In heaven, Jesus and his armies assemble and ready themselves for battle. Then they wait for the Jews to cry out for the Messiah to rescue them.

On earth, it is only when all hope is lost that the Jews finally cry for God's salvation and the Messiah's appearance. When he hears their cry, Jesus returns and starts the transition from the great tribulation into his millennial reign (see figure 9). As Jesus approaches the earth, an angel prepares the way by calling all fowls and beasts to the supper of God, which will be served in the valley of Megiddo. Then, everyone on earth witnesses Jesus returning in the clouds in great glory and power. Without delay, the antichrist, the kings, and their armies turn to fight Jesus and his armies. First, Jesus throws the antichrist and the false prophet into the lake of fire, where they remain its sole residents for a thousand years. Then Jesus fights his enemies while he sends his armies out to fulfill their sole directive: occupation. Jesus alone wins this victory as he demolishes the world's armies. His enemy's blood now freely flows and turns Jesus' pure, white clothing to crimson red. The best efforts of his enemies prove fruitless, as their weapons do not hurt or even slow either Jesus or his armies.

Figure 9: Timeline of Events Following Jesus' Return

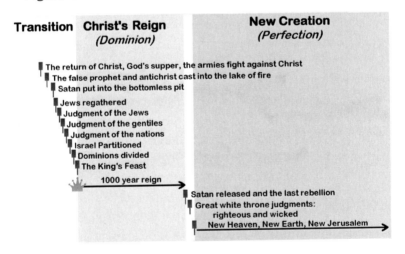

When the fighting ends, an angel binds and casts Satan into the bottomless pit. The bottomless pit previously holding the antichrist and many fallen angels now incarcerates Satan throughout Jesus' millennial reign. After Satan no longer presents any danger to the Jews, Jesus goes to the wilderness, unseals the prepared place, and brings those Jews back to Jerusalem without even pausing long enough to change his clothing.

Dominion

The next few months are hectic as Jesus gathers Jews from all corners of the earth, brings them back to the land of Israel, and judges each against the terms and conditions of their marriage covenant. From these judgments, each Jew receives Jesus' rewards or death in hell. Afterward, he judges Gentiles based on their willingness to accept his ruling authority. Those refusing forfeit their lives. The judgment of nations follows. Jesus groups Gentile nations into sheep (right hand) and goats (left hand) according to their treatment of Israel. He destroys the goat nations while preserving the sheep nations. After Jesus judges the nations, he partitions Israel and the surviving Jews receive their land allotments. The transition period ends with the appointment of millennial rulers over all of the earth's jurisdictions. The king ends the transition with a grand feast for the earth's occupants, the last of God's three great feasts (the marriage feast, God's supper, and the king's feast).

Peace, safety, and prosperity mark Jesus' thousand-year reign. Some highlights of his reign include the end of war, Jesus' peace covenant with humanity, Jesus' everlasting kingdom, and the building of the final temple. At the end of this thousand years, an amazing sequence of events unfolds when God releases Satan from the bottomless pit and Satan inspires humanity's final rebellion. As the rebellious armies camp outside Jerusalem, preparing to attack, God destroys them with fire descending from heaven. The armies' destruction ends Satan's role in the history of humanity as God casts him into the lake of fire, where the antichrist and the false prophet have already been suffering for a thousand years.

The curtain now closes on the existing creation as fire destroys them. Next, the great white throne judgments purge all remnants of sin. Jesus sits on this throne and individually judges people based on their works in two separate judgments. In the obscure first judgment, God rewards the righteous who died after the great tribulation. In the second judgment, the wicked of all ages are judged. All those standing before Jesus in this second set of trials receive the same sentence: eternal life in the lake of fire. Here, they suffer forever from all sorts of punishments, including fire, darkness, disease, flesh-devouring worms, and separation from God. Their bodies continually renew themselves so their pain never subsides or ends.

Perfection

God now replaces the destroyed creation with a new, glorious one. It consists of the new heaven, new earth, and new Jerusalem. Virtually everything known about these new places comes from Revelation 21-22. They are places of indescribable, incomprehensible beauty and value. Precious jewels and pure, transparent gold form key building materials for major parts of new Jerusalem, including its foundation and streets. The city of new Jerusalem is huge. It reaches heights of 1400 miles and has a base spanning 1400 miles per side. The glory of God continuously fills it with light, and it is a true twenty-four hour a day, seven day a week city, where the light never goes out. It is the center of all worship activities, and the river of life flows freely from the dual throne of God the Father and the Son. Everyone entering the city is able to enjoy the river's healing properties. Along the river of life's banks grows the tree of life, which yields twelve types of fruits twelve times a year. Outside the city is the lake of fire, a constant reminder of the consequences of sin.

The prophecies of the Bible end here, with the righteous in the new creation joyfully spending eternity with God and the wicked suffering forever in the lake of fire.

Each of the following chapters provides detailed investigations of the different prophetic periods. Starting with the church age and continuing through eternity, they expand on many of this chapter's missing details and provide background to many of this chapter's interpretations.

The Church Age (Preparation)

Revelation's road map starts with the church age. The church age begins shortly after Jesus' resurrection and continues until the rapture. During this time, the church preaches the Gospel of Christ to the four corners of the earth and God's new covenant (salvation by faith) replaces the old covenant (Old Testament law). Birthed out of Jesus' sacrifice, the church works to methodically prepare the world for the Bible's fullness of time when Jesus takes his earthly throne. By the end of the church age, nations, political alliances, governmental systems, spiritual apathy, and technologies are all in place for fulfilling tribulation prophecies.

This chapter reviews the church age prophecies contained in the first three chapters of Revelation. The prophecies in these chapters cover this period exclusively from the church's perspective. As shown in the next chapter, other church age prophecies cover this period from a Jewish perspective.

Introduction to the Revelation of Jesus Christ

Section reference: Revelation 1:1–8.

Revelation's introduction immediately stakes out its contents, veracity, and intended audience. It identifies its contents as prophecy through its title (Revelation of Jesus Christ) and the revealing of things to come. Heightening the prophetic anticipation, these verses also point to Jesus' triumphal, glorious second coming. As a work of prophecy, Revelation, and more importantly, its author, must conform to the Old Testament standards for prophets: perfect accuracy and first commandment adherence. Since most of its prophecies are yet unfulfilled, the focus on validating Revelation's veracity must center on its author.

Unique among the Bible's books, Revelation claims to be a collaborative effort. Its prestigious lineage starts with God the Father, who conceived it and gave it to Jesus Christ. This presents the first of many of Revelation's difficult mysteries. If Jesus is God, why does God the Father need to give it to him? Based on Matthew 24:36, some suggest Jesus did not have the details of this Revelation while he was on earth. This view suggests Jesus only received the complete Revelation when he went to heaven. This interpretation is difficult because Jesus' end-time teachings (e.g., Matthew 24) demonstrate his mastery of eschatology in general and last days events specifically. More likely, God the Father shared the vision's content with Jesus sometime prior to his birth in Bethlehem.

After receiving this vision, Jesus gives it to its human transcriber through an emissary: God's angel. While not directly identified, the angel's role of revealing the vision to John is suggestive of the role of the Holy Spirit, who teaches and reveals all truths to people (John 14:26). This idea is reinforced when John employs a mysterious reference—"the seven spirits which are before his throne"—in his salutation to the Asian churches. While some proffer that these are seven angels (perhaps even the seven seen later with the trumpet and vial judgments), this is probably a reference to Isaiah's seven spirits,[1] a probable reference to the Holy Spirit. If the angel is the Holy Spirit, then John receives the visions of Revelation with the full force, power, and unity of the Holy Trinity: Father, Son, and Holy Spirit. John seems to immediately emphasize the Holy Trinity's role in this work when the salutation mentions each member individually:

God the Father ("him which is, and which was, and which is to come"), the Holy Spirit ("the seven spirits which are before his throne"), and Jesus Christ. This sets a tone seen throughout the entire book of Revelation where each member of the Godhead plays active, visible roles in bringing its visions to fruition and sets this book apart from all other books of the Bible.

The book's final credibility rests on its human author and his creditability as both an accurate witness and recorder. This author identifies himself simply as John but is widely thought to be Jesus' beloved disciple, the author of the gospel of John and the three epistles of John. If the Apostle John is its human author, the book's veracity is beyond question.

The last key point of these verses is Revelation's audience: seven churches located in Asia Minor, the modern country of Turkey. These churches play prominent roles, as each receives a letter from Jesus. During the first century, letters (epistles) written to churches were copied and circulated among all churches for everyone's edification and instruction. Probably, the book of Revelation was handled in a similar fashion, suggesting Revelation had a second, broader audience: all Christians.

While Revelation's salutation is unique from other New Testament epistles, John also includes the commonly used epistle greeting, "Grace be unto you, and peace." Sometimes, mercy was added between grace and peace, but in every case the order of the salutation never deviates from the sequence: grace, mercy, and peace. This salutation is a simple picture of salvation since God's grace first provided atonement for sin and when this mercy is applied it produces peace with God. This greeting informs all readers that Revelation's unnamed blessings are for God's redeemed who read, hear, and keep Revelation's prophecies. So important is it that it is repeated a second time in the book's epilogue. The first two verbs, read and hear, speak of the process of searching Scripture, which is a characteristic highly esteemed by God (Acts 17:11). The last verb, keep, speaks of the process of putting faith into action, as emphasized in James 1:22-25.

Before proceeding, it is useful to explore a few minor points in these introductory verses. First, Revelation's titles convey part of the story, providing subtle timeline and narrative clues. For example, this salutation provides an extensive list of Jesus' titles. Of these, the most intriguing title is the "prince of the kings of the earth." Later, in Revelation 17:14 and 19:16, his title changes from prince to king. As a prince, there remains the expectation of ascension to a throne, and it appears, at least for now, Jesus portrays himself not as the king but as the heir apparent.

Church Age Overview

Section reference: Revelation 1:9-16.

Banished by Emperor Domitian to the island of Patmos around AD 95 for faithfully preaching the Gospel of Christ, John is in the spirit on the Lord's day when he receives this vision. Being in the spirit probably indicates he is praising and worshiping God despite hardships, while the Lord's day is significant because it frames Revelation's prophecies to the seventh millennium: the Day of the Lord. John's worship is interrupted by a great voice sounding like a trumpet, foreboding the rapture's trumpet. Through three of his titles, the speaker identifies himself as Jesus Christ and commands John to write everything he sees in a book and send the book to seven churches in Asia Minor located within approximately one hundred miles of each other (see figure 10):

1. Ephesus
2. Smyrna
3. Pergamos
4. Thyatira
5. Sardis
6. Philadelphia
7. Laodicea

Figure 10: The Seven Churches of Revelation

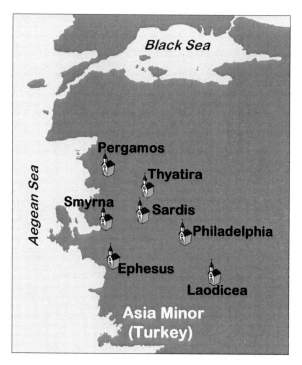

Next, John sees a glorious vision of Jesus. The vision not only conveys aspects of Jesus' character and majesty but also flavors each of the church's letters by giving insights into the church's favor or disfavor, depending on which detail is used. The garment down to the foot and the golden girdle on his chest he wears shows him as humanity's high priest (Hebrews 3:1, Hebrews 6:20, Psalm 110:4, Isaiah 11:5, and Genesis 14:18-20). His snow white head and hair portray him as a man full of the wisdom of the ages (Leviticus 19:32). His eyes being like a flame of fire indicates that he constantly seeks the truth and executes judgment (1 Peter 3:12 and Isaiah 10:17). His feet like fine brass demonstrate he destroys Satan and sin while simultaneously protecting the righteous from the furnaces of persecution (John 3:14, Exodus 38:3, Numbers 21:9, Matthew 27:46, and Daniel 3:20-23). His voice like many waters suggests he is the source of the water of life (John 4:5-15, James 3:12, and

Revelation 21:6). The sharp, two-edged sword from his mouth is the Word of God (Hebrews 4:12, Luke 4:4, and Deuteronomy 10:16). His countenance like the sun shows his close fellowship with his Father (Exodus 34:29-35 and Matthew 17:1-2). Finally, the seven golden candlesticks and the seven stars portray Jesus as the church's close friend and protector.

At this point, John has not mentioned seeing any of the trappings of Jesus' royalty. This omission is all the more glaring when one considers Jesus' description in Revelation 19, where John describes him as having many crowns, ruling with a rod of iron, and having the title of "King of kings and Lord of lords." These omissions seem to match Jesus title of "the prince of the kings of the earth" from Revelation 1:5 and once again suggest Jesus has yet to ascend his rightful throne.

© Pat Marvenko Smith - www.revelationillustrated.com

Revelation's next two chapters contain the seven letters. They give insights into the first-century church's strengths and weaknesses and a prophetic overview of the progressive development of the church. Each letter shows the church's dominant characteristics during seven phases of development. Just as all seven churches existed simultaneously during the first century, it is possible to find examples of each church type in any church phase. For example, today, it is easy to find the persecuted church (Smyrna) even though the dominant church type is the apathetic, lukewarm church (Laodicea). The dominant church type of a church phase defines it, not the sundry different exceptions.

The following sections separately explore each church and the church period it represents. Since many of the letters refer or allude to locally significant features of the church's city, a short description of each first-century city precedes the analysis of the church's letter.

Ephesus

Section reference: Revelation 2:1-7.

The first stop on the church age road map is the church of Ephesus. At the time this letter was written, Ephesus was at its zenith as one of the largest and most impressive cities of the ancient world. Its population of 250,000 to 500,000 (estimated) made it one of the largest cities of its time. Its geography, natural resources, and manmade features made it a political, religious, and commercial center. Chief among its assets was its artificial harbor, capable of supporting the largest ships of its day. It sat on the Cayster River somewhere between the mouth of the river and a point three miles inland. To the north lay the Hermus River, and to the south the Maaeander River. It laid on four of the most important Roman roads in Asia Minor. These provided excellent access to the Hermus and Maaeander River basins as well as the rest of Asia Minor. These transportation systems made Ephesus one of the most accessible cities in Asia. Ephesus also rested in an exceptionally fertile valley between two hills: Prion and Coressus.

Ephesus was the primary harbor for Rome's Asia province. As such, Roman law compelled Roman governors to enter this province through Ephesus. The Roman governor of the province resided in Ephesus even though Pergamum was the official capital. Effectively, this made Ephesus the de facto capital of Asia. It had the privilege of self-rule, and consequently, no Roman garrisons were stationed there. Today, its ruins sit near the Turkish city of Selcuk but nowhere near a harbor, as silt from the Cayster River slowly filled it over centuries of neglect. The city is now six to seven miles inland.

Perhaps the greatest source of Ephesus' city pride was its most prominent landmark: the Temple of Artemis. Considered by many to be the greatest of the seven wonders of the ancient world, it drew vast numbers of religious pilgrims and was an important source of revenue for the city. The temple was made of the finest marble and other materials. It sat majestically on a hill, giving an impressive view to those approaching. The temple's interior was 425 feet long and 290 wide. Its one hundred and twenty-seven richly sculptured pillars, each said to be the life's work of a single king, supported the roof. It was covered and filled with the finest carvings, statues, and paintings.

The primary purpose of the temple was the worship of the fertility goddess Artemis (Diana). Statues of Diana show her naked from the waist up. From the front, row upon row of breasts cover her chest. Thousands served Diana as priests, priestesses, eunuchs, and slaves. The priestesses were thinly veiled prostitutes selling their sexual favors to those worshiping the goddess. Many profited from this service, including the temple's staff, merchants, and artists. Diana merchandizing (e.g., figurines) was big business and nearly caused a riot when merchants feared Paul's preaching threatened their revenue streams (Acts 19). Prior to the first-century introduction of Christianity, the worship of Diana (or similar goddesses) was the dominant religion in many parts of the region.

In Ephesus' letter, Jesus draws on the image of him holding the angels and standing in the middle of the candlesticks. This image sets the letter's tone and reminds the church he is protecting them and fellowshipping with them. Thus, he approaches the church of Ephesus as a lover trying to revive his mate's love by reminding her of the depth and breadth of his love. Here, Jesus calls the one he loves to return to him with all her heart.

The letter then moves to the church's appraisal. It is one of three mixed reviews. Only two churches receive unblemished reviews while two receive no praise. With each review, Jesus sends a clear message: he is watching and judging.  Ephesus' review starts with their good works, including their labors; their hatred of evil, including the deeds of the Nicolaitanes; and their love of the truth. This shows the Ephesians have worked diligently and patiently without succumbing to depression or fatigue. Jesus acknowledges their unselfish motives, their zeal, and their defense of the faith. Jesus singles out their testing of false apostles for special praise. Apostles were one of five church offices established in Ephesians 4:11. Two of these, the apostles and the prophets, were critical for establishing the church. Many believe these were active only in first century while the other three (evangelists, pastors, and teachers) are active throughout the church age. Like prophets, apostles had special qualifications that could be tested and verified. Some generally accepted apostolic qualifications include:

- eyewitnesses to Jesus life on earth

- personally called to the office by Jesus

- words and writings possess the power of the prophets

- authority proven through the working of miracles

Significantly, only this letter makes any mention of the apostles. Since false prophets and false apostles had the potential to destroy the early church, their identification was critical to protecting it and keeping its doctrine pure. The Ephesians understood this and zealously guarded the church's integrity.

With the praise concluded, Jesus moves to Ephesus' shortcomings. In this case, Jesus lists only one complaint: they have left their first love. The Greek word for love in this context is agape (Strong's G26), the superior form of love that God alone has truly mastered. This indictment suggests the church of Ephesus had gotten so busy laboring they had simply failed to spend the time with Jesus necessary for nurturing their relationship and renewing their love. This is similar to the husband, who spends so much time at work that he fails to spend any time with his wife and family until one day he discovers the love has died and he has lost his family. Likewise, it is easy for the bride of Christ to get so busy working for Jesus that she fails to spend any time with him and eventually loses her love for him. This seems to be what happened to the early church, as they got so involved in spreading the Gospel that they simply forgot their love. It is a risk all Christians face daily and must vigilantly guard against.

As a zealous groom, Jesus pleads with the church to return to its loving fellowship with him, but he also warns he will not wait forever. Eventually, his jealousy provokes him to remove the church's candlestick. This broken fellowship may seem a small thing, especially in light of their tremendous work, but to Jesus (and his Father), it is intolerable. Consider God's promise to Israel:

> Because thou servedst not the Lord thy God with joyfulness, and with gladness of heart, for the abundance of all things; therefore shalt thou serve thine enemies which the Lord shall send against thee, in hunger, and in thirst, and in nakedness, and in want of all things: and he shall put a yoke of iron upon thy neck, until he have destroyed thee.
>
> Deuteronomy 28:47-48

When Israel loses her love and zeal for God, she suffers under the harsh rule of their enemies. When the church loses her love, Jesus removes her candlestick, and the church dies. Apparently, the first-century Ephesians never regained their love for Jesus since this church has been gone for a long time. Consequently, numerous generations in the area have not had ready access to the Gospel of Christ.

Before he concludes, Jesus commends the church one last

time because they hate the works of the Nicolaitanes. (Notice how carefully Jesus chooses his words; there is no hatred of the people, only of their works.) The Nicolaitanes are an obscure sect, as are their origins and beliefs. The Bible mentions them only twice: here in the letter to the Ephesians and in the third letter to the church of Pergamum. The Nicolaitanes' name comes *clergy* from Greek root words meaning to conquer the people (niko, to conquer, and laos, the people or the laity). The letter to Pergamum also mentions another false doctrine, Balaam, that may give clues to this doctrine. Balaam comes from Hebrew root words meaning "lord of the people" or "destroyer of the people." The names of both sects suggest their doctrines ensnare and enslave people. While not conclusively known, some suggest the sect of Nicolaitanes used the liberty of Christ to sin freely and that the Nicolaitanes had virtually no moral standards, especially concerning sexual activities.

Jesus concludes this letter with the same phrase used in each of the seven letters: "Let him hear what the Spirit saith unto the churches…" The instructions of each letter come from the Holy Spirit and are for the edification of all Christians, not just those in this church. During the great tribulation, Revelation 13:9 changes this phrase to simply, "Let him hear." The absence of both the church and the Holy Spirit in this great tribulation declaration are yet another confirmation that by then, the rapture has already occurred.

Each letter also concludes with a final promise for those who overcome. The word overcome conveys the importance of winning battles, not just fighting them. With this, Jesus sets a high standard, where Christians must not only confront the problems of life, but must also defeat them. Romans 8:37 confirms this by telling Christians to be "more than conquerors." "More than conquerors" are armies who not only win battles but so thoroughly defeat their enemies that they are unopposed and are able take the spoils of war and enact new political policies. Jesus makes it clear he expects Christians to overcome the world, not be subject to it.

The final promises of the first three letters speak of the gift of eternal life. In this letter, the promise is for Christians to eat of the tree of life. This is the same tree rejected by Adam and Eve in the garden of Eden (Genesis 3:22-24). Today, it is in paradise, where Jesus went after his crucifixion (Luke 23:43) and Paul heard words unlawful for men to utter (2 Corinthians 12:4). After God creates the new heaven and earth, it grows in new Jerusalem.

Ephesus represents the first church period, the age of the apostles, which ended as the apostles died. The start of the Ephesus church period is generally set on the day of Pentecost in Acts 2. Its end is typically set sometime around AD 100, with the death of the last of the apostles.

Table 6 shows a summary of the church of Ephesus. This busy church was full of works and zealously defended the faith and fought hard to keep doctrine pure. As shown by the presence of the Temple of Artemis, ardent pagan worship confronted them. Their zeal and fervor for Jesus caused them to become so busy that they lost their fervent, deep love for Jesus. Jesus calls this church to come back to him. If they do not return, he will remove their candlestick. For those overcoming, Jesus lets them eat from the tree of life.

Table 6: Ephesus Church Summary

Ephesus	
City Characteristics:	Large, powerful city noted for Temple of Artemis (Diana), one of the seven wonders of the world. Primary harbor for Rome's Asia province.
Church Summary:	The zealous apostolic church that got so busy doing the work of God and defending the faith that they lost their love for God.
Represented Age:	Up to AD 100
Jesus' titles:	Holds the seven stars in his right hand and walks in the midst of the seven golden candlesticks (protection and fellowship).
Commendations:	**Condemnations:**
Cannot bear evil people. Tried false prophets. Patient. Much labors. Hate Nicolaitanes' deeds.	Left first love.
Rewards:	**Punishments:**
Those who overcome eat of the tree of life	Unless they repent and do the first works He will remove their candlestick.

Smyrna

Section reference: Revelation 2:8-11.

The next stop on the prophetic timeline is the church at Smyrna. Founded in 1000 BC, Smyrna is a city that survived and thrived despite adversity. Numerous fires and earthquakes through the millennia destroyed significant portions of it. The most notable of these occurred around 600 BC. Afterward, it lay dormant for three centuries until rebuilt in 290 BC by one of Alexander's generals. It was a matter of civic pride that it had died and been brought back to life. Many considered it the most beautiful of all Greek cities. It sloped down the hill of Pagus, meeting the sea, and as one approached the city, buildings at the top of Pagus' rounded hill looked like a crown. This attribute earned the hilltop the nickname of "the crown of Smyrna."

As a city, Smyrna idolized Rome and built a temple to worship this city in 195 BC. A century later, Roman general Sulla's army faced bitter winter weather without proper clothing. On hearing of the soldier's plight, the citizens of Smyrna literally gave the army the clothes off their backs. In AD 26, Rome rewarded Smyrna's loyalty with a temple dedicated to the emperor Tiberius. In the second century, an earthquake destroyed much of the city, and Emperor Marcus Aurelius rebuilt it yet again.

Smyrna's name comes from myrrh, and this foreshadows its difficulties. The fragrance myrrh was one of the city's chief products, and it is often associated with pain and suffering because of its use in embalming fluids and painkillers. It has a rich biblical history:

- Myrrh traders bought Joseph (Genesis 37:25)
- Israel sent it to appease the ruler of Egypt (Genesis 43:11)
- It is a key component of the temple's holy anointing oil (Exodus 30:23)
- It was offered to Jesus as he was dying on the cross (Mark 15:23)
- It was used to prepare Jesus' body for burial (John 19:39–40)
- It was used to prepare the marriage bed (Song of Solomon)
- It was given to Jesus at his birth (Matthew 2:11)

The gift of myrrh at Jesus' birth painted a picture of his death and suffering while gifts of gold and frankincense spoke of his deity. In the future, people no longer give Jesus gifts of myrrh, only gold and frankincense (Isaiah 60:6). This gift is now inappropriate since he is no longer destined to suffer and die.

Today, the city is still alive and known as Izmir (a variation on Smyrna). Its population is roughly 2,500,000, which makes it one of the largest in Asia Minor. Its ancient harbor has filled and now rests beneath a modern bazaar. New buildings cover much of the old city, including the stadium.

The letter to the church of Smyrna is the shortest and one of only two unblemished appraisals. This church refused to worship Caesar as God and suffered for it. Polycarp was an early pastor of this church and is famous for uttering, "Eighty and six years have I served him, and he never did me any harm. How can I deny him?" in response to a demand to deny Jesus to save his life.

For Smyrna, Jesus identifies himself with the titles of "the first and the last" and "which was dead, and is alive" to remind the church of his eternal nature. He reassures the church that, no matter what tribulations they face, he is there with them. More importantly, he reminds them he is the first fruits of the grave. He has already endured and overcome the persecution this church suffers, and he gives them the strength to overcome everything befalling them.

Jesus tells the church he knows their works, tribulations, poverty, and the blasphemy of the liars of the synagogue of Satan. Their works show they are a busy church, constantly striving to fulfill God's will. The city repays their good deeds with tribulations and poverty. The Greek work for tribulation, thlipsis (Strong's G2347), also means pressure or persecution. This is Revelation's persecuted church, and  this persecution resulted in great poverty, which made them unable to meet the basic needs of themselves and their families.

Without the ability to work, earn wages, and probably own property, they would have no choice but to depend on charity, which, in this environment, would be difficult to find. Despite their physical poverty, Jesus calls them wealthy. Later, he calls the wealthiest church (in terms of physical possessions) poor. The poverty of this church is temporary whereas the poverty of the last church is eternal. God is stockpiling great rewards for Smyrna's Christians in heaven.

The indictment of those saying they are Jews but are of the synagogue of Satan is likely a fulfillment of John 16:2, where Jesus foretold people thinking they were doing God's will when persecuting his church. Jesus testifies they are actually doing Satan's will. This is the first of two times these letters mention the Jews, and on both occasions, they oppose faultless churches.

Jesus comforts Smyrna's Christians, telling them not to fear. He urges them to be faithful, even if it costs them their lives while he warns Satan will lead a ten-day persecution of the church. During this time, their persecutions will increase beyond work restrictions to include prison and execution. Jesus promises a reward for those who are faithful: a crown of life. This is one of five crowns listed in the New Testament:

- the incorruptible crown (1 Corinthians 9:24–27)
- the crown of rejoicing (1 Thessalonians 2:19–20)
- the crown of life (James 1:12; Revelation 2:10)
- the crown of righteousness (2 Timothy 4:8)
- the crown of glory (1 Peter 5:2–4)

Since the New Testament spreads the descriptions of these crowns into different locations, it is difficult to determine whether they are attributes of a single crown or separate crowns. In Revelation 19, Jesus wears many crowns; however, these represent dominion over nations and do not yield any clues on how many crowns the righteous receive.

The letter ends with Revelation's standard blessing for Christians who hear what the Spirit of God is telling the churches. Again, the blessing is dependent upon overcoming the world. This time, those who overcome receive protection from any harm from the second death: Revelation 20's lake of fire. Those who go into this lake never leave it, and they enter with eternal bodies that are impossible to destroy. Only the unsaved (those not born-again) are sentenced to the second death. The simple rule of thumb is:

- born twice (physical and spiritual), die once (physical)
- born once (physical), die twice (physical and spiritual)

The Smyrna church period represents the early church persecuted by the Roman Empire. The city of Smyrna is representative of the Roman Empire. Their devotion to Rome, their religious systems, and their persecution of those who do not worship the state deity are consistent with the city of Rome. Most agree the Smyrna church period started around AD 100 and continued through the death of Diocletian in AD 312 The general agreement for the church period is the ten days of church persecution represents the persecution of the church by ten different Roman emperors. Ten emperors often listed as Christianity's persecutors include:

1. Nero (AD 64–68): Crucified and threw Christians into pits with wild animals; executed Paul and possibly Peter.

2. Domitian (AD 90–96): Killed thousands in Rome; banished John to the Isle of Patmos.

3. Trajan (AD 104–117): Outlawed Christianity; burned Ignatius at the stake.

4. Marcus Aurelius (AD 161–180): Tortured and beheaded Christians.

5. Severus (AD 200–211): Burned, crucified, and beheaded Christians.

6. Maximinius (AD 235–237): Executed Christians.

7. Decius (AD 250–253): Tried to wipe out Christianity and executed those he could find.

8. Valerian (AD 257–260): Tried to wipe out
   Christianity; executed the bishop of Carthage.

9. Aurelian (AD 270–275): Persecuted
   Christians any way he could.

10. Diocletian (AD 303–312): Burned the Scriptures.

This list suggests this period starts prior to AD 100 or this period overlaps the prior church age. Between the reigns of many of these emperors, there were short gaps that allowed a little reprieve for the early Christians. These reprieves, though, did not alleviate or reduce their poverty since legal restrictions still limited their ability to earn wages and own property. Estimates suggest this period may have witnessed as many as 5 million Christian martyrs.

Table 7 shows a summary of the church of Smyrna, which was one of two churches without condemnation. As the myrrh produced in the region, they produced a sweet fragrance from their sufferings. For ten days, they endured tremendous persecution. They worked hard but faced great opposition from both pagan and Jew. They are a very poor church, but they have stockpiled tremendous wealth where it matters most: heaven.

Table 7: Smyrna Church Summary

Smyrna	
City Characteristics:	Name comes Myrrh, a plant associated with suffering. Myrrh was a chief product. Survived and thrived despite adversity. It had died and come back to life. Many pagan temples.
Church Summary:	The first of two faultless churches. This is the persecuted church marked by its physical poverty and spiritual wealth.
Represented Age:	AD 100–312 [Persecuted by ten emperors]
Jesus' titles:	The first and the last, which was dead, and is alive (Jesus eternal nature)

Commendations:	Condemnations:
Works. Tribulation. Physical poverty. Spiritual wealth. Attacks from Jews and synagogue of Satan.	None

Rewards:	Punishments:
Be faithful unto death → Crown of life. Those who overcome are not hurt by the second death.	None

Pergamos

Section reference: Revelation 2:12-17.

The third church is Pergamos, the official capital of Asia Minor. Pergamos and Pergamum are alternate names for this city: Pergamos is the feminine form and Pergamum is the neutral form. Pergamos is located about 100 miles north of Ephesus, with Smyrna about halfway between the two. Unlike Ephesus and Smyrna, it has no port because it is about 15 miles from the Aegean Sea. It is located in the Caicus River basin but is three miles away from the river. Two tributaries of the Caicus River—the Selinus and the Kteios—fed Pergamos, but neither tributary was navigable. The Selinus flowed through the city while the Kteios flowed along its walls. Pergamos also did not sit on any major trade routes. The lack of good ports, navigable waters, and highways with heavy trade traffic severely hampered commerce. Naturally, unlike Smyrna and Ephesus, Pergamos was not a trading or commercial center, though they were noted for their ointments, pottery, and parchment.

By the end of the first century, Pergamos had been the capital of Rome's Asia province for about 250 years. Its stature as the region's longstanding capital caused many to consider it the greatest city in Asia. Even during Roman rule, Pergamos viewed itself as the defender of Greek culture in Asia Minor. It was an important center for culture and learning. Its large library, second only to Alexandria in size, contained over two hundred thousand volumes at its peak and had a 44' by 52' reading room. Legend has it that, due to issues arriving from its rivalry with the Alexandria library, it had to develop an alternative source of writing tablets for its books. When Egypt refused to give Pergamos papyrus, Pergamos refined the use of parchment. The name parchment may even be a derivative of the city's name. Later, Mark Anthony permanently ended this rivalry when he gave Pergamos' entire book collection to Cleopatra for Alexandria's library.

Pergamos was a center of worship for four deities: Athena, Asklepios, Dionysis, and Zeus. Each had its own beautiful temple built by Pergamos' citizens. The most notable of these was the altar of Zeus, which was a 90 feet wide, 90 feet deep, and 40 feet tall structure placed on a hill in such a way that, from a distance, it looked like a giant throne.

Pergamos still exists today as a city of approximately fifty thousand with the name of Bergama (a Turkish derivative of Pergamum), and its chief exports are cotton, wool, and leather.

To the church of Pergamos, Jesus introduces himself as the one with the sharp sword with two edges, the Word of God. Its presence indicates Jesus is either reaching out to the lost or purging the sins of the church. Unfortunately, the text of the letter shows it is the latter.

Jesus commends the church of Pergamos for not denying his name or the faith, even at the cost of their lives. Jesus also tells them he knows they live in a stronghold of Satan that has both his seat and dwelling. While no consensus exists on these references, many suggest Satan's seat may be the altar of Zeus, the sanctuary of Asklepios, or the temples of the emperors. Visually, the altar of Zeus looks like a seat and is a natural candidate. In these same verses, Jesus also refers to the martyr Antipas, who was probably one of the early leaders of the church, but few facts about him survive. Tradition claims the citizens of Pergamos roasted him to death inside a brass bull during the reign of Emperor Domitian.

Jesus faults this church for having members holding the hated doctrines of Balaam and the Nicolaitanes. The verb hold suggests these members actively believe and teach these false doctrines. Their influence within the church causes other members to depart from the faith and corrupts church  doctrine. Numbers 22-31 provides clues to the doctrine of Balaam. Balaam was a prophet for hire brought by Balak, king of Moab, to curse the Jews. When the angel of the Lord prevented Balaam from cursing the Jews, Balaam counseled Balak to intermingle the two peoples. The idea was Moab's women would marry Israel's men and then exert their influence to cause the children of Israel to abandon God by committing fornication, worshipping idols, and eating things sacrificed to the idols. Balak followed Balaam's counsel, and his advice inflicted great damage on Israel's relationship with God. As a result, God inflicted great judgments on the Jews. The second doctrine mentioned in this letter, that of the Nicolaitanes, was also found in the church of Ephesus. An important difference between these churches is Ephesus hated this doctrine and Pergamos tolerated it.

Jesus calls on the church to repent. If they do not, Jesus comes quickly, brandishing his sword, the Word of God, to cut away both the sin and sinners. It is unfortunate many Christians, including those in Pergamos, do not understand their actions are tempting Jesus to use his sword against them. In their minds, Jesus' unconditional love keeps them safe from his retribution. However, this letter makes it clear there are severe consequences for tolerating, entertaining, and following false doctrines.

The promise to those who overcome is twofold: hidden manna and a new name written on stone. Manna was special bread that tasted like honey and fed the children of Israel during their wanderings in the wilderness. This bread appeared outside the camp every morning except the Sabbath so the Jews could gather it for their day's meals (Exodus 16). This manna fed their bodies while the hidden manna, which also came daily, fed the believer's spirit. The hidden manna is the bread of life promised by Jesus in John 6:35.

The symbolism of a new name in stone is rich and insightful. People normally receive new names when they are adopted (names of the parents) or get married (name of the husband). Christians receive new names at their adoption, and these names reflect both their Father and Spouse. Since these new names are permanent, Jesus writes them in stone. The names are new and probably replace Christian's present names while presumably they eventually forget their old names. As new names, they do not carry the weight of their past sins, and the white stones symbolize their newly gained purity. An ancient court ritual may also suggest the white stone's meaning. In these courts, jurors dropped pebbles into an urn to determine the defendant's guilt—black pebbles for guilty and white pebbles for innocent. The majority of pebbles, white or black, determined the verdict. Christian's stones are white, showing the cleansing effects of Jesus' blood.

The Pergamos church period starts with Emperor Constantine's Edict of Toleration AD 312 and continues to approximately

AD 600. Due to its gradual transition into the next church period, a precise end date is difficult but many scholars seem to tie it to the rise of Gregory I to the papacy in AD 590 or Pope Sabianus' death in AD 606. With the Edict of Toleration, Constantine became Pontifax Maximus, the head of the church. He unified both the church and state under one authority. Overnight, the Christians went from persecuted to esteemed. Wholesale, forced conversions of soldiers and others occurred. Pagan temples became churches, and countless churches were constructed from the stones of other pagan temples. Many priests of idols (paid by Rome) converted to Christianity and brought with them the rituals, traditions, and idols of their prior religions. This is probably the source of the doctrinal errors of Balaam and the Nicolaitans, but some consider the Nicolaitans' doctrine as the new hierarchy of the priestly ruling class.

This age saw the first ecumenical councils, restriction of doctrinal inquiry, and the introduction of civil penalties for departures from accepted norms. While not as severe as the torture and death of the Middle Ages, penalties still included deposition, confiscation, and banishment. This age also saw the inception of many new and false teachings.

Table 8 shows a summary of the church of Pergamos. This church was situated in Satan's stronghold but faithfully lifted up Jesus and defended the faith, even when it cost members their lives. However, it tolerated false doctrines. Two doctrines in particular—the doctrines of Balaam and the Nicolaitanes—permeate this church. Jesus calls this church to repent so he does not have to brandish his sword against them.

Table 8: Pergamos Church Summary

Pergamos	
City Characteristics:	Capital of Rome's Asia province and considered by some to be the greatest city in the region. Maintained large library, second only to Alexandria. Center of worship for four deities. Emperor worship very pronounced.
Church Summary:	A faithful church that tolerates false doctrine.
Represented Age:	AD 312–600
Jesus' titles:	The sharp sword with two edges (judge).

Commendations:	Condemnations:
Does not deny Jesus' name or the faith. Home of Antipas the faithful martyr. Satan's seat is located where they live.	People hold the doctrine of Balaam and the Nicolaitanes. Eat things sacrificed unto idols. Commit fornication.

Rewards:	Punishments:
Those who overcome eat of the hidden manna and receive a white stone with new, unknown name.	Unless they repent, He will quickly fight against them with the sword of His mouth.

Thyatira

Section reference: Revelation 2:18–29.

The fourth church, Thyatira, receives the longest letter. It was a city built to be destroyed. It was strategically placed in a long valley running north to south that connected the river valleys of the Caicus and Hermus rivers. One of Alexander's successors built this city as a remote outpost to protect Pergamos. The road from Pergamos went east and then southeast out from Pergamos to reach Thyatira, a distance of about forty miles. As a gateway to Pergamos, its mission was to delay attacks while Pergamos prepared its defenses. Placed by the river Lycus on relatively flat terrain, it had no natural and few manmade defenses. Consequently, this city was destroyed and rebuilt several times.

Under Roman dominion, Thyatira flourished and became a wealthy commercial center. Its location, originally a liability, now became an asset. It was a key connection point for Pergamum, Laodicea, Smyrna, and the interior regions of the Asian province. In the first century, Thyatira was reaching its peak prosperity.

Thyatira had numerous trade guilds (an early version of trade unions), with separate guilds existing for virtually every industry. Guild membership was mandatory for all business owners and workers. While the principle industries were wool production and dyed goods, many other guilds existed for several industries, including linen production, garment manufacturing, leather works, tanneries, pottery, bakeries, slave trading, and copper works. Each guild had its own patron deity, and the guilds held annual feasts in honor of its patron deity, with meat sacrifices and other pagan rituals. The dyer's guild built a reputation for its use of a special purple made from madder root. Known today as Turkish red, this is the purple Lydia of Thyatira sold in Philippi (Acts 16:14).

Unlike the other cities seen so far, Thyatira was not an important religious center and there was no sizable Jewish population. The primary god worshipped in Thyatira was the sun god, Apollo, but the biggest religious challenge to the early Christians was from the guilds. The dilemma facing Thyatira's Christians was jobs verses faithfulness to God. Today, Thyatira is a town of about ninety thousand, known by the name Akhisar.

In this letter, Jesus sets a tone of judgment by identifying himself with two symbols: eyes like a flame of fire and feet like fine brass. His eyes search for truth and rightly discern good and evil while his feet of brass stand poised to crush evil wherever found. Thyatira's appraisal is the most mixed of any of the churches. They receive both tremendous praise and condemnation.

Jesus commends Thyatira for their charity, service, faith, patience, and works. Charity can also be translated as love since its root is agape, the same love lost by the Ephesians. Interestingly, both faith and patience are steppingstones on Roman 5:1-5's agape love road map: faith, grace, tribulation, patience, experience, hope, and agape (love). This makes it natural to assume anyone commended for agape love is also praise worthy for each of the other six. Jesus further commends the Christians at Thyatira for their works and service, which likely have been demonstrated by their ministering to the needs of others. These works actually increase over time, and this is direct proof of both their faith and their love (James 2:17-18).

Jesus condemns Thyatira for allowing the false prophet Jezebel to teach in the church. Her influence is the logical progression from the compromises made by the church of Pergamos in their doctrine, particularly in tolerating the doctrine of Balaam. Following Balaam's advice to intermarry Moabite women with Jewish men, Jezebel, the daughter of Zidonian's king, married Ahab, the king of Israel. She led Israel into pagan worship of Baal, seduced Ahab to transgress the law freely, and declared war on the men of God. First Kings 18 and 2 Kings 9 shows Jezebel persecuted, hunted, and killed God's true prophets. Eventually, her enemies killed her, dogs devoured her, and her bones rotted in the streets.

As Jezebel was not a Jew, the Jezebel of Thyatira is not a Christian, though she calls herself a prophet and, by implication, a believer. It is not clear whether the church recognizes her lack of qualifications as a prophet, teacher, or believer. If they failed to see through her facade, their first sin is not testing and proving her claim to be a prophet (as the Ephesians zealously did). Consequently, her teachings seduced many church members into sin, most probably including sexual fornications and eating things sacrificed to idols. Jesus returns to the tone of the letter, judgment, persecuting Jezebel, her lovers, and her adulterous offspring. He is searching hearts (eyes of flaming fire) and rewarding works (feet of fine brass). His judgments fall only on those guilty of spiritual adultery, sparing the innocent.

Jesus closes the letter with instructions and blessings for the church's faithful. He first instructs them to hold fast until he returns. Some interpret this statement as signifying the church of Thyatira remains on the earth until the rapture. However, Jesus' focus here is one of judgment, and for those overcoming the world and proving worthy by their works, he promises special blessings. These include receiving the morning star (another name for Jesus, see Revelation 22:16), becoming rulers over nations, and ruling with rods of iron. Like the potter in Jeremiah 18:3-6, their citizens will be as pots in the hands of the potter. In Jeremiah, the pot is Israel, but in the future, it will include all nations.

The church period of Thyatira represents the Middle Ages. It starts with the end of the Pergamos church period around AD 600 and continues to the beginning of the reformation around AD 1500. During this time, warlike Asian heathen barbarians subjected Europe to a series of invasions and occupations while Islam's political and spiritual spheres of influence grew to engulf increasingly larger portions of Western Asia, the Middle East, and North Africa. The church's signature works of the Middle Ages occurred in Europe, where it was instrumental in winning the hearts and souls of several diverse groups of people. Rome's fall and the end of its established societal order introduced many new challenges to the Gospel's European promulgation. Gone were the days of highly educated, centralized population centers. Missionaries now had to explore the wildernesses, seeking the lost who often lacked even rudimentary levels of education. As a result, the church not only spread the Gospel but also laid societal foundations in the areas of education, literature, and art. Through this time, the church became a disciplinary institution characterized by its legalistic, hierarchical, ritualistic, and romantic character. The medieval church founded universities; built lofty cathedrals; stirred up the Crusades; and meddled in the affairs of sovereign nations, often dictating who could and could not reign. Like Thyatira, the strength of the medieval church was their love, faith, and works. Through the Middle Ages, the church's works grew in magnitude and number, so their works at the end were greater than at the beginning.

The medieval church also institutionalized many of the rituals and doctrinal errors of the Pergamos church age. At the same time, it was difficult, if not impossible, for laypeople to challenge the clergy since physical and language barriers blocked access to Scriptures. Few copies of the Bible existed, and access to these was limited to priests. Not surprisingly, this volatile combination led to several church crises, with the most pronounced occurring in the tenth, eleventh, and fourteenth centuries. Eventually, priesthood corruption culminated in the infamous papacies of Alexander VI (Borgia, 1492-1503), Julius II (1503-1513), and Leo X (1513-1521).

As the Middle Ages progressed, anti-Catholic opposition was met with increasingly severe punishments, including torture and death. As the power of the church grew, religious and secular authority became concentrated in the hands of a few individuals. Often, the members of the church faced the same dilemma faced by the actual church of Thyatira: spiritual purity versus the need to meet life's physical needs through employment under the onerous terms of local trade guilds. Even within the church, those seeking the truth often found themselves at odds with the very priests entrusted with protecting and proclaiming it.

Table 9 shows a summary of the church of Thyatira. This was a church full of great love and works. They faced many battles between the flesh and spirit as the influence of the trade guilds coerced them to serve the guild's pagan gods to earn a living. Offsetting their great works was their tolerance of the teachings of the false prophet, Jezebel. She seduced many to eat things sacrificed to idols and commit fornications. Thyatira and Ephesus are interesting contrasts. Ephesus lost its love while Jesus commends Thyatira for its love. Ephesus did not tolerate false doctrine while Thyatira allows Jezebel to seduce and corrupt the church. Both fell short of God's standards.

Table 9: Thyatira Church Summary

Thyatira	
City Characteristics:	Built to be destroyed. Protected Pergamum from attack. Destroyed and rebuilt several times. Trade guilds affected livelihood – forced choice of jobs versus God.
Church Summary:	A church of love and works but permeated by the teaching of false doctrines.
Represented Age:	AD 600–1500
Jesus' titles:	Son of God, who hath his eyes like unto a flame of fire, and his feet are like fine brass (judge).
Commendations:	**Condemnations:**
Great love, charity, faith, service, patience, and works that increase over time.	Allows female false prophet, Jezebel, to teach and seduce people to eat things sacrificed to idols and commit fornication.
Rewards:	**Punishments:**
Those who overcome rule over nations in strength (rod of iron) and receive the morning star.	Unless they repent, God will kill her children and give to everyone according to their works.

Sardis

Section reference: Revelation 3:1–6.

The fifth church, Sardis, is the first of two without any commendations. By the late first century, Sardis had already enjoyed a rich and colorful history, but its best days were already behind it. It had been the capital of the wealthy nation of Lydia and one of the greatest cities in the ancient world. It was located in the fertile Hermus River valley about 30 miles south of Thyatira. It was on the western end of the royal road that led east to the Persian capital city of Susa. Nearby were hot springs said to be the place where gods gave life to the dead. The city itself sat on top of the northern slope of Mount Tmolus, which stood 1000 to 1500 feet above the valley. Its design and strategic placement on Mount Tmolus made it virtually impregnable. The mount had smooth, nearly perpendicular rock walls on three sides. One could only approach the city from the south, along a steep and difficult path. The Pactolus River formed a moat that flowed at the base of Mount Tmolus. Triple walls around the city gave it an added measure of security. The walls, the city's design, and the city's location limited its ability to expand. In response, a new city sprouted up at the base of Mount Tmolus while the old city served as a refuge from danger. Ironically, the safety offered by Sardis became the reason for its fall.

Sardis reached its zenith in the sixth century BC under King Croesus. It was so widely recognized as a wealthy city that the saying "rich as Croesus" came into common usage. While Croesus led Sardis to its greatest heights, he also caused its fall to the Persians. As he heard of the growth in power and wealth of the Persians, Croesus grew more and more fearful of their threat. He decided he had to attack before the Persians grew any stronger. As was common for kings of his era, he consulted the oracle at Delphi before making battle plans. The oracle purportedly told Croesus, "If you cross the Halys you will destroy a great Empire." Croesus assumed the oracle meant Persia and apparently, never considered this cryptic answer could refer to Sardis. He attacked the Persians, suffered an embarrassing defeat, and retreated to the safety of Sardis. Angry, Cyrus, the king of Persia, was determined to extract a measure of revenge, so he pursued Croesus back to Sardis and laid siege to the city. Herodotus (Book 1) tells an astonishing story of Sardis's defeat where Hyroeades observed a soldier scaling one of the rock walls to retrieve a helmet. He also observed no guards were posted on these walls and later led a group of Persians up this path.

By attacking Cyrus and not posting watches on all approaches, Croesus brought Sardis's downfall. After Sardis's fall, Croesus was condemned to die by fire. Herodotus records that Cyrus reprieved Croesus as he stood on the wood pile prepared for his execution when Croesus told Cyrus the soldiers were not plundering Croesus' wealth but Cyrus'. Shortly after, Cyrus stopped the plundering and spared Sardis any further destruction. Incomprehensibly, Sardis falls again in 218 BC in a similar manner.

In the first century, Sardis was fabulously wealthy. Part of the wealth came from gold in the Pactolus River. Sardis used this gold to mint coins, which were widely used for commerce. Other sources of Sardis's wealth included their wool production (they claimed to have discovered how to dye wool), fruit production, and the garment industry. They were also close to trade routes and became a commercial center.

Sardis contained a magnificent temple for Artemis that may have rivaled the one in Ephesus. After Emperor Tiberius rebuilt Sardis, they built a temple in his honor. Today, the small village of Sartmustafa (a derivative of Sardis) stands among Sardis's ruins, and the closest town is Salihli.

Sardis's letter starts with Jesus identifying himself as the one having the seven Spirits of God and the seven stars. To a church receiving no commendations, Jesus simply tells the church he has the Holy Spirit and protects the leaders of the churches. He does not identify himself as either a judge or an avenger. Sardis's depravity suggests there is no fear of God in the church; and without it, threats have little effect. Neither Sardis nor Laodicea (the other uncommended church) possess the fear of God or show any desire to serve him. In both cases, Jesus encourages them to reestablish fellowship with him. To Sardis, he shows himself as exactly what a dead church needs most: life (the Spirits of God and light).

Jesus tells Sardis he is watching them and their activities. For this church, this is not good news. Like the city they live in, they have a reputation that is vastly different from reality. Sardis

5 Sardis

was known as a wealthy, prosperous city but in fact, was decaying, with its best days long past. Likewise, the church of Sardis was once a vibrant, active church but has now decayed to death. They still have the reputation of living, but this is nothing more than a reputation. Not surprisingly, Jesus is not pleased with what he sees and gives them a recipe for revival:

1. *Watch*

2. *Strengthen* the things which remain that are ready to die

3. *Remember* therefore how thou hast received and heard

4. *Hold* fast

5. *Repent*

The first and most emphasized point is the need to watch. Twice, the city of Sardis fell because they failed to deploy guards, and its church is likewise guilty of not watching. Twice, Jesus warns them that he comes as a thief. These words evoke the rapture imagery, causing some to believe the Sardis church lasts to the rapture.

It also recalls Ezekiel 33:1-12, where God made Ezekiel the watchman for Israel. Likewise, the church is the New Testament's watchman. Ezekiel was responsible for sounding the alarm to warn people to repent from their sins and now, as Sardis's letter demonstrates, the church bears this responsibility. Slothful watchmen do not alert the citizens as danger approaches, and by their inaction, are responsible for the deaths and injuries inflicted on those they were protecting. The church's inattentiveness causes death and injury to the citizens of Sardis, whom they should have protected. Instead of laying up treasures to their accounts in heaven, they have laid up the condemnation of the blood of the innocents, who should have had the opportunity to protect themselves from the coming danger of eternal judgments.

The revival recipe's second step (strengthening) demonstrates that until one dies, there is still hope. The third step (remembering) improves people's fellowship with God through thankfulness, holiness (remembering God's gifts), and obedience (fear of the Lord/God's judgments). The fourth step (holding fast) is a battlefield term describing the repelling of an attack without retreat, regardless of the odds or costs. Similarly, the church is to watch in anticipation of an attack, hold fast during an attack, and never retreat. The last step (repentance) is a call for people to turn away from their sins, not simply apologize for them. This fivefold prescription can save the spiritual life of any backslidden church or individual.

Surprisingly, even this dead church has a few pure and faithful members. The small number of faithful believers in the midst of large numbers of spiritually dead suggests the days of Elijah when Elijah thought he was the only one left serving God. However, God told Elijah that even in those dark days, a remnant of seven thousand remained (1 Kings 19:18). The promise of the faithful walking with Jesus recalls Enoch, who was taken to heaven for walking with God (Genesis 5:24 and Amos 3:3). Jesus promises to give Sardis's faithful: white raiment, names in the Book of Life, and a positive character reference to God the Father. The white raiment honors their purity while the character reference draws on the promises of Matthew 10:32-33 and Mark 8:38 (Jesus' shame). Interestingly, twice in the seven letters, Jesus encourages the church to attend to their clothing needs and both times in letters addressed to the churches without praise: Sardis and Laodicea.

The church of Sardis is generally accepted to represent the reformation period of roughly AD 1500 to AD 1750. Many mark the beginning of this period with Martin Luther's posting of his Ninety-five Theses on October 31, 1517 and its conclusion sometime around the great awakening. This period saw many reformers and reformation movements. Chief of these was Martin Luther, but many others were instrumental. Reformation movements started in many quarters, including Germany and Switzerland, but eventually spread throughout most of the world. Three fundamental principles drove it: the supremacy of the Scriptures (especially over traditions), salvation by faith (the supremacy of faith over works), and the priesthood of the believers (the supremacy of Christians over an exclusive priesthood). In particular, they rejected several traditions, including the papacy, the worship of saints and relics, transubstantiation, prayers and masses for the dead, purgatory, and indulgences.

The Catholic Church responded to the reformation with the Council of Trent (1545-1563), which provided some priesthood reforms, but with the dogma of papal absolutism they firmly entrenched themselves against Protestants. Later, the Vatican council of 1870 took the natural step of extending these "reforms" into papal infallibility, as papal directives were effectively elevated to scriptural stature. This is level of authority was never bestowed on any group in either the Old or New Testaments and elevated the papacy above the laws governing all prophets, including the greatest: Jesus.

Like Sardis, people deadened by the weight of both doctrinal errors and corruption fill the Reformation church. Their desire to maintain power and their appearance of holiness puts them at opposition to God and prevents them from watching. Just like the church of Sardis, some (e.g., Martin Luther) diligently seek to serve God. These men start the revivals leading into the next church age, the perfect church of Philadelphia.

Table 10 shows a summary of the church of Sardis. This church was very much like its community: prone to not watch for danger. It has the reputation of being alive but is dead. Jesus gives them a five-step revival program and reminds them he is coming as a thief, unexpectedly.

Table 10: Sardis Church Summary

Sardis	
City Characteristics:	Virtually impregnable city that fell twice due to failing to post watchmen. Very wealthy but decaying city. Contained Artemis Temple rivaling the one in Ephesus.
Church Summary:	The first of two churches without any praise. It is a church that on the outside appears alive but is actually dead. Possibly a wealthy church. Even in this church there are some worthy members.
Represented Age:	AD 1500 –1750
Jesus' titles:	The one with seven Spirits of God and the seven stars (life).
Commendations:	**Condemnations:**
None	Appear alive but are dead.
Rewards:	**Punishments:**
Those who overcome will be clothed in white raiment, name not blotted out of book of life, Jesus testifies of them to the Father.	Watch, strengthen, remember, hold fast, repent, or Jesus will come as a thief.

Philadelphia

Section reference: Revelation 3:7-13.

The church age reaches its zenith with its sixth church, Philadelphia. This "city of brotherly love" lays about 30 miles from Sardis and 105 miles from Smyrna, both of which lie in the

Hermus River valley. Philadelphia lays on the Coagmis River, a branch off the Hermus. It sits on an easily defensible 800-foot-high hill at the junction of several important trade routes. Its location earned it the nickname "gateway to the east" and enabled it to become an important and wealthy trading center. Its importance increased as the coastal cities declined. Volcanic activity gave Philadelphia some of its more distinctive features, including the cliffs behind it, called Devitt ("inkwells"). It was on the edge of the Katakekaumene (the "burned land") volcanic region, and this land was ideally suited for vineyards.

Founded by the Greeks in 189 BC, it is the youngest of the seven cities and served as a missionary outpost for Hellenism and as a center for Greek culture and language. Lydia and Phrygia were the focal cities for this missionary outreach, which was so effective that by AD 19, the Greek language had fully displaced the Lydian language. Along with Sardis, Philadelphia suffered a major earthquake in AD 17. It continued to suffer severe aftershocks for over a year, and most of the inhabitants lived in huts and booths outside the city until the aftershocks finally ended. Like Sardis, Emperor Tiberius helped rebuild Philadelphia, and in appreciation, the citizens of Philadelphia assisted in building the temple to Tiberius in Sardis. Also in honor of Emperor Tiberius's generosity, they renamed the city to Neocaesarea. Later, they changed it again to Flavia and people referred to Philadelphia by both names (Neocaesarea and Flavia) through the second and third centuries. In 1190, Fredrick Barbarossa entered Philadelphia. The Turks besieged it in 1306 and 1324, but they remained independent until 1390. In 1403, Tamerlane captured the city and, reportedly, built a wall on the bodies of the victims. The city exists today under the name Alasehir and has a population of roughly forty-five thousand people.

The church of Philadelphia is often called the perfect church because of the lack of condemnations in its letter. To this perfect church, Jesus identifies himself with three titles previously unseen in Revelation: holy, true, and holding the key of David. Surprisingly, only three times does Revelation call Jesus holy: here, by the tribulation saints in Revelation 6, and by the great tribulation saints in Revelation 15. In contrast, the second title, true, is common throughout Revelation, and in many of these cases, they call him "true and faithful." Both of these titles are rather self-evident because Jesus' nature is one of both holiness and truthfulness. The last title—the holder of the key of David—requires some explanation, as it is a reference to Isaiah 22:20-22. In this messianic prophecy, Eliakim held the palace's keys, and only he could open or shut its doors. Likewise, Jesus holds the keys to God's palace, the key of the house of David (royalty). On earth and in heaven, Jesus opens and shuts doors as he sees fit. Only for the church of Philadelphia does Jesus say he open doors.

Some view the church of Philadelphia's open door as proving this church age continues up to the rapture. However, while Jesus promises no man can shut this door, he does not promise he will not shut it.  He opened the door because of the church's deeds, and presumably, if this changes, Jesus will choose to close the door himself. The door's opening and closing is exclusively Jesus' decision, but his decisions are influenced by people's actions. This is readily evident in the Old Testament when God gave the Jews the choice of blessings or curses and by their actions, the Jews chose which they received. Likewise, the churches, by their actions, determine whether they receive blessings (in this case, open doors) or curses (closed doors). Furthermore, it is inconceivable to think Jesus would leave an open door for a corrupt church.

Jesus commends the church of Philadelphia for keeping his Word and not denying his name. Throughout the Bible, the greatest compliments are often the simplest. To the church of Thyatira, Jesus wrote the longest letter, listing many commendations, but there were also serious flaws. For Philadelphia and Smyrna, he uses few words to bestow great honor. In a similar fashion, God has paid great but simple compliments to some of the heroes of the faith: Enoch simply walked with God (Genesis 5:22), Noah found grace in God's eyes (Genesis 6:8), and David was a man after God's own heart (Acts 13:22).

The church of Philadelphia did not pick over the Word of God, choosing to respect only the pieces appealing to them, but according to Jesus, they kept the full counsel (every part of the Bible). This church steadfastly refuses to compromise, continuously searches the Scriptures' truth, and never denies Jesus. They are always doing God's work, but they avoid falling into the trap of the Ephesians. Their love for Jesus is as fresh as ever, and their hearts are faithful to God. One can derive many more attributes from Jesus' simple praises, but it is sufficient to say this is a vibrant, active, productive church achieving results far beyond its size and resources.

Jesus tells the church they have little strength. How can a church so highly praised by Jesus have little strength? Does not God strengthen the hand of the righteous? Yes, but the point of this statement is not one of the church's weakness but of the magnitude of the church's accomplishments with respect to its size. This fulfills the parable of the mustard seed in Matthew 13:31-32 and Matthew 17:20, where Jesus teaches anything is possible with faith the size of a mustard seed. Like a mustard tree, the church of Philadelphia has become a mighty tree that feeds, protects, and nourishes many far beyond the influence suggested by their small size.

Both faultless churches, Smyrna and Philadelphia, face the synagogue of Satan's opposition. From the beginning, one of the church's greatest obstacles has been religious Jews. Scribes, Pharisees, and Sadducees opposed Jesus. They plotted his crucifixion, persecuted the apostles, persecuted the early church fathers, and persecuted the early church in general. These misguided souls always felt they were doing God's work, but Jesus boldly declared them spiritually dead (Matthew 23:27-29). The centuries have not reduced the friction between these Jews and the church (even toward its Jewish members). Even in the next to last church age, they are actively opposing the works of this perfect church. As the church's effectiveness increases, so does its opposition. Eventually, Jesus forces these Jews to fall prostrate in humility at the feet of the saints. They will be humbled to learn the God they claimed to serve so zealously loves and ordained the very church they gleefully persecuted.

Jesus promises this church he will keep them from the hour of temptation in return for keeping his Word. This time comes upon the whole world as it tries, tests, and judges the people of the world. Humanity's greatest temptation is probably the unholy trinity's seductive enticements for people to worship the antichrist and his image and receive his mark. Since these temptations affect the entire earth at one time, it is likely the hour of temptation is another name for the seven-year tribulation. It is significant the church is kept away from this time and not protected through it as he did with Shadrach, Meshach, and Abednego in the fiery furnace of Daniel 3.

Like the churches of Thyatira and Sardis, Jesus tells the church of Philadelphia to hold fast but this time he also instructs them to protect their crown rewards. This may sound passive, but it requires constant diligence and quick reaction to attacks. The letter concludes with blessings for those who overcome:

- will be pillars in the temple of God
- shall not go out anymore
- shall have names written on them:
    - God the Father
    - New Jerusalem
    - the new name Jesus gives them

The pillar suggests strength, permanence, and importance. Because it is in the temple of God, this shows they will always be in God's presence, living with him. Revelation 21 fulfills this promise in new Jerusalem, the home of God the Father, Jesus, and the bride. Like a pillar, the bride never has to leave the presence of God. By writing the various names on the faithful, Jesus is marking them as his people.

Philadelphia is generally accepted to represent the church

period from the time around the great awakening, about AD 1750, to the end of the great rivals, about AD 1900. This was a time of great missionary outreaches as a few people "of little strength" used God's power to perform great and miraculous works. It was a time when the church sought and taught the truth and people of great faith built great churches and great schools. Edwin J. Orr sums up this period well in his book, *The Rebirth of America*:

> In the mid 1800s, people began to be converted at the rate of 10,000 a week in New York City. The movement spread throughout New England. Church bells would bring people to prayer at eight in the morning, twelve noon, and six in the evening. The revival went up the Hudson and down the Mohawk. Baptists had so many people to baptize, they couldn't get them into their churches. They went down to the river, cut a big square in the ice, and baptized them in cold water. In one year (1857), more than one million people were converted. The revival crossed the Atlantic, broke out in Northern Ireland and Scotland and Wales and England, South Africa, South India—anywhere there was an evangelical cause, there was revival—and its effect was felt for 40 years.[2]

Table II shows a summary of the church of Philadelphia. It was like its city and had a missionary zeal. The name of its city suggests it was a church full of love, and its actions demonstrate this. Jesus opened doors for them to go through in spreading the Gospel, and their results were far greater than their numbers. Like the church of Smyrna, great opposition accompanied these opportunities, and Satan and false religious Jews opposed them. Unlike the church of Smyrna, this church overcame their enemies not through their deaths but through their lives and God's power in them.

Table 11: Philadelphia Church Summary

Philadelphia	
City Characteristics:	Founded as a missionary outpost for Hellenism and a center for Greek culture and language. Successfully displaced Lydia language with Greek.
Church Summary:	The second of two faultless churches. Also known as the "perfect" church of brotherly love. It has an open door, tremendous works, and great love.
Represented Age:	AD 1750–1900
Jesus' titles:	He that is holy, true, has the key of David, opens and no man shuts, and shuts and no man opens.

Commendations:	Condemnations:
Kept his word and did not deny His name. They have an open door before them that no man can shut. Have little strength but great works. Opposed by false Jews and Satan. Hold fast to crowns. Do not let anyone steal. Kept from the hour of temptation.	None

Rewards:	Punishments:
Those who overcome made a pillar in God's temple, new name, God's name and new Jerusalem written on.	None

Laodicea

Section reference: Revelation 3:14–22.

The seventh and final church, Laodicea, receives no commendations and the most severe reprimand for any church. Purportedly, this was not Laodicea's first letter, but an earlier one from Paul did not survive the ages. The city itself was founded by the Seleucid ruler Antiochus II, who named it after his first wife. Its name means "justice of the people," a popular name for cities of that age. Its original settlers were from Syria and included remnants of the Babylonian Jews. Laodicea lies approximately 100 miles east of Ephesus and 40 miles from Philadelphia. It is located on a plateau several hundred feet high, and its geography made it nearly impregnable, except for its one great vulnerability: a total absence of local water. Stone pipelines running from a nearby city in the Lycus valley provided the city's water. This was an exotic and expensive solution for the time. However, during times of war, she was extremely vulnerable, as enemies could easily stop the water. Located nearby were two cities linked to Laodicea in the New Testament, Colossae, located about ten miles east, and Hierapolis, located about six miles south (Colossians 4:13). In contrast to Laodicea's imported water, both had local water sources. Where Laodicea's water likely arrived lukewarm, Colossae's water was noted for being cold and pure and Hierapolis was noted for its natural hot springs.

Laodicea was located at the junction of two important roads. One was an east-west thoroughfare leading from Ephesus into the interior of Asia. The other ran north to south from Pergamos to the Mediterranean Sea. Laodicea leveraged its location to become an important commercial and banking center. It became so wealthy that when struck by a devastating earthquake in AD 60, they refused help from Rome and paid for all reconstruction themselves. They also developed several renowned industries and were particularly famous for a special variety of soft, black wool. They had an important medical school associated with the nearby temple of the Phrygian god

Men Karou. They produced a large pharmaceutical business, and its chief pharmaceutical exports were eye and ear salves. The ruins of the city now have the name of Eski Hissar (old castle) and lie near the modern town of Denizli.

To this church, Jesus introduces himself as the Amen, the faithful and true witness, and the beginning of the creation of God. Like the church of Sardis, Jesus' focus is restoration, not judgment, and these titles all emphasize the credibility of his testimony. This letter is not pleasant to receive, but Jesus is telling the church everything in the letter is true and there are no exaggerations, deceptions, or distortions.

Without commendations, Jesus goes straight to their condemnations as he compares their love for him to the city's lukewarm water. Like the city, this church has no source of water, as the Holy Spirit's spiritual water is conspicuously absent. Jesus prefers enemies (the cold water) to the lukewarm water of indifference that fills the hearts of this church. He hates these hearts so much he will spew them out. Spew comes from the Greek word emeo (Strong's G1692), which is the root for emetic and literally means regurgitate. While not a pretty picture, it graphically portrays God's disgust at Laodicea's spiritual condition.

Jesus clearly lays out the church's fundamental issue: their love of physical wealth and the apathy it creates. In their minds, they have everything they need, and they are so confident in their riches and possessions that they are not introspective about their lives and their spiritual condition. As a warning, Paul warned Laodicea's sister city, Colossae to, "Set your affection on things above, not on things on the earth" (Colossians 3:2). In 1 Timothy 6:7-12, Paul sent another warning to be content with having one's needs (food and clothing) met. He further warns against the love of money by saying those who strive to be rich fall into temptation.

Laodicea's wealth became a snare drowning men in destruction and perdition. Their love for wealth has so corrupted them they are incapable of discerning spiritual truths or their spiritual condition: wretched, miserable, poor, blind, and naked. Their wretched and miserable states demonstrates their separation from God (Romans 7:24, 1 Corinthians 15:19). Even though they have great physical wealth, their poverty speaks of their spiritual needs and their inability to see the truth. Laodicea stands in stark contrast with the church of Smyrna, which was physically poor but spiritually wealthy, and their nakedness vividly tells of their lack of works, service, ministering, deeds, or study. The picture of Laodicea is surreal. They live among great prosperity and possess great wealth but are poor. They live in the middle of an area known for its eye treatments but are blind. They live in a city known for its black wool but are naked.

Jesus pleads with the Laodiceans to buy pure, refined gold (tried in the fire) and white raiment from him so they will no longer be poor and naked. Jesus knows only riches laid up in heaven survive forever and counsels this church to anoint their eyes so they will no longer be spiritually blind. He enunciates his love for them by reminding them that he judges and corrects those he loves, including them.

Jesus concludes this letter with a call for people's salvation and a pronouncement of blessings for believers. The call for salvation is not just for the church period of Laodicea but also the entire church age. Placed strategically just prior to the rapture, it is the clarion call of the church age issued to all humanity. Jesus actively knocks on hearts, pleading with people to invite him in so he can fellowship with them and save them from judgment. Interestingly, Jesus wants to enjoy the close fellowship of the day's principal meal (last meal of the day). This meal is also a picture of the Lamb's marriage feast, another picture of salvation.

Again, the blessings are for those who overcome. This time, he promises ruling dominions, or kingships. This is a common promise in Revelation and the third (and last) of the church's rewards but is presented only after Jesus assumes his earthly throne. Interestingly, in the church of Laodicea's letter, Jesus mentioned all three components of the church's rewards: clothing, riches, and dominions.

Laodicea concludes the church age. This period starts with the conclusion of the great revivals, roughly AD 1900, and continues to present. It is a time marked by tremendous physical wealth but few spiritual fruits. As Laodicea does not have its own source of water, this church is missing its water (the Spirit of God). During this period, many churches "liberalized" their doctrinal positions while reducing the role of Scriptures in preaching and teaching. At this time, the great missionary zeal of Philadelphia became only a distant memory.

Never has access to Scripture been so readily available, but this church's members may be the most ignorant about God's Word. Worse, their wealth has sapped their desire to learn. This church's physical wealth (and their reliance on it) sets the stage for the seven-year tribulation, especially the battle of Armageddon. This battle purges the earth of many things, including people's reliance on physical wealth when, at its height, people throw away their riches. It is significant the last church period before the tribulation is afflicted with the same love of money crushed in the seven-year tribulation.

Table 12 shows a summary of the church of Laodicea which has many similarities to its city. They are missing a local source of water; the water they pipe in is lukewarm. They are physically wealthy and do not believe they have any needs. However, Jesus calls them spiritually blind, naked, and poor. Jesus counsels them to purchase gold, white raiment, and eye salve to alleviate their spiritual condition. Unless they become zealous and repent, God will spew them out of his mouth as the foul-tasting water they are. Even with all of these shortcomings, Jesus promises those who overcome will rule with him.

Table 12: Laodicea Church Summary

Laodicea	
City Characteristics:	Virtually impregnable city. Lack of water made it vulnerable. Wealthy city. Renowned for special wool and eye salve.
Church Summary:	The last church prior to the rapture. An indifferent church with tremendous material wealth and no praise. It is characterized by a lack of love, works, and spiritual poverty. Most of its members will stand before God naked and without rewards.
Represented Age:	AD 1900–present
Jesus' titles:	Amen, faithful, true witness, beginning of God's creation.

Commendations:	Condemnations:
None	Lukewarm. Rich with many possessions. No physical needs but plenty of spiritual needs: poor, blind, and naked.

Rewards:	Punishments:
Those who overcome will sit with Jesus on His throne. Those who open their door → Jesus enters, fellowships with them, and enjoys the principal meal with them.	Unless they become zealous, repent, and buy from Jesus refined gold, white raiment, and eye salve, God will spue them out of His mouth.

As the last church period, it is possible to find additional clues about this church age from other passages. For example, 1 Timothy 4:1-5 shows in the last days some Christians become hypocritical liars by departing from the faith and going after false doctrines and teachings. These "Christians" not only follow false doctrines but also teach them and seek converts. They can do this because they have seared away their conscience and it can no longer convict and correct. This theme continues in 2 Timothy 4:3-4, as these verses speak of people lusting, heaping, and itching for false doctrine. This passage suggests they accumulate, perhaps even hoard, teachers, but these teachers only teach what these people want to hear: fables satisfying their lusts and soothing their itching ears.

Church Age Conclusion

Revelation's church age prophecies revolve around seven churches. Each was active at the time of John's vision. Each received letters from Jesus that also provided a prophetic overview of the church age. They broke the church age into seven distinct periods:

1. Ephesus (to 100 AD): the apostolic church that was so busy working they lost their love for God

2. Smyrna (AD 100 to AD 312): the "faultless" persecuted church

3. Pergamos (AD 312 to AD 600): a faithful church that tolerated false doctrine

4. Thyatira (AD 600 to AD 1500): a church of love and works that was permeated by the teaching of false doctrines

5. Sardis (AD 1500 to AD 1750): the dead church without any praise but some worthy members

6. Philadelphia (AD 1750 to AD 1900): the "perfect" church of brotherly love that possessed an open door and tremendous works

7. Laodicea (AD 1900 to present): the indifferent church without love for Jesus and possessing no works

Just as all seven churches were active in the first century, examples of all seven probably existed during every church period. The dates shown above are approximate and not universally accepted.

In these letters, three churches received mixed reviews, two received perfect marks, and two received failing grades. Jesus counseled only the churches without praise—Sardis and Laodicea—to get life's necessities, raiment, since only they were so spiritually poor they did could not meet these basic needs. Interestingly, both spiritually poor churches were materially rich. It is a little puzzling that Jesus never mentions the necessity of food. Perhaps it is because, as he states in John 6:35, he is the bread of life and also, in John 4:14, he is the source for the water of life.

In contrast, Jesus warned the two unblemished churches—Smyrna and Philadelphia—not to let anyone take their crowns. Their necessities were so secure that Jesus focused on their rewards, or luxuries of life. Jesus demonstrates the crown's high standards through their omission in the other five churches. Interestingly, Jesus mentions Jewish opposition only for these two perfect churches. Seemingly, their tremendous works also brought out tremendous opposition not felt by the other five churches.

The next event on the prophetic timeline is the rapture. Before moving on to the rapture and the tribulation's start, the next chapter looks at prophecies illuminating God's church age plans for the Jews. These prophecies run parallel to Revelation 1-3, but their omission from Revelation is striking.

Israel during the Church Age (Preparation)

Revelation's church age description could easily lead one to conclude that the church has replaced the role of Abraham's descendents or even that God has rejected the Jews. After all, only twice in Revelation 1-3 are the Jews even mentioned, and in both occasions, they persecute perfect churches. Fortunately, the rest of the Bible provides many clues concerning their disposition. Sadly, the passages paint a generally horrific landscape of their plights and sufferings. More importantly, these passages explain God's role in their pain and suffering, why Israel has fallen under his judgment, and the nation's final disposition. This chapter explores Israel's church age trials and tribulations (their distress), the nation's promised rebirth, the infant nation's opposition and trials (their birth pangs), and the important reestablishment of sacrificial worship.

Israel's Great Distress

In Jesus' future millennial reign, Israel will be the world's premier nation and will finally enjoy the full extent of Deuteronomy's blessings (Deuteronomy 28:1-14). Then, they will be God's conduit for blessings to overflow from them to all Gentiles. Now, they are living in the last phase of a terrible time of persecution and tragedy. The prophecies concerning the present time of trouble cover an important period in Israel's history and set the stage for many key end-time prophecies. It is an unfortunate fact that much of this material has been abused to justify persecution of the Jews or teach forms of replacement theology (other groups have taken Israel's place in God's plan), especially since these verses show God's corrective, not destructive, punishment of Israel.

At the proper time, God will restore his wife, Israel, to her rightful position. Until then, he continues to exercise spousal discipline, correcting and rebuking his wife. This right is his alone, and anyone taking liberties with her risks his wrath. This point is evident, as God unconditionally promises to bless those who bless the Jews and curse those who curse them. Even as they wallow under God's curses, God zealously watches over his wife and there is never any excuse or defense for afflicting them.

Christians predisposed against the Jews should consider the critical role Jews have played in promulgating the Gospel. Not only did they pen the predominate portions of both the Old and New Testaments of the Bible but also were its primary characters and audience. In other words, the Bible was written by Jews, about Jews, and for Jews. On top of this, virtually every early church leader was a Jew, and without their efforts, Gentile Christianity would never have been grafted onto this Jewish tree (Romans 11). Further, Romans 11:1-2 is unequivocal that God has not rejected or replaced the Jews. The book of Romans further explains that even at the height of God's punishment, not all Jews are rebellious. It illustrates this point by recalling when Elijah thought only he was faithful, God testified that there were seven thousand (1 Kings 19). Similarly, Romans 11:5 states a faithful remnant remains even during the church age dispersion. The fact God has not and will not forsake or replace Israel is also confirmed in Deuteronomy 4:30-31, where, even in the darkest moments of the last days, God desires to forgive Israel and restore her as though nothing has happened. Understanding these basic facts about God's relationship to Israel and the accountability of Gentiles, Christian and non-Christian, for their actions against God's wife is an important foundation to lay prior to looking at this difficult period in Israel's history.

The tone for Israel's last two thousand years was set on the eighth day of Jesus' life, when his parents took him to the temple for his circumcision. There, Simeon met them and foretold the impact Jesus' birth had on Israel, including Israel's fall and rise again (Luke 2:34). Through all of this, Jesus is a lightning rod of controversy (a sign) whom many oppose. The Bible portrays Israel's fall through many symbolic representations:

- an adulterous wife (Ezekiel 16, Jeremiah 30:14–15)
- dross (Ezekiel 22:17–22)
- an unproductive vineyard (Isaiah 5:1–7)
- an unproductive fig tree (Hosea 9:10, Mark 11:12–21)
- her two falls (Isaiah 29:1, Ezekiel 16:23, Ezekiel 24:6–14, Deuteronomy 28)

Each of these justify God, placing the blame for next section's curses on his unfaithful wife. These curses haunt her throughout the church age.

Israel's Curses

While the Old Testament pronounces both blessings and curses on Israel, the curses far outnumber the blessings. For example, in Deuteronomy 28, fourteen verses contain blessings while fifty-four verses contain curses, and many of these are polar opposites of the blessings. For example, Israel's obedience causes God's blessings to overtake them (Deuteronomy 28:2) while Israel's disobedience causes God's curses to overtake them (Deuteronomy 28:45). In addition, God's joy in blessing the Jews changes to joy in cursing them (Deuteronomy 28:63). God's curses on Israel include:

- Judgment from heaven (heaven of brass) (Deuteronomy 28:23)

- No one is able to save them from the curses (Deuteronomy 28:29)
- Israel's labors:
  - They shall live a hard life (earth of iron)
  - They shall suffer severe droughts (Deuteronomy 28:24)
  - Their food is destroyed by blasting and mildew (Deuteronomy 28:22)
  - They shall not prosper (Deuteronomy 28:29)
  - They shall be only oppressed and spoiled (Deuteronomy 28:29)
  - They shall plant vineyards and not get the harvest (Deuteronomy 28:30, Micah 6:14)
  - Their farm animals (ox, ass, and sheep) shall be violently taken away and given to others (Deuteronomy 28:31)
  - Others shall have the fruit of the land and their labors (Deuteronomy 28:33)
  - Locusts shall eat the grain harvest, trees, and the fruit of the land (Deuteronomy 28:38, 42)
  - Worms shall devour their grapes (Deuteronomy 28:39)
  - Their olive trees shall cast off their fruit before it is ripe (Deuteronomy 28:40)
  - They shall eat and not be satisfied (Micah 6:14)
- Israel's health:
  - They shall suffer from deadly pestilence (disease) (Deuteronomy 28:21)
  - They shall suffer from consumption, fever, inflammation, and hot fever (Deuteronomy 28:22)
  - Many shall have unhealable skin diseases, including the botch of Egypt, emerods, scab, and the itch (Deuteronomy 28:27)
  - They shall suffer from all the diseases of Egypt plus all manner of diseases and plagues (Deuteronomy 28:60–61)

- Israel's effectiveness in war:
  - They shall flee seven ways (Deuteronomy 28:25)
  - Their carcasses shall rot in the field and be consumed by wild animals (Deuteronomy 28:26)
  - During sieges, they shall eat their children for food (Deuteronomy 28:53)
  - During sieges, men shall hate their brothers, wives, and children and shall leave them (Deuteronomy 28:54)
- Israel's families:
  - Their children are cursed (Deuteronomy 28:18)
  - Men marry and another man has sex with his wife (Deuteronomy 28:30)
  - They shall build a house and not live in it (Deuteronomy 28:30)
  - Their sons and daughters are taken away, given to others, and they will watch in vain every day to see them again (Deuteronomy 28:32, 41)
- Israel's mental health:
  - They shall suffer from various psychological diseases, including madness, blindness, and astonishment of heart (Deuteronomy 28:28)
  - They shall grope at noonday like a blind man (Deuteronomy 28:29)
  - The things they shall see shall make them mad (Deuteronomy 28:34)
- Israel's relationships to other nations:
  - They shall be an astonishment, a proverb, and a byword among all nations (Deuteronomy 28:37)
  - They shall be made low and the stranger made high (Deuteronomy 28:43)
  - They shall be borrowers and not lenders (Deuteronomy 28:44)

- They shall serve their enemies in hunger, thirst, and nakedness (Deuteronomy 28:48)

- They shall be under the harsh rule of their enemies (yoke of iron) (Deuteronomy 28:48)

- There shall be few Jews left (Deuteronomy 28:62)

- They shall be scattered among all the nations of the earth (Deuteronomy 28:64)

- They shall find neither ease or rest wherever they are driven (Deuteronomy 28:65)

- Wherever they are driven, they shall have trembling hearts, sorrowful minds, fearful hearts, and have no confidence their lives will continue from morning to evening or from evening to morning (Deuteronomy 28:65–67)

- They shall be scattered through the dispersion of the Romans (Deuteronomy 28:68, 32:26; Ezekiel 22:15; Hosea 9:17)

While this is not a comprehensive or exhaustive list, it is nonetheless extremely formidable. No rational person would desire to endure these curses, but this is precisely what has happened to the Jews for the last two thousand years.

Romans 11:11-12 shows an obscure fact of Israel's fall: it was ordained by God. Through their fall, the church carries the Gospel to the Gentiles. As God's grace comes to the Gentiles, the Jews become jealous. Prior to this, it was always the Jews making God jealous, but now they suffer the jealousy. Israel's fall is so complete that they become enemies of the Gospel (Romans 11:28). However, God warns Gentiles Israel's fall is only temporary and they need to be humble and not boast of their new position (Romans 11:17-21).

When will Israel's curses end? Jeremiah 16:18 shows they suffer the curses until, as a nation, they have paid twice for their sins. Hosea 3:4-5 explains this period lasts a long time (many days). Hosea goes on to explain that when it ends, the royal lineage of David once again resides on the throne. This does not occur until the last days when Jesus ends the times of the Gentiles and takes his earthly throne. Clearly, God is not finished with Israel, though his judgments are severe.

Israel's Rebirth

God's punishments start reaching their climatic conclusion when he begins gathering the Jews from the uttermost parts of the earth back to the land he gave them over three thousand years ago. This process starts gradually and continues until all Jews are back in Israel following Jesus' return. During this time, the gathering is temporally interrupted by wars that once again disperse many out of the land of Israel. The Jews' gathering and Israel's national rebirth are probably the most important precursors to end-time events. Without the nation of Israel, many end-time prophecies are impossible to fulfill. Israel's rebirth is so important that of all the end-time indicators, it alone implies a specific timeframe. This is shown in Jesus' parable of the fig tree (Matthew 24:32-35). Earlier, Jesus had cursed and killed the fig tree when he was hungry. This foreshadowed Israel's death through the Roman dispersion (Matthew 21:19-20). Now, Jesus restores hope by promising the fig tree will live again and the generation seeing the fig tree's budding will not pass before Jesus' return. This is similar to one of Ezekiel's prophecies where he described Israel's rebirth as budding forth and ties it to "that day" (Ezekiel 29:21).

Jesus' budding fig tree parable has been both critical to deciphering end-time prophecies and controversial, as debate swirls around its potential misuse for end-time date setters. Afraid of being  labeled date setters, many prophecy students shy away from applying this parable's timeframe to current events. Others maintain Jesus' words did not outline a specific timeframe for Jesus' return but simply indicate that once Jews return to their land not all will again be disbursed prior to Jesus return. Regardless, like the millennial day theory, there are several difficulties using this parable to set dates. For example, what constitutes "the fig tree's budding?" Several possibilities exist. The three most popular seem to be Israel's independence on May 14, 1948, Jerusalem's unification under Jewish control (1967), and Jerusalem becoming the nation's capital (1950). Israel's independence in 1948 tends to be the most universally accepted.

The definition of "this generation shall not pass" is even more problematic. Forty years is often suggested because it is the time Israel wandered in the wilderness (Numbers 14:33). Others use the lifespan of people found in Psalm 90:10 as a basis for setting this at seventy to eighty years. Still others suggest it could last as long as anyone who saw the fig tree's budding remains alive. The last definition could potentially push the timeframe beyond one hundred years. Most scholars lean toward the Psalms definition of seventy to eighty years, but there is no consensus.

Combining these various definitions of both the fig tree's budding and the generation's length, the prophecy window could close as early as 1988 (1948 plus forty years) or after 2067 (1967 plus one hundred years)—a range of over eighty years! If this parable does indicate a time span, it significantly reduces the possible range of dates for Jesus' return over that seen with the millennial day, but it is not suitable for date setting. Even the most popular opinions restrict Jesus' return to earlier than 2028 (eighty years after the nation's 1948 founding) but still leaves years of uncertainty. Even this date should be considered cautiously and in the light of other end-time prophecies.

There are many verses showing God gathering the Jews to Israel from every nation and outpost in the world. While these verses agree in terms of the Jews' return, they often seem to contradict in details. For example, Micah 2:12 shows a great multitude of men where Isaiah 10:21-22 shows a small remnant. Likely, the gathering occurs in many phases, and each passage describes a different aspect of this process. A prominent theory dealing with the apparent contradictions is there are not one but two end-time gatherings: one before the tribulation (in disbelief) and one after (in belief).[1] Passages included in the disbelief gathering are Ezekiel 20:33-38, Ezekiel 22:17-22, Ezekiel 36:22-24, Ezekiel 37-38, Isaiah 11:11-12, and Zephaniah 2:1-2. Passages included in the belief gathering are Deuteronomy 4:29-31, Deuteronomy 30:1-10, Isaiah 27:12-13, Isaiah 43:5-7, Jeremiah 16:14-15, Jeremiah 31:7-10, Ezekiel 11:14-18, Amos 9:14-15, Zechariah 10:8-12, and Matthew 24:31. The deportation of half of Jerusalem's Jews during the battle of Armageddon strengthens this theory (Zechariah 14:2), as these Jews must come back to the land of Israel upon Jesus' return.

Israel's Birth Pangs

The birth pangs of Israel are the pains and sufferings of the nation as it struggles first for its survival and then to give birth to its new king, the ruler of all nations. The imagery of birth pangs comes from Revelation 12's depiction of a woman (Israel) in the last moments of travail, struggling to produce her offspring: the new king. This section focuses only on the portion of the birth-pang prophecies leading up to the tribulation. The lack of a Revelation-style road map for this period tends to cause interpretation difficulties. The clearly known parts of the birth pangs include the reestablishment of the nation with the gathering of the Jews, Israel fighting many different wars, and Israel eventually dropping their defensive positions when they believe they are finally safe.

Birth-pang Prophecy Challenges

Though many general prophecies exist (like Israel's curses during the last two millennia), this timeframe does not appear to contain many specific historically significant prophetic events. Prophecies of a general nature present special challenges in determining both their applicability to specific periods and their prophetic horizon. One must determine whether the prophecy had a prior fulfillment and if it did, whether it could have multiple fulfillments. Incomplete historical records can make these determinations especially challenging.

Identifying Israel's pretribulation foes is another birth-pang prophecy challenge. Unlike the seven-year tribulation, where Israel's wars are global in nature, most of Israel's pre-tribulation battles have local scopes and require the identification of regional ethnic groups and nations. The fact that ancient names for nations are often quite different from their modern ones compounds this issue. Through the centuries, the people forming nations have been conquered, dispersed, killed, and subdued. Consequently, it is often difficult to say with certainty which modern countries are the subject of detailed prophesies.

Illustrating this difficulty, consider the following list of biblical names for ancient countries in and around Israel: Moab, Tyre, Ammon, Sidon, Egypt, Syria/Damascus, Philistines (Gaza, Ashdod, Ekron), and Edom (Idumea). How many of these are familiar? What modern nations do they represent? Where are their geographic locations? The Philistines are an excellent representation of these difficulties. This nation appears often in prophecies, including many apparent end-time prophecies. Do the Philistines exist today, and if so, who are they? In the past, the Romans conquered them, and some believe the Maccabees destroyed them. Could the modern Palestinians be the descendents of the ancient Philistines? They do live in the same geographic region and possess the same ancient hatreds of Israel. Some researchers emphatically argue against it, saying modern Palestinians are nothing more than a diverse collection of Arabs originating from many countries, without a common ancestry. Resolution of questions surrounding the Philistines is difficult and representative of other possible birth-pang prophecies pronounced on other nations. Despite these difficulties, the birth-pang prophecies section attempts to provide some prophetic insights into Israel's birth pangs.

Birth-pang Prophecies

Generally, birth-pang prophecies portray Israel as a nation forced to confront and overcome various enemies. During this time, Israel fights a progression of wars against increasingly stronger armies. These wars culminate with two cataclysmic battles during the seven-year tribulation, but even prior to this, Israel successfully contends with many regional adversaries. Zechariah 12:5-8 is set "in that day" and alludes to Israel's end-time military prowess. This passage's highlights include:

- Jerusalem shall be inhabited again
- Judah shall devour all its enemies
- God saves Judah first
- In battle, each inhabitant of Jerusalem shall be as David
- In battle, the house of David shall be as the angel of the Lord

Zechariah's focus on Judah and Jerusalem and not Israel as a whole helps fuel speculation of Israel's possible end-time division into two nations. This is especially true since Revelation 7 clearly shows at least twelve of the thirteen tribes present in Israel during this time.

Passages such as this show Israel has many end-time enemies and fights many wars but provide precious few specifics about these wars (e.g., who, when, or where). What they do show is the Jews are valiant fighters, as these passages compare Israel's fighting abilities to David, who defeated a lion, a bear, and Goliath. As mentioned earlier, there are striking similarities between David's conquests and three of Daniel's four beasts. These similarities become even more interesting when Hosea 13:6-8 predicts all four afflict Ephraim (the northern tribes). By directing these pronouncements against Ephraim, Hosea seems to also support the proposition of the end-time division of the nation of Israel. Interestingly, Hosea shows the leopard only observing and not attacking (at least individually). This seems to be consistent with both the story of Goliath and Amos 5:18-19, which omit references to the leopard. From these passages, it appears the leopard is the most reluctant of the four beasts to attack this nation while the other beasts each afflict Israel: the lion in Israel's war of independence, the bear in Ezekiel's future battle of Gog and Magog, and the last beast in the battle of Armageddon.

Establishing Sacrificial Worship

While Israel's rebirth completes a critical piece of the prophetic timeline, several lesser pieces still need to come together before the fulfillments of certain key tribulation events are possible. These include:

- Israel acquiring great wealth
- Israel believing they are safe and at peace
- Religious leaders acquiring power to enact and enforce religious laws
- Religious leaders restarting sacrificial worship

The first two—Israel's great wealth and her belief in her peace and safety—are prerequisites for Ezekiel's battle of Gog and Magog. Israel's wealth is the reason for this invasion (see the sixth seal's section of the tribulation chapter), and it is her belief that she is finally safe that increase her vulnerability to attack. The religious leaders' rise to power is necessary for the enactment of wide-sweeping religious laws, including the reintroduction of Sabbatical travel restrictions, which will impede Jews fleeing to the mountains during the great tribulation. Finally, the reestablishment of sacrificial worship must occur before the antichrist can commit three despicable acts against the temple mount: the abomination of desolation, the stopping of the daily sacrifice, and the treading down of the temple's courtyard. Though each of these prerequisites are important, the one that generates the most interest and speculation is the reestablishment of sacrificial worship.

Sacrificial worship will require:

- the creation of temple vessels
- the creation of articles of the priesthood, including the High Priest's ephod
- the training of priests
- finding or building the furnishings of the tabernacle
- finding the ark of the covenant
- the construction and cleansing of the temple edifice

Israel's enthusiasm for reestablishing sacrificial worship is obvious when one considers how far efforts to address these issues have gone. Many of the temple's vessels and priesthood articles are reportedly available, including both the ephod and breastplate. Potential priests are reportedly being trained, and many people are searching for both the tabernacle furnishings and the ark of the covenant. The search for the ark is particularly interesting, as rumors about its location swirl including Ethiopia, Vatican vaults, and hidden passages in Solomon's temple mount.

By far, the greatest obstacle for sacrificial worship would appear to be the construction of the worship edifice, but even after it is erected, a couple of other obstacles remain: identification of a suitable red heifer for cleansing the tabernacle and the fabrication of the incense of the golden altar. The Bible places strict requirements on the selection of a red heifer. In 2002, the religious world was abuzz with news of the birth of a qualified candidate, but it was later disqualified. The making of the temple's incense may also prove problematic since only a single Levite family knew its secret ingredients, formula, and processes.

Concerning the worship edifice, Old Testament sacrificial worship was held on altars without any edifice, on the brazen altar of the tabernacle (tent) of Moses (and later, the tabernacle of David), and the brazen altars of Jerusalem's two majestic temples. The vast majority of prophecy experts expect the construction of another temple for sacrificial worship. They watch daily for any indications that the start of construction may be imminent.

A minority opinion holds the Jews erect the tabernacle (tent) to support sacrificial worship during the seven-year tribulation.

Jeremiah 7:4 infers there will be three temples by repeating references to the temple three times. Naturally, the next question is how many temples have there been? Most scholars ignore temple renovations when counting the number of different temples and count a temple only at its initial dedication. Even if subsequent renovations dramatically changed its appearance (e.g., Herod's reconstruction), it is still the same temple. By this numbering method, there have been two past temples (Solomon's and Ezra's), leaving just one future temple. Other numbering schemes that include reconstruction in the overall count push the count total up significantly and simply do not fit Jeremiah's prophecies. Zechariah 6:12-15 makes it clear Jesus builds the last of Jeremiah's temples. Jesus can only build this temple after he returns (following the full tribulation).

If this last temple is not erected until after the full tribulation is over, how can the antichrist desecrate it? Ezekiel 37:26-28 provides some clues, as God promises to set his sanctuary (holy of holies) and tabernacle (the edifice housing the sanctuary) in their midst forever. Throughout the Old Testament, tabernacle's Hebrew root word consistently refers to a tent, and the Old Testament does not use this word in conjunction with any permanent temple.[2] Ezekiel's future tabernacle is probably a cloth structure instead of a permanent temple. This tabernacle reference is sandwiched between the last day prophecies of the valley of dry bones and the invasion of Magog. Its position suggests it is an end-time worship edifice, which is used before, during, and after the seven-year tribulation (at least until replaced with Jesus' temple).

Revelation 13:6 also suggests the Jews will use a temporary structure like the tabernacle. The Greek root word for this passage's tabernacle is skene (Strong's G4633), which translates as a tent or cloth hut. This verse is placed in the great tribulation and again implies the seven-year tribulation tabernacle is a temporary, movable structure like a tent and not a permanent structure like a temple.

Amos 9:11 gives additional clues about the possible use of the cloth tabernacle, as Amos explicitly calls the worship structure the tabernacle of David. What structure is this? After all, David desired to build a temple, but God stopped him. After that, David accumulated much of the material used in the construction of the first temple and passed his temple dreams and instructions on to his son, Solomon. Throughout his life, David had to worship in the tabernacle. The natural assumption is that he was worshipping in Moses' tabernacle, but 1 Chronicles 15:1 suggests differently, as David made a place for the ark of God. Since the ark always went into the holy of holies, this implies David made a new tabernacle to replace the tabernacle of Moses. If he did, then Israel could only have used this tabernacle for, at most, fifty years (based on the length of David's reign as king and the time Solomon spent building the temple). This is just a fraction of the time Israel used Moses' tabernacle and may indicate God had future plans for it, perhaps including its future reuse in the last days.

Amos 9:11 indicates when the Jews erect David's tabernacle, God performs some interesting miracles: closing up the breaches, raising the ruins, and rebuilding it as in ancient days. To close breaches and raise ruins, a portion of the original materials must be present otherwise there is nothing to close or raise. When viewed in light of the promise to close the breaches and raise the ruins, the promise to rebuild David's tabernacle is to not only rebuild it in the same style but also using the original materials. Except for the temple's foundation, nothing remains of either the first or the second temple's original construction materials, not even one stone on top of another. This is not a breach but total destruction, and it is hard to envision a scenario where either Solomon's temple or the second temple could be reconstructed in a way to fulfill Amos' prophecy. However, if the tabernacle of 1 Chronicles 15:1 were discovered, its original construction materials would be present though one would expect the ravages of time to have reduced its condition to a state of fragile ruins full of rips, tears, and decayed material.

This would necessitate the tabernacle to be handled with the same level of care used for the dead sea scrolls. Instead, Amos' prophecy suggests that God not only restores the old tabernacle to the point that it can be erected again but also, its condition is the same as when it was taken down thousands of years ago. Isaiah 33:20 provides further support for Amos's prophecy by showing the use of stakes and cords, emphasizing the tent and temporary natures of this structure.

In 1 Chronicles 22:6-10, God stopped David from building the first temple because he was a man of war. Today, Israel is a nation of war with Ezekiel's great army quite active. It is not a nation of peace, and if God did not allow David to construct the first temple, then it seems highly unlikely God allows the current nation of Israel to build any temple before Jesus' return.

Summarizing, there is ample evidence to suggest the Jews do not build a permanent temple prior to or during the tribulation. The most likely scenario consists of the Jews finding and erecting David's tabernacle just prior to the tribulation. Since this is a cloth structure, it can be set up quickly, with little or no warning. Even so, the priests need training, the temple vessels must be made, the priestly garments created, the ark of the covenant and temple furnishings found, and the temple cleansed. This tabernacle remains in use throughout the full tribulation and continues even after Jesus' return, as he uses it until he completes construction work on his temple (Isaiah 16:5).

Israel's Church Age Summary

The church age is a dark period in Israel's history, as the Jews endure God's curses. Nowhere do they find peace, safety, or prosperity for more than short periods. Hated wherever they go, the Jew's trials and tribulations cause them to be unwilling witnesses for God. Toward the end of the church age, God starts gathering the Jews back to the promised land, where eventually they become a nation with a strong army. They need this powerful army to withstand their many enemies, including the last days' superpowers: the four beasts of Daniel.

The Rapture

The church age climaxes with the much-anticipated rapture. At that moment, Jesus takes all Christians to heaven while whoever is left behind faces the terror and uncertainty of the tribulation. The following explores the rapture's mysteries by starting with an overview of the world's wickedness before proceeding onto the rapture and the subsequent pretribulation events in heaven.

The World's Condition Prior to the Rapture

Israel's national rebirth occurs during perilous times (2 Timothy 3:1). In fact, Jesus compared the world at this time to the days before the flood of Noah and the destruction of Sodom in the days of Lot (Luke 17:26-33). Starting with Noah, the Bible shows the preflood people carrying out normal daily routines, oblivious to the coming destruction. Daily, the ark's construction occurred in plain sight, yet Noah's warnings went unheeded. On the surface, their activities do not seem out of the ordinary; however, Genesis 6:5 shows these people spent all of their time thinking of ways to enjoy the short-term pleasures of sin (Hebrews 11:25). Matthew 15:19 shows these thoughts eventually produced murderers, adulterers, fornicators, thieves, liars, and enemies of God. Other clues from Luke 17:26-33 include:

- "They did eat," suggesting gluttony
- "They did drink," suggesting drunkenness
- "They married wives," (plural) and "they were given in marriage," suggesting marriages of convenience with no permanence

In short, the people of Noah's day lived for the pleasures of sin, and these actions are repeated in the last days.

The men of Sodom's day were not any better. They also appear to be guilty of gluttony and drunkenness, without any regard for their creator. "They bought, they sold, they planted, they builded," suggests a materialistic society focused on gain and wealth. Ezekiel 16:49-50 strengthens the charges of materialism against Sodom with two statements: "Abundance of idleness," and "Neither did she strengthen the hand of the poor and needy." Abundance of idleness implies abundant wealth while their treatment of the poor and needy demonstrates their greed and lust. Other failings listed here and in Jude 1:7-8 include unbridled pride, abominations (typically sacrifices to strange gods), fornications (sex outside of marriage), and desiring strange flesh (lack of control over one's body, desires, and lusts manifested through all sorts of deviant sexual activities). Additionally, Sodom's pride results in her separation from God (1 John 2:16) and primes her for destruction (Proverbs 16:18).

The combination of Noah and Sodom presents a troubling picture of humanity on the eve of Jesus' return. It is one of complete debauchery but is consistent with other detailed descriptions of last days' people. Another less obvious part of the prophecy deals with the righteous during this time. For both Noah and Lot, their testimonies produced little fruit, as only eight souls survived the flood and only three survived Sodom's destruction. In Lot's case, he chose to live in Sodom, and this decision vexed his soul (2 Peter 2:6-8), causing him to lose his testimony even among his own family. Prior to entering Sodom, this man led a group so large that Abraham and Lot separated due to infighting between the two groups for limited pastures and water. Abraham's pleading for God's mercy on Sodom implies just how large Lot's group may have been. He opens his negotiations at fifty people before finally working down to just ten (Genesis 18:16-33). Unfortunately, what Abraham did not know was that since Lot had left Abraham's side he succumbed to Sodom's lifestyle, losing both his zeal for God and his testimony. No longer did he lead his servants, their families, or even his own family. Their love for Sodom (a type of the world) was so great the angels had to expel Lot and his family before they could complete their work (Genesis 19:16). Even then, Lot lost his wife because of her love for Sodom (Genesis 19:26).

Notice also that neither the worldwide flood nor the destruction of Sodom came until God protected his people: Noah in the ark and Lot outside of Sodom. First Peter 3:20 confirms God waited, delaying the flood, until all of the righteous were safely enclosed the ark. Just as God removed Noah, Lot, and the rest of the righteous before pouring out his past judgments, God will remove the righteous prior to the tribulation's future judgments (1 Thessalonians 5:9).

Elsewhere, the Bible describes the pre-rapture generation as:

- lovers of their own selves (love of self displaces all other loves) (2 Timothy 3:2)

- covetous (2 Timothy 3:2)

- boasters (2 Timothy 3:2)

- proud (2 Timothy 3:2)

- blasphemers (2 Timothy 3:2)

- disobedient to parents (2 Timothy 3:2)

- unthankful (2 Timothy 3:2)

- unholy (2 Timothy 3:2)

- without natural affection (Natural forms of love have disappeared such as parents' for their children, spouses' for each other, natural sexual attractions, and godly affections) (2 Timothy 3:3)

- trucebreakers (even refusing to enter truces or reconcile) (2 Timothy 3:3)

- false accusers (2 Timothy 3:3)

- incontinent (no self-control) (2 Timothy 3:3)

- fierce and merciless (2 Timothy 3:3)

- despisers of those who are good (2 Timothy 3:3)

- traitors and betrayers (2 Timothy 3:4)

- heady (headstrong, passionately self-destructive) (2 Timothy 3:4)

- high-minded (prideful) (2 Timothy 3:4)

- lovers of pleasures (Hebrews 11:25) more than lovers of God (2 Timothy 3:4)

- having a form of godliness, but denying the power thereof (2 Timothy 3:5)

- predatory: creep into houses and lead captive silly sinful women laden away (2 Timothy 3:6); and teeth as swords and teeth as knives to devour the poor and needy (Proverbs 30:14)

- ungrateful: curse their father (Proverbs 30:11) and mother (Proverbs 30:11)

- pure in their own eyes (Proverbs 30:12)

Additionally, there are many false prophets and doctrines (Luke 21:8), many wars (wars and rumors of war) (Luke 21:9-10), and many who persecute the righteous (Luke 21:12-16).

At this time, people will seek peace but find war (1 Thessalonians 5:3). The greatest example occurs just prior to the battle of Armageddon, where the antichrist's assumption of power gives the appearance of the arrival of a golden age of peace and prosperity. In reality, it leads to the worst catastrophes and wars ever unleashed on earth. Others examples can easily be found from the last century. World War I was "the war to end all wars." Atomic bombs gave the world MAD (mutually assured destruction), where the repercussions of war were considered so great no one would ever fight another war. People have often believed they were entering a golden age of peace only to be bitterly disappointed. Only when Jesus sits on his throne is this golden age achieved.

During this time, people scoff at God and his prophecies (2 Peter 3:3-4 and Jude 1:18-19). They not only question prophecy's veracity but also mock it and those who believe it. They quickly toss aside God's promises, saying if Jesus has not returned in two thousand years, then clearly he will never return. Skepticism greets all warnings about Jesus' return, as people come up with all sorts of reasons to disbelieve, including regurgitating the past errors of disproved date setters. Like the people of Sodom, they follow their own sensual lusts, and this makes the idea of a God's judgment both inconvenient and dangerous. They will do anything to persuade themselves they have nothing to fear.

Daniel 12:4 shows it is also a time seeing a dramatic expansion of knowledge, an apt description of the current knowledge explosion. Estimates vary, but many believe knowledge is doubling every couple of years. Daniel does not indicate how this knowledge is applied, but 2 Timothy 3:7 shows this new knowledge is not increasing people's wisdom. Rather, it is a time where knowledge is growing but people are unable to find either wisdom or truth, a dangerous combination.

Daniel 12:4's description of travel suggests transportation systems are both fast and extremely prevalent. This stands in stark contrast to most of human history. Until the nineteenth century, travel was limited to slow sea vessels, walking, or animal-powered vehicles (horses, mules, horse-drawn carriages, and carts). A day's journey was a standard measure of distance consisting of approximately 20 miles. If one were able to maintain this pace, it would take a little over 150 days to traverse the United States from coast to coast (over 170 days if one observes the Sabbatical restrictions). These travel times created many hardships and kept most people from traveling more than 50 miles from their place of birth. The introduction of steam trains reduced travel times from months to weeks. Since then, the world has seen the rapid introduction of automobiles, powered boats, planes, high-speed rail, and spacecraft. All have significantly reduced travel times and rendered the concept of a day's journey archaic. Today, the 150-day journey of two hundred years ago only takes a week, a few days, or a few hours, depending on which method of transportation is used. Now, a leisurely, twenty-minute Sunday afternoon drive has replaced the hard day's journey. Further advances in transportation technology may further reduce travel times, but they cannot match the dramatic changes already seen. The ease and speed of travel has opened a variety of new opportunities to many. Today, people are literally fulfilling Daniel's description of running back and forth across the earth in ways impossible to imagine just two hundred years ago.

As seen, the days leading up to and following the rapture are perilous times, where people's thoughts are on pleasure and not God. They delight in their sins and seek ways to increase their pleasure through them. Their advances in many fields of knowledge and technology help convince them they do not need to repent, so they ridicule discussions of Jesus, his return, and God's judgment. Despite the many signs of impending doom, they continue with their normal lives, ambivalent of the imminent danger. Just as the people of Noah's day did not panic until the floods started, neither will the people of this day panic until it is too late to avoid the seven-year tribulation's judgments.

The Hope for Revival

Despite the challenges presented by the world's condition and the church's Laodicean indifference just prior to the rapture, many Christians hold high hopes for a major revival prior to the rapture. They base this hope in part on the promise of God's grace as seen in Romans 5:20. "Moreover the law entered, that the offence might abound. But where sin abounded, grace did much more abound." Outside of perhaps the time preceding Noah's flood and Sodom's destruction, when will sin abound

any more than the seven-year tribulation and the period immediately preceding it? This abundance of sin guarantees God's
grace will be at its peak during this time. Many Christians
expect to see God's grace exhibited not only by the forgiveness
of sin but also by the Holy Spirit's activities in reaching and
converting large numbers of the world's lost masses. Joel 2:28-
29 end-time prophecies strengthen these expectations, as God
promises the Holy Spirit will operate in unprecedented ways.
While the context of the verses do not indicate whether the
Holy Spirit's activities transpire before or during the seven-year
tribulation, it is clear his actions precede Jesus' return. Most
likely, the fulfillment of Joel's prophecies starts prior to the full
tribulation and continues through it.

Extra-biblical statements further fuel expectations of a
major end-time revival. For example, in 1889, the famous missionary to China, James Hudson Taylor, reportedly foretold two
future world wars and a major worldwide revival. This revival
just prior to Jesus' return would emanate in Russia before spreading to Europe and then the rest of the world. Bishop Aristo-
coli also made similar pronouncements about a future Russian
revival lighting the way for the rest of the world. Whether predictions like these prove legitimate, they continue to serve as
hope and inspiration to missionaries throughout the world and
help nourish the hopes of a coming worldwide revival.

The Rapture

Section reference: Revelation 4:1-2.

The first two verses in Revelation 4 mark a dramatic change
in the perspective and focus in Revelation's narrative. Revelation 1-3 have covered the "things thou hast seen and the things
which are..." (Revelation 1:19). Their primary focus has been on
the past and present. From here on, everything John sees occurs
in the future: "Things which must be hereafter..." Though
Revelation 1-3 mentions the church nineteen times, it neglects
to mention the church again until its epilogue in chapter 22.

Where John has been describing events from an earthly perspective, he now shifts to a heavenly one. What triggers such significant changes in the Revelation narrative? Some of the clues found in these first two verses of Revelation 4 include:

- a door opened in heaven
- voice like a trumpet
- command to come up hither
- caught up to heaven before the throne of God

© Pat Marvenko Smith - www.revelationillustrated.com

Compare this description to 1 Thessalonians 4:13-17, where Jesus descends from heaven and calls all Christians, dead and alive, to meet him in the clouds. His command is accompanied by the shout of an archangel and God's trumpet. In Revelation, a door opens in heaven, and in 1 Thessalonians, Jesus descends from heaven. In Revelation, there is a voice like a trumpet, and in 1 Thessalonians, there is the trumpet of God. In Revelation, God commands John to go up to heaven, and in 1 Thessalonians, Jesus commands the church to meet him in the air. These parallels suggest these two passages describe the same event: the church's rapture. While the word rapture does not appear in the Bible, its meaning (to be carried away bodily or spiritually) is clearly embodied in these passages, which helps explain why the word rapture has become the commonly used term for this event. As the church is absent from the earth after the rapture, the church is also absent from Revelation after Revelation 4:1-2. John's presence in heaven and the church's absence in Revelation suggests the church is now safely in heaven with God. Only the rapture fits all of the changes and descriptions of Revelation 4:1-2.

Hosea 13:14 speaks of the rapture as God ransoming people from death and the grave. Second Timothy 2:11-12 promises in the same way, as Jesus was raised from the dead to reign as king, Christians will live and reign as kings with him. Paul provides another view of the rapture.

> Behold, I show you a mystery; We shall not all sleep, but we shall all be changed, In a moment, in the twinkling of an eye, at the last trump: for the trumpet shall sound, and the dead shall be raised incorruptible, and we shall be changed.
>
> 1 Corinthians 15:51-52

In the same way, Rosh Hashanah's trumpets usher in the seventh month of the Jewish calendar (the Sabbatical month), the rapture's trumpets usher in the Day of the Lord (the start of the Sabbatical millennium). The rapture's trumpets call Christians to meet Jesus at the beginning of the seventh millennial day, but its description as the last trumpet adds an element of mystery to the description. Is this the last trumpet ever blown, the last recorded in the Bible, the last of a specific type, or the last in a cycle? This mystery contributes to alternate theories of the rapture's placement with respect to the seven-year tribulation. By suggesting the rapture's trumpet is either the last trumpet ever blown or the last recorded in the Bible, it leads some to conclude it cannot occur until the seventh judgment trumpet of Revelation 11.

Those holding this and similar views believe the rapture occurs either during the middle of the seven-year tribulation (midtribulation) or at the end of the seven-year tribulation (posttribulation). Complicating this position are posttribulation biblical references of trumpets blown during Jesus' reign (e.g., Isaiah 27:13).

Since these trumpets can only sound after the seven-year tribulation is over (and the possible times for both has passed), even midtribulation and posttribulation rapture theories have the same issues with the meaning of 1 Corinthians 15:51's last trumpet as the pretribulation rapture theory. One can only conclude the rapture trumpets are neither the last trumpets ever blown or even the last trumpets referenced in the Bible. The mystery of the last trumpet is probably a reference to the last trumpet of the annual holy days: Rosh Hashanah or the trumpets blown on every fiftieth Day of Atonement (tenth day of seventh month) in conjunction with the observance of jubilee (Leviticus 25).

During the rapture, all Christians are rapidly changed. This happens in the twinkling of an eye (a blink), about an eighth of a second. This surprisingly short period is even more amazing considering the many changes occurring during it. For example, Matthew 22:30 shows people will no longer marry and implies there are no more sexual distinctions while Philippians 3:21 promises glorious new bodies. These new bodies are needed since currently sin stains the existing ones, making them vile. The rapture transforms the existing bodies from their current, sin marred, mortal states to pure, immortal ones with interesting changes. These changes are readily apparent in John 20:19-31, where Jesus appears in his immortal body and his apostles can see and touch it, but he just appears in rooms without opening doors. Somehow, this immortal body can move freely through solid walls yet still be touched as though solid. His body was still marred by the wounds he suffered on the cross but at the same time glorified in immortality. Today, Christians groan to possess this immortal body (1 Corinthians 15:50 and 2

Corinthians 5:1-4), as they can inherit the kingdom of God, go to heaven, and see the Father's face (Exodus 33:20).

1 Corinthians 15:42-44 shows many changes in the new bodies: corrupt becomes incorrupt, dishonorable becomes glorious, weak becomes powerful, and natural (carnal) becomes spiritual. A subtle point of these changes is the body's affect on people's behavior. It is easy to appreciate the new bodies are not stained by sin simply because they are new. However, if people sinned in these new bodies, what would happen? They too would be stained and vile. Whoever sinned would be back to where they started, but this time, like the fallen angels, without any provision for God's restoration. However, these bodies are not just incorrupt but also incorruptible. No one is able to dishonor and stain them with sin. How can people have free will and creativity yet not sin? This is a mystery of God, but it is clear the body's permanent, sinless nature somehow makes it impossible for people to sin. It will now be impossible for saints to lie, cheat, steal, commit perverse acts, or commit any other sin due to this new spiritual, eternal, heavenly, incorruptible body.

At Jesus' second coming, his army in these new bodies is able to march without missing a step while enemies try to destroy them (Joel 2:7-9). No weapon is able to kill, injure, or even slow them down. No one and no human barrier is able to resist these new bodies. These changes are hard to imagine or comprehend, but they give clues to how comprehensive these change are.

The church age chapter's summary mentioned Jesus' omission of food as a necessity of life and pointed out that Jesus is both the bread and the source of the water of life. Consequently, these new bodies no longer seem to require food or water. This is not to imply people no longer eat, for all resurrected people will enjoy a wonderful marriage feast in heaven. It simply means people no longer have to eat to survive. It is interesting to note that before man's fall in the garden of Eden, food was a necessity but clothing was not. Now, in the resurrected bodies, clothing is a necessity but food is not.

When will the rapture occur? Jesus promises it occurs sometime during the last day (John 6:39-40). Unfortunately, this only shows the rapture's approach. This prophecy does not contain sufficient information to pinpoint its exact timing. In point of fact, Matthew 24:36 explains it not known by the angels, the Holy Spirit, and even Jesus but only the Father. It is a point often emphasized in Scripture (e.g., Mark 13:32-37, Matthew 24:42-51) because the rapture comes suddenly without warning, like a thief in the night (1 Thessalonians 5:2-4).

The imagery of the bridegroom getting his bride further supports the rapture's suddenness. After his engagement, the groom was responsible for the preparation of a place for his new family. Since the groom inherits his land from his father, he prepares the place on his father's land. With his hormones and desires to be with his wife raging, it was naturally tempting for the groom to get anxious and want to pick up his bride before the place was fully prepared. It was the father's duty to prevent this by deciding when it was time to get the bride. Effectively, this kept both the groom and bride from knowing the exact date of the marriage. Similarly, Jesus has returned to his Father's house to prepare a place for believers (John 14:1-4). As the groom, Jesus promises to prepare a place for his bride, and as he prepares, he awaits the Father's instructions to get his bride. Though he may know the preparations are virtually complete, he does not know when his Father will send him. Unfortunately, date setters (people who name the time of the rapture) have discredited prophecy in their failed attempts to pinpoint this date. Through their efforts, people have quit jobs and sold everything they have in an attempt to be ready while damaging the credibility of all prophecies in the eyes of non-believers. Beyond the fact that this a date known only to the Father, it is especially disappointing that many of these dates were set prior to the Israel's rebirth, a scriptural impossibility. Exhaustive eschatology studies can give one the clues to identify the signs pointing to the coming rapture and help students avoid the folly of date setting.

So far, these passages detailed the rapture from the view

of one caught in it. A natural question is, "How will those left behind see and react to it?" Psalm 12:1 speaks of the righteous' disappearance, where they disappear (cease). Many people speculate that when this occurs, those left on earth will panic due to the resulting confusion, but Isaiah 57:1-2 suggests otherwise. When the righteous and merciful are taken away (perish), those left do not even ponder why it happened (lay it to heart). It never occurs to them that they may have been removed from the coming evil (the full tribulation).

It is natural to wonder how it would be possible for the church to disappear without causing panic and confusion. The stories of Noah and Lot may provide possible answers. In both cases, the percentage of people removed was very small, and no one believed their testimony of the coming danger. In fact, Lot's own sons-in-law felt he was mocking them when he warned of the coming danger. Another possibility can be seen in the teachings of occult and New Age groups, where different explanations are already being proffered long before the actual event. For example, some UFO groups believe the new age cannot dawn until the mother ship removes a group of people. In some stories, the group removed are the spiritually backward. In others, they are the spiritually mature. Either way, their disappearance opens the door for the dawning of their new age of Aquarius.

While the people of earth are apathetic, the rapture affects them in a couple of significant ways: the Holy Spirit's restraint of Satan's works are greatly relaxed and the son of perdition (antichrist) is revealed (2 Thessalonians 2:6-7). With the church no longer on earth, he no longer works through these men and his opposition to the son of perdition lessens. Without the opposition of the Holy Spirit, Revelation 13's three beasts start their work with minimal opposition, and it is a bad time to be left on earth.

Summarizing, Revelation 4:1-2 describes the church age's curtain call: the rapture. While this event hardly seems to cause a ripple on the world scene, it loosens the restraints on Satan and prepares the way for the son of perdition and the tribulation. As the righteous transit to the clouds, God transforms their bodies from their natural, carnal state into heavenly spiritual bodies. All believers, dead and alive, meet Jesus and return with him to heaven and the place he has prepared for them. All of the events of the next few sections precede the tribulation's start and occur in heaven. The Bible gives few clues to tell how much time expires between the rapture and the start of the tribulation. Estimates for this timeframe range from none up to twenty years. Likely, there will be a measurable but short period between the rapture of Revelation 4:1-2 and the start of the tribulation in Revelation 6:1.

The Church's Rewards
Section reference: Revelation 4:4

Immediately following the rapture, twenty-four elders representing the righteous (including the just retrieved church) are before the throne wearing white raiment and crowns. This is the first of three rewards for the church listed in the New Testament: clothing (white raiment and crowns), riches (gold, silver, and precious stones), and dominions (geographical area and people to rule). Sometime between the rapture of Revelation 4:1-2 and the elder's appearance here before God's throne, the righteous have received this reward. The other two rewards are not mentioned, but many people believe Jesus also gives the riches rewards and perhaps the dominions rewards at the same time. Revelation suggests another possibility, where Jesus separately awards the riches at the start of the great tribulation and the dominions in the transition period for his millennial reign.

The fundamental difference between raiment and crowns is the difference between necessities of life and abundant blessings. Raiment is one of 1 Timothy 6:8's necessities. Without it, guests attempting to attend the Lamb's marriage supper are cast out of heaven and into hell (Matthew 22:11-13), demonstrating that proper raiment is probably more important in heaven than on earth. Crowns complete the royal ensemble but are for only the most deserving.

Zechariah 3:1-5 paints a fascinating picture of Joshua receiving his clothing reward. Wearing filthy, sin-laden garments, Joshua, as a type of the righteous, stands in front of the angel of the Lord, who issues several declarations:

- Joshua's iniquity has been removed from him (past tense)
- Joshua is to be given a change of raiment
- Joshua is to have a mitre (a diadem or crown) placed on his head

Similarly, the righteous will stand before God in their filthy, sin-laden clothes, and as always, Satan will be standing there, resisting and accusing each of them. Though Jesus previously removed their iniquity (sin), its effects, as evidenced by the stained clothing, still linger. Now these effects are forever purged as Joshua receives garments befitting royalty. Amazingly, through this entire judgment, Satan is not only present but also attempting to stop or at least diminish each person's rewards. As incredible as it may sound, God has not expelled Satan from heaven and does not expel him until the middle of the seven-year tribulation in Revelation 12. This means Satan will likely be in heaven to witness and oppose both the saint's clothing and riches judgments.

A mystery of this judgment occurs in Revelation 3:18. This passage suggests not everyone receives clothing and some people stand naked before the throne of God. Since God's clothing is symbolic of Jesus' salvation, it is not clear how people could stand before this throne naked and still  be worthy of heaven. Perhaps these verses are simply an appeal for people to repent. Even if they were naked before God, one would assume that somehow they will eventually acquire clothing, but it is not clear when and how.

Another mystery surrounding the reward judgments is when the church receives its inheritance (Ephesians 1:13-14). Apparently separate from the three rewards, the church receives this inheritance based on its relationship to the Father through Jesus Christ. Unlike works or performance-based rewards, this unearned acquisition of ownership comes solely through inheritance. This inheritance differs from modern inheritance in some critical ways. Today, heirs in western societies only receive their inheritance on the death of the testator(s). In the absence of other legal vehicles, heirs are not able to use, manage, or control these assets prior of the testator's death. Even when other provisions are in place, the heirs' legal rights over their future property are limited. In contrast, Old Testament laws gave living sons ownership rights when they reached the age of majority. The story of the prodigal son reflects this living inheritance when the younger son asks for his possessions. In Luke 15:12, the younger son had a clear expectation that the property was not only his but also he had every right to take control and use it as he saw fit before the death of his father. The father divided the property according to the law and gave a third to the son (two parts for the older and one part for the younger) though it is not clear whether the father's compliance with this request represents his legal responsibilities or his generosity. Either way, his son receives a third of his estate, wastes it all, finally comes to his senses, and returns to his father to beg for his forgiveness. The father welcomed him back and put on a celebratory feast. When the older son complained about the attention given to the wayward son, the father comforted him by reminding him everything belonged to him (Luke 15:31). It is important to understand that this was not a platitude but reflected the legal condition of the estate. Since the younger son took his portion of the inheritance, all that was left legally belonged to the elder son.

Galatians 4:1-7 shows the living heirs were entitled to their inheritance where, prior to receiving their inheritance at the age of majority, the son's legal position is closer to that of a servant or even more accurately, a slave. When the church reaches the age of majority (probably when the church receives their new bodies) they receive their inheritance.

While not completely clear what portions of God's estate believers inherit, Mark 10:17-21 does show part of it is eternal life. The Jews' recognition of this fact in this passage, along with Jesus' lack of correction, affirms its validity. Clearly, part of the church's inherited estate is eternal life, but another part may be the estate of heaven. When the father told the prodigal son's brother that everything he had was his, it suggested that God withholds nothing from his heirs, including heaven.

Worship at God's Throne

Section reference: Revelation 4:2–11.

After the rapture, the first thing John sees is a glorious vision of God on his throne in all his majesty, sovereignty, and power. Most commentators identify Jesus as the one sitting on the throne, but Revelation 5:7 creates problems for this interpretation when Jesus, the Lamb, takes a book from the one on the throne. If he takes the book from the one on the throne, then someone else must be sitting on it. This leaves God the Father as its most likely occupant. In both Revelation 6:16 and 7:9, there are two different entities: the one on the throne and the Lamb. These descriptions are consistent with this vision and do not change until Revelation 21–22 when the throne is the habitation of both God the Father and the Lamb. The seven burning lamps in front of the throne contain the seven Spirits of God, the Holy Spirit; and with Jesus' appearance in Revelation 5, each member of the Holy Trinity is present at this throne.

This vision compares God's appearance to both jasper and sardine stone. Jasper is a clear quartz crystal, which Revelation 21:11 compares to the glory of God. Some suggest its descriptions in Revelation are closer to diamond than jasper. Sardine is a red stone that appears only once in the Bible, but another possible name for sardine is sardius, which does appear elsewhere. Both sardius and jasper  are in the high priest's breastplate; Ezekiel 28's Eden, the garden of God; and individual layers of new Jerusalem's foundation.

Surrounding the throne is a rainbow, a symbol of God's promises following Noah's flood to never again destroy the earth with water. This is especially comforting considering the catastrophes the world endures over the coming seven-year tribulation. The lightning, thunder, and voices that come from the throne often accompany the judgments of God on the earth during the full tribulation, and their presence portends God's coming wrath. In front of the throne is a sea like glass or crystal, which speaks of purity and peacefulness (no waves).

Arrayed around the throne are the twenty-four elders in their raiment and crown rewards. They likely represent the righteous of all ages but could represent just the church. Their presence recalls the twenty-four orders of Levites who took turns serving in the temple (1 Chronicles 24:1-19). Throughout Scripture, elders are always men and never angels. Elders served different roles within the nation of Israel and the church. Within the nation of Israel, they are civil leaders. This role continues into the New Testament until the establishment of the church when elders served as religious leaders. These different roles lead to the natural question of whether these heavenly elders represent the Old Testament civil leaders or the New Testament religious leaders. Their testimony in Revelation 5:10 suggest they are both because God is tearing down the separations of church and state, having made them both kings and priests.

© Pat Marvenko Smith - www.revelationillustrated.com

In and around the throne are four unique beasts. Many believe these are the cherubim described in Ezekiel 1 and 10. They first appeared in Genesis when they protected the tree of life from humanity. They also protected the mercy seat of the ark of the covenant and the holy of holies (embroidered on the curtains). Revelation's beasts have six wings while the cherubim have four wings. While there are many similarities in these descriptions, this single difference suggests these are different beings, perhaps even the seraphim of Isaiah 6:2. Few details about seraphim are available, but they are probably worshipers while cherubim are protectors.

The beast's first praise is, "Holy, holy, holy, Lord God Almighty." The three holies confirms the presence of each member of the Holy Trinity, and "Lord God Almighty," confirms the mystery that they are one God (see also Isaiah 6:3). The throngs in heaven then praise him for his eternal existence (past, present, and future) and give him glory, honor, and thanks. As soon as the beasts finish, the twenty-four elders, representing all of the righteous in heaven, fall down before God Almighty and worship him by casting their crowns before his throne and saying the Lord is worthy to receive glory, honor, and power. Where the beasts give God thanks, the elders proclaim his worthiness for power. The elders then acknowledge God has made all things for his pleasure.

Search for One Worthy to Open the Sealed Book

Section reference: Revelation 5.

Revelation 5 introduces the earth's title deed,[1] a book with seven seals held in the right hand of God the Father. Next, a strong angel, likely Revelation 10's mighty angel, issues a proclamation initiating a search for anyone worthy to open it. Only one is found: Jesus. It is not until he steps forward to take the book that John finally sees him in the midst of the throne. Interestingly, John provides no explanation why he failed to see or even note Jesus' presence prior to this.

The elders call Jesus by two titles (the Lion of the tribe of Judah and the Root of David), proclaiming his royal lineage while showing his redemptive work as Savior (the slain Lamb, with seven horns, seven eyes, and the seven Spirits of God). Jesus' horns speak of his power, and the seven  horns suggest complete power, the power only God Almighty possesses. Seven eyes, which are the seven Spirits of God, suggest not only Jesus' omnipotence but also the Holy Spirit's overflowing presence in him. Revelation 1 showed Jesus in the midst of church (the candlesticks). Now, Revelation 5 shows him in the midst of the throne of God. Where is the church? Since the rapture, the church is now with Jesus in heaven surrounding the throne of God.

As Jesus takes the book, he receives three groups of praises:

- The four beasts and the twenty-four elders sing a new song

- Many angels, the beasts, and the elders speak the Lamb's praises

- Every creature in heaven, on the earth, under the earth, and in the sea speak the Lamb's praises

The twenty-four elders are now holding harps and vials containing the prayers of the saints. These vials are seen again in Revelation 8's censer judgments and later in Revelation 16's seven vial judgments.

The elders praise Jesus for his worthiness and his past redemptive deeds, including his death. They testify that they represent Jesus' redemptive work, including people from every kindred, tongue, people, and nation. Their statements are past tense, further suggesting the rapture's completion. Finally, they praise Jesus for his future deeds: making them kings and priests who shall reign on earth. The praises continue as 100 million angels (one of few biblical clues to the angelic host's size) chime in with a sevenfold praise of Jesus: power, riches, wisdom, strength, honor, glory, and blessing. The praises reach their climax as all saints and creation's creatures proclaim a fourfold blessing. For unspecified reasons, the fourfold blessing does not include the blessings of riches, wisdom, and strength. This last scene is reminiscent of Jesus' arrival in Jerusalem on Palm Sunday (Luke 19:39-40), when Jesus told the Pharisees that even if the people were quiet, the stones would cry out. Here, John shows this prophecy's fulfillment, as all of God's creation praises Jesus. It is not clear whether all creatures include all men on earth but considering people's animosity and rebellion against God, it seems improbable for them to be included.

Revelation 5 ends with the angelic beasts affirming the praises with a simple amen and the elders prostrating themselves in praise before the throne of God for a third time. At this time, the church is in heaven, the people on earth are indifferent, and Jesus stands poised to reclaim the earth by opening the sealed book.

The Tribulation (Redemption and Coronation)

The tribulation encompasses two of Revelation's themes: redemption (seven seal judgments) and coronation (seven trumpet judgments). It starts with the antichrist's unveiling and lasts three and a half years. This period sees an amazing sequence of events, including the arrival of the four horsemen of the apocalypse, a major war, many catastrophes, demons released from the bottomless pit, and a 200-million-man army set loose to rampage against their neighbors and ancient enemies. The transition into the great tribulation contains so many dramatic, rapid-fire events that they demand a separate chapter and are covered in the following midtribulation chapter.

Seals One to Four: The Four Horsemen of the Apocalypse

Now possessing the sealed book, Jesus starts triggering tribulation's initial events by breaking its seals. The first four seals introduce four horsemen, collectively known as the four horsemen of the apocalypse. They spread misery and death wherever they ride throughout the earth. The imagery contained in Revelation is so striking that they are common subjects of apocalyptic artwork, and most tribulation pictures contain some version of them. Each of these four seals introduces one of the riders each astride a differently colored horse:

© Pat Marvenko Smith - www.revelationillustrated.com

Horseman 1:	rides a white horse and introduces the son of perdition
Horseman 2:	rides a red horse and brings war
Horseman 3:	rides a black horse and brings famine
Horseman 4:	rides a pale horse and brings death

Their work starts at the advent of the tribulation and presumably continues until Jesus' return. Riding throughout the earth, they continue taking God's judgment to the farthest reaches of the globe until their gruesome work has claimed a quarter of the world's population.

Zechariah 6:1-8 paints a similar image. Zechariah's horses leave from a mountain of brass, foreshadowing the unnamed judgments they take with them. Zechariah's horses and Revelation riders are so similar yet also remarkably different that their comparison naturally sparks scholarly debate.

1/3 | Seals 1-4: The Four Horsemen: Imitation, War, Famine, Death

Seal One: The Son of Perdition

Section reference: Revelation 6:1-2.

When Jesus breaks the first seal, he irreversibly sets the tribulation's actions in motion, introduces the first rider, begins the earth's redemption, and commences earth's most tumultuous period: the seven-year tribulation. The Bible dedicates more prophecy to these years than any other period, and these initial events barely hint at its coming dangers and catastrophes.

Ominous thunder forebodes the coming judgments as the first rider arrives on a white horse, carries the military might of a bow, wears the political authority of a crown, and goes out conquering and subjugating. Discussions of these descriptions generally center on what is missing: arrows or even a quiver for them. In other words, he carries a bow but no ammunition. Some suggest this shows he has the trappings of military power without the wherewithal to execute it. Another possibility is this shows his preference is to acquire power through coercion rather than force.

This rider takes his bow and immediately sets out on a course to acquire and expand his dominion throughout the earth. His insatiable appetite for power drives him to continuously seek opportunities to acquire more and helps identify him as the son of perdition, otherwise known as the antichrist. Along with the church's rapture and Israel's rebirth, the antichrist's unveiling is one of the most anticipated tribulation indicators. The following is likely this event's most quoted passage.

Let no man deceive you by any means: for that day shall not come, except there come a falling away first, and that man of sin be revealed, the son of perdition; who opposeth and exalteth himself above all that is called God, or that is worshipped; so that he as God sitteth in the temple of God, showing himself that he is God.

2 Thessalonians 2:3-4

"Falling away first" probably reflects the worldwide apostasy besetting humanity as this time approaches, though some suggest it refers to the rapture. Apostasy afflicted the last day's church, Laodicea, and will only grow after the rapture removes all Christians. One of this verse's key points is it links this revealing to "that day," the Day of the Lord. Combined with what is known of the duration of his activities (seven years, Daniel 9:27) and his reign's end at the end of the full tribulation, when Jesus throws him into the lake of fire, the son of perdition's unveiling must occur at the beginning of the tribulation, most probably here in the first seal. Even if this seal does not represent his unveiling, it still must occur now at the beginning of the tribulation.

Second Thessalonians 2:3-4 portrays the antichrist as the ultimate rebel, fighting God every way possible and eventually proclaiming himself god, demanding people's worship, and sitting in the holy of holies as god. Second Thessalonians 2:8-12 describes him as a liar who uses Satan's power to produce miracles, illusions, and signs to fool people. Just as magicians in Pharaoh's courts imitated some of Moses' miracles, the antichrist imitates miracles of God and uses every possible deception to deceive and enslave as many people as possible.

Daniel 11:21-24 portrays him as a vile flatterer who makes and breaks covenants to obtain power and kingdoms. He can never be trusted, as he will say anything to anyone. He talks of peace but instead brings war and forcibly takes riches and spoils. Psalm 12:8 shows that as he ascends to power, the wicked are everywhere. As the tribulation moves forward, he sets his sights on the innocent and righteous, whom he persecutes without mercy.

Summarizing, the antichrist:

- has the appearance of military might
- receives political authority
- has an insatiable appetite for power
- opposes God
- proclaims himself God
- demands worship
- sits as God in the holy of holies
- is a liar
- uses Satan's power to perform miracles
- is a vile person
- comes in peace but brings war
- makes and breaks covenants
- obtains kingdoms through flatteries
- takes spoils and riches
- promotes the wicked
- persecutes the righteous

Recognizing the Son of Perdition

While it is natural to be curious of his identity, so far, Revelation has provided precious few clues. Fortunately, more are supplied as the antichrist takes center stage during the great tribulation, and speculation about his possible identity is deferred until then. Elsewhere, the Bible does give some basic tests to prove his identity. For example, 2 John 1:7 claims those who do not profess Jesus Christ has come in the flesh are deceivers and an antichrist. Undoubtedly, this applies to not just the tribulation's infamous antichrist but also anyone who does this. Conversely, anyone failing this test is not the antichrist.

Significantly, God does not leave the identification of the antichrist to chance as he sends two witnesses to boldly expose the beast's identity and his plans. He sends these two witnesses (not one) to satisfy legal requirements for testimony (Deuteronomy 19:15). The antichrist hates these witnesses but must endure them for 1260 days (just less than three and a half years), until God permits him to kill them. While not clearly specified, it is likely they start their ministry as soon as the antichrist rides on the scene.

The Son of Perdition's Deeds

Daniel 9:27 mentions signature deeds the antichrist performs during Daniel's seventieth week: a covenant he brokers (and later breaks), stopping the daily sacrificial worship, and the abomination of desolation. Early in the tribulation, he establishes the covenant, and it remains in effect through the full tribulation. Some suggest the confirmation of the covenant is not a new covenant but simply the enforcement of an existing pact. Likely, this is the antichrist's first act and is probably executed even before Jesus breaks the second seal. Isaiah 28:14-18 reveals this is a covenant with death and hell, which a stone (Jesus) destroys using hail and water. Isaiah pegs the tribe of Ephraim, with the complicity of priests and prophets, as entering into this despicable covenant on behalf of Israel. Void of spiritual wisdom, these drunkard fools deceive the Jews (Isaiah 28:1-13) and Ephraim's role in entering the antichrist's covenant may explain why Revelation 7 omits them from the list of tribulation tribes.

The Bible leaves the nature of this covenant to speculation, but it is reasonable to assume it is a peace treaty that finally guarantees Israel the basic internal and external safety and security they have so desperately craved since their inception in 1948. Based on past agreements (e.g., the Oslo accord), Israel has shown a willingness to make draconian concessions in their pursuit of this dream. Likely, the antichrist uses their yearning against them to extract many concessions and potentially, Israel could grant an "independent" third party, like the antichrist, binding arbitration authority to resolve regional disputes. If true, Israel gains the illusion of peace and safety but pays an astronomically high price by relinquishing some or all of its autonomy (1 Thessalonians 5:3). By appearing to bring peace and safety, the antichrist's influence and reputation as a miracle worker skyrockets. Using this covenant as a launching pad, he starts gaining and consolidating power until he eventually rules over all nations during the second half of the seventieth week of Daniel (the great tribulation).

Daniel 9:27 shows that the antichrist eventually breaks this covenant through the abomination of desolation. By this time, he has already stopped the daily sacrifice and turned the courtyard of the tabernacle over to the Gentiles. The exact nature of this abomination is debatable, but its effects are significant, far-reaching, and set in motion the chain of events leading to the battle of Armageddon. The antichrist's actions appear somewhat subdued during the tribulation's three and a half years, but when he takes his temporary throne during the great tribulation, he triggers many of God's judgments.

The Great Imitator

Throughout the full tribulation, the antichrist imitates Jesus Christ, whose throne he desperately wants to take. Despite the testimonies of the two witnesses, he seeks to deceive the world into believing he is the earth's rightful heir, the promised Messiah. Table 13 shows many of the ways he imitates Jesus, as revealed now in the first seal judgment and throughout the rest of Revelation's narrative.

Table 13: Antichrist's Imitations of Jesus

	Jesus	Antichrist
Rides (Revelation)	White Horse	White Horse
Weapons	Sword	Bow (no arrows?)
Actions	Comes in War Brings Peace	Comes in Peace Brings War
Character	Speaks Truth	Speaks Lies
Power	Authority of God	Authority of Satan
Deity	Is God	Proclaims himself God
Dominion	Earth	Earth
Throne	Jerusalem	Jerusalem
Persecutes	Wicked	Righteous
Rewards	Righteous Nations Righteous People	Wicked Nations Wicked People
Chief Witness	Elijah	False Prophet
Heritage	Judah	?

Beyond this table of biblically supportable imitations, extra-biblical events suggest there are more. For example, like Hitler's satanically inspired vision, it is likely that he will plan for his reign to last one thousand years. In fact, there are several strong parallels between the antichrist's rise to power and Hitler's. Hitler came to power mainly through political means, though the threat of paramilitary action was always present. He used deceit, lies, and the power of persuasion to influence people. Once in power, he took what he wanted from whom he wanted and used these possessions as he saw fit. His hatred for both God and his people was seemingly boundless. The biggest drawback in this comparison is the realization that Hitler is only an antichrist imitator. Any evil Hitler committed pales next to the future deeds of this maniac.

The Question of Heritage and the Tribe of Dan

Table 13's last item raises the question of the antichrist's heritage. This interesting and contentious question originated with the blessings Israel gave to his children just prior to his death. Of most interest are the blessings given to Judah and Dan. First, Genesis 49:8-12 promises that Judah will be the tribe of royalty and specifically, the tribe of the Messiah. It has been the tribe of Boaz (the husband of Ruth), David, Solomon, the kings of Judah, and Jesus. Judah's descendents ruled over all or part of the kingdom of Israel until the Babylonian captivity. Jesus' lineage from Judah is so important that both the Gospels of Matthew and Luke include proof of it. With the first-century destruction of Jewish genealogical records, it became difficult for a Messianic imitator to trace his heritage to Judah.

Next, Genesis 49:16-18 promises Dan "shall judge his people, as one of the tribes of Israel..." This conjures up images of Israel's Old Testament judges, who ruled Israel prior to the kings. The judges, starting with Moses and ending with Samuel, led the nation for hundreds of years. They came from every tribe and often led the nation for their lifetimes. Like these judges of old, the tribe of Dan judges his people and presumably, the other tribes of Israel. However, this judge is a serpent, a deadly, venomous adder that strikes the horse's heels and causes the rider to fall off the back of his horse. These images recall the prophecies in the garden of Eden against the serpent (Genesis 3:14-15). That serpent bruised Jesus' heel at the cross of Calvary, but God promised that Jesus will ultimately bruise his head. It appears that, once again, Satan, this time through the tribe of Dan, causes Israel to stumble and fall backward from God.

Dan's serpent is suggestive of the brazen serpent Moses created to save the children of Israel from deadly serpents in the wilderness (Numbers 21:6-9). In John 3:14-15, Jesus claimed to be this brazen serpent. As brass, Jesus is judged; and as a serpent, he became sin on the cross at Calvary. Jesus bore humanity's sin burden and was judged as sin by God the Father. At that time, he was separated from his Father, who could not even look at him (Habakkuk 1:13), which is why he cried out "Eli, Eli, lama sabachthani?" That is to say, "My God, my God, why hast thou forsaken me?" (Matthew 27:46)

Without doubt, the primary application of this illustration is salvation where people receive healing from sin's deadly wounds by simply looking to Jesus, their brazen serpent, for salvation. However, there is also an important secondary, end-time application. In it, the children of Israel receive deadly wounds from the poisonous serpent of Dan, but again, they can live by simply looking to Jesus for their redemption.

Along with Ephraim, Dan is one of two tribes omitted in Revelation 7's list of tribes. Dan, whose name means judged, was the firstborn of Bilhah, a handmaid, or slave, of Rachel. As firstborn, he may have been eligible to claim special inheritance rights, but these passed to the tribes of Judah and Joseph, both born of free women. Judah received the Messianic blessings while Joseph received the double-portion inheritance (two tribes, Manasseh and Ephraim, instead of one). Amos 8:13-14 shows that during the full tribulation ("that day"), Dan tries to usurp Judah's throne. He will lead Israel to worship his gods, and those doing so will fall and never rise again. Since God raises all who place their trust and confidence in him, it is clear that Dan is leading them to worship false gods (probably Satan). These verses point to the possibility that the antichrist comes from the tribe of Dan, but these prophecies could also speak of another of the Revelation's beasts: the false prophet. Either way, it might not be possible for people on earth to know that one or the other is from the tribe of Dan because Israel no longer possesses accurate genealogical records. Today, DNA testing offers some hope for resolving this issue.

Some have suggested that Israel's thirteenth judge, the Nazarite Samson (Judges 13-16), is the judge foretold in the prophecies of Dan in Genesis 49:16-18. While Samson was full of character flaws, he does not appear to fit these prophecies because he does not fulfill any of the following:

- He did not rule in a deceitful or wicked manner.
- His power clearly came from God, not Satan.
- He did not betray or wound his brothers (only himself).
- He did not lead them from worshipping God.
- He did not live in the Day of the Lord.

Besides Samson, the Bible provides no candidates for the fulfillment of the prophecies against Dan. This only leaves the future beasts of Revelation 13: the antichrist or the false prophet.[1]

Seal Two: War

Section reference: Revelation 6:3-4.

The second seal brings the second horseman riding a red horse. This rider receives a great sword to remove peace wherever he rides and he wields it to turn nation against nation and neighbor against neighbor. Even where different ethnic groups have peacefully coexisted for hundreds of years, he stirs up ancient hatreds and unleashes regional tensions. The Bible, with its Israel-centric nature, omits most of this rider's wars since they do not directly involve the nation or the land of Israel, but this omission does not diminish either their scope (worldwide), their severity, or the affected ethnic groups.

Many suggest the first half of the seven-year tribulation is a time of relative peace, and in comparison to the great tribulation, this is reasonable, but this rider's activities assure that outside of the great tribulation, this is the most horrendous period of wars the earth ever sees.

Seal Three: Famine

Section reference: Revelation 6:5-6.

The third seal reveals a horseman riding a black horse. This rider carries the instruments of trade (balances) in his hand and uses them to measure and sell a penny's worth of wheat and barley. In today's monetary system, a penny is not a large sum of money, but Matthew 20:1-2 demonstrates it represents a full day's wages. A measure is a single person's rations for one day (about one quart). This sets the price for a day's worth of wheat at an entire day's wages. Likewise, a day's wages purchases only three quarts of barley. Considering five pounds of processed flour (not raw wheat) currently sells for few dollars, hyperinflation has sent the cost of wheat from pennies to tens of dollars, perhaps hundreds of dollars. These descriptions paint a picture of tremendous food shortages and famine. While not stated, it seems reasonable to assume these are consequences of the wars caused by the second rider since historically war leads to food shortages and ultimately, famine.

The protection of the oil and wine may be an indication the luxuries of life are still available but are now very precious. However, this passage's oil is actually olive oil, often symbolic of the Holy Spirit. When combining this with the fact that wine often represents the fruit of God's people, one is led to the conclusion that God tells the third rider not to harm his people during the seven-year tribulation. God set this precedent when he protected Israel while he plagued Egypt and Pharaoh (Exodus 9:24-26) and does not abandon it now.

Seal Four: Death

Section reference: Revelation 6:7–8.

When Jesus breaks the fourth seal, he reveals the last, and only named, horseman of the apocalypse: Death. To some, this rider's pale horse suggests a physically weak horse rather than a pale color, but most commentators believe pale does refer to its color—perhaps a gray or a color associated with death such as a pale green. Pale green is likely since the word chlorine comes from pale's root Greek word chloros (Strong's G5515). Fortunately, the actual physical traits of the horse do not seem to affect the description of the horseman or his activities.

Before the end of the full tribulation, Death kills 25 percent of the world's population, or about 1.6 billion people. While he performs his gruesome work with beasts and something simply called death, he also utilizes the work of the second (kills with the sword) and third horsemen (kills with hunger). Perhaps the first horseman also joins in, but no direct evidence appears in this description. Ezekiel 14:21 may give a clue of the form of "death" brought by this last horseman when he adds pestilence to the list. Elsewhere, the Greek word for death, thanatos (Strong's G2288), does not describe death from a specific cause but from all causes. This makes it likely that this rider's death refers to any form of death not explicitly listed, including pestilence. Since his victims are destined for hell, it appears that, like the third horseman, the righteous are protected from his work.

This ends the descriptions of the four horseman of the apocalypse and their activities through the seven-year tribulation. Since the workers of imitation, war, famine, and death are not mentioned again, it is easy to overlook their ongoing activities. However, this oversight, especially in light of Death's destruction of 1.6 to 2 billion people, diminishes the abject hopelessness and horror they inflict on the world for seven years. Though it is not always clear how the horseman's activities intertwine with future judgments, it is clear that, prior to Jesus' return, they make life on earth unbearable for the wicked.

Seal Five: Persecution of the Righteous

Section reference: Revelation 6:9-11, Revelation 7:9-17.

Revelation now changes its focus to earth's remaining righteous. When Jesus breaks the fifth seal, bodiless souls appear under an altar in heaven. These are martyrs slain for the Word of God and their testimony. Their presence in heaven proves they can only be the souls of righteous people but they cannot be the church because the church received their new bodies when the rapture occurred in Revelation 4:1-2. These righteous can only be those who have died since the rapture and are, therefore, tribulation saints. Apparently, these saints rejected the first rider's demands, followed God, lived their lives according to God's commandments, and testified of Jesus. For this, they became the horseman's mortal enemies and received an earthly reward of death, probably by beheading (Revelation 20:4).

Contrast the cries of these saints for God's vengeance on those who persecute and shed their blood against the church's response to persecution as epitomized by Stephen's dying words, which focused on forgiveness and echoed those Jesus uttered on the cross (Acts 7:55-60). Now the tribulation saints cry not

> 1/4 Seal 5: Tribulation Saints Revealed

for forgiveness but for revenge. This call reflects a significant post-rapture change. No longer does God patiently wait for the wicked to repent. Now he pours out judgment after judgment until they finally succumb to Jesus' authority. As Stephen's cries for God's mercy on his persecutors was a reflection of God's attitude toward the wicked, the tribulation saint's cries for vengeance are now a reflection of God's new attitude.

At first, John saw just the martyrs' souls (no bodies). After their cries, he sees them receiving the reward of the righteous: white robes. Since their bodiless souls have no need of garments, their reception of the white robes implies their souls now reside in physical bodies and sometime in these verses, they must have received their new perfect eternal bodies. After receiving their robes, these saints receive instructions to wait until the rest of the saints of the full tribulation die and join them in heaven. Unlike the church, who had to wait for the rapture for their resurrection, God resurrects, transfigures, and gives these saints their white robe raiment rewards immediately following their deaths. At some point in the full tribulation (possibly the marriage supper), this immediate resurrection ends, and afterward, all the dead must wait until the final judgments at the great white throne.

This creates an interesting contrast between the white robe rewards of the tribulation saints and the last church age, Laodicea. God counseled the Laodiceans to buy white raiment so they could cover their nakedness, but the tribulation saints receive their reward without question or comment. Presumably through their deaths, these saints have already shown themselves worthy.

Later, Revelation 7:9-17 suggests these saints are a staggering multitude, as John was able to estimate the population of 100 million angels but these saints are so numerous he claims no man can count them. Considering the church is not on earth and new believers are quickly martyred, how is it possible for there to be so many full-tribulation saints? Perhaps they are the fruits of the two witnesses and God's servants (the unraptured Jews). Perhaps it is the fear of God and his judgments, or repulsion over the antichrist's actions. However, it is evident that even in the midst of the great sins of the tribulation, God's grace is pleading with men to repent and return to him. Notably, this great multitude of saints comes from all nations, all kindreds, all people, and all tongues, which demonstrates the complete penetration of the Gospel throughout the earth. Nations denote national boundaries, kindreds denote a common ancestry such as a race or tribe, and people denote a blended group and can consist of multiple kindreds or span across national borders. Tongues indicate language is not a barrier to salvation. In short, the Gospel's preaching reaches the entire world, excluding no one.

Now clothed in their white robes, this uncountable multitude stands before the throne of God and before the Lamb.

They hold palm leaves in their hands, recalling the palm leaves used to worship Jesus as he entered Jerusalem on Palm Sunday (John 12:13). In both words and actions, the full-tribulation saints acknowledge Jesus' deity and praise both Father and Son. Two differences between the church, as represented by the twenty-four elders, and the full-tribulation saints are:

- The church wears their crown rewards and the full-tribulation saints hold palm leaves
- The church stands around the throne and the full-tribulation saints stand in front of it

Standing before God's throne, these saints cry out salvation to God the Father, who sits on the throne, and the Lamb. Even the praises of the full-tribulation saints recognize the separation of the throne of God and the Lamb and confirm Jesus has yet to assume his throne. Immediately afterward, the angels and the elders worship the Lord with a sevenfold blessing: blessing, glory, wisdom, thanksgiving, honor, power, and might.

This blessing is almost identical to the angels' sevenfold blessing of Revelation 5:12, where the only real difference is this list contains thanksgiving and Revelation 5:12's list contains riches. (Might and strength come from the same Greek word.) Perhaps this indicates the riches God treasures most are the thanksgiving from those he created. When the praise is complete, one of the elders explains the multitude is the righteous dying during the seven-year tribulation. Starting now and continuing throughout the entire seven-year tribulation, each arriving wedding guest must receive and wear clothing washed white in Jesus' blood, which signifies their reward of eternal life. God protects, comforts, removes their sorrows, and provides their needs: white raiment, the bread of life, and the water of life. They get to continually live and serve in his presence, before his throne, and in his temple.

A commonly asked question is whether people can receive salvation during the seven-year tribulation. The events of the fifth seal and Revelation 7 emphatically affirms that indeed they can, but their salvation comes at a heavy cost: their lives. A second, similar question is whether people who had the opportunity to receive salvation before the seven-year tribulation can reconsider and receive it during the seven-year tribulation. Second Thessalonians 2:10-12 is normally quoted in response to this question. These verses support the argument that people who have heard and rejected the Gospel cannot receive salvation after the rapture since God sends strong delusion to cloud their thoughts to the point where it is impossible for them to receive salvation. This position opens questions about the point of no return for a nonbeliever. When has a person so thoroughly rejected the Gospel they no longer have an opportunity to receive salvation? Does it happen if they heard the name of Jesus, heard a single sermon delivered under the Holy Spirit's authority, or merely heard of salvation? While the answers to these questions are solely in God's hands, it is easy to agree that people who rejected the Gospel while there were minimal consequences will find it difficult, probably impossible, to change their minds when it costs them their lives.

Seal Six: Magog's Invasion

Section reference: Revelation 6:12-17.

Up to now, all tribulation activities have started at the tribulation's beginning and continued until Jesus' return. They foreshadowed future problems humanity faces but provided few details of actual events. Here in the sixth seal, this changes dramatically as Jesus initiates a devastating series of events: a great earthquake, the sun's light changed, the moon's light changed, things falling to the earth, the sky rippling like a scroll, and islands and mountains moved out their places. These events are so hideous they drive people into mountains and rocks for safety.

What does this seal unleash? What causes all of this devastation? The answers are not immediately clear, but the seal's description contains important clues. One clue is the people's reaction to the catastrophes, as everyone from every class of life hides themselves in dens and mountains. On the surface, this is an odd reaction to earthquakes. Earthquake survival plans typically call for people to move out into open areas or into structurally strengthened parts of buildings (e.g., doorways). Also, the duration of earthquakes do not generally allow the large-scale evacuations described here. Most people simply do not live or work close enough to any type of den or mountain to be able to get to them before the average earthquake ends. If the dens and caves are actually modern centralized underground shelters, then evacuation times become an even greater issues. As seen by coastal evacuations before hurricanes, most evacuation plans require many hours and often days to organize and implement. The travel difficulties associated with active earthquakes make any evacuation during an earthquake even less likely. Typically, emergency personnel only execute evacuation plans when there is sufficient warning to get people to safety, not during the disaster itself. The fact people are in shelters in the dens and mountains (or their modern equivalent: underground bomb shelters) suggests they knew of the danger and were able to hide themselves before it came.

The next clue is the stars of heaven cast something to the earth in a manner consistent with a fig tree casting its unripe figs when shaken by strong winds. Recalling the fig tree is symbolic of Israel, Israel is apparently pivotal to the sixth seal's events. The fig tree produces the castoff fruit, but since it is unripe, it is not the spiritual fruit God demands of Israel but something quite different. Whatever these fruits are, a mighty wind propels them great distances and through the heavens at high speeds. Here, the Greek word for heaven, ouranos (Strong's G3772), means sky or heaven. Putting it all together, the nation of Israel casts off things they have created as mighty winds carry them, shining like stars, through the sky at high speeds and across great distances.

These castoff fruits produce some significant effects when they cause heaven to depart like a scroll. The rippling like a scroll suggests shock waves of a type and magnitude unseen and unimaginable until the advent of modern nuclear weaponry. These castoffs also move mountains and islands out of their places. If the first effect is the result of nuclear weapons exploding, then the second could also be a natural consequence of the same explosions. Thirdly, these fruits could be the cause of the darkening of the sun and moon, which is reminiscent of Kuwait after the 1991 Gulf War when Saddam Hussein set the oil fields on fire. Until extinguished, smoke from the fires so thoroughly blackened the days that pictures from the area matched the sixth seal's descriptions very closely.

All of these clues suggest world events cause people to evacuate into underground bomb shelters in anticipation of nuclear war, and Israel is the focal point as she launches a variety of nuclear weapons that travel great distances at high speeds to the homes of their enemies. The explosions of these weapons causes shockwaves,  moves mountains and islands, triggers earthquakes, and launches billowing smoke and debris into the air. This darkens the sun and makes the moon appear red. As these catastrophes unfold around them, the reactions of those in the shelters are telling. They cry out for their shelters to protect them from the face of God the Father (sitting on the throne) and the wrath of the Lamb. Even these shelters' occupants seem to recognize Jesus is not yet on the throne. The shelter's occupants also recognize something not seen so far in Revelation: Jesus' wrath. Apparently, they understand the Day of the Lord has come and they are not able to stand up to him. By the end of the seven-year tribulation, their attitudes will have changed, and many will fight against Jesus in a vain attempt to stop his return.

This is the first of several great earthquakes affecting mountains and islands. This time, the earthquakes only move them. In Revelation 16:20, another earthquake eliminates islands and mountains. The later earthquake occurs during the height of the great tribulation at the start of the battle of Armageddon. This is also the first of five times the sun darkens during the seven-year tribulation. The second occurs in Revelation 8:12, the fourth trumpet judgment; the third occurs in the fifth trumpet judgment in Revelation 9; the fourth occurs in the fifth vial judgment in Revelation 16:10-11; and the last is not found in Revelation, but Old Testament prophets foretold its occurrence during Jesus' return.

Comparison: The Sixth Seal versus the Battle of Magog

The most likely reason for these events is a catastrophic war caused by Magog's invasion of Israel (Ezekiel 38-39). The leader of Magog, Gog, leads many nations in this attack on Israel, and like Revelation's sixth seal judgment, God's wrath rains down from the heavens and shakes the earth. Table 14 compares seven critical details tying Revelation's sixth seal to Magog's invasion. These commonalities form a persuasive, but not conclusive, argument that these describe the same event. The timing of this battle is often debated, as different scholars place this battle prior to the tribulation, others place it in the great tribulation prior to the battle of Armageddon, and still others place it as part of the battle of Armageddon.

Table 14: Comparison: Magog Invasion versus Seal Six War

Detail	Revelation	Ezekiel
Day of God's wrath	"And said to the mountains and rocks, 'Fall on us, and hide us from the face of him that sitteth on the throne, and from the wrath of the Lamb: For the great day of his wrath is come; and who shall be able to stand?'" (6:13)	"For in my jealousy and in the fire of my wrath have I spoken" (38:19)
Last days	"And I beheld when he had opened the sixth seal."	"And thou shalt come up against my people of Israel, as a cloud to cover the land; it shall be in the latter days, and I will bring thee against my land, that the heathen may know me, when I shall be sanctified in thee, O Gog, before their eyes." (38:16) "And it shall come to pass in that day, that I will give unto Gog a place there of graves in Israel." (39:11)
Battle takes place in Israel	"The stars of heaven fell unto the earth, even as a fig tree casteth her untimely figs, when she is shaken of a mighty wind." (6:13)	"After many days thou shalt be visited: in the latter years thou shalt come into the land that is brought back from the sword, and is gathered out of many people, against the mountains of Israel, which have been always waste: but it is brought forth out of the nations, and they shall dwell safely all of them." (38:8)

Table 14: Continued

Detail	Revelation	Ezekiel
Destruction reigned from the air	"The stars of heaven fell unto the earth, even as a fig tree casteth her untimely figs, when she is shaken of a mighty wind." (6:13)	"I will rain upon him, and upon his bands, and upon the many people that are with him, an overflowing rain, and great hailstones, fire, and brimstone." (38:22)
Tremendous shaking of the earth	"And I beheld when he had opened the sixth seal, and, lo, there was a great earthquake." (6:12)	Surely in that day there shall be a great shaking in the land of Israel; So that the fishes of the sea, and the fowls of the heaven, and the beasts of the field, and all creeping things that creep upon the earth, and all the men that are upon the face of the earth, shall shake at my presence, and the mountains shall be thrown down, and the steep places shall fall, and every wall shall fall to the ground. (38:19-20)
Mountains thrown down	"And every mountain and island were moved out of their places." (6:14)	"Surely in that day there shall be a great shaking in the land of Israel; So that the fishes of the sea, and the fowls of the heaven, and the beasts of the field, and all creeping things that creep upon the earth, and all the men that are upon the face of the earth, shall shake at my presence, and the mountains shall be thrown down, and the steep places shall fall, and every wall shall fall to the ground." (38:19-20)
God is Magnified	"And said to the mountains and rocks, 'Fall on us, and hide us from the face of him that sitteth on the throne, and from the wrath of the Lamb: For the great day of his wrath is come; and who shall be able to stand?'" (16-17)	"Thus will I magnify myself, and sanctify myself; and I will be known in the eyes of many nations, and they shall know that I am the Lord." (38:23)

Ezekiel's descriptions of this battle's aftermath further supports its placement at the sixth seal as Israel's captured weapons provide the country's fuel for seven years, the full tribulation's duration (Ezekiel 39:9-10). If this invasion occurs in the great tribulation, then Israel continues burning these weapons well into Jesus' reign. Although it is a possibility, it seems unlikely Israel needs to rely on this source of energy after his return. More likely, this battle occurs at the beginning of the tribulation so Israel can exploit their spoils of war for the full duration of Daniel's seventieth week.

Additionally, this war leaves untold multitudes of dead invaders polluting the mountains of Israel. Ezekiel describes a burial process where men receive continual employment for seven months (Ezekiel 39:13-16). Satan's ejection from heaven in the middle of the seven-year tribulation puts Israel under such great, constant duress for the last three and a half years of the full tribulation that it seems highly unlikely Israel could be able to support this kind of burial activity then. It is far more likely Israel can execute this orderly burial process only during the early stages of the tribulation, while they still cling to the hope of peace and safety.

Ezekiel's description of the battlefield cleanup is completely different from the battle of Armageddon's battlefield cleanup described in Revelation 19:17-18, where birds and wild animals devour the armies' remains. The differences of these battlefields are also telling. The battle of Armageddon occurs in a valley while Ezekiel's battle occurs in the mountains, the same place Jesus told the Jews to flee for safety from the battle of Armageddon. Since Jesus will not send people to the battlefield for safety, it is natural to conclude the invasion of Magog must occur before the battle of Armageddon commences.

Another issue with placing this battle in the great tribulation is the list of allies. In the battle of Armageddon, Israel has no allies, as every nation fights against them. In this battle, Israel has allies and a limited, though daunting, number of enemies. This fact alone shows the battle of Magog is a separate war from the battle of Armageddon, which must be finished prior to latter's start. Ezekiel 38:1-7 lists Israel's invaders. Most notable among these is the invader's leader, Gog, and his country, Magog (also translated as Rosh). Both are the source of tremendous speculation.

Magog is generally accepted as modern Russia, and this conclusion is strengthened by Moscow's location virtually due north of Jerusalem (Jerusalem is at about 35E longitude, and Moscow is at about 37E longitude). Table 15 summarizes the list all of Israel's invaders and their modern names and locations. Note these enemies form northern and southern alliances attacking Israel from two directions, forcing Israel to fight a multiple-front war.

To all of this, Ezekiel 38:4 adds an intriguing mystery: the countries leading this invasion had planned to attack Israel at an earlier time but for some reason gave up and returned home. Now God is pulling them back to Israel for their destruction. If Magog and his allies had their earlier plans thwarted, when did or does this occur? If rumors of war plans highlighting Russia's past intentions to invade Israel proved true, then these plans could fulfill this prophecy. Fortunately, Israel's invasion of Lebanon in 1982 interrupted these rumored plans. Lack of substantiation of these rumors leaves questions of Magog's first intentions to speculation.

Unlike, the future battle of Armageddon, Israel has allies in this battle (Ezekiel 38:13) but their response is confusing. Ezekiel shows them only asking questions as though they are only seeking diplomatic solutions. He does not mention them coming to Israel's assistance. Probably, these nations reluctantly participate in the battle, but based on this passage, their participation is far from certain. Table 16 provides the full list of allies and their likely modern names and locations.

Table 15: Nations Aligned against Israel: Magog Invasion

Nations Aligned against Israel	
Biblical Reference	**Modern Name**
Magog (Ezekiel 38:2)	A land located north of Jerusalem (likely Moscow, Russia)
Meshech (Ezekiel 38:2)	Believed to have settled in Asia Minor (modern Turkey)
Tubal (Ezekiel 38:2)	Believed to have settled in Asia Minor (modern Turkey)
Persia (Ezekiel 38:5)	Ancient empire based in modern Iran
Ethiopia (Ezekiel 38:5)	Ethiopia
Libya (Ezekiel 38:5)	Libya
Gomer (Ezekiel 38:6)	Believed to have settled in Asia Minor (modern Turkey)
Togarmah (Ezekiel 38:6)	Believed to have settled in Asia Minor (Both Turkey and Armenia are considered possibilities)

Table 16: Nations Aligned with Israel: Magog Invasion

Friends of Israel	
Biblical Reference	**Modern Name**
Sheba	Believed to have settled on the Arabian peninsula (probably modern Saudi Arabia).
Dedan	Believed to have settled on the Arabian peninsula (probably modern Saudi Arabia or Yemen). (Could extend to other countries on the Arabian coast along the Arabian sea or Persian Gulf.)
the merchants of Tarshish	Trading partners covering a diverse geographic region. There are many questions concerning which countries was part of this trading alliance. Most believe that, as a minimum, the countries along the southern part of Europe are included. Some extend this to northern Europe and beyond. A reasonable assumption is the merchants represent the modern EU.
all the young lions	A clear reference to younger members of the Tarshish trading alliance. The comparison to young lions suggests they are former colonies of the lion (England). (Probably includes a wide variety of countries including USA, Canada, South Africa, New Zealand, and Australia.)

The Battle's Preparation

Ezekiel lays out several prerequisites for Magog's invasion, including:

1. Israel's national rebirth (Ezekiel 37:1-14)

2. restoration of sacrificial worship (Ezekiel 37:27-28)

3. establishment of pro and anti-Israel military alliances (Ezekiel 38:1-13)

4. Israel's wealth (Ezekiel 38:12-13)

5. Israel's relaxation of their national security (Ezekiel 38:8, 11, 14)

Only Israel's national rebirth is currently in place. This is important since Ezekiel 38:8 locates the primary battlefield as Israel's mountains. This passage describes this battlefield as laying barren for a long time, until its people are brought back from many nations.

The second prerequisite of sacrificial worship could start quickly under the right circumstances. Priesthood preparations are currently well under way, and the primary obstacle remains the worship facility's erection on the temple mount. Assuming the full tribulation's worship facility is the tabernacle, this could be resolved quickly once the Jews discover the ancient tabernacle. After this, the priests would only need to cleanse and dedicate the tabernacle before sacrificial worship commences. Clearly, there are many other issues with this scenario, such as the Jews gaining free and unfettered access to the temple mount; the discovery of the tabernacle's furnishings, including the ark of the covenant; and the creation of key materials for the tabernacle, including the tabernacle's specially blended lamp oil, the priest's ointments, and the ashes of the red heifer. People have already been diligently trying to solve these and many others issues associated with setting up the sacrificial worship.

The third prerequisite's military alliances are currently close to reality. For the friendly alliance, many of the EU countries, the United States, Australia, Saudi Arabia, and small Arab countries along the coast of the Arabian Sea and Persian Gulf banded together to fight two wars in Iraq. The second war saw some friction within the alliance but nothing irreparable. Among Israel's future enemies, Iran and Libya are already staunch opponents of Israel. Turkey and Ethiopia are problematic, but both are becoming Muslim countries with sentiments leaning against Israel. In the second gulf war, Turkey was very late in offering any help to the allies because of concerns of possible reactions of their internal Muslim population. Today, Iran is reportedly working toward consolidating the Muslim leanings of each of these countries to create political alliances similar to those of Ezekiel 38. All of this may be somewhat irrelevant since the attack's suddenness seems to catch Israel completely by surprise and suggests the invader's alliances may come together equally quickly.

The fourth prerequisite requires Israel's acquisition of enough wealth to entice the invasion. Twice, Ezekiel indicts the invaders for their greed (Ezekiel 38:9-13). The first time, God indicts Gog's motive for the war: to take a spoil and prey (take Israel's wealth by force). The second time, Israel's allies respond to Gog's attack by asking him if he has come to take a spoil and prey. Not only does God declare Gog's motives but also the motives are so intuitively obvious that other countries immediately deduce them. Today, an attack might generate numerous speculations concerning the invader's motives (e.g., religious, defense of regional allies, and hatred of the Jews) but none would include the invader's greed. Something changes before the war's start to make greed the obvious and dominant reason for attacking Israel.

Currently, Israel has few natural resources, and its GDP is only about $17,000 per person. Compared to many other countries in the region, this GDP is good but not outstanding and is not suggestive of the source of enough riches to entice an invasion of the magnitude described in Ezekiel 38. Israelis have long lamented God gave them land in just about the only place in the region without oil. Despite this, some who have studied the biblical accounts of Sodom and Gomorrah believe these accounts show strong evidence there is oil in Israel, perhaps exceeding all others in the region. The possible source of this wealth is explored further in the following sections.

The final prerequisite, Israel believing they are safe, is based on Ezekiel 38:9-13's description of Israel living in unprotected (unwalled) villages. Until modern warfare rendered them impotent, walls around towns, villages, and cities provided the city's primary military protection. When people were afraid of their enemies, they prepared for war and built or fortified these walls.

Israel's apparent lack of military preparedness demonstrates Israel's confidence they are finally safe from their enemies. This is one of three references in Ezekiel 38 stating Israel's confidence in their safety, and these repetitions emphasize Israel's strong expectation of peace. Considering Israel's currently strong military readiness, it seems impossible to see them reducing their military alert levels this significantly, but Ezekiel shows them relaxing their guard prior to the start of this war. They reduce their defensive alert status and may have started dismantling their security forces. Likely, this confidence in their national security is at least partly the result of the antichrist's confirmation of the peace covenant.

The Battle and Its Aftermath

Ezekiel 38:14-17 shows Gog launching the invasion by leading his great army south to attack the mountains of northern Israel. The army is so great they cover the land of Israel like a cloud. Figure 19 shows this battlefield and a second one found elsewhere (the plains of Edom). In this passage, God not only takes responsibility for driving the invaders into Israel but also enumerates his reasons:

- A sign for the heathen (people of the world)
- So he is magnified (Ezekiel 38:23) and sanctified among all people
- To fulfill the prophets' words

When these armies decide to invade, God's anger burns almost uncontrollably and makes everyone on the earth shake in fear (Ezekiel 38:18-20). His fury, jealousy, and wrath compel him to freely inflict his judgments on the invaders. He starts with a mighty earthquake, which causes every wall in Israel to crumple, mountains to move and fall, and all living creatures (man, beast, fowl, and fish) to fear God. God's judgments continue as he rains fire, great hailstones, and brimstone on the invaders (Ezekiel 38:21-23). Limitations of ancient Hebrew and the ancients' lack of understanding of modern weapons systems cloud these descriptions, making them difficult to decipher. Possibly, these could describe modern weaponry such as missiles, bombs, and artillery. The straight interpretation of volcanic type activity may be accurate, but in the context of this devastating war, modern weaponry seems a more likely interpretation.

Figure 19: Magog's Invasion of Israel

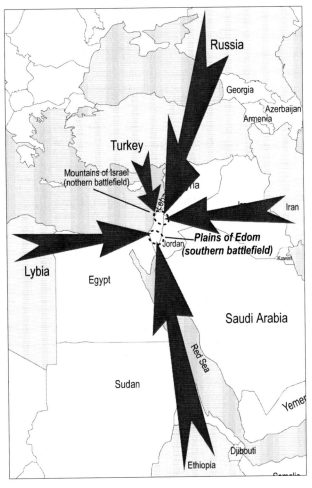

If there is any doubt of the war's outcome, the description of its culmination and the devastation wreaked on the participating armies in Ezekiel 39:1-8 eliminates it. God decimates the invading armies and destroys five-sixths of the nation of Magog. The dead of the invading armies litter the mountains of Israel while the animals eat the flesh of the fallen. Magog's destruction is not limited to the battlefield but extends to its homeland as God's fiery judgments consume their land. As the battle progresses, the war's ravages go beyond the participating nations to include mysterious places simply called the islands. Wherever the islands are, their inhabitants are living their lives without any cares, and this carelessness indicates they expect neither an attack nor God's judgment for their sinful behavior.

Due to nuisances of the Hebrew language, Old Testament island references may refer to actual islands or almost any land adjacent to water, including coastal areas and river valleys. In fact, each of these possibilities can be found rendered for this passage in one or more major Bible translations. Even assuming islands are the correct translation, lands not considered islands today might still be implied. Since Israel sits on land composing three major continents, the other four continents could be considered islands. After all, each is much smaller than the combined land mass of Europe, Asia, and Africa and are only reachable across large expanses of water. This opens up many lands as possible options for these islands, including anything from a tiny atoll to any of the four other continents: North America, South America, Australia, and Antarctica.

Based on the information presented thus far and current geopolitical conditions, the war might unfold in the following manner:

- A conventional invasion starts with coordinated northern and southern fronts driving deep into the land of Israel (figure 19).

- Attempting to end the invasion, Israel's friends quickly start diplomatic efforts.

- The invasion catches Israel unprepared, quickly overwhelming their conventional capabilities.

- In desperation, Israel resorts to using its last option: nuclear bombs and missiles (their unripe fruit).

- Now under nuclear attack, the invaders respond in kind, launching their nuclear weapons at preprogrammed targets (the careless islands).

- The war continues to escalate as the careless islands now respond by launching their own nuclear weapons against their attackers.

- The ensuing, full-scale nuclear war destroys five-sixths of the land of Magog (Russia), crushes the other invaders, decimates the careless islands, and creates a political vacuum the antichrist, China, and others can exploit for the duration of the seven-year tribulation.

While clearly speculative, these possibilities are nonetheless extremely sobering considering this is the nightmare nuclear war feared since the advent of atomic bombs. While Ezekiel's prophecies may unfold quite differently, the devastation suffered by Magog is clearly consistent with the devastation expected from a full-scale nuclear war.

Ezekiel does not stop the war's descriptions with the battle-field but continues into its aftermath, including the burial of the invading armies and the disposition of their weapons and spoils. Israel buries the dead polluting their land for seven months, and burns the captured weapons for seven years (Ezekiel 39:9-16). The war also increases Israel's wealth as they confiscate much of the wealth of the invading nations by spoiling those desiring to pillage them. Israel kills so many invaders within their borders that an entire valley must be set aside just for their burial. Israel changes the name of this valley, located east of the Sea of Galilee, to Hamongog in recognition of those buried in it. The smell arising from the valley of Hamongog's dead is so overwhelming that people traveling through the area are repulsed and cover their faces for relief from its horrendous stench.

Ezekiel's account of Israel's burial methods for the invading armies' dead is nothing short of amazing. A full-time staff administers the burying process and organizes the workers into crews that only make sense with modern transportation and construction technologies. When a day's journey was only twenty miles, the process of moving massive numbers of dead from the battlefield to a valley miles away would be untenable. One round trip could easily take a week and only result in the burial of just a few corpses at a time. At that rate, this task could consume the nation for years. For this reason, ancient armies left virtually all battlefield casualties where they fell. It was simply impossible to bring the dead home for burial. The burial process Ezekiel describes can only be accomplished using modern technologies like earthmovers, trucks, cars, centralized communications centers, and telecommunications. It starts with scouting teams searching the country for bodies and continues with spotters marking the body's locations with road signs and recording its location in a centralized data bank. Back at the command center, supervisors assign and schedule burial crew's activities. Later, the burial crews pick up the bodies and transport them back to the burial valley. This description stands out for many reasons.

- the staggering number of dead

- the massive burial grounds (a complete valley)

- the large-scale burial production techniques employed

Other Magog Battle Details

Ezekiel was not the only Old Testament prophet who spoke of this war. For example, Isaiah 2:5-16 describes people fleeing to the rocks for protection from God's wrath. This occurs in the Day of Lord when Israel's land is full of treasures (Ezekiel's spoil). The treasures of Israel, the wrath of God, and the setting in the Day of the Lord tie this description to the Magog invasion of Ezekiel while the people fleeing to rocks for protection, the wrath of God, and its setting in the Day of the Lord tie it to Revelation's sixth seal.

This passage introduces two new points: people's worship of idols and the judgment on the ships of Tarshish. The land of Israel is full of idols and idol worshippers. The same people who refuse to humble themselves before God do not think twice about worshipping these useless gods, but God demands people worship him and him alone. This singular worship only occurs during Jesus' reign, and until then, God pours his wrath out on both idols and their proud worshippers. Later in this same chapter of Isaiah, men enter the rocks a second time. At "that time," they will permanently throw away their idols. Earlier, Ezekiel listed Tarshish as one of Israel's allies. Now Isaiah lists them as one of the war's casualties. Perhaps this is a clue to the identity of Ezekiel's mysterious isles seen in the aftermath's description.

Isaiah 34:1-4 adds some remarkable details to the sixth seal's descriptions. As in the sixth seal, Isaiah shows:

- shockwaves rolling through the sky as a scroll being rolled together

- figs falling off a fig tree

- the wrath of God on many nations

- the mountains melted

Isaiah also uses another symbol for God's people: the vine. Just as the fig tree loses its figs, the vine loses its leaves. Both suggest the same firing of weapons seen in the sixth seal. The slain fall throughout the land and like Ezekiel's description, create an awful stench. Isaiah 34:5-6 gives the battle's southern battlefield: Bozrah and Idumea. Both are places in Edom, which was located directly southwest of Israel. It is along the probable invasion route of the southern alliance (Isaiah 34:7-15). The battle utterly destroys this area, reducing it to an uninhabitable wilderness only fit for unclean animals. and renders the area impassable forever. Throughout the rest of the seven-year tribulation and Jesus' full millennial reign, people are not able to enter or pass through this former battlefield. Unlike Ezekiel's battlefields, no one clears the plains of Edom because workers are never able to enter the area. Isaiah paints a picture of an unparalleled environmental disaster with burning pitch (a commonly used Old Testament word for crude oil) filling the streams and covering this land. Unlike Kuwait's individual oil well fires after the first Gulf War, huge lakes of crude oil burn uncontrollably. These fires never stop because inexhaustible supplies of oil constantly replenish these lakes and streams. Air, water, and surface pollution spew out at unprecedented rates. The damage is so great that many would predict dire consequences for the earth and all humanity. However, these fires will continue burning unabated throughout the golden age of humanity (Jesus' reign) when lifespans increase and health issues diminish despite this disaster's lingering effects.

Reasonably, this oil could be the source of Israel's prewar wealth. This as yet undiscovered oil field is obviously massive and probably dwarfs any prior discoveries since it contains enough oil reserves to continuously burn out of control for over a thousand years. The discovery and development of this oil field would infuse Israel with incredible wealth and serve as motivation for Magog's armies, especially if it deprives the invaders of one of their key sources of cash flow. Another possibility for their wealth is minerals mined from the Dead Sea. Many believe it is loaded with rich reserves of gold and silver, and planned Dead Sea developments will greatly simplify its mining. One more theory centers on hidden treasures found in some Dead Sea scrolls, especially the copper scrolls. Any or all of these might be sufficient to establish Israel as one of the world's wealthiest nations and serve as motivation for Magog's attacks early in the tribulation.

The Burden of Damascus

A mystery of end-time prophecy is the placement of Isaiah 17:1-4's burden of Damascus. The language in this passage is unmistakable. A city that claims to be one of the longest, continuously inhabited cities in the world is completely, totally destroyed. It is no longer occupied, is no longer a city, and only ruble remains. The total destruction invokes images of unbridled modern warfare. While these verses provide few clues about when this occurs, three possibilities seem most likely: pretribulation during Israel's birth pangs, the invasion of Magog, or the battle of Armageddon. Shortly after foretelling Damascus's doom, Isaiah seems to suggest the invasion of Magog as nations come to steal Israel's wealth, but instead God quickly destroys them, and overnight, the enemies of Israel are gone (Isaiah 17:12-14). This suggests Damascus is destroyed just before or during this war.

Since the invading armies of the northern alliance will likely have to pass through Syria on their march to Israel, their presence in Syria could easily lead to Damascus's destruction. Jeremiah 49:23-27 provides additional information on Damascus's destruction. Here, it shows fire destroying Damascus, which is eerily reminiscent of the destruction of Magog and the isles.

Tribulation Ministry Established

Section reference: Revelation 7:1-8.

Between the sixth and seventh seals, God suspends all judgments and even stops the wind while 144,000 Jews receive the protection of his seal. No detailed descriptions of the seals or their functions are given, but clearly they serve to protect the bearer from any harm, including the seven-year tribulation judgments and the great tribulation's three beasts. Their seals are suggestive of a powerful spiritual version of the peculiar clothing worn by Jews on their hands and foreheads (Deuteronomy 11:18). Similarly, God's seals go on the foreheads of these 144,000 Jews.

Shortly, the antichrist will imitate this mark and require everyone to have his counterfeit mark permanently engraved on their right hand or forehead (Revelation 13). Though similar, the two marks have opposite effects. God's mark protects the bear-

1
6 144,000 Jews Sealed by God

er's life while the beast's mark condemns its bearers to eternal death in the lake of fire and exposes them to the full weight of God's wrath.

Here, God carefully handpicks Jews of pure character and behavior (Revelation 14:1-5) from each of twelve of Israel's tribes to be his witnesses on earth. Table 17 shows Israel's tribes organized by maternal heritage, maternal birth sequence, overall birth sequence (parenthetical numbers), and the number of sealed people. Joseph's double-portion inheritance is evident in this list as each of his sons, Ephraim and Manasseh, stand as full, independent tribes, increasing the number of tribes from twelve to thirteen. Throughout the Bible, lists of the tribes are often reduced to God's perfect number of governmental perfection (twelve) through the omission of a tribe. In this case, the omitted tribe is Dan, and their omission is likely an indictment of his traitorous full-tribulation role in betraying the other tribes. An interesting subtlety of this list is Ephraim's replacement by Joseph, his father. Since there were twelve thousand already sealed from the tribe of Ephraim's brother, Manasseh, then it makes sense that Joseph's tribe is composed only of members of the tribe of Ephraim. Like Dan's omission, Ephraim's replacement may also be an indictment of his traitorous full-tribulation role in implementing the covenant with death and hell (Isaiah 28).

Table 17: Revelation 7 Tribes Sealed

Leah (free)	
Tribe	Number Sealed
Reuben (1)	12,000
Simeon (2)	12,000
Levi (3)	12,000
Judah (4)	12,000
Issachar (9)	12,000
Zebulun (10)	12,000

Rachel (free)	
Tribe	Number Sealed
Joseph (11) – Ephraim	12,000
Joseph (11) – Manasseh	12,000
Benjamin (12)	12,000

Zilpah (bond)	
Tribe	Number Sealed
Gad (7)	12,000
Asher (8)	12,000

Bilhah (bond)	
Tribe	Number Sealed
Dan (5)	0
Naphtali (6)	12,000

As this list clearly specifies, each of these men is a direct blood descendent of one of the sons of Israel (Jacob). Though many claim to be replacements for the Jews listed here, by calling out these men by their genealogical roots, God eliminates this possibility.

Seal Seven: The Seven Trumpet Judgments

Section reference: Revelation 8:1-6.

When Jesus breaks the last seal, the earth's title deed finally lays bare as Jesus claims his rightful property. A half hour of heavenly silence greets this event, though both the reason for the silence and the significance of its duration has perplexed scholars for generations. Most suspect heaven is silent in dreadful anticipation of God's coming judgments. More likely, it is out of respect, as Jesus comes out of his holy habitation to claim his inheritance: the earth (Zechariah 2:12-13).

© Pat Marvenko Smith - www.revelationillustrated.com

After the silence, seven angels receive the seven trumpets of the coronation theme. The last three of these trumpets represent judgments so severe that angels proclaim three woes (Revelation 8:13). The word woe is an exclamation of grief, and throughout the Bible, God reserves it for uniquely harsh forms of judgment. The same root Greek word ouai (Strong's G3759) is sometimes translated in Revelation as "alas." In either translation, the meaning remains the same: God's crushing judgment is coming. These last three terrible judgments are collectively known as the three great woe judgments.

Many people suspect the first four angels of the trumpet judgments are the same angels of Revelation 7:1-3. They base this conclusion on the angel's instructions (Revelation 7:3) and the division of the trumpet judgments into two groups (four lesser judgments and three greater judgments). While the speculation is interesting, this question seems to have little, if any, bearing on the narrative.

After the angels receive their trumpets, Revelation presents mysteries concerning an altar, incense, and prayers. An eighth angel holding a golden censer comes before the golden altar in heaven and receives incense to offer with the prayers of the saints. The golden altar's material shows this is not an altar intended for blood sacrifices since it is made of a precious metal, not the metal of judgment (brass). Therefore, it is intended for precious things, like the prayers of saints. Interestingly, this heavenly altar has an earthly counterpart, a somewhat obscure tabernacle altar: the golden altar in the inner sanctuary. This altar was located in the inner sanctuary just outside the holy of holies and burns only a special blend of spices and oils made according to God's personal recipe (Exodus 30:23-25). The high priest was responsible for tending the altar daily to make sure the incense burned perpetually and no unacceptable incense (strange incense) contaminated it.

The Old Testament provides the incense's basic ingredients but omits its production details (Exodus 30:34-38). Only priests were allowed to make this oil and then only for tabernacle use. Penalties for violating this law were high, as anyone attempting to copy it or use it for any unlawful purposes was banished. The Levite family responsible for producing the incense zealously guarded its secrets. In the past, attempts by other priests and alchemists to replicate the formula failed when the family entrusted with its secrets refused to assist. Purportedly, the alternate formulas were never able to replicate the straight stream of smoke ascending directly to heaven produced by the true formula. To avoid the appearance of evil, the family guarding these secrets refused to wear perfume of any type and required pledges from any women marrying into the family to abstain from using perfumes.

As the inner sanctuary's golden altar would perpetually burn this specific incense, heaven's golden altar perpetually carries the prayers of the saints to the throne sweetened by the angel's incense. Romans 8:26-27 shows this incense is the Holy Spirit who makes intercession for believers, changes their groans into prayers, and then carries these prayers to heaven. The Holy Spirit purifies and sweetens the prayers of the saints before he takes them to the throne of God. Like the burning incense, the Holy Spirit takes the believers' prayers straight to God's throne.

Revelation's golden censer is reminiscent of the high priest's golden censer used to carry incense from the golden altar with him into the holy of holies. The cloud of the incense was to cover the mercy seat to keep the priest from dying (Leviticus 16:12-13).

During Kahor's rebellion (Numbers 16), Kahor and his followers burned strange incense in their censers, but this counterfeit formula proved incapable of protecting them from God's wrath, as these rebels died by having the earth open her mouth and swallow them directly into hell. As the incense in the golden censers protects the priest, the incense of the righteous (the Holy Spirit) protects saints from God's judgments when he fills their golden censers (their earthly bodies). No incense other than the Holy Spirit can protect people since he calls people to salvation and then eternally secures it. This is probably why Jesus warns against losing this incense by blaspheming the Holy Spirit (Matthew 12:31-32).

Whose prayers are in the golden altar? Perhaps they are the prayers of the saints of all ages, the prayers of Christians, or the prayers of the tribulation saints whose prayers for vengeance started when the fifth seal was broken. Since the incense on the golden altar in the inner sanctuary burns daily, it is likely these prayers are solely those of the tribulation saints.

An eighth angel brings another set of judgments when he takes some of the burning incense from the golden altar, puts it into the golden censer, and throws it to the earth. When it hits, there are voices, thunder, lightning, and an earthquake. Except for voices, all are self-evident, though their scope and magnitude are unclear. The Greek word for voices, phone (Strong's G5456), can also be translated as noises or sounds, depending on its context. In a normal context, noises or sounds would probably be better translations, but later in Revelation 10, thunders speak. Here, it probably refers to any noises significantly different from thunders. This judgment reveals the second of five different sets of earthquakes listed in the book of Revelation. Two earthquakes occur in the tribulation, one occurs in the midtribulation and two occur in the great tribulation. Table 18 shows when these different aspects of the golden censer judgments occur elsewhere in Revelation.

Why would the prayers of the saints create the judgments shown here? Perhaps it is God's vengeance and payment for the world's abuse of believers. Throughout the church age, saints heaped coals of fire on their enemy's heads by not repaying transgressions in kind (Romans 12:19-21). Now, the golden censer could be God's repayment. Another possibility is the censer judgment could be retaliation for the antichrist stopping the daily sacrifice. Revelation does not mention it, but Daniel explains it occurs in the seven-year tribulation, 2300 days before the cleansing of the temple. If seven days are required for the temple's consecration, then the daily sacrifices end 2293 days before Jesus' return or just a little under a year after the start of the seven-year tribulation.

Table 18: Revelation Judgments: Earthquakes and Signs in the Sky

		Voices	Thundering	Lightning	Earthquake
Tribulation					
Seal 1	Rev 6:1		✓		
Seal 6	Rev 6:12				✓
Seal 7 (Golden Censer)	Rev 8:5	✓	✓	✓	✓
7 Thunders	Rev 10:3-4	✓	✓		
Midtribulation					
resurrection of the two witness	Rev 11:12-13	✓			✓
Great Tribulation					
Trumpet 7	Rev 11:19	✓	✓	✓	✓
Vial 7	Rev 16:18	✓	✓	✓	✓
Worship					
Post rapture worship	Rev 4:5	✓	✓		
Pre marriage feast worship	Rev 19:6	✓	✓		
Post-Trib worship with 144,000	Rev 14:2	✓	✓		

At the onset of the trumpet judgments, it is useful to consider an alternative interpretation of Revelation's three groups
of judgments (seals, trumpets, and vials). This well-known

interpretation holds that the three are parallel passages and each presents different views of the same events on earth. This interpretation presents several challenges. First, John wrote Revelation as a narrative smoothly flowing from one event into the next. Another issue arises when one tries to itemize the judgments because the patterns among the three sets of judgments are good but not perfect fits. For example, the sixth seal contains a war while the wars of the trumpet and vial judgments are in the seventh judgments.

The symbolism behind the seal judgments was Jesus' redemption of the earth, the opening of earth's title deed. Do the trumpet judgments have similar symbolism and, if so, what is it? Clues are in the way trumpets are employed throughout the Bible.

- leading praise, worship, and atonement (Psalm 150:3, 1 Chronicles 13:8, and Numbers 10:10)

- calling people to meet God (Revelation 4:1-2, Exodus 19:17-19, and Matthew 24:31)

- calling people to observe days: atonement, solemn, and beginnings of months (Leviticus 25:9, Leviticus 23:24-27, and Numbers 10:10)

- calling on God for deliverance (Numbers 10:9)

- calling people to assembly or arms (Numbers 10:1-7, Ezekiel 33:1-6, and 1 Corinthians 14:8)

- calling troops to attack or retreat

- announcing a new king's coronation

While one can argue for virtually every one of these roles applying to Revelation's trumpet judgments, the strongest candidates are the last two: calling troops to attack or retreat and announcing a new king's coronation. The following sections consider the possible prophetic applications of these two.

Trumpets Used for Sounding Attack or Retreat

Like many other nations, the Jews used trumpets to give battle-field directions, including retreat and attack. For example, they used them in the battle of Jericho (Joshua 6:4-6). In this battle, priests blew the trumpets to tell people to attack on the seventh day after they had marched around the city seven times. After completing the seventh circuit around the city, they shouted and blew the seven trumpets. Then all the men of Israel attacked as the walls fell.

Combined with the millennial day, this story has interesting prophetic applications. On the seventh day, seven trumpets are blown and the great city of Jericho falls. Likewise, on the seventh millennial day, the seven trumpet judgments are blown and the great city of Mystery Babylon falls. These trumpets do appear to have prophetic applications and ties to Revelation's seven trumpet judgments.

Trumpets Used for New King's Coronation Announcement

Old Testament trumpets accompanied the coronation of new kings. For example, trumpets announced Joash's coronation (2 Chronicles 23:13). Athaliah, an interloper who usurped the throne, tried to destroy all rightful heirs to the throne. When the one survivor, Joash, is crowned king, trumpets announce the end of Athaliah's reign.

In the full tribulation, an interloper, the son of perdition, attempts to usurp Jesus' throne, but his aspirations are dashed when the trumpet judgments announce Jesus' coronation and his failure. As will become clear, Revelation's seven trumpets are primarily coronation trumpets, and they introduce the coronation theme.

Trumpets One to Four: The Minor Judgments
Section reference: Revelation 8:7-12.

The first angel's trumpet brings hail and fire mingled with blood raining onto the earth, destroying a third of all plant life. This cryptic description might be the debris from volcanic eruptions raining down from the sky with the burning volcanic rock looking like hail and destroying vegetation. The allusion to blood may refer to the blood from the animals and people it kills. A volcanic eruption this large could be a contributory factor to the coming fourth trumpet's darkening of the skies.

This trumpet bears a strong resemblance to Moses' seventh plague, where God rained hail mingled with fire on the Egyptians (Exodus 9:22-24). Prior to the plague, Moses warned people to protect themselves and their animals. God-fearing people took action (Exodus 9:19-21) and those who did not suffered catastrophic

losses (Exodus 9:25). This plague features many of the same elements of Revelation's first trumpet judgment, including hail and fire burning up green grass and trees. The blood mingled with the hail and fire is similar to Moses' seventh plague. During the tribulation, two witnesses like Elijah and Moses minister as they did in the Old Testament. Perhaps Moses, or a successor, once again warns those who fear God to take protective action before this judgment comes.

The second angel's trumpet causes a great mountain to be thrown into saltwaters. Likewise, the third angel's trumpet causes a great star to pollute fresh waters. The interpretation of both the second trumpet's great mountain and the third trumpet's great star are tricky. The second trumpet suggests a meteor while the third, wormwood, uses the same language found in the sixth seal and suggests some form of military weapon. Wormwood is an archaic term referring to very bitter herbs. If the sixth seal refers to nuclear missiles and bombs, then perhaps the third trumpet refers to missiles or bombs loaded with chemical or biological weapons. While the root causes of these catastrophes are unclear, there can be no doubt that a third of all of the world's waters become unusable, a third of the shipping and sea life is destroyed through both the fiery mountain's impact and resulting secondary effects (tidal waves, etc.), and many perish due to poisoned water. An interesting sidebar that has fascinated students of prophecy for years is the fact that the name of the site of the nuclear meltdown in Russia, Chernobyl, means wormwood. This probably has nothing to do with the third trumpet, but it has fueled speculation about Chernobyl's role in the trumpet judgments.

On at least three occasions during the seven-year tribulation, God turns water into blood: the trumpet judgments, the vial judgments, and the work of the two witnesses. These differ mainly in their scope. These judgments are

20 | Trump 3: Third of Fresh Waters Become Bitter

similar to the first plague God poured out on the Egyptians when all of Egypt's waters became blood for seven days (Exodus 7:20-21). By contrast, Revelation does not specify the trumpet judgments' duration.

The fourth angel's trumpet brings darkness for the second time in the tribulation, and it is possible this darkness is the direct result of the first three trumpet judgments. At this time, only two-thirds of the light of the sun

21 | Trump 4: Sun/Moon light Darkend by a Third

and moon makes it through the atmosphere's pollutants. Judgments of darkness, like the fourth trumpet, speak of people's separation from God and specifically their spiritual darkness. John called Jesus the light shining in the world's darkness (John 1:5, 3:19). This darkness was never more illustrative of humanity's separation from God than when it befell the earth at Jesus' crucifixion (Matthew 27:45). This darkness proved that this brazen serpent of sin had been fully isolated from God the Father, whose eyes are too pure to even look at sin (Habakkuk 1:13). Darkness also covered the earth at creation (Genesis 1:2), painting a picture of God's creation possibly ravaged by sin. In the future, darkness separates the wicked from God in the lake of fire, a place of utter darkness (Jude 1:13). This contrasts with the dwelling place of righteous (new Jerusalem), which is a place of perpetual light (Revelation 22:5).

Trumpet Five: The First Great Woe (the Bottomless Pit Opens)

Section reference: Revelation 9:1-12.

The fifth angel's trumpet brings the first of the three great woes. Now, a star possessing the pit's keys falls from heaven to earth and frees the bottomless pit's forces from their prolonged captivity. The star's fall from heaven conjures up images of the sixth seal's stars, but this star is clearly some sort of creature since John refers to it as "him." John does not identify the fallen star, but clues from the text encourage speculation. Jesus provided a key clue in Luke 10:18 when he described Satan as lightning falling from heaven. Isaiah uses another of Satan's many names, Lucifer, in association with another star fallen from heaven. Isaiah makes it clear this fall was not accidental but instead, God forcibly threw him down because of his open rebellion. He took a mighty gamble when he sought to gain all power and authority but ended up losing everything. Throughout Revelation, there is a systematic fulfillment of Isaiah's prophecy as God expels Satan from heaven, defeats him at Armageddon, locks him in the bottomless pit, and throws him into the lake of fire. Today, he bides his time by opposing God and his people in every way possible.

These descriptions point to Satan as the fifth trumpet's fallen star, but why is Satan given the keys to the bottomless pit? Also, does God reclaim these keys, and if so, when? If Satan still possesses the keys when he is incarcerated in the bottomless pit, what would prevent him from using

them to escape? For the last two questions, it is reasonable to assume God takes back all that is rightfully his, including the keys to the bottomless pit, before Satan is locked away. For now, it is sufficient to know God has given Satan the pit's keys so he can empty it of its occupants (with the possible exception of four held until the next trumpet) and angry, vengeful beasts never seen by anyone are now freed to torment humanity.

When the bottomless pit opens, smoke and locusts ascend, darkening the sun and sky. Smoke suggests the lingering effects of God's fiery furnace judgment on the pit's prisoners: locusts. These locusts inflict tremendous damage similar to that in Exodus 10:14-15's eighth plague. A key difference though is that Moses' locusts only attacked vegetation, but these attack the flesh of all men except those with God's seal, Revelation 7's 144,000. Though their description is difficult, these locusts are logically fallen angels, and the effects of their release speak of their sheer volume, the polluting effects of their sin, and their separation from God.

Their bites are as painful as a scorpion's first sting but not so poisonous that they cause death, even when stung repeatedly. Apparently, bodies do not build up any immunity, since each sting hurts as much as the first. Bite after bite, for five painful months, the pain never subsides as the locusts continually, sadistically inflict pain. It is little wonder that many people seek relief through suicide, but sadly for them, the fourth horseman, Death, has apparently suspended his work.

The descriptions of the fifth trumpet's locusts are among the most difficult in the Bible. Different commentators have proffered many possible explanations, including allegories of modern weapons of war (e.g., helicopters). Their descriptions give the following general impressions:

- Horses prepared for battle suggest power, strength, and speed
- Faces of men suggest intelligence
- Hair of women suggest outward attractiveness
- Teeth of lions suggest power and perhaps, cruelty
- Breastplates of iron suggest strength and invincibility
- Crowns like gold suggest authority and royalty
- Sound of chariots suggest calamity, chaos, and confusion

There is a king over these locusts, who is a destroyer or a destroying angel, alternative names for Satan, the ruler of all fallen angels.

Trumpet Six: The Second Great Woe (Kings of the East)

Section reference: Revelation 9:13–21.

The sixth angel's trumpet brings the second of the three woe judgments. This woe starts at Revelation 8's golden altar, which contains prayers and incense, when a voice from its horns commands the sixth trumpet's angel to release four angels bound in the Euphrates River. This voice probably belongs to the altar's incense, the Holy Spirit, and the four angels he commands released are probably fallen angels. Since the Bible contains no evidence of God binding sin-free creatures, any other potential identification of these angels is difficult; but if they are fallen angels, why are they held in the Euphrates River instead of the bottomless pit? Is this a second holding place for fallen angels or maybe the location of the bottomless pit's entrance? If it is the bottomless pit's entrance, why did the fallen star in the fifth trumpet not release these angels? For now, the answers to these and similar questions must be left to speculation.

Interestingly, the Euphrates River has been a focal point for history. It came out of the garden of Eden; was the center of the Assyrian, Babylonian, and Medo-Persian empires; was the eastern border of the Roman Empire; and in the future, becomes Israel's eastern border (Deuteronomy 11:24). It now plays a role in releasing a terrible army that destroys a third of the world. Later, it again plays a role in enabling this army to march against Jerusalem.

The four released angels have a terrible mission: kill a third of the people on earth. Combined with the people killed by the fourth seal's horseman, half of the earth's population entering the tribulation perishes by the end of the seven-year tribulation. Compare this with Jesus' description of two being together and one is taken and one remains (Luke 17:34-37). Traditionally interpreted as conveying the rapture's suddenness and apparent random removal of people, these verses actually seem to confirm the human loss inflicted by the full tribulation.

The four angels lead a terrible 200-million-man army,[2] serving as its four heads. Only one country lying east of Israel past the Euphrates River is capable of fielding an army of this size: China. Today, China is actively arming itself with the latest in military technology through both acquisition and development. The four angels lead this army in rampaging against ancient enemies surrounding them, though Revelation does not list any of their victims or opponents. Parallels can be drawn between this army's action in the seven-year tribulation and Japan's actions in World War II when Japan conquered and subjugated countries around them for years before attacking the country that would bring their downfall: the United States. In a similar fashion, this army attacks their neighbors before turning their attentions to the enemy that is ultimately responsible for its fall: Israel (see sixth vial judgment). This army benefits from the fallout of the sixth seal, where at least one and maybe two major military powers have been neutralized. This frees them from the fear of retaliation.

It is interesting to notice the parallels between this sixth trumpet judgment, the sixth seal judgment, and the sixth vial judgment, as each ushers in war: the battle of Magog, the unleashing of the 200-million-man army, and the assembling of the armies for the battle of Armageddon.

The sixth trumpet judgment concludes with God pausing to see if the people on the earth are repentant. The implication is that if they are repentant, then the judgments can end. Unfortunately, God finds idol and devil worship, murders, sorceries, fornications, and thefts. More importantly, there is no repentance, and God's judgments continue. Before the great tribulation is over, God checks two more times. He continues to look for reasons to avoid executing all his planned judgments but fails to find them. Ultimately, he has no option but to follow through with each dreadful plague, curse, and judgment.

The Seven Thunders, God's Decree

Section reference: Revelation 10:1-11.

Prior to the seventh trumpet's third woe judgment, a mighty angel carrying an open book comes to earth to declare some specific decrees. When he speaks, seven thunder judgments join in, and their unknown messages produce this chapter's most famous mystery. However, the clearly described events of this chapter have far-reaching ramifications and reduce the mysteries of the thunders to interesting side notes.

The traditional interpretation of this vision is that the angel is Jesus Christ and the book is the earth's evidence of purchase he received in Revelation 5 and opened in Revelation 6-8. On the surface, this makes perfect sense, but there are several underlying difficulties with both the interpretation of the angel and the book. The exploration of these mysteries starts with the search for possible identities of the angel.

The Mystery of the Angel

The mighty angel stands on the earth with one foot on the ground and one on the sea. When he refers to the blowing of the seventh trumpet in future tense ("But in the days of the voice of the seventh angel, when he shall begin to sound…"), he fixes this vision prior to the end of the seven-year tribulation and, more importantly, Jesus' return. Identifying the angel as Jesus creates conflicts with the promise of Jesus' return in Acts 1:9-11, where the angels said Jesus returns the same way (and probably the same place: Mount Olivet) he left. Jesus' second coming in Revelation 19 fulfills this prophecy. How can the mighty angel be Jesus when his next coming is at the end of the full tribulation? Perhaps this vision is only symbolism, but then the next dilemma quickly surfaces. Throughout Revelation, John shows absolute reverence for Jesus. Though John refers to Jesus by many different titles, he never leaves any doubt of Jesus' identity, nor does he ever seem to refer to Jesus as an angel when the subject is not in question. Most who maintain this is Jesus base their position on the open book in the hand of the angel. The last book referenced in Revelation was the earth's title deed, which Jesus just finished opening. If this is the same book, then it is reasonable to assume this is Jesus. However, even the identity of the book is not self-evident, and the next section covers these questions separately.

© Pat Marvenko Smith - www.revelationillustrated.com

The next most common interpretation of the mighty angel is precisely that he is an angel. Maybe he is Gabriel, Michael, or some other powerful unnamed angel; but he is an angelic being. This simple interpretation also presents its own dilemmas. This angel swears an oath. Nowhere else in the Bible does an angel swear an oath. Men swear oaths. God swears oaths. Angels do not swear oaths. In addition, the oath involves promises to do things only God has the power to perform. Even Abraham's servant refused to swear an oath for matters beyond his control in the search for Isaac's bride (Genesis 24:3-9). When Abraham released his servant from responsibility for the woman's answer, his servant freely swore the oath. This angel swears his oath without qualification or reservation. This suggests he personally possesses the power to bring the provisions of this oath to fruition. As will be shown later, no angel (or any other created for that matter) being has this power or authority.

The mighty angel's qualities reinforce the idea the angel is not one of the angelic beings, but God. The clouds for clothes, pillars of fire for feet, the rainbow, and the face shining as the sun are all symbols of God and his mercy. Exodus 13:21-22 shows both the clouds and pillar of fire as God led Israel in the wilderness. In the wilderness, the Lord God was in the pillar of cloud and the pillar of fire that guided Israel and was a sign of God's mercy, protection, and deliverance of Israel. Numbers 9:15-16 also shows them when the tabernacle is set up. The clouds and fire at the tabernacle show God's presence in his house and, in particular, the holy of holies. Just as they show God's power in the wilderness, they now show God's power in the tabernacle.

This angel's rainbow is another powerful symbol of God. God gave it as a token of his promise never to use water to destroy humanity again (Genesis 9:12-17). The rainbow shows God freely bound himself to this covenant.

The angel's face shining as the sun is an indication of being in God the Father's immediate presence. The glory of God's face reflects in the faces of those who have been near him. It showed in Moses' face after he returned from Mount Sinai in

Exodus 34:29-30. In Matthew 17:1-3, Jesus' face is also transformed, reflecting the glory of God. In Psalm 80, David three times implores the Shepherd of Israel to shine forth and to have his face shine on Israel so they may be saved. Throughout history, people have gotten hints of the glory of God as it shone through the faces of his servants. His glory radiating from their faces shows someone has been in the presence of the Father. The mighty angel's shining face shows either he is the Father or has recently been in his immediate presence. However, as Moses discovered, no man has seen or can see God's face without perishing (Exodus 33:20).

The mighty angel's oath, clothing, feet, rainbow, and face all suggest he is God the Father, but the fact he is an angel suggests he is a created being, not creator. However, there is one angel in the Bible recognized as God: the angel of the Lord. The Bible shows him:

- stopping Abraham from sacrificing his son (Genesis 22)
- appearing to Moses in the burning bush (Exodus 3)
- confronting Balaam and his ass as he went to see the king of Moab (Numbers 22)
- recognized by Gideon as God (Judges 6)
- defending Jerusalem from the Assyrians (2 Kings 19, Isaiah 37)
- promising to rebuild Jerusalem and the temple after the Babylonian captivity (Zechariah 1)
- participating in the garment and crown judgments (Zechariah 3)
- instructing Joseph concerning the conception and birth of Jesus (Matthew 1)
- rolling back the stone from Jesus' tomb (Matthew 28)
- telling Zacharias of the birth of John the Baptist (Luke 1)
- announcing Jesus' birth to the shepherds (Luke 2)
- killing King Herod (Acts 12)

By announcing Jesus' birth, rolling the stone from Jesus' tomb, and working on earth after Jesus' ascension, the Bible demonstrates the angel of the Lord is not Jesus. Since men live after seeing him, he cannot be God the Father. This leaves the Holy Spirit, the Comforter, as the angel of the Lord. As both an angel and God, he meets all criteria for the mighty angel. So likely, this mighty angel is the Holy Spirit, and as evidenced by his feet of fire, clothing, the rainbow, and his shining face, he comes to the earth under the full power and authority of the current king, God the Father. Next, the mysteries of his little book help explain his mission.

The Mystery of the Little Book

As previously mentioned, the simplest and most obvious conclusion is the open book is earth's title deed. However, John does not call earth's title deed a little book. Looking at the Greek word for this little book yields some surprises. The Greek word bibliaridion (Strong's G974) represents a small booklet or a very small book. This specific word is not the same word used in any reference for earth's title deed. In fact, it occurs nowhere else in Revelation or even the New Testament. It is not used to reference the book of Revelation, the Book of Life, or the books at the judgment seat,[3] but only references this mighty angel's book. The inference is this little book is different from all other books in the New Testament, but the text provides precious few clues to the book's purpose or contents.

The end of Revelation 10 provides a small sliver of a clue when the mighty angel tells John to eat the small book. When he does, it is sweet in his mouth but bitter in his belly. After he eats the book, the mighty angel tells him to "prophesy again before many peoples, and nations, and tongues, and kings." Ezekiel 2:8-3:7 contains a remarkably similar passage. Like John, Ezekiel is to eat the roll whose taste was sweet as honey. Also like John, Ezekiel is to speak God's words (prophecy) to Israel. Remarkably, the root word used for Ezekiel's roll is almost as rare as its New Testament counterpart. This word, the Hebrew megillah (Strong's H4040), has an Aramaic root and this combination occurs in only two other Old Testament passages: Zechariah 5:1-4 and Ezra 6:1-3.

The roll in Zechariah 5:1-4 pronounces curses on the wicked. Its immense size (thirty feet by fifteen feet) seems to indicate it has little in common with Revelation's little book. On the other hand, Ezra's roll provides several surprising and intriguing clues. In Ezra 6:1-3, an exhaustive search is required to find a roll containing a royal decree when the Jews building the second temple were challenged concerning the legality of their actions. At this time, they found a royal decree ordering the rebuilding of Jerusalem's temple and setting the building's outside dimensions. This decree was authored by a king prior to Darius, recorded on one of these rolls, and stored in the royal record's vaults.

Ezra's roll suggests Revelation's little book could contain one or more royal decrees. What could these decrees be? The mighty angel's oath gives some clues. He starts his oath by lifting his hand to heaven and swearing by the creator of the universe and all therein there will be time no longer. If he swears by the creator of the universe, does this not prove he is not God? In short, no. Hebrews 6:13 shows God swears by himself. When he swears to something, he swears by his name because there is nothing greater. Now, in Revelation, he swears by himself that there shall be time no longer, which is simply another way of saying there will be no more delay. He swears to execute his royal decrees as quickly as possible after the seventh trumpet sounds. At that time, God's mysteries are fulfilled and, by implication, the time of prophets ends.

If the mighty angel carries out his work at the seventh trumpet, then the actions after its sounding naturally suggest the contents of his royal decrees. The next chapter reveals the first event following the seventh trumpet's sounding is Jesus' coronation. Therefore, it is reasonable to assume the mighty angel swears to place Jesus on his throne as King of kings and Lord of lords, an act only God can perform.

Solomon's coronation illustrates the actions of the mighty angel and gives additional clues of these royal decrees. In the final days of his reign, King David had grown weak and vulnerable. He also had promised the throne to his son, Solomon, but a rival tried to take advantage of David's condition and claim the throne (1 Kings 1:5). The rival was Adonijah, another son of David but not the heir. He uses the term "I will," which demonstrates the pride characteristic of Satan (Isaiah 14). First Kings 1:9-10 shows Adonijah setting up his own altar and performing unlawful sacrificial worship. Adonijah calls all the men of Israel to the sacrifice except the rightful heirs and his supporters. Solomon's mother asks King David whether he knows of Adonijah's actions, whether David had authorized them, and whether David replaced Solomon as king (1 Kings 1:15-18). Per their plan, the prophet Nathan then enters and confirms the testimony of Solomon's mother (1 Kings 1:24-27).

Upon learning of this treachery, David immediately swears he will honor his vow to Solomon and Solomon will rule from the throne of Israel (1 Kings 1:29-30). David does not stop at simply confirming the promise but orders an action unprecedented and never repeated in the ascension of the kings of Israel and Judah: Solomon's coronation prior to the former king's death. He gives orders to his servants to immediately make provisions to coronate Solomon, and they put Solomon on a mule, blow the trumpets, and say, "God save King Solomon," (1 Kings 1:33-35). Adonijah discovers his brother's coronation when he hears the blaring of the trumpets and the rejoicing of Jerusalem's people (1 Kings 1:41-46).

Strong parallels exist between the coronations of Jesus and Solomon. Like David, the standing king (God the Father) has selected his rightful heir: Jesus Christ. Like the proud Adonijah, a usurper full of pride, the antichrist, lays claim to the throne. As Adonijah set up his illegitimate throne and attempted to rule Israel before Solomon legally ascended to it, the antichrist sets up his own equally illegitimate throne and attempts to rule the earth from it before Jesus' coronation. In both cases, when the king hears of the usurper's treachery, he declares his intentions of installing the rightful heir on the throne and orders his servants to hold the coronation ceremony immediately, without waiting for the king's death. For Jesus, the servant carrying out the executive order is none other than God's Holy Spirit, the faithful Comforter who has always lifted Jesus up (John 16:7-16).

Also prior to his death, David gave Solomon several charges concerning the construction of God's temple (1 Chronicles 22:6). Likewise, Jesus receives the charge to construct the final temple and its plans from his Father.

It is finally time to speculate on the decrees contained in the mighty angel's little book. This little book contains one and possibly, two decrees:

- The Holy Spirit's charge to immediately coronate Jesus
- Jesus' charge to build the third temple

Given the context of the mighty angel's actions, the first decree is a virtual certainty while the second is a strong possibility. The royal decree and the mighty angel's actions are about to fulfill the prophecy of Luke 1:31-33 calling for Jesus to rule all nations from David's throne. Psalm 2:7-8 also confirms this by declaring God has given Jesus the heathen for his inheritance to the farthest reaches of the earth.

Revelation 10's mighty angel is the Holy Spirit, who:

1. comes from heaven with royal decrees (small book)

2. claims his rightful authority over the entire planet

3. makes unknown proclamations
   accompanied by seven thunders

4. swears when the seventh trumpet blows he will execute the royal decrees and reveal the mysteries of God

5. commands John to eat and preach the decrees

While the proclamation of the mighty angel and the seven thunders are unknown, the rest of the vision tells an incredible story. Whether the thunder's unknown proclamations remain hidden because they are too detailed or for some other reason, their suppression should not detract from the wonderful information provided and the mysteries revealed by the rest of the vision.

The first half of the seven-year tribulation is an amazing time in human history. It contains events more terrifying than any previously seen in history. During this period, there are many devastating wars, with most of them unrecorded because they occur outside the prophetic context of Israel and Jerusalem. However, the existence of these many wars is clear from the actions of the four horsemen of the apocalypse. Even a casual glance at these events makes it hard to understand how Bible scholars throughout the ages could characterize this as a time of peace. However, this opinion is understandable when compared to the coming devastation of the great tribulation.

The Midtribulation (Coronation)

The events of Revelation 11-12 form a transition into the great tribulation. These two chapters contain several key events, which happen rapidly. Many of these start or end a period of three and a half years. Eliminating any time scale confusion, John alternatively gives the times as days, months and years, but all define the same length of time: three and a half years. The measuring of the temple starts one of these periods while the next event, the killing of the two witnesses, ends another. In total, these two events span the tribulation's full seven years. The rapidity of these events is best understood by recognizing that the last event (the persecution of the woman) also starts a period of three and a half years that must coincide with the period started by the first event (the measuring of the temple).

Based on Daniel 9:27, most have marked the abomination of desolation as the seven-year tribulation's midpoint and consequently associate it with Israel fleeing to the wilderness. Contrarily, this analysis identifies the seven-year tribulation's midpoint as the seventh trumpet and suggests the abomination of desolation does not occur until after the great tribulation is underway. Since the abomination of desolation is the focus of many midtribulation teachings, the next section covers the abomination and its placement on the prophetic timeline. After this, the midtribulation descriptions start with the measuring of the tribulation's temple.

The Abomination of Desolation

Before speculating about the abomination of desolation, one should understand abominations in general. Throughout the Bible, there are a wide range of behaviors called abominations such as pride, lying, murder, wicked imaginations, eagerness to sin, sowing of discord (Proverbs 6:16-19), things highly esteemed among men; those who refuse to hear the law; blemished sacrifices; offerings from male or female prostitution; false measurements; the thoughts, ways, and sacrifices of the wicked; those who condemn the righteous or justify the wicked; and sodomy. However, the dominant use of this term concerns the making, keeping, and worshipping of idols and other false gods. God strongly condemns this regardless who performs it, Jew or Gentile.

Daniel 8-12 mentions the abomination of desolation several times. It is an act so vile that Jerusalem and Israel come to the verge of total annihilation before God's final intervention rescues them. It is so central to the great tribulation that Jesus left directions to those witnessing it (Matthew 24:15, Mark 13:14).

This act, described in Daniel 11:30-31, is performed by none other than the antichrist, who hates the holy covenant (Deuteronomy's marriage covenant between God and Israel). When the antichrist returns from a failed military campaign, he focuses his anger and indignation toward the covenant he despises and hates. He schemes and concocts plans to break the covenant by:

- polluting the sanctuary
- taking away the daily sacrifice
- placing the abomination that makes desolate

In this passage, sanctuary can refer to the entire temple mount, the inner sanctuary, or the holy of holies. The entire temple mount includes the holy of holies, the inner and outer sanctuary, the altar, and the courtyard of the Gentiles. Daniel does not specify which part or parts of the sanctuary are polluted, where the abomination is placed, or what the abomination is.

Other abomination descriptions yield precious few additional clues to either its identity or where the antichrist places it. While Daniel gives great latitude to its identity, Jesus spoke as though it would be intuitively obvious (Mark 13:14-18). Many look to Antiochus IV's second century BC actions of as a possible fulfillment of Daniel's abomination. At that time, he stopped the sacrifices, burned copies of the law, forced the monthly sacrifice of unclean animals (swine) on the brazen altar, built an altar to Zeus on the brazen altar, and forced the Jews to stop the religious practices ordained in Deuteronomy. Undoubtedly, the sacrifice of swine on the brazen alter was a blatant abomination, but the worship of Zeus and the erection of his altar were its equals. Others look at Caligula's desires to establish idol worship by erecting a statue of himself inside God's temple. For Caesars, the practice of placing this type of statue into temples and shrines throughout the ancient world was not uncommon. These historical accounts demonstrate that the desire of people to profane God's temple is not new, and they give clues to the possible source of the future abomination occurring in the midst of Daniel's seventieth week.

Daniel 11:36-39 provides a few more clues, as the antichrist worships strange gods, gives his wealth to them, calls himself God, claims to be greater than God, and hates both God and his people. His love of false gods and hatred of God Almighty suggests the following possibilities: an idol dedicated to the antichrist, an idol dedicated to the god of forces, or sacrifices to false gods. Historical precedence strengthens the case for either the erection of an idol on the temple mount or sacrifices to false gods.

Daniel 8:9-14 provides another key piece of information: there is a 2300-day period commencing with the daily sacrifice's cessation and extending to the sanctuary's cleansing. The sanctuary's cleansing, or consecration, is historically a seven-day process, which can only be initiated by the priests after the little horn's removal. This means the earliest the priests can complete this cleansing is seven days after the antichrist's imprisonment in the lake of fire following Jesus' return to earth. As shown in Table 19, this 2300-day period is only one of several critical, full-tribulation time spans. Each gives a slightly different view of the relationship of various full-tribulation events, all of which must fit together precisely. Analysis of these time spans provides crucial clues to the timing of the abomination of desolation and, ultimately, its identity.

Daniel 12:11-12 is the basis for two of Table 19's entries. The first is a 1290-day period from the taking away (stopping) of the sacrifices (Daniel 8 and Daniel 11) until the abomination of desolation. Traditionally, many have assumed these two events are the same, but Daniel 12:11 indicates they are actually separated by roughly forty-three months.

The second period is 1,335 days long, and unlike the first, Daniel does not explicitly identify its beginning and ending event. Instead, the implication is the second period's onset coincides with that of the first (Daniel 12:11) and ends with the mysterious "Blessed is he that waiteth" event. This suggests the second period starts with the abomination of desolation while its end event (when people are "blessed" if they are still alive) implies all events of the full tribulation (including the final war with its killing and destruction) are past. It also infers Jesus' early millennial reign judgments along with their associated death sentences are also finished. If either of these conditions is not true, then these proclamations make no sense since people may still have possible death sentences hanging over their heads. This second timeframe probably provides clues to the time required for Jesus to complete the transition period, including many judgments starting with his return. Daniel 7:12 may also suggest the length of this transition (a season and a time; three months plus one year) but this point is not clear.

Three of Table 19's last five entries come from Revelation:

- the temple and the holy city are trodden underfoot for forty-two months (Revelation 11:2)
- the children of Israel are protected in the wilderness for three and a half years (Revelation 12:14)
- the ministry of the two witnesses lasts 1260 days (Revelation 11:3)

The different time spans used to measure these events suggest subtle differences in their durations. Smaller units are inherently more precise while larger time spans are less so due to their larger rounding errors. Times given in years (also called times) have precision to months while times given in months are precise to weeks and times given in days are precise to hours. The last two entries are the time the antichrist reigns (Daniel 7:25) while the last is the length of Daniel's seventieth week.

Table 19 now has eight durations relating ten different events. From these entries, it should be possible to construct a detailed timeline showing the relationships of all Table 19 events and the time separating them. Before assembling this detailed timeline, it is important to note that all entries must be simultaneously satisfied or the detailed timeline cannot be valid. This last restriction is critical because it triggers challenges to some classically held positions on the event sequences.

Of the ten events, half are obvious. Jesus' return occurs seven years after the tribulation's beginning (g). The antichrist starts his reign three and half years prior to Jesus' return (h). The Jews are sealed in the wilderness 1260 days prior to Jesus' return (a). The temple is downtrodden for forty-two months prior to Jesus' return (b). Next, the two witnesses start their ministry at least 1260 days prior to the Jews being sealed in the wilderness (c) and there could be up to half a month delay between their deaths and the sealing of the place in the wilderness. The half of a month is the maximum time between the start of the temple desecration, which occurs prior to their deaths, and the sealing of the place in the wilderness (42 months versus 1260 days). So, the witnesses start testifying 2520 to 2535 days prior to Jesus' return and die 1260 to 1275 days prior to Jesus' return.

Table 19: Full-Tribulation Event Durations

Event	Duration	Start	End
(a) Protection in wilderness (Revelation 12:6,14)	1260 days / 3 ½ years	Persecution of the woman (Israel)	Jesus' return
(b) Treading down of the temple and the holy city (Revelation 11:2)	42 months	Prior to death of two witnesses	Jesus' return
(c) Ministry of 2 Witnesses (Revelation 11:3)	1260 days	Revealing of the antichrist? Start of the tribulation?	Death of the two witnesses
(d) End of daily sacrifice to the abomination of desolation (Daniel 12:11)	1290 days	End of daily sacrifice	The abomination of desolation
(e) Blessed are those who wait until the end (Daniel 12:12)	1335 days	End of daily sacrifice? The abomination of desolation?	End of Jesus' transition? Jesus' return?
(f) End of the daily sacrifice to the cleansing of the temple (Daniel 8:11-14)	2300 days	End of daily sacrifice	Cleansing of the temple (Jesus' return)
(g) Tribulation (Daniel 9:24-27)	7 years	Revealing of the son of perdition	Jesus' return
(h) Antichrist's reign (Daniel 7:25)	3 ½ years	Antichrist starts ruling	Jesus' return

Next, the abomination of desolation occurs 1290 days after the end of the daily sacrifice (d), which itself occurs 2300 days prior to the cleansing of the temple (f). The minimum time required to cleanse the temple is seven days. Assuming the antichrist will block this cleansing as long as he rules, then this cannot happen earlier than seven days after Jesus' return. This means the daily sacrifice ends no earlier than 2293 days prior to Jesus' return and the abomination of desolation no earlier than 1003 days. Curiously, these calculations push the abomination of desolation almost a year after the start of the great tribulation, when the Jews are sealed in the place in the wilderness.

The last entry to consider (e) is the most obscure. As previously mentioned, the termination event of "Blessed are those who wait" likely refers to the end of Jesus' transition period. Since this period commences 1335 days prior, this seems to eliminate the possibility that it starts with the daily sacrifice's end. This leaves the abomination of desolation as the probable start and means the "Blessed are those who wait" is at least 332 days after Jesus' return. Interestingly, Daniel 7:12 adds another possible wrinkle to this analysis, as it suggests a slightly longer transition period lasting a season and a time (fifteen months). This longer transition delays the following events by approximately 118 days: the daily sacrifice's end, the abomination of desolation, the temple's cleansing, and "Blessed are those who wait."

Table 20 summarizes the prior discussions with separate columns for both the short (332 days) and long (450 days) transitions. While this table leaves the abomination in the midst of the seventieth week of Daniel, it is not in the exact middle, where most place it. This seems to conflict with Jesus' warnings to the Jews in Mark 13:14-18 (also see Matthew 24:14-22) where they are to immediately flee when they see the abomination of desolation. Delays due to getting supplies, nursing babies, Sabbatical travel restrictions (currently nonexistent), or winter weather (Matthew 24:20) will have ramifications so severe that they will suffer woe (as in the last three trumpet judgments). Traditionally, Jesus' place of refuge is considered to be the safe place of Revelation 12 and Isaiah 63. Since Table 20 shows God sealing the safe place prior to the abomination of desolation, either the table is in error or there is a second place of refuge for those fleeing after the abomination of desolation.

Table 20: Full-Tribulation Timeline Events with Respect to Jesus' Return

Event	Time until Jesus' return (earliest possible)	Time until Jesus' return (15 month transition)
2 witnesses start testifying	Greater than 2520 days	Greater than 2520 days
Daily sacrifice stopped	2293 days	2175 days
Rule of the antichrist	3.5 years	3.5 years
Treading down of the temple and the holy city	42 months	42 months
Death of the 2 witnesses	Greater than 1260 days and less than 42 months	Greater than 1260 days and less than 42 months
Jews Flee to wilderness	1260 days	1260 days
Abomination of Desolation	1003 days	885 days
Jesus' return	0 days	0 days
Cleansing of the temple	-7 days	-225 days
Blessing for those waiting until the end (judgments)	-332 days	-450 days

In Revelation 12:6 and 12:14, the safe place is in the wilderness, but Matthew 24:16's place of refuge is the mountains. Not only are the English words (wilderness versus mountains) different but so are their Greek roots. The Greek word for wilderness, eremos (Strong's G2048), translates in different forms, including desert, desolate, and solitary but never as mountain. The Greek word for mountain, oros (Strong's G3735), translates as mount or hill but never as wilderness. They do not appear to be the same place, though some might point out that mountains and desert can simultaneously refer to the same place such as mountains in the desert.

The strength of this argument weakens in the face of Luke 21:20-24, where Jesus warned the Jews to flee to the mountains when armies encompass Jerusalem. This is a possible dual horizon prophecy, with the Roman dispersion providing the first fulfillment but leaving its definitive fulfillment until the full tribulation's battle of Armageddon immediately preceding Jesus' return. Just as for the abomination of desolation, Jesus tells the Jews to flee to the mountains, but these armies do not gather outside Jerusalem until the sixth vial judgment of Revelation 16:12-16, well after the Jews have been sealed in the safe place. Here, there can be no doubt Jesus is referring to a different place than the one mentioned in Revelation 12. Since Jesus tells the Jews to flee to the same place on both occasions, it is clear Jesus does not tell the Jews to flee to the Revelation 12's safe place when the abomination of desolation occurs. This also implies God seals the place in the wilderness before the abomination of desolation, confirming Table 20. Those fleeing after the abomination of desolation flee to the mountains surrounding Jerusalem. Not surprisingly, these are the same mountains where David sought refuge from Saul. It is interesting that in the last days, when Israel fights like David, the Jews flee to the same place of refuge David used.

Looking for possible abomination of desolation candidates following the safe place's sealing (Revelation 13-18), an interesting candidate immediately jumps out in Revelation 13:14-15: the image of the antichrist. This image deceives many since it is not only lifelike but seems to live and people either worship it or die. While the Bible is silent on the point, it likely is placed on the temple mount, perhaps even in the holy of holies. The fallout of this image's creation is woven throughout most of the following great tribulation events. In one, an angel explicitly preaches against the image to every person on earth (Revelation 14:9), as he warns those worshipping the image will end up crushed in the winepress of God's wrath. The false prophet constructs this image early in the great tribulation (consistent with Table 20), and it seems to cause desolations consistent with Daniel's descriptions. The image becomes a focal point of the remainder of the great tribulation, and many of the great tribulation's catastrophes are direct results of God's judgments for its creation and worship. For these reasons, this analysis shows the abomination of desolation occurring during the great tribulation.

Jerusalem's Temple Measured and Downtrodden

Section reference: Revelation 11:1-2.

Returning to the timeline, John receives instructions to measure Jerusalem's temple. This emphasizes its physical existence while the inexplicable omission of the measurement's results suggests its temporary nature. The presence of worshippers demonstrates Jews are actively using this facility when the antichrist issues his decree giving Gentiles unfettered access to the outer court, also known as the courtyard of the Gentiles. These intrusions continue unabated for forty-two months until the great tribulation ends. For now, the inner sanctuary with the holy of holies and the court with the brazen altar remain off limits, but this likely changes later with the abomination of desolation. The Bible provides few details of the Gentile's activities in the outer sanctuary, but one could see them moving or removing temple landmarks, setting up tourist vendor stands, setting up anti-God and pro-antichrist propaganda booths, and holding various religious ceremonies for false gods and idols.

One of the more disturbing aspects of these verses is the implied loss of Jewish autonomy, not only on the temple mount but through-out Jerusalem and even pos-sibly through-out Israel. These losses of autonomy probably contribute to the desires of Jews to flee to a place of refuge shortly in Revelation 12.

26 **Tabernacle's Courtyard Trodden**

The Ministry of the Two Witnesses

Section reference: Revelation 11:3-14.

The activities of the sixth trumpet close with the deaths of two witnesses who have been prophesying for 1260 days. They appear to be God's last prophets, and their deaths officially close the days of prophets since, as the mighty angel testified, the seventh trumpet reveals the mysteries of God.

The witnesses' description as olive trees alludes back to Zechariah 4 and suggests their Jewish ancestry. Their descriptions as candlesticks alludes to any of a host of special candlesticks found throughout the Bible, including the temple's golden candlesticks, the candlestick in Zechariah 4, Jesus' candlestick illustrations (Matthew 5:14-16), and the seven churches' candlesticks (Revelation 1-3). In each case, the candlesticks shine their light (Jesus Christ) in a dark world, and the candlesticks highlight the two witnesses' relentless proclamation of Christ's Gospel. While their impact is worldwide, they remain humble, as evidenced by their modest clothing made from sackcloth, an inferior material that today is used for packaging.

God empowers these two men with the ability to perform many miracles, including:

- stopping rain
- turning water into blood
- smiting the earth with all sorts of plagues as often as they choose

These miracles provide the chief clues to the witnesses' identities because the miracles of Old Testament prophets were often their identifying signatures. For example, killing warriors with a donkey's jawbone and the destruction of a false god's house of worship by pushing over two of its pillars were signature miracles of Samson (Judges 15-16), and the sun standing still in the sky was a signature miracle of Joshua (Joshua 10:12-14). Revelation's two witnesses repeat signature miracles of Elijah and Moses. Like Elijah, they have the power to stop the rain (1 Kings 17:1). Like Moses, they can turn water into blood and smite the earth with sundry plagues (Exodus 5-14).

Could these two witnesses be Elijah and Moses? As one of only two Old Testament people taken to heaven without dying (the other was Enoch from Genesis' pre-flood days), Elijah appears to be a prime candidate. Other prophecies, such as Malachi 4:5-6, suggest Elijah's premillennial return in the Day of the Lord. Importantly, Malachi calls Elijah by name in this passage, not as a messenger. During Jesus' first coming, many, including Jesus' disciples, questioned why Elijah had not fulfilled this prophecy. Jesus addressed this in Matthew 17:10-14 when he told his disciples Elijah had come and they understood he spoke of John the Baptist. Since Jesus' first coming did not occur during the Day of the Lord, why did Jesus not correct his disciples about Elijah preparing the way? Perhaps another of Malachi's prophecies contains the answer. Malachi 3:1 shows an unnamed messenger preparing the way. Unlike the later prophecy (Malachi 4:5-6), this prophecy neither calls Elijah by name nor ties its fulfillment to Jesus' return. Could the first promise (Malachi 3:1) refer to Jesus' first coming and the second promise to Jesus' return? If this is the case, then John the Baptist is the messenger of Malachi 3:1 and Elijah's return is still to come.

Comparisons between Elijah and John the Baptist are natural since both were great prophets who prepared the world for Jesus' arrivals and wore similar distinctive trademark clothing (2 Kings 1:8, Matthew 3:4). When these similarities are combined with expectations of a single Messianic (Jesus) appearance, confusion naturally emerged, surrounding the prophetic roles of Elijah and John. Now it is clear they are not only different roles but also probably different individuals.

The second witness' identity is more difficult and has been the source of much speculation. Again, the witnesses' miracles suggest an obvious candidate: Moses. His appearance at the mount of transfiguration (Matthew 17:1-5) with Jesus and Elijah reinforces this idea, but the biggest obstacle for this theory is Moses' death in Joshua 1:1. If Moses is the second witness, then it appears he may be the only person to have his body suffer the corruption of death (dead for more than three days) on two occasions. In all other cases, only immortal bodies replace people's mortal, corruptible bodies after the mortal has suffered through three days of corruption. If Moses is the second witness, then God probably protected his body from corruption after his death and has preserved that body for several thousand years. As unlikely as this scenario seems, an intriguing passage in Jude 1:9 shows the archangel Michael contending with Satan over Moses body. With the mysteries surrounding the final disposal of Moses' body, is it possible Michael rescued Moses' body to preserve it for the tribulation? Is this why Moses appeared at the mount of transfiguration? Only time will tell.

Two other candidates often proffered for the second witness include Enoch and a modern-day successor to Moses (like John the Baptist was a successor to Elijah). Enoch is a possibility since he, like Elijah, did not die. People discount him because he was not a Jew, not a prophet, and had no recorded miracles. The presence of a witness like Elijah at Jesus' first coming suggests the second witness may likewise be a successor to Moses, but this possibility seems doubtful. If the first witness were the ancient Elijah, why would the second witness be a contemporary?

Another common theory is the two witnesses are both end-time contemporaries imbued with the power of Elijah and Moses. It is difficult to align this last theory and Malachi 4:5-6 (though Dr. Fruchtenbaum presents a strong case that Elijah returns prior to the tribulation and the work of the two witnesses[1]). This leads to the conclusion that the most straightforward identification of the witnesses is also the most likely: they are Elijah and Moses who have returned to serve God once more.

Whoever these witnesses are, God protects them from their enemies with fire emanating from the witnesses' mouths. Psalm 18:6-8 shows a similar fire coming out of God's mouth. Later, Jesus uses this fire during the battle of Armageddon. For now, the two witnesses not only minister with God's power but also under his protection. This only serves to frustrate and anger their chief enemies (the antichrist and Satan), who have hated them and anxiously waited for an opportunity to eliminate them.

After 1260 days, the antichrist is finally able to satisfy his lusts when God removes his protective shield and he destroys the witnesses. In triumph, he lets their bodies rot in the streets where they fell in the city that God calls Sodom, Egypt, and the city of Jesus' crucifixion: Jerusalem. By calling her Sodom, God declares she is sinful and spiritually dead. By calling her Egypt, he declares she is carnal and worldly. The witnesses' deaths trigger worldwide celebrations and gift exchanges. Just as full-tribulation saints come from every definable group of people, those rejoicing over the witnesses' deaths also come from every definable group.

Throughout their 1260-day ministry, television and other media has amplified the two prophets' uncompromising boldness in proclaiming God's Word by reluctantly broadcasting

End of 2 Witnesses' Minstry (1260 days)

their words and actions into homes worldwide. While Revelation provides no details of their messages, the reactions of the messages' recipients speak volumes. The antichrist hates these witnesses and seeks opportunities to destroy them. This suggests they have been revealing his identity, his intentions, God's judgments against him, and his destiny. By the world's joy following the witnesses' deaths, it is obvious they have condemned the world of its sin and the plagues punishing their sins have only served to further infuriate them. Judging by the nations' anger following Jesus' coronation, it is likely they have proclaimed the new king's (Jesus Christ's) upcoming coronation. Probably, from the moment of the antichrist's appearance after Jesus broke the first seal, the two witnesses have foretold Jesus' reign and prepared the world for it.

After lying on the streets lifeless and motionless for three and a half days (one day for each coming year of judgment in the great tribulation), the Spirit of life from God enters them, stands them on their feet, and calls them to heaven. In contrast with the church's instantaneous and unobservable rapture, these men slowly ascend while their enemies tremble in fear. Unlike the church's rapture, news organizations will probably catch their ascension on tape and constantly replay it for several days afterward. Within an hour of their ascension, a great earthquake hits Jerusalem, destroying ten percent of the city and killing seven thousand people. Those left are terrified and finally give God his glory, but this long overdue, single act of worship is not enough to avoid the judgments coming during the next three and a half years. The second woe judgment is complete, but the seventh trumpet is about to bring the third and last woe.

Trumpet Seven: Jesus Christ Crowned King of Kings

Section reference: Revelation 11:15-19.

The seventh trumpet brings the much-anticipated and glorious coronation of Jesus Christ. The anticipation for this moment has been building from the time Jesus started claiming his rightful property (the earth) by breaking the seals of earth's title deed. Since then, the two witnesses, the seven trumpets, and the mighty angel continued to build it. His coronation has now arrived with all the pomp and circumstance due a great king, starting with the grand and glorious seventh trumpet's proud proclamation. Then great, magnificent voices of unknown origin fill the heavens with their declarations of Jesus' coronation and his new position as king over all of the kingdoms of the earth. His reign now officially starting, will never end. By the time the elders start worshiping, Jesus has already received and accepted his crown, his new title, his great power, and his new responsibilities.

Jesus' coronation is the fulfillment of Hebrews 1:8-13, where God the Father transfers his kingdom to his Son, Jesus Christ, and gives his Son the glory due him. He testifies to his Son's character (loves righteousness), his nature (he is God), and his past (he laid the foundations of the earth; "before Abraham was, I Am," John 8:58). God also anoints Jesus with the oil of gladness and promises him there will be no end to his reign. Finally, God directs Jesus to sit at his right hand until all of Jesus' enemies have been subdued. (One of the great tribulation's focuses.) Daniel 7:13-14 shows another view of the coronation, where the ancient of days (God the Father) gives the Son of man three things: dominion, glory, and a kingdom. Jesus receives all of these in heaven. His dominion is the earth and all humanity; he rules over them, and they will serve him. Yet again, Daniel affirms the eternal nature of Jesus' throne, a point also affirmed by David in Psalm 145:13.

Trump 7: Jesus' Coronation

The throngs in heaven greet the coronation with praise and worship. Again, the twenty-four elders represent the saints in worshipping before God's throne. This is the fourth of five times they worship God in the book of Revelation:

- after the rapture
- after the lamb of God is deemed worthy to open the sealed book
- after the resurrection and reward of the tribulation saints
- after the coronation of Jesus
- after the fall of Mystery Babylon

This time, they say, "We give thee thanks, O Lord God Almighty, which art, and wast, and art to come; because thou hast taken to thee thy great power, and hast reigned." Other translations render the last phrase "hast reigned" as "begun to reign," which is more consistent with this coronation scene. The elders first acknowledge Jesus' eternal existence before focusing on his reign when they praise Jesus for assuming his new authority (taking power).

© Pat Marvenko Smith - www.revelationillustrated.com

On the earth, the reaction is markedly different, as the nations are angry. Why are they angry? Primarily because they know the time of God's wrath and judgment has come. They also know the time of the dead has come, a cryptic way of saying Jesus and his saints are returning to rule the earth. How do the nations know Jesus is now king? Perhaps it is the great voices in heaven announcing Jesus' coronation. Perhaps they find out the same way Adonijah learned of Solomon's coronation (through the blowing of the coronation trumpets). There are not enough details to know, but their reactions make it clear they understand what has transpired in heaven and how it affects them.

Psalm 2, Jesus' coronation psalm, shows the reaction of the earth's people: rage and vain imaginations. Their anger (rage) brings rebellion (imagine a vain thing), and the rulers of the earth make plans to oppose Jesus to keep him from subjugating them. God's reaction is clear and strong: he laughs at them, he puts them in derision (a form of mockery), he speaks to them only in wrath, he plagues (vexes) them in his wrath (sore pleasure), he sets Jesus on the throne in Jerusalem, and he breaks them with a rod of iron. Either the people kiss the Son or suffer his wrath, but as always, God promises blessings for those putting their trust in Jesus.

Revelation 11:18 suggests the judgment of the righteous between the wrath of God and the destruction of the unrighteous. (The judgment of the wicked waits until the great white throne judgments in Revelation 20.) The judged are the dead, the prophets, the saints, and those who fear the name of God. After receiving their crown and raiment judgments following the rapture, the righteous now receive the works reward judgment promised in 1 Corinthians 3:9-15. Throughout their lives, every person's works are recorded in a book of works (Revelation 20:12). At the righteous' reward judgment, God purges sin out of this book by burning its combustible materials (wood, hay, and stubble), leaving only the works of righteousness, precious materials like gold, silver, and precious stones. God tells Christians to prepare for this day of judgment by laying up riches for eternal life through good works (1 Timothy 6:17-19). In Luke 12:31-34, Jesus tells believers to build up this treasure in heaven. Believer's riches are safer in heaven than any earthly bank. This treasure is safe from thieves, deterioration, rot, insects, and age—plus, the reward's amount is far greater than any possible sacrifices. Matthew 19:27-30 promises huge rewards for everything sacrificed: a hundredfold.

This is not a 100 percent return (onefold) but one hundred times greater. Most people would be thrilled to receive a 100 percent guaranteed return on their investment. If they could find these types of investment vehicles, funds for risky investments would dry up. However, the kingdom of heaven is a guaranteed investment with astronomical returns. Amazingly, the same people who carefully work to maximize the returns on their earthly investments often fail miserably in their heavenly investments. Like the Laodicean church, they will have no rewards to show for their life's work on this day. Neither the fear of the Lord, love for the Savior, nor the promise of rewards has motivated them to live their lives righteously.

Following the reward judgments, John sees God's heavenly temple opened. It contains the ark of the testament, which

is likely a heavenly companion of the ark of the covenant. The Bible only mentions the ark of the testament here and provides few details about it. Today, people are searching worldwide to find the earthly ark, which contains the mercy seat, the rod of Aaron, the Ten Commandments, and the manna from heaven. Some suggest it is not lost but is the ark of the testament in heaven. If so, it likely does not return until Jesus returns. Others believe this is a different ark and the ark of Moses is symbolic of the one in heaven. The answer to this mystery must wait, but the later theory (two arks) seems the more plausible of the two, especially in light of the two golden altars already seen.

Revelation 11 ends as God pours more judgments out on the earth. There is another earthquake, accompanied by great hail, lightning, thunder, and

noises. These judgments are only the first of many for humanity's rejection of their new king.

The War in Heaven and the Last Woe

Section reference: Revelation 12:1-12.

Revelation 12 begins with a great wonder in heaven: a woman clothed with the sun, the moon under her feet, and a crown of twelve stars. Joseph had a dream where the sun, moon, and eleven stars made obeisance to him (Genesis 37:9-10). The sun and moon were his parents, and Genesis' eleven stars represent Joseph's eleven brothers, the other tribes of Israel. In Revelation, there is a crown of twelve stars, one star for each of Israel's twelve tribes, including Joseph. This crown identifies the woman as God's wife, Israel. She is pregnant and, through the pains of childbirth, gives birth to a male child who rules all nations with a rod of iron. Notice the subtle distinction of this child who is a king, not a Lamb. Most view this vision as looking backward to Jesus' birth to Mary, but that child was a Lamb prepared for sacrifice, not a king. This vision is current, not past, and its placement here confirms Jesus' coronation after the seventh trumpet and sets the stage for the war in heaven.

The vision continues with the introduction of the second great wonder in heaven: the child's enemy. This enemy is a great, red dragon whose tail casts a third of heaven's stars to earth. Revelation 20:2 clearly identifies the dragon as Satan. His red color illustrates his sinful nature, and the stars speak of the hosts of angels he led as one of three archangels (Michael and Gabriel being the other two). As will be seen shortly, his seven heads, ten horns, and seven crowns link him to the antichrist and Mystery Babylon.

Today, many countries and religions celebrate this dragon. Pictures, models, and costumes portray him. Often, he is attempting to capture a golden orb, a symbol of authority, in his mouth. Legend has it that if the dragon is successful in capturing it, he overcomes his adversary. The dragon and his supporters believe his adversary is only temporarily winning this battle, so in a desperate attempt to win the battle, the dragon continually tries to capture that orb. Likewise, the real dragon,

Satan, has been using every weapon at his disposal to fight his adversary: God Almighty. He is trying to steal God's orb and rule in his stead, and he will try anything in the vain hope of defeating God. He has pinned his greatest hopes on invalidating God's plans.

Satan's attempts to undermine God's plans were on full display in World War II Germany. He inspired Hitler's actions and plans as part of a larger spiritual battle. If Satan could eliminate all Jews, then it would be impossible for God to fulfill the prophecies surrounding the "end times." Without the Jews, there are no 144,000 Jews sealed, there is no sacrificial worship, and there is no battle of Armageddon. Without the fulfillment of these things, then God would fail to meet the standards of his law and would fall to Satan's flawed state. It is Satan's hope to bring God down to this state so he can get his judgment postponed or eliminated. Fortunately, God has always known the dragon's tactics and strategies, and though no price is too high for the dragon to pay to protect himself, his schemes cannot succeed.

© Pat Marvenko Smith - www.revelationillustrated.com

Here in Revelation 12, the dragon is waiting to devour the woman's child as soon as it is born. He desires to destroy the true king before he can take the throne Satan has so desperately craved these many years. In this vision, Jesus' birth is not like his first coming, where he was physically born of Mary. This time the nation of Israel is in the throes of labor to produce the new king. God protects the king by taking him out of the clutches of his enemy, placing him on his throne, and shielding him from attack. For the first time in Revelation, John sees Jesus on his throne. Without a doubt, he is now King of kings.

After the vision, the woman Israel flees into the wilderness to a place prepared for her. This is the first of two times in this chapter where Israel flees to the wilderness. The first time, God protects them for 1260 days. The second time, God protects them for three and a half years. The first occurs prior to the war in heaven while the second occurs after the war. People start fleeing after Jesus' coronation (first time) and continue fleeing after the war (second time) until the place is sealed. Those inside are protected from the dragon's wrath and leave those outside at the mercy of the unholy trinity and the great tribulation's judgments.

The wilderness' prepared place needs to be a well-recognized destination for large numbers of people to decide independently to seek its protection. It must be prepared to handle the needs of a massive number of people for at least 1,260 days. It must be defensible enough to withstand Satan's great tribulation attacks, and it

must be in a desert or desolate wilderness. Isaiah 63:1-6 shows the place is in Edom, which is southeast of Israel, with its most famous landmark being the ancient city of Petra. Due to the surrounding terrain, Petra is defensible. Carved out of red rock, it is so unique that it sometimes serves as an exotic movie location for major films. Petra is the most likely location possibility for Revelation's place prepared in the wilderness, but Edom's permanent fires and impassable lands, courtesy of the sixth seal's war of Magog, are likely to complicate the Jew's flight to her safety.

Figure 20: Picture of Petra
(Possible Site of Jewish Refuge)

Satan's attack on Jesus starts a war in heaven between Michael and his angels and the dragon and his angels. Michael and his angels win a decisive victory and permanently cast the dragon and his angels out of heaven, exiling them down to earth. Many Christians are surprised to find out that Satan is in heaven today. They are even more surprised to learn that Satan not only has free access to heaven during the tribulation but also witnesses Jesus' coronation and two of the believer's judgments. His access to both heaven and the throne of God are consistent with the rest of Scripture. Job 1:6-9 shows Satan in heaven accusing Job before God. He has clearly accused all righteous people before God, just as he did with Job. Apparently, he never sleeps, accusing them day and night. Consumed with his hatred of God's people, he apparently never rests in his pursuit of their destruction. Those whom he accused overcome him by the blood of the Lamb (Jesus); their testimony; and their willingness to sacrifice all, including their lives, for the Lamb.

When Michael casts them out of heaven, everyone in heaven rejoices, as a loud voice proclaims that all of those living in heaven should rejoice. The same voice proclaims four things have now come: salvation, strength, the kingdom of God, and the power of Christ. This declaration underscores a dramatic change in God's actions toward

3/3 War in Heaven - Satan Exiled

his enemy and humanity. The days of God's long-suffering are over (2 Peter 3:9-10). Shortly, God forces everyone to decide whom they will serve, God or Satan. No one is able to defer this decision, and the consequences of this decision are life and death, both physically and spiritually.

The voice finishes by proclaiming the start of third and final woe: Satan's expulsion to earth. It is a woe because Satan's anger is greater than ever and he is motivated to avenge himself while he can. He is also well aware from Scripture that he has three and a half years left and is no longer able to leave earth. Here, he must remain, waiting for the true king's return and his ultimate judgment. Now, the sole remaining outlets for his wrath are the persecution of God's people and the damnation of people's souls to hell and the lake of fire. For the rest of the great tribulation, almost no one on earth is safe from his wrath.

The Dragon Attacks Israel

Section reference: Revelation 12:13-17.

Full of wrath and rage, the dragon turns his complete attention to God's people and Israel in particular. If he cannot destroy God, he at least attempts to destroy God's chosen people: Israel.

When Satan starts persecuting Israel, both the desire and urgency to flee to the place prepared for them reaches a crescendo. Those fleeing use airlifts to reach the place in the wilderness, but this only continues for a short time. Before long, Satan tries to destroy those who have fled by drowning them, but he is thwarted, as the earth just soaks up the water. When he sees his failure, he refocuses his attention to the remnant who, until  Jesus' return, must bear the full brunt of his wrath. Among those remaining are the 144,000 sealed in Revelation 7.

When Satan attacks the place prepared in the wilderness, God seals it. Those who flee after this have to flee to much less secure places, specifically the mountains of Israel. They will not have the benefit of the prior preparations found in Petra and will probably have trouble getting food and other necessities. Like David fleeing from Saul, they will probably have to stay on the move to keep their pursuers at bay. Even then,  they will be safer in the mountains than in the cities.

Isaiah 26:17-21 foretells God's people entering the prepared place, shutting the doors behind them, and remaining in it while God pours  his judgment on the world. This passage also describes Israel as a pregnant woman in the throes of childbirth and a time where the dead are alive (as shown in Revelation 4's discussion of the rapture).

The Great Tribulation (Decision and Subjugation)

The great tribulation, the second half of the seven-year tribulation, sees the antichrist's rise to power; the introduction of the false prophet; the erection of the image of the beast; the introduction of a new worldwide monetary system, the mark of the beast; the great wheat and tare harvest; the fall of Mystery Babylon; the Lamb's wedding; the marriage supper; and Jesus' return. Woven throughout these chapters are many difficult images. John explains some of the images in Revelation's narrative while others require exhaustive research. Some of the symbols are so fundamental to unraveling the great tribulation's secrets they demand special exploration prior to reviewing the great tribulation as a whole. The following sections explore the mysteries of the great tribulation beasts (dragon, the beast of the sea, the false prophet, and Mystery Babylon) and key distinguishing features (heads, horns, and crowns).

The Great Tribulation Beasts

During the great tribulation, four villains dominate the earth's activities: the three members of the unholy trinity and Mystery Babylon. As shown in Revelation 16:13, the unholy trinity consists of: the dragon, the beast, and the false prophet. The beast was introduced earlier under a different name, the first horseman of the apocalypse, while the dragon appeared in the war in heaven. Now, two new characters come onstage: the false prophet, who legitimizes the beast's authority, and Mystery Babylon, who provides the beast his seat of power. Additionally, many new clues now emerge about these characters' identities and actions.

The principle member of the unholy trinity, the dragon, is red with seven heads, ten horns, and seven crowns (Revelation 12:3-4). He has several names, including the serpent, the devil, Satan, and the deceiver of the whole world. He shares all his power, authority, and throne with the other members of the unholy trinity: the two beasts. The first of these two beasts, also called the beast of the sea, rises from the sea, having seven heads with a name of blasphemy, ten horns, ten crowns, the appearance of a leopard, feet like a bear, and a mouth like a lion (Revelation 13:1-3). The third and last member of the unholy trinity, the false prophet, is a beast who has two lamb's horns, speaks like a dragon, and performs wonders and miracles (Revelation 13:11). The last of the four characters, Mystery Babylon, is a whore who sits upon a beast and many waters, wears scarlet raiment and jewels of royalty but without crowns, seduces the kings of the earth, and has a name on her forehead: "Mystery, Babylon the great, the mother of harlots and abominations of the earth," (Revelation 17:1-6). The dangerous beast she sits on is scarlet, full of the names of blasphemy, and, like the first beast, has seven heads and ten horns.

Table 21 summarizes the symbolic descriptions for each of these four characters and adds a similar beast from Daniel 7. Several of these images contain the head, horn, and crown symbols, making the interpretation of these images critical to decoding the four characters' descriptions. The following sections explore these mysteries before analyzing the descriptive implications for each.

Table 21: Great Tribulation Beast Details

	Dragon Rev. 12:3-4	Beast of the Sea Rev. 13:3	Daniel's 4th Beast Dan. 7:1-8
Other Names	Satan, serpent, Devil (Rev. 12:9); Lucifer (Isa. 14:12)	Antichrist (1 John 2:18); Son of Perdition (2 Thes. 2:3)	
Heads	7	7	
Horns	10	10	10, 1 little, 3 destroyed
Crowns	7	10	
Color	Red		
Animals	Dragon	Leopard with bear's feet and lion's mouth	Iron teeth; eyes of a man. [3 other beasts: lion, bear, leopard]
Location		Sea	
Clothing			
Other	Third of the stars cast to earth	One head wounded to death (by sword Rev. 13:14)) and healed; power given by dragon; power for 42 months (Rev. 13:5); beast is in bottomless pit (Rev. 17:8)	Nails of brass (Dan. 7:19); devoured and stamped residue with feet; mouth speaking great things; rules 3 and ½ years

	Another Beast Rev. 13:11-15	Mystery Babylon Rev. 17:1-6
Other Names	False prophet (Rev. 16:13)	Mother of Harlots and Abominations of the earth
Heads		7 (on the dangerous beast)
Horns	2	10 (on the dangerous beast)
Crowns		
Color		Scarlet dangerous beast
Animals	Lamb and speaks like a dragon	Sat on scarlet, dangerous beast that had 7 heads and 10 horns
Location		Wilderness
Clothing		Purple and scarlet with gold precious stones and pearls
Other	Power to perform miracles, including calling fire from heaven and giving power to the image of the beast	Golden cup full of abominations and fornications; kings and inhabitants drink of her fortification; drunken with the blood of saints and martyrs

The Mysteries of the Heads

Revelation 17:8-11 provides two interpretations for the seven heads. The first ties the seven heads to Mystery Babylon's seven mountains. This interpretation is specific to Mystery Babylon, and these mountains are explored later. The second interpretation, germane to both the dragon and the beast of the sea, represents seven historical human kings.

The head's seven kings ruled over a wide span of time, with five ruling prior to John, one being John's contemporary, and the last is a future ruler who lasts only a short time. The existence of an eighth king that is of the seven shows there are eight separate reigns but with only seven kings; one of the kings must reign twice. There are numerous conflicting theories concerning these kings' identities. One holds these kings represent seven historical kingdoms (nations). The arguments for this position can be very compelling, but references elsewhere in Revelation show the eighth king is a man, the son of perdition, not a nation. If one king is a man, then all seven must be men. The seven kings may also represent nations, but the heads' primary symbolic representation must be the kings and not the countries they represent.

The most straightforward interpretation is the heads represent seven historic kings, but who are they? The easiest to identify is the king contemporary to John, the sixth king. Based on the probable date of this vision, most believe the sixth king is either Domitian or Nero, with Domitian being the favorite.

The first five kings are more difficult, with many possible candidates existing among the Egyptians, the Assyrians, the Babylonians, the Medes, the Persians, the Greeks, and the Romans. Daniel 8's single-horned goat seems to provide the best clues to their identities. This goat comes from the west to destroy a two-horned ram and becomes very strong. Eventually, its horn is broken into four parts (Daniel 8:5-8). The archangel Gabriel explained the ram represents the Media-Persian Empire, which overthrew the Babylonian empire around 539 BC (Daniel 8:19-22). The Medes and Persians shared power with the Persians, eventually becoming the dominant nation. Located in what is today Iran (as also was Media), Persia remained the dominant empire until destroyed by the single-horned goat, Alexander the Great's Greece.

While the goat represents Greece, its single horn represents its leader, Alexander the Great. Alexander broke all Persian opposition in three principle battles from 334 BC through 331 BC (Granicus, 334 BC; Isus, 333 BC; and Gaugemela, 331 BC). Following

Alexander's premature death at the age of thirty-two, his kingdom was split among his four generals: Cassander, Lysimachus, Seleucus, and Ptolemy. These generals are the four smaller horns replacing Alexander's big single horn. Since the generals were all Grecian, the vision did not replace the goat, only the horns.

As important as these prophecies were in outlining ancient history, they play an equally important role in end-time prophecy as they narrow the potential list of antichrist candidates. Daniel 8:9-12 shows a little horn emerging from the goat's horns. This little horn becomes very strong, especially toward the south and east (interestingly the same geographical areas captured by Alexander). It turns its attention to the pleasant land (Israel); challenges the host of heaven, God, the angels, and the saints; causes some of the stars of heaven (angels) to be cast to the earth (likely a reference to Revelation 12); takes away the daily sacrifice; tears down the sanctuary; and commits the transgression (the abomination of desolation). These descriptions show this little horn is the antichrist, and despite his evil deeds, he prospers for a time.

Daniel 8:23-25 places the fulfillment of the little horn vision in the last days when a king comes to power and destroys both mighty people and the holy people (Jews). Gabriel further explains that this future king will be a mighty ruler but his power comes from another source: Satan. His pride will be legendary, as evidenced by his belief that he can not only resist Jesus (Prince of princes) but also defeat him. His power is based on deceit and fraud (craft), and he uses peace, or its promise, as a weapon to destroy many.

Historically, many have identified this little horn as Antiochus Epiphanes due to his actions in spoiling the temple and stopping the daily sacrifice in the second century BC, but he is not the definitive fulfillment because he is not one of the five horns and he did this long before the last days. Several characteristics of the little horn identify him with the future son of perdition:

- Mighty power comes from another source (The beast gets his power from the dragon in Revelation 13.)
- Magnifies himself in his heart (Daniel 11:36)
- Stands against the Prince of princes (otherwise known as the Lamb and Jesus Christ, Revelation 17:14)
- Destroys many (Daniel 8:24-25)
- Comes to power peaceably (Daniel 11:21-24)
- Causes craft (deceit) to prosper (Daniel 8:25)

Daniel's passages tie five kings, Alexander and his four generals, to the antichrist. Are Daniel's five Grecian kings the first five kings of Revelation 17? It is difficult to say, but at least one king, Alexander the Great, is undoubtedly common to both lists.

Could the antichrist be a descendent of Daniel's kings? Revelation 17:8 gives some odd clues when it states the beast "was, and is not; and shall ascend out of the bottomless pit..." Notice the similarities to John 8:58 where Jesus said, "Before Abraham was, I am." Verb tense is critical in both verses. In the latter, Jesus proclaims he lives (present tense) when Abraham lived (past tense). For the former, the antichrist predated John (was), no longer lived (present tense), and will live again (shall ascend; future tense).

As shown in Revelation 11:7, the antichrist is currently in the bottomless pit. Clearly, God releases the beast from the pit just in time for the tribulation. Some believe the beast contained in the bottomless pit is the demonic force responsible for his success. Instead, the text suggests God preserves one of the prior human kings in the bottomless pit for this day. Revelation 13:3 explains the antichrist, the eighth king, has a death wound that has healed, a point confirmed by the false prophet's testimony (Revelation 13:14). Interestingly, the people of the world not only understand he received a deadly wound but they are also in awe of his recovery.

Different explanations for the beast's deadly wound have surfaced, and one of the most popular is the seventh king receives this wound and is then revived, perhaps through a pseudo resurrection. This theory seems unlikely for a couple of reasons. First, the seventh king is a future king, but the beast is a past king held in the bottomless pit. Second, modern medical practices have made miraculous recoveries almost commonplace. For example, in the 1980s, both Ronald Reagan and the pope lived through almost deadly gunshot wounds. While their recoveries were both remarkable, neither generated the groundswell of public adoration nor worship that people during the great tribulation will heap on the beast. This naturally leads one to wonder what is so remarkable about the beast's wound that people will worship him en masse, especially in light of skepticism caused by the news media's exaggeration of facts so commonplace today.

Some theorize the seven kings represent the demonic forces empowering the ancient kingdoms and their kings. Like the first theory, the seventh king suffers a deadly wound but recovers. This theory does not overcome any issues of the first theory while it creates a quandary with the interpretation of the eighth king. When and how does the eighth demonic spirit replace the seventh spirit presumably possessing the beast? Both of these theories suffer from the issue of seven kings and eight reigns. If the seventh king is also the eighth, what would cause the Bible to count his reign a second time? Still another theory holds the beast represents an ancient nation brought back to life. This theory is unlikely since the Bible does not show nations going into or coming out of the bottomless pit.

The most direct theory is also the most difficult to accept. It leads to the conclusion the antichrist is one of five men, Alexander the Great and his four generals, and he is currently in the bottomless pit awaiting his future release at the start of the tribulation. This theory goes against virtually all accepted analyses and this author's predisposition. If Alexander, or one of his generals, did return and prove his identity, then his return would indeed provoke great commotion and wonder among the people of the world. His return thousands of years after his death would fit the description of the deadly wound, which is healed and could easily elicit the worldwide response seen in Revelation 13 and Revelation 17:8.

Assuming the bottomless pit is indeed currently incarcerating this little horn, the most likely candidate is the principle horn of Daniel's five horns: Alexander the Great. Alexander was born into the Greek royal family of Philip II in 357 BC, and his mother, Olympias, told Alexander his father was actually Zeus, king of the gods. Ancients knew Zeus by many names (e.g., Ammon) but his position as a false god (Isaiah 44:6) and the king of other equally false gods suggests he is none other that Satan, the king of all fallen angels including those released from the bottomless pit after the fifth trumpet sounded. There is no evidence Alexander put much stock into his mother's accounts until he visited the oracle at Siweh in Egypt. During an arduous journey to seek the oracle's guidance, two talking snakes reportedly saved the traveling party from death. On his arrival at Siweh, the priests treated Alexander as a god and allowed Alexander alone to enter the outer sanctuary without changing into special ceremonial temple clothing. The priests recognized Alexander as the son of Zeus (though there is some dispute this was nothing more than a language issue) and invited him directly into the inner sanctuary to consult the oracle. After his visit to the oracle, Alexander began speaking of his "secret" father, Zeus, and did little to stop people from worshipping him as god.

As Alexander conquered territories, he was content to leave friendly administrations in place but was quick to punish and destroy any who rebelled against him. Contrary to popular opinion, he died before fulfilling all of his goals, as his armies refused to follow him into the depths of India. He ended up returning to Babylon, where he prepared an army to explore and conquer Arabia. As a great leader who regularly put his life at risk by leading battles from the front lines, he received many wounds on the battlefield, some almost fatal. His military conquests gained him unparalleled wealth, which he used to whet his seemingly boundless appetite for all sorts of debaucheries.

Once he even burned a city in a drunken fit (though details of this event are sketchy at best), an action that shamed his countrymen back home. Alexander's appetite for the world's pleasures may have only been exceeded by his desire to serve and worship false gods. He performed blood sacrifices and built places of worship, altars, and temples to many of them. Throughout his life, he was always cautious to not offend the gods, and his queries to the oracles were, in part, directed at finding the gods he should honor at each point in his journeys.

Alexander died at the age of thirty-two in Babylon near the Euphrates River. The cause of his death was an unknown disease, but rumors still persist that he was actually poisoned. After his death, his officers spread the story that Alexander did not die; he just left the company of men. One of the more intriguing aspects of his legacy is the uncertainty of the current location of his body and is the source of much speculation and research.

Though Alexander is a sound candidate for the beast, the idea that the bottomless pit releases a former human king, whether Alexander or anyone else, it has incarcerated for thousands of years seems on the surface to be nothing more than reckless fanciful imaginations. Why would God treat the son of perdition differently from all other men in history? Why would he preserve this man from all others? Literal interpretations of these Scriptures have often reached this conclusion, but they are so preposterous and troubling that most believe the interpretation is wrong and choose other theories in its place.

A popular alternative theory for the antichrist's identity centers on the title "the son of perdition." A search of Scripture finds "son of perdition" mentioned only twice. The first time is in John 17:12, where Jesus called Judas Iscariot the son of perdition. Based on this simple fact, many assume the antichrist is Judas. Even if true, the bottomless pit must also incarcerate him. This is a position inconsistent with the other references on the antichrist. If the bottomless pit holds any man, it must be one of Daniel's Greek horns and not Judas Iscariot.

Summarizing the seven heads, the Bible gave two interpretations of the symbolic heads. The first applies only to Mystery Babylon, giving a geographical clue about the city (seven mountains) and the second shows the seven heads represent seven kings. Five kings predate the writing of the book of Revelation. One ruled during John's day, and one is a future king. One of the kings rules twice, the second time as the eighth king, and this king is the beast, the antichrist. This king received a deadly wound from which he recovered. This section mentioned several theories concerning the interpretation of the eighth king. Each leads to different conclusions about the antichrist's identification, with Alexander the Great being the most direct interpretation presented but also the most difficult and troubling.

The Mysteries of the Ten Horns

Revelation 17:12-14 explains the ten mysterious horns of the antichrist, the dragon, and Mystery Babylon's dangerous beast represent ten future kings. These are the beast's end-time contemporaries who rule with him during the seven-year tribulation and give him their autonomy, power, and authority (Daniel 7:24-25). The beast uses their delegated power to rule the world and make war with the Lamb, Jesus Christ, but their relationship is complex at best. Ultimately, the beast destroys three of them for rebelling against him (Daniel 7:8, 7:24-25), and in the end, the remaining seven destroy his seat of power, Mystery Babylon (Revelation 17:16-17).

The hatred the seven surviving kings have toward Mystery Babylon is most likely because of their contentious relationship with the beast, and it drives them to utterly destroy her by fire. The section on the antichrist covers various theories concerning these kings and the nations they rule.

The Mysteries of the Crowns

Unlike the seven heads and ten horns, Scripture does not explain the crowns. They appear in Revelation's visions but not in Daniel's visions. The Greek root word for these crowns, diadema (Strong's

G1238), specifically refers to a royal diadem crown, signifying ruling authority over a nation or similar dominion. The New Testament shows this type of crown in only three places: the dragon's description (Revelation 12:3), the beast of the sea's description (Revelation 13:1), and Jesus' description as he prepares to return to earth (Revelation 19:12). The dragon has seven crowns, the beast has ten crowns, and Jesus has many crowns. The dragon's crowns probably speak of the seven kings (the mysterious seven heads) he has ordained through the ages. The beast's ten crowns probably speaks of the ruling authority of the prior section's ten horns. Jesus' many crowns tell of his absolute sovereignty as the earth's rightful, legal ruler, and they are the crowns of all the earth's nations. The beast receives the dragon's crowns only to have Jesus confiscate them on his return.

The Dragon

The first of the great tribulation's four terrible villains, the dragon, is the easiest to identify. He is red, has seven heads, ten horns, and seven crowns. His red color speaks of his sinful nature while his ten horns point to the ten end-time kings he uses to empower the antichrist. His seven heads and seven crowns suggest the seven kings he has empowered throughout history. Revelation 12:9 identifies the dragon as Satan. He led his angels into rebellion and was cast out of heaven by the archangel Michael.

The Beast (of the Sea)

Revelation 13:1-3 describes the second villain, the second member of the unholy trinity, as a beast rising out of the sea. Unlike the four beasts standing before God's throne, this beast is dangerous and has:

- seven heads with the name of blasphemy on them
- ten horns
- ten crowns
- the dragon's power, seat, and great authority

- a body like a leopard
- feet like a bear
- a mouth like a lion

The ten horns tie him to the ten great tribulation kings who empower him while the ten crowns attest to their dominions. The seven heads identify this beast as one of seven kings empowered by dragon, and the name of blasphemy on them demonstrates the profane actions each has committed. The sea the beast rises out of is not water but humanity (Revelation 17:15). This confirms he is a man who manages to distinguish himself above all others.

This beast receives his authority and power from the dragon who places all his resources under the beast's control, including Satan's fallen angels. Imagine the power he wields as he is able to do things no man has ever done by directing demonic legions, fallen angels, and using Satan's powers to meet his deepest desires. Considering God kept legions of these fallen angels safely locked away in the bottomless pit until the fifth trumpet judgment, this is something even Satan could not do until now.

The leopard, the bear, and the lion are the first three of Daniel's four end-time beasts (Daniel 7) and link this beast to the fourth and dreadful beast who is overthrown by the ancient of days. Daniel 7:17-18 lays the groundwork for understanding these beasts by stating they are four kings whose reigns are ended by Jesus. Many theories exist about the identity of the four kings and their kingdoms. Most interpretation efforts focus on identifying their kingdoms since this task is far more practical than naming the kings.

By far, the most prevalent interpretation of Daniel's four beasts builds on the interpretation of another of Daniel's visions: the statue with the golden head and its feet of clay (Daniel 2). Briefly, the interpretation of the statue shows the major empires having dominion over Israel: Babylon, Media-Persia, Greece, Rome, and a future empire partly derived from the prior empire (Rome). The application of this interpretation to the four beasts has produced the following possibilities:

	Option 1	Option 2
1. Lion	Babylon	Babylon
2. Bear	Media-Persia	Media
3. Leopard	Greece	Persia
4. Dreadful beast	Rome	Greece

A far less popular theory is that each beast represents an end-time nation and its ruler. This theory holds that the statue with the golden head and Daniel's four beasts cover different prophetic periods. The image covers historical empires while the four beasts cover last days' world powers. The number of passages showing several of these beasts appearing together supports this theory.

- Revelation 13:1-2: leopard, bear, lion, and the beast rising out of the sea

- Hosea 13:6-8: lion, leopard, bear, and a wild beast (all seen just before God becomes their king)

- Amos 5:18-20: lion, bear, and a serpent

- Zechariah 12:8-9/1 Samuel 17:31-37: feeblest among Israel fights as David who defeated a lion, a bear, and Goliath

- Proverbs 28:15: lion, bear, and a wicked ruler

The difficulties in identifying the nations represented by Daniel's beasts (the leopard in particular) have hampered this theory. Especially troubling is the scarcity of interpretational clues contained in either the book of Daniel or the rest of the Bible. This dearth of clues certainly makes it understandable why so many gravitate to the first interpretation. In fact, this scarcity forces the following analysis to look beyond the Bible for clues. By necessity, these discussions assume that these are the last days, and today's geopolitical climate is foretold by these beasts.

Daniel 7:3-4 describes the first of these beasts as a lion with wings of an eagle. The lion has long been the symbol for England and is the most likely this symbol's nation. This lion has wings of an eagle, which are removed, made to stand on its own feet like a man, and given the heart of a man. Like this lion, England once had the eagle's wings of the United States. Just as the eagle wings were a part of the lion and became a separate entity, the United States was a part of England and became an independent country represented by its national symbol: the eagle. The eagle's heart could represent either the United State's life or its charity. The United States and other nations separating out of England might be the young lions referred to in Ezekiel 38:13 and in various references in Jeremiah, Nahum, Ezekiel, and Zechariah.

Daniel 7:5 describes the second beast as a flesh-devouring bear. This is an apt description of the Russian bear who has been cruel and merciless to its enemies and citizens. Under Stalin and Lenin, it put millions of Russians to death. During World War II, it gained a reputation for being unmerciful to its enemies; and during the cold war, they provided the world with the iron curtain and brutal repressions of uprisings. Daniel's bear lies on one side while watching from the other (raises itself up on one side), suggesting a nation having a border needing little defense. Likewise, Russia has never been invaded across its northern border. Only during the cold war was this border threatened and then only by air attacks. Never has Russia ever been concerned her enemies would, or even could, launch land-based attacks across this border. It has three ribs in its mouth, and these lack satisfactory explanations in either historical or end-time world powers theories. The best theory suggests the three ribs represent three cruel rulers that "devour much flesh." If this is the case, Lenin and Stalin are two viable candidates, and the third might be its future leader, Gog, who leads the sixth seal's invasion of Israel.

Daniel 7:6 describes the third beast as a leopard with four bird wings, four heads, and a dominion (control of people and territory). The leopard is by far the most difficult of the four beasts. It is absent from many biblical references containing both a lion and bear, such as Amos 5 and the story of David and Goliath. Unlike the other beasts, the leopard does not seem to independently threaten Israel; even in Hosea, he is only an observer of the other beasts (Hosea 13:7). This seems consistent with the list of Israel's end-time wars, as Israel's initial struggles for statehood came against the English lion, their sixth seal's war was fought against the Russian bear (Magog), and their desperate battle for survival in the battle of Armageddon is against the terrible and dreadful beast (the antichrist) and his worldwide armies. Though the leopard is a major last days nation, it does not independently wage war against Israel.

Scouring the Bible for possible end-time powers represented by the leopard, one comes across the sixth trumpet's 200-million-man army, which is responsible for the destruction of a third of the world and Revelation 16's kings of the east (likely this same army). Is it possible the Old Testament fails to mention an army that destroys a quarter of the world's population, or could this be the mysterious leopard? At first glance, this appears a bad fit since it is the red dragon, not the leopard, most commonly associated with China. However, there are some intriguing possibilities. First, China has many different species of leopards, and several are native only to China. Second, in 1998, China developed a new generation jet fighter and named it the flying leopard. They were so proud of this accomplishment, they made a film in honor of its development. The name of the fighter is eerily reminiscent of the World War II American fighter squadron based in China known as the flying tigers. The sixth trumpet contains clues suggesting China is possibly the leopard. One of these is the four angels released from the Euphrates River to lead the army. These are likely the four heads of Daniel's leopard. If China is the leopard, then several open prophecy questions would be resolved and means Daniel's first three beasts represent the twentieth and twenty-first century's great world powers: United States/England (lion), Russia (bear), and China (leopard).

Daniel 7:7-9 describes the last beast as dreadful, terrible, and strong. This beast's strength appears overwhelming. Even its teeth (made of iron instead of enamel) make it strong and enable it to devour like the bear. These teeth tie him to the golden-headed statue's final nation: its feet of clay mixed with iron. This beast is a destruction machine; whatever his teeth do not devour, he breaks into pieces and crushes with his feet. Daniel 7:23 shows he eventually devours the whole earth. His ten horns represent the ten kings and the kingdoms forming the beast's power base. They also tie him to the golden-headed statue's ten toes (the final nation). This same passage shows the little horn destroys three of the ten kings. This beast and the statue are eventually destroyed by the ancient of days. The ancient of days' description nicely mirrors the description of Jesus in Revelation 1:13-15, but as is so often the case, these descriptions could equally apply to God the Father. Daniel 7:13-14 clarifies this is the Father, as the ancient of days overthrows the beast before taking his throne and giving it to the Son of man.[1]

Daniel 7:19-22 provides an additional detail: nails of brass. It also identifies the little horn, as the antichrist shows him speaking great things (compare to the beast of the sea's blasphemies), prevailing in war against the saints, and being destroyed by the ancient of days.

Daniel's fourth beast has intrigued students of prophecy because it gives clues to the antichrist's power base and identity. Daniel 7:24-25 describes him changing times and laws, suggesting he demands changes to the Bible, the holy days, and the observance of the holy days. It also gives the duration of his reign: three and a half years (time, one year; times, two years; and dividing of times, half a year). The duration of his reign given here is consistent with Revelation's beast of the sea account but differs from the generally accepted seven-year duration derived from Daniel 9:27. Since Daniel 9:27 speaks of the covenant's duration, not the beast's actual reign, it seems reasonable for the beast's reign to span only half of the seven-year tribulation.

The inception of the European Market, now the European Union (EU), created a buzz of excitement for prophecy students in anticipation that this would evolve into the beast's political machinery. The EU is composed of independent nations who agree to abide by the rules of law created by treaty and the council of the EU. The government is composed of legislative councils, courts, and a presidency rotated among the member nations. Conceptually, this political structure conforms to the description of the ten-horned beast. The EU started with six member nations in 1951 as the European Coal and Steel Community (ECSC). Currently, there are twenty-seven member nations (see Table 22) with others under consideration. The EU believes an important challenge for their member states is the development of a military, which can be at the disposal of the EU leadership to help resolve various domestic and international crises.

Table 22: European Union Member Nations

Belgium (1951)	West Germany (1951)	Luxembourg (1951)
France (1951)	Italy (1951)	Netherlands (1951)
Denmark (1973)	Ireland (1973)	United Kingdom (1973)
Greece (1981)	Spain (1986)	Portugal (1986)
Austria (1995)	Finland (1995)	Sweden (1995)
Cyprus (2004)	Czech Republic (2004)	Estonia (2004)
Hungary (2004)	Latvia (2004)	Lithuania (2004)
Malta (2004)	Poland (2004)	Slovakia (2004)
Slovenia (2004)	Bulgaria (2007)	Romania (2007)
Croatia (TBD)	Turkey (TBD)	Former Yugoslav Republic of Macedonia (TBD)

For the EU to be the fourth beast, several issues must be resolved. Primarily, the number of member nations in the EU is too great. Most expect this to occur by the EU trimming its member nations down to ten. Another possibility is a stream-lined decision-making process where the representatives of only ten nations are in the council. Alternatively, the EU may subdivide its member nations into ten regional ruling districts. Assuming the EU will transform into a ten-ruler confederation of some type, it still needs a strong, centralized military, though the armed forces of many of its member nations could easily provide the basis for these centralized forces.

The EU's political organization (particularly its rotating presidency) would help someone like the antichrist rise to power. Several times, rulers have used constitutional means to come to power and then discarded the constitution to maintain power. The antichrist could come to power through the rotation of the presidency, declare emergency powers, and never step down. Only time will tell if the fourth beast's ten horns represent the EU.

Besides the EU, at least one other theory for the ten horns has gotten some traction. It involves the United Nation's division of the earth into ten economic regions called kingdoms with the multiple nations in each kingdom ruled under a single governmental authority. Today, this governmental scheme seems farfetched since nations so fiercely defend their independence, and it is unlikely they would yield their sovereignty to a single ruler.

When God (the ancient of days) destroys this last beast, Daniel 7:10-14 shows him sparing the lives of the first three beasts for a season and time (roughly fifteen months). The description of the fourth beast's destruction in flames matches Revelation's account of the antichrist's destruction in the lake of fire. The first three beasts' short-term survival seems to imply their long-term fate lies in the judgment of nations while other Scripture suggests each survive this judgment and enter Jesus' millennial reign. Prior to describing the beast's demise, Daniel 7:10-14 speaks of another judgment, likely the judgment of the saints in heaven preceding

Jesus' return. The rest of the descriptions in this passage concern Jesus' victory at the battle of Armageddon and the establishment of his kingdom. These descriptions are again remarkably consistent with Revelation 19-20.

A last detail about the antichrist is the number of his name: 666 (Revelation 13:18). This prophetic clue has probably generated more speculation than any other Bible prophecy as it has spawned innumerable theories, counting schemes, and investigations. Almost no prominent politician has escaped its scrutiny as various calculations of the numeric value of their names unfairly make some of them antichrist candidates. Though often interesting and compelling, the prophetic merit of these conjectures does not match their entertainment value as they are almost exclusively carried out in total isolation from all other antichrist prophecies, particularly the prophecies stating he is currently in the bottomless pit. Unless the one in the bottomless pit is a demonic force, these searches are in vain.

The False Prophet

Revelation 13:11-12 provides what appears to be the Bible's only description of the last member of the unholy trinity: the false prophet. Like the other beasts, his description is shrouded in mystery. Like the antichrist, the false prophet is a dangerous beast. Unlike the antichrist, this beast is a religious leader who does not have any national dominion. His two horns are particularly difficult to understand. In Daniel 8, there was a two-horned ram symbolizing the Media-Persian empire. Since the ram represents an empire and the false prophet has no dominion, this two-horned beast does not seem to provide any insights into the false prophet's horns. Elsewhere, horns represent authority, usually kings, and the lamb represents Jesus. Combining these, a horn of a lamb suggests someone with religious authority, probably Christian. The two horns suggest he has the authority over two religions. Perhaps these two horns represent the two covenants, Judaism and Christianity, and the false prophet's authoritative credentials to both. For Christianity, this suggests the pope or someone holding a similar position in another denomination, and for Judaism, this suggests the high priest. Another possibility is the two horns represent different denominations. For example, a unity movement could bring the authority of two Christian denominations (e.g., Anglican and Catholic) together under a single ruling authority.

The false prophet acts in manners consistent with Old Testament false prophets. He claims to speak for God, but his words are those of the dragon (Satan). He throws all his credibility behind the antichrist and exercises the power of the dragon to perform a variety of miracles. Two of his miracles are direct imitations of the works of Elijah: calling fire down from heaven (1 Kings 18) and giving life (1 Kings 17). His imitation of Elijah is not accidental or coincidental. In his efforts to legitimize the first horseman's imitation of Jesus, the false prophet impersonates Elijah to deceive people into believing he is fulfilling Micah's last days' prophecy for Elijah's return (Micah 4:5). In so doing, he persuades people that the beast is the promised Messiah. His impersonation of the Jewish prophet Elijah lends credibility to the idea that one of his horns represents the religious authority of Judaism.

This beast is instrumental in consolidating power under the antichrist. Before the great tribulation ends, he institutes monetary and religious policies that condemn many to eternity in the lake of fire. His actions are so despicable that God sends angels to preach against him. Among men, only two enter the lake of fire before the great white throne judgments, and this dubious honor falls to these last two utterly evil and dangerous beasts: the antichrist and the false prophet.

Mystery Babylon

Revelation 17:1-6 introduces the last of the great tribulation's infamous actors: Mystery Babylon. Mystery Babylon is described as a whore who sits on many waters and seven mountains (the seven heads as shown earlier) in the wilderness. Like the beast's sea, Revelation 17:15 shows Mystery Babylon sits on the sea of humanity. Differences in the Greek root words for the beast's sea and Mystery Babylon's waters[2] suggest differences between these two bodies of humanity, but the significance of these differences are not readily obvious—though they may be due to the physical bodies of water surrounding Mystery Babylon, enabling her to be a world-class trade port.

© Pat Marvenko Smith - www.revelationillustrated.com

She also sits on a dangerous scarlet beast who is full of the names of blasphemy and has seven heads and ten horns. These suggest she rides the beast of the sea, the antichrist, to regain her worldwide prominence. Undoubtedly, their futures are inextricably linked, as she receives prestige from the beast while giving him his throne.

Mystery Babylon dresses in only the most expensive clothing and fine jewelry. The quality of her clothing and her ostentatious jewelry shows her lovers have been most generous to her while the color of her clothing speaks of her royalty (purple) and her sin (scarlet). Even her clothing's color attests to her immense wealth since prior to the last few hundred years, only the wealthiest of people could afford dyed clothing. She has a name written on her forehead—"Mystery, Babylon the Great, the Mother of Harlots and abominations of the earth"—that references an ancient city and suggests she is a city. This point is confirmed by Revelation 17:18, which goes on to state that she reigns over the kings of the earth. Even with this, the Mystery portion of her title clouds her identity, suggesting she is not ancient Babylon but she has ties to ancient Babylon.

As a whore, Mystery Babylon fornicates with the kings of the earth and entices the kings of the earth to join her drunken revelry. Her intoxicating beverage of choice is not alcohol but the blood of the righteous (saints and martyrs). This foul wine of repugnant sin, abominations, and fornications fills her golden cup and is continuously replenished as she seduces people from every ethnic group (Revelation 17:15). Where she and her lovers become intoxicated on the blood of the righteous, in the future, the guests at God's supper (the great tribulation's battle of Armageddon) will become intoxicated on her blood and that of her lovers.

While God views her as a sluttish whore, she views herself as an immortal queen who will never know sorrow and is immune from God's judgments (Revelation 18:7). This attitude is more likely found in ancient cities with long histories than young, immature cities, which normally suffer from inferiority complexes and constantly need to prove their importance. Supporting the notion that she is an ancient city is God's indictment of her treatment of the apostles and prophets (Revelation 18:20). Since apostles were contemporaries of Jesus and lived only in the first century, Mystery Babylon must be not only an ancient city, but also a thriving, first-century city.

While lovers made Mystery Babylon wealthy, she also made them rich (Revelation 18:15). Revelation 18:11-13 lists the goods and services she bought and sold. Most are innocent enough, but some are ominous such as slaves and the souls of men. This suggests the seven-year tribulation could see the resumption of open slave trading, but it could also only refer to her past sins. The trading in souls is obscure and suggests people willingly trade away their souls for her pleasures. Does this sound farfetched? With the introduction of the mark of the beast later in the great tribulation, people will trade their souls for food (the mark of the beast, Revelation 13-14). If they trade their souls for food, what would stop them from trading their souls for pleasure?

The reaction of the merchants to Mystery Babylon's destruction exceeds expectations for simply losing a trading partner. Clearly, this city has compensated them extremely well for their compromises, and these rewards probably reflect the antichrist's cronyism. Daniel 11:39 shows him dividing the land for gain. This infers he first gains control of the property and then sells and gives it away as he chooses. Two methods of gaining the property are likely: purchase and confiscation by force. The focus on the land's division for gain conveys the antichrist confiscates it, divides it, and gives it to his cronies. This is the modus operandi used by Hitler in Nazi Germany when his cronies were rewarded with property of all types taken from "enemies" of the state. Daniel 11:39 suggests the antichrist repeats this, as he freely rewards his friends, punishes his enemies, and makes the merchants wealthy through this systematic pillaging of people's possessions.

Several events in ancient Babylon foreshadow its future namesake, Mystery Babylon. Ancient Babylon was guilty of several sins ultimately provoking God to deliver them into the hands of their enemies, including:

- the erection of a 90-foot tall, golden image with a death penalty law requiring all to worship it (Daniel 3)
- King Nebuchadnezzar's great pride (Daniel 4)
- the desecration of the golden vessels of God's temple (Daniel 5)

Remarkably, similar episodes occur during the seven-year tribulation when the false prophet builds an image of the beast (Revelation 13), the false prophet enacts laws forcing worship of the beast's image, the antichrist's pride exceeds that of the king of Babylon, the antichrist gives the outer courts of the temple over to the abuse of Gentiles, the beast stops the daily sacrifice, and the beast implements the abomination of desolation. Undoubtedly, these desecrations involving the temple and its sacrifices will be as great as any committed in ancient Babylon.

However, the key linkage between ancient and Mystery Babylon is found in Nebuchadnezzar's image with the golden head (Daniel 2:28-36). A key to this passage is its fulfillment in the latter days. The image has the following characteristics:

- great, bright, and terrible
- head of fine gold
- breast and arms of silver
- belly and thighs of brass
- legs of iron
- feet and ten toes of iron and clay
- image utterly destroyed at its feet by a stone not cut with human hands
- stone becomes a mountain and fills the whole earth

Fortunately, Daniel interprets this confusing image (Daniel 2:37-45). Each of the image's five separate portions represent a different kingdom. Each kingdom replaces the next until the kingdom of God overthrows them all. Each is also composed of a different material, and each successive portion of the image becomes progressively less precious. Daniel interprets the head as the king of ancient Babylon, Nebuchadnezzar. Each successive portion of the image represents a kingdom rising after Babylon's fall. The following list contains the parts of the statue and two popular views about the nations each represents.

	Option 1	Option 2
Head of fine gold:	Babylon / Nebuchadnezzar	
Breast and arms of silver:	Media-Persia	Media
Belly and thighs of brass:	Greece	Persia
Legs of iron:	Rome	Greece
Feet and ten toes of iron/clay:	Daniel 7's ten horns of the fourth beast and, by extension, Revelation 13's beast and Mystery Babylon	

Option 1 is the more widely accepted of the two due to its inclusion of Rome and its recognition that Media-Persia jointly ruled (though primary authority transitioned from Media to Persia during their reign). Rome's eventual division into two parts further supports its inclusion in the image's list of nations as the legs of iron. Particularly interesting is the last kingdom, which is only partly strong and is the weakest of the five. Its strength comes from the leg's material (iron) and implies it descends from the kingdom represented by the image's legs. The feet's ten toes are suggestive of the fourth beast's ten horns and the ten nations that give power to the antichrist. Its weakness comes from the image's only nonmetallic material (clay) and reinforces the idea that the antichrist's power base is partially strong and partially weak. These ten nations tie this image to the antichrist, whom Mystery Babylon rides in her return to world prominence. The entire image is destroyed by the stone cut without hands. This stone attacks only the image's feet but destroys the entire image, including its head: Babylon. Through this image, ancient Babylon is linked to its successor, Mystery Babylon, and both fall in the last days at the hands of God.

Who is this whore Mystery Babylon? So far, there have been several clues to her identity:

- great, wealthy, powerful, wicked city
- first-century city that persecuted the apostles
- sits on seven hills
- city of the beast's power
- located in the wilderness
- trading city
- makes merchants wealthy
- expects long life

Her location is particularly confusing. She is located in the wilderness, but the details of her destruction show her close proximity to water (Jeremiah 51:42). It is not clear whether her surrounding lands are currently a wilderness or if this is only true after her destruction. If she is currently in a wilderness, then few cities in the world (including those in the EU) meet this requirement.

Some have wondered whether she could be Jerusalem. The simple answer is no since Revelation 18:21-23 shows God destroys Mystery Babylon and she remains uninhabited forever. She never again sees candlelight, bride, or bridegroom. During the millennial reign, Jesus reigns in Jerusalem and the whole world flocks to it. Since Jesus and the Jews inhabit Jerusalem continually throughout his reign and Mystery Babylon is uninhabited, Jerusalem cannot be Mystery Babylon.

Beyond Jerusalem, many other theories exist for Mystery Babylon's identity, but none is fully satisfactory. The most prominent and enduring is Rome. Those holding this position base it primarily on its seven mountains and the residual iron left in the feet from the fourth kingdom of iron: Rome. Others suggest it is a rebuilt Babylon or a city in the same area, such as Baghdad. This would fit the wilderness description, but it is not a major port of trade, descended from the fourth kingdom, or a persecutor of the apostles. Some proffer major trading ports such as New York and Tokyo strictly on the strength of their world trade status and others suggest EU cities (e.g., Brussels) based on the partly iron toes. For each of these possibilities, many of the tests also fail.

Only time will tell which city is Mystery Babylon, but with the information today, Rome remains the best candidate. Its seven hills (Aventine, Caelian, Capitoline, Esquiline, Palatine, Quirinal, and Viminal) are famous, and its ties to the fourth kingdom are obvious. She is an ancient city with a history of persecuting the apostles and prophets. Her age and history could very well lead her to believe she would live forever. She is a city located close to both air and sea ports and has a long history as a center of trade. Her ready access to the Mediterranean Sea along the Tevere River makes her vulnerable to destruction by raging seas, as described by Jeremiah, and as head of the Catholic Church, Rome could be instrumental to the plans and activities of both the antichrist and the false prophet.

This concludes the exploration of the mysteries of the heads, horns, crowns, dragon, beast of the sea, false prophet, and Mystery Babylon. The next section resumes the timeline narrative with the start of the decision theme, the first of two of the dreadful great tribulation's themes.

The Antichrist Takes Power

Section reference: Revelation 13:1-10.

After his defeat at Michael's hands, his confinement on earth, and his failure to destroy the Jews in the wilderness, Satan turns his attention to solidifying control over the earth. He empowers two men to enslave, control, and rule according to his wishes. This unholy alliance works to consolidate all power under a single man, persecute the righteous, and deceive the world into worshipping the false gods of the beast and the dragon. Revelation 13:1-10 shows the dragon throwing his full support behind the antichrist and giving him three things: power, seat, and great authority. Through the first three and a half years of the full tribulation, the antichrist has played an active secondary role, but now Satan thrusts him to center stage.

Satan exploits the beast's sword wound and his miraculous recovery from it to generate a ground  swell of support, resulting in the world worshiping the dragon and the antichrist. They ask, "Who is like the beast?" asking, "Who is able to make war with the beast?" Desperate for deliverance from the ravages of the tribulation, the world's people grasp at the hope they offer. Many, but clearly not all, people worship the beast and the source of his power, the dragon.

The beast's rise to power began when the first seal was broken and he came onto the scene as a man of peace who confirmed a covenant with Israel. However, he was actually a man of the vilest character to whom no vow or bond is sacred and only does things for the common good when it is to his advantage. Even now, his character is on display, as he has already started breaking the covenant made with Israel three and a half years earlier. He needs to convince people that he alone has the answers to all of the world's problems while he eternally subjugates and enslaves their souls. In a manner similar to Hitler's use of the depression, the antichrist uses the crisis of the tribulation to come to prominence and power. Even today, Hitler receives praises for his efforts in building a great highway system, bringing the country out of a depression, and rebuilding the country's infrastructure. Likewise, the antichrist appears to do good things, but Daniel 11:23 makes it clear this is just an illusion. Daniel 11:21 shows this beast is a liar who uses flatteries to enable him to acquire power peacefully but then uses this power to loot, steal, rob, and persecute those who oppose him (the righteous and the innocent). Eventually, he brings both himself and his followers to utter destruction.

Through his deceit, he gains control over a power base of

ten rulers, and from this base, he eventually controls all nations, peoples, and languages. Through this time, he gains control over Daniel's lion, bear, and leopard. No one on earth is exempt from his brief but cruel reign of forty-two months. Fortunately, the brevity of his reign constrains his ability to solidify and consolidate his power. He wages war against any who oppose or reject him, destroys as many saints as possible, and devours the poor as a lion and a bear (Proverbs 28:15).

© Pat Marvenko Smith - www.revelationillustrated.com

Throughout the great tribulation, the antichrist uses his newly acquired position and power to escalate his war against the God he hates. His anger is evident as he speaks great blasphemous things against: God, God's name, God's tabernacle (Greek skene (Strong's G4633), tent or cloth hut), and those in heaven. Daniel 11:36-38 shows him putting his hatred against God into action as he does his own will (as opposed to God's or men's will), exalts himself above all, proclaims himself above every god, speaks against God, and honors the god of forces (Satan) with valuables. With every word, he challenges God's authority, attempts to deceive the earth's inhabitants, spews his venomous hatred against God, and attempts to elevate himself by tearing down and destroying others. This last tactic of Satan and his operatives stands in direct contrast to God's methods of edifying people (1 Corinthians 8:1, 1 Thessalonians 5:11) and his directions to his people to become great by first being the least (serving) (Luke 9:48).

John ends the antichrist's introduction with a warning for all to hear: people will reap what they sow. Those persecuting, enslaving, and killing others will suffer the same fate. This warning is especially urgent due to the coming worldwide persecution of the righteous spearheaded by the antichrist.

The False Prophet Revealed

Section reference: Revelation 13:11-14.

Now John observes the second beast (the false prophet) arising from the earth. His rising recalls man's creation in Genesis and affirms the false prophet's human nature. Though his miracles may suggest otherwise, he is only a man and nothing more. To legitimize the beast's throne, he claims to be a prophet of God. His infamy exceeds all of history's other false prophets, including the magicians at Pharaoh's court, and the counselors at Nebuchadnezzar's palace. He receives all of the antichrist's power, including that given by the dragon. He uses this power to edify both the dragon and the beast so they can deceive the world into worshipping and serving them. He performs great miracles, not ordinary slight of hand magician's tricks, but unexplainable miracles as grand and logic defying as any found in the Old Testament. Now, for the first time, all three members of the unholy trinity (the dragon, the beast, and the false prophet) are together, cooperating, and fully sharing power.

The Beast Invades Egypt

Sometime after the antichrist's acquisition of power, he starts performing many of the deeds foretold by Daniel. One action having far-reaching consequences (his invasion of Egypt) does not appear in Revelation. This leaves its position on the prophetic timeline open to speculation. References in Daniel suggest the first of two invasions occurs after the unholy trinity has consolidated its power and before the final countdown to Armageddon kicks off with the abomination of desolation. Another possibility is this invasion is a byproduct of the sixth seal's war, but Egypt's exclusion from the list of Magog allies discounts this possibility. His invasions of Egypt[3] are particularly important because the effects of this invasion continue well into Jesus' millennial reign.

Daniel 11 provides three separate references to the kings of the south after the antichrist's rise to power in verse 21. The first two appear to refer to two separate invasions, and the last appears to be a summary of the first. The first (Daniel 11:25-28) shows him overpowering the king of the south with a great army.

38 | Antichrist's Invasion of Egypt

He loots the countries of the south and returns with great wealth. Daniel 11:29-31 shows him returning a second time but with far different results. The second invasion fails primarily because Chittim sends ships to oppose the invasion. Chittim is modern Cyprus and is normally associated with two prominent countries that have occupied and controlled it: Rome and Greece. If the ten horns are some version of the EU, then Chittim could be a subset of the EU nations. This suggests the invasion fails due to opposition internally within the antichrist's seat of power. This opposition provokes the beast's anger, and his retaliation against the perpetrators probably leads directly to the beast plucking the three horns. For some unknown reason, this defeat heightens the antichrist's hatred of the covenant between God and Israel (the holy covenant). This hatred leads directly to his rejection of the covenant and the abomination of desolation. This description is eerily reminiscent of Hitler, who blamed his failures and those of Germany on the Jews. His use of the Jews as scapegoats only intensified his "final solution" activities.

The last reference (Daniel 11:40-44) describes a series of battles. First, the king of the south and the king of the north enter the glorious land and many countries are overthrown, a possible Magog invasion reference. Then, the antichrist's confiscation of Egypt's gold, silver, and precious things alludes to his first invasion of Egypt while the tidings out of the north appear to allude to the failed second invasion and the destruction of the three horns. The passage ends with the antichrist's destruction at Jesus' hands in the battle of Armageddon.

Ezekiel expends portions of several chapters (29 through 32) on the invasion of Egypt. For example, in Ezekiel 29:8-15, God punishes Egypt by the sword, not by a natural disaster or "an act of God." The effects to the land and nation of Egypt are devastating:

- The land is absolutely, completely wasted and desolated (nothing is left untouched)
- The land is uninhabitable for forty years by both man and beast
- The nation of Egypt is scattered and dispersed among the nations for forty years

When the forty years are completed, God brings them back to the land of Egypt, where they will again be a nation, albeit a minor one. Never again will they be an influential power broker, lead alliances, or direct the actions of other nations.

The forty years are interesting. In this age of nuclear weapons, the possibility that war exiles people for forty years is not surprising, and this could easily represent the time for radioactive fallout to safely decay. While this seems reasonable, it is strange that similar descriptions do not appear with either the invasion of Magog or the battle of Armageddon. Whether this suggests the use of nuclear weapons in one battle and not the others is unclear, though the descriptions of fires in Egypt and at least one of its cities are consistent with the damages of nuclear weapons.

Surprisingly, the theft of Egypt's wealth appears to be God's reward to the antichrist for services rendered. This is seen in Ezekiel 29:19-21 as Nebuchadnezzar (a type of the antichrist) receives Egypt's riches as wages at a time when Israel is budding (the last days). This creates an baffling paradox, as, even in his boundless angry hatred of God, the antichrist has somehow performed God's will. God provides no clues to how the antichrist labors on God's behalf—simply that he has. Perhaps God is punishing these nations for their ancient hatred of Israel. Truly, this puzzling mystery must be left to speculation.

Ezekiel 30 paints a graphic picture of this invasion. First, Ezekiel 30:3 sets the time frame: the Day of the Lord. Then it names the invaders' leader: Nebuchadnezzar king of Babylon (Ezekiel 30:10). It then lists the nations suffering under the king's heavy hand: Egypt, Ethiopia, Libya, Lydia (Lud), the mingled people, Chub, and their allies (Ezekiel 30:4-5). The first three of these nations are also in Daniel 11:43's descriptions. Ezekiel 30:6-7 shows the countries and cities laid waste through fire and the devastation of war. Ezekiel 30:12-24 shows the invasion also causes rivers to dry up, idols to be destroyed, and dispersion of the Egyptians throughout the world.

Summarizing, the invasions of Egypt occurs in the Day of the Lord, is one of the rare seven-year tribulation prophecies not found in Revelation. The invasions, led by the future king of Babylon (the antichrist), probably occur after the antichrist's rise to power but before the abomination of desolation. He attacks not only Egypt but also the surrounding countries such as Libya and Ethiopia. He loots the countries and returns very wealthy with many Egyptian slaves. The war's devastation probably forces other Egyptians to leave, and they are unable to return to their land until forty years have expired. This means their exile continues even after Jesus Christ is on the throne and all fighting has long ceased. The antichrist's second invasion fails due to the opposition of adversarial nations, perhaps even EU member countries. Between the two attacks, the invaded countries are devastated. Egypt's cities are wasted, and its land is uninhabitable for forty years. Unlike the land of Edom (and later Mystery Babylon), where wild beasts but not people will live in the land, neither beasts nor people live in Egypt for forty years, though both eventually return.

The Abomination of Desolation

Section reference: Revelation 13:14–15.

Immediately after his introduction, the false prophet launches his programs to solidify the beast's power. He attempts to identify and eliminate all opposition (passive or active) to the beast. The first step is the design, creation, and erection of an image of the beast. When completed, the false prophet somehow makes the statue appear to live. It not only speaks but also apparently sees, hears, understands, and reasons. Whenever anyone refuses to worship it, it even has the power to have them executed. One can only imagine the full capabilities of this image, but it is certainly within the realm of possibility that it is able to carry on conversations, move, and show emotions.

The Bible leaves details of the image's technologies to the imagination. Two possibilities include demonic forces or modern artificial intelligence (AI). Currently, AI technology is not capable of matching this level of sophistication, but this field is rapidly advancing.

Future technologies may make it possible to create an image of this sophistication, but the time required to design and build the circuitry for the image may still make its use impractical. The use of demonic forces is more consistent with both the source of the false prophet's power (the dragon) and the image's description. The text suggests the image has breath and, by implication, a soul. It would be hard to construe electronics, no matter how sophisticated, as a soul. Demonic activity, as recorded in the New Testament, would seem to be more consistent with this description, especially in light of the rampant demonic activity seen elsewhere throughout the seven-year tribulation (e.g., the fifth trumpet and the sixth seal).

Regardless of the source and extent of the image's powers and abilities, the image plays a critical role in great tribulation events. Significantly, the false prophet is able to enact laws requiring its worship with refusal bringing death, presumably by beheading. However, those acquiescing risk God's wrath. Already, people have to choose between death and God's wrath. Soon, the stakes will be raised even higher.

This image of the beast provides yet another link between ancient and Mystery Babylon, as kings of both eras built statues and enacted laws, with death penalty laws forcing their worship. As described in Daniel 3:1, ancient Babylon's statue was 90 feet tall, 9 feet wide, and inspired by the vision of the image with the head of gold. Nebuchadnezzar honored himself by constructing the entire image out of gold and then proclaimed that on pain of death everyone would stop and worship the statue whenever his musicians played (Daniel 3:4-7). Predictably, some refused, including three Jews: Shadrach, Meshach, and Abednego. These three stood before Nebuchadnezzar's judgment seat, where they were given a final opportunity to appease Nebuchadnezzar but refused. Nebuchadnezzar's anger was so great that he not only ordered their deaths but also ordered the guards to throw them into a furnace heated seven times hotter than normal. Oddly, the furnace's heat kills all who get near it except the three bound Jews. This leads to a well-known miracle: Nebuchadnezzar sees four unfettered men walking freely, and they are impervious to both the flames and the heat. Amazingly, he recognized the fourth man as the Son of God (Daniel 3:13-27).

In a similar fashion, the false prophet creates an image that people worship or die. The big differences between the images erected by Nebuchadnezzar and the false prophet are:

- the false prophet's image is in the likeness of the antichrist while the model for Nebuchadnezzar's image is unknown (probably Nebuchadnezzar)

- musicians led the worship of the image in ancient Babylon while the false prophet leads the worship of the image of the beast

- the image in ancient Babylon is lifeless while the false prophet's image appears to live
- only people in ancient Babylon worshiped the image while people throughout the world worship the future image
- in ancient Babylon, people are burned alive for refusing to worship the image while in Mystery Babylon they are probably beheaded (Revelation 20:4)

Like ancient Babylon, there will be those who risk their lives by refusing to worship the image, and many will be executed.[4]

Undoubtedly, the erection of the image of the beast is an abomination. It also will lead to the desolations of the winepress of God's wrath, also known as the battle of Armageddon. This is probably Daniel's abomination of desolation, and the false prophet builds and erects it under the authority, approval, and direction of the antichrist. The statue triggers such destruction and chaos that Jesus told the Jews to flee to the mountains when it occurs (Matthew 24:15-22) because it ushers in the greatest tribulation the world has ever seen. While not stated in Revelation, the most likely dwelling place for the image of the beast is the temple's courtyard or inner sanctuary on the temple mount.

The Mark of the Beast

Section reference: Revelation 13:16-18.

Next, the false prophet enacts the second prong of his program to enslave people: the mark of the beast. This counterfeit to Revelation 7's seal of God is a new "forgery proof," cashless monetary system. It replaces all existing monetary systems in the world and renders all paper monies worthless. This system makes it impossible to conduct business or even buy food or water

4 0 Mark of the Beast Introduced

without it on either the forehead or right hand. In contrast to God's seal, which protects life, the beast's seal brings eternal death (lake of fire).

The nuances of the Greek language permit the mark to be located in a range of places, including the right hand or implanted on either the hand or the wrist.[5] This mark has the beast's number (666) associated with it. Six is the number for man (the day of his creation, Genesis 1:26-28) and is often associated with imperfection or sin while the number 3 is associated with God. Many consider three 3's (333) a number for God, and some suggest this shows either the antichrist's claim to be twice as powerful as God or the depths of his sin.

Current speculation is that the mark is a barcode of some type, printed on the skin or a biotechnology chip placed under the skin. Those who favor the barcode point out that UPC codes found on commercial products contain two fields separated by the symbols for the number 6. The code also starts and ends with a six, yielding UPC symbols with 666 embedded in them. Those who favor the chip implant claim the Greek language describes implants and point to the massive amounts of information required for complex identification and banking systems. Implanted chips similar to those in smart cards could greatly assist these systems. Regardless of the physical form of the mark, the networks, infrastructures, and point-of-sale equipment have to extend to the four corners of the globe. It is not hard to envision cashless monetary systems like this in developed countries where ATM machines and credit cards are commonly used, but underdeveloped countries, where most daily business continues to be transacted via cash or barter exchanges, would seem to present significant barriers to its introduction.

The Reward of the 144,000

Section reference: Revelation 14:1-5.

Following the introduction of the mark of the beast, there is a curious pause where God itemizes the character of Revelation 7's 144,000 sealed servants and details their rewards. They are seen with Jesus on Mount Zion. Since Jesus does not return for another five chapters, this event's placement here is odd; but its placement following the Jews fleeing to the wildernesses' safe place and the mountains suggests these men did not flee with their brethren. Rather, with God's seal protecting them, they boldly, openly witness for the full tribulation's duration, knowing they are safe from both the unholy trinity and the judgments of God.

The character of these men is beyond reproach, as they are virgins who watch every word from their mouth and are fault-less before God. Out of their mouths flows only the living water of God, as they do not curse, lie, or gossip. How many Christians meet this standard? Their rewards include temporal life, eternal life, and a song that is theirs alone. Their presence with Jesus on Mount Zion[6] shows all survive the great tribulation despite the actions of the unholy trinity. The voice sounding like many waters calling them to heaven is reminiscent of Jesus' description in Revelation 1 and conveys a picture of eternal life (Jesus' water of life). Immediately after hearing this voice, the witnesses are before God's throne, the beasts, and the elders. Since these are in heaven, it is clear God has called the 144,000 witnesses up to his heavenly throne in their own private rapture. To enable them to stand in God's presence, God completes their reward of life by replacing their temporal bodies with their perfect eternal bodies. These witnesses are only the second group of people (after the church members living at the time of the rapture) to receive eternal life without dying; and they receive it in the third of Revelation's three raptures (the church in Revelation 4:1-2, the two witnesses in Revelation 11, and the 144,000 in Revelation 14).

God's Ultimatum: The Time of Decision

Section reference: Revelation 14:6-13.

The worship of both the beast and his image along with the intro-duction of his mark brings a final ultimatum from God. His time of long-suffering has ended, and he will no longer afford people the luxury of deferring their spiritual decisions (2 Peter 3:9). God uses three angels to deliver his ultimatum in three messages:

1. Fear God, give glory to him, and worship the God of creation.

2. Mystery Babylon is judged and is fallen.

3. God's judgment will fall on anyone receiving the mark of the beast and worshiping the beast or his image.

Each angel preaches a message to everyone throughout the earth in their own languages. The first angel's proclamation fulfills Jesus' end-times prophecy of the preaching of the Gospel throughout the earth (Matthew 24:14). Despite their best efforts, the church has never accomplished what these three angels will: the simultaneous worldwide preaching of the Gospel to every person in their own language. This definitive fulfillment of Jesus' prophecy only occurs after the rapture, not before, as most often taught. The next verse (Matthew 24:15) further supports this position, as Jesus ties the worldwide preaching of the Gospel to the great tribulation by warning of the abomination of desolation.

The first angel calls men to repent, turn back to God, reject the unholy trinity, and reject the beast's image while the third angel proclaims judgment  on those rejecting the message of the first angel. People demonstrate their rejection of God by:

- worshipping the beast

- worshipping the image of the beast

- receiving the mark of the beast (on either the forehead or the hand)

Once they meet all three conditions, then the judgments pronounced by the angel are borne by them. (It is debatable whether people must meet all three conditions, but the text suggests this interpretation.) The judgments include drinking of the wine of the wrath of God and never-ending torment by fire and brimstone (hell and the lake of fire). The wine of God's wrath refers to the great tribulation in general and the battle of Armageddon specifically. The Gospel preached by the first and third angels could not be any simpler: choose God and eternal life or Satan and eternal damnation.

Another heavenly voice (not one of the angels) proclaims the righteous dying during the great tribulation will rest, be blessed, and be rewarded for their works. These righteous will also be guests at the marriage feast of the Lamb, and God the Father will offer them white garments washed in the blood of the Lamb, eternal life, and eternity in heaven. The second angel's message pronounces Mystery Babylon's fall.

The great tribulation has now reached a fateful point where it is impossible for people to straddle the fence concerning their love for God. Everyone has to choose sides, and those choosing God face a death sentence through beheading or starvation. Those choosing expediency temporarily preserve their physical lives but die the second death in the lake of fire. Now, people must reveal their true nature (righteous or wicked). This theme continues throughout the rest of Revelation 14 and includes God's great harvest and the winepress of his wrath. These events also sift the wicked from the righteous.

The Great Harvest of Wheat and Tares

Section reference: Revelation 14:14-19.

God follows the three angels' ultimatum with actions. First comes the great harvests and then the winepress of God's wrath. Through these, God actively culls out and punishes the wicked. The great harvest features the Son of Man and an angel using separate sickles to harvest the earth's people. Jesus Christ harvests the righteous in the first harvest while wearing a crown for the first time in Revelation. Interestingly, this is a stephanos crown, not the royal diadema crowns worn by the dragon (Revelation 12:3); the beast (Revelation 13:1); and in the future, Jesus himself (Revelation 19:12).[7] Stephanos crowns serve several New Testament purposes, not the least of which are the rewards of the righteous and Jesus' crown of shame (crown of thorns) at his crucifixion.

Jesus reaps his harvest from the same place he met his bride at the rapture: the clouds. He has again left heaven to come to the earth and like the rapture, does not set foot on it. Unlike Revelation 10's mighty angel, Jesus does not wear the clouds but sits on them. When it is time

to reap, an angel comes out of the temple and commands Jesus to use his sickle. Which angel directs Jesus? It would seem natural to assume it is either God the Father or the Holy Spirit since they are God and, therefore, Jesus' equal. Since it is an angel, it is natural to identify him as Revelation 10's mighty angel, but there is simply not enough information.

The second harvest is carried out by two other angels and immediately follows Jesus' harvest. One angel, the grim reaper, carries a sickle and waits for the other angel's command. This last angel is in charge of fire, suggesting he is in charge of the gates of hell and the lake of fire. Jesus taught of these harvests in several places, including Mark 4:26-29 and Matthew 13:24-30. In Matthew 13:24-30, he focused on two harvests: wheat and tares. As he explains in Matthew 13:37-43, this kingdom of heaven parable shows God the Father sowing good seed (wheat) while his enemy, Satan, plants bad seed (tares). In their early growth stages, wheat and tares are virtually indistinguishable. To protect the wheat, God ordered his servants to let both grow to maturity in the fields. When harvested, the wheat goes into God's barn (heaven) while the wicked are burned. Now in the great tribulation, this parable finally comes into focus. Satan has tainted God's fields with the seeds of sin, and God let the good and bad seed grow to maturity when their differences become obvious.

Joel 3:12-14 gives not only a description of this harvest but also its location: the valley of Jehoshaphat (also know as the valley of Megiddo). This valley of decision is the same location as the battle of Armageddon, one of the most identifiable events of the great tribulation. The harvest and the valley of decision are alternate names and descriptions of this war.

Winepress of God's Wrath

Section reference: Revelation 14:19-20.

Revelation 14 ends with the terrible winepress of God's wrath, which crushes the second harvest's wicked into juice. The juice of the  wicked flows so widely that at its peak, following Jesus' return in Revelation 19:15, it floods an area spanning 200 miles and reaching depths of four to five feet throughout the valley of Megiddo. Isaiah 63:1-6 shows Jesus returning from Bozrah in red apparel after treading this winepress by himself. Just prior to his return in Revelation 19:15, Jesus wears white garments. Now, however, his clothing has been stained red from his gruesome work in treading God's winepress of wrath and wading in its juices (men's blood). Why is he coming from Edom? After he has eliminated the threats against them, Jesus rescues them from the place protecting the Jews in the wilderness (Revelation 12). An interesting side point to note from this story is the contrast of people's blood staining Jesus' clothing while in the fifth seal, Jesus' blood removes stains from people's clothing.

Wheat in the Barns

Section reference: Revelation 15:1-8.

Revelation 15 commingles warnings of the seven vial judgments' impending doom and descriptions of the great harvest's  wheat (saints) in the barn (heaven). Their joint presence indicates the harvest continues throughout the vial judgments. The wheat's victories over great tribulation foes (the beast, his image...) proves they are the great harvest's martyrs. The sea of glass mingled with fire shows they are from the sea of humanity, overcome tribulation (fire), and obtained peace with God (glass). They now sing a song that is a combination of the song of Moses and the song of the Lamb. This suggests they have the hope and promises of both covenants and likely include Jew and Gentile. Their song looks forward to the end of God's judgments and Jesus' earthly return when they declare all will fear God and all nations shall worship Jesus.

The Seven Vial Judgments: God's Wrath of Subjugation

Revelation 15's warnings of the seven vial judgments' impending doom introduces God's last plagues in the form of seven golden vials. These vials of wrath start the last of the full tribulation's themes: subjugation. They are not just the last plagues of the great tribulation but also God's last plagues ever. In Revelation 5, the prayers of pretribulation saints filled golden vials, but now these vials overflow with God's wrath. Is there a correlation between the prayers of the saints and the wrath of God? Romans 12:18-21 provides a clue: Christians are to overcome evil with good and at no time are they to take vengeance or wrath on their enemies. Instead, this is to be left to God. As Revelation 16:5-7 shows, eventually God converts the prayers of the saints (including their trials and tribulations) into his wrath and avenges his saints. Here, the angel testifies God changes their water into blood because of the blood of the saints and prophets they have shed. If there is any doubt about the appropriateness of the wrath of God, the voice of the Holy Spirit from the altar (Revelation 16:7) should dispel it, as he testifies the wrath from the vials is both true and righteous. The good news is this is the end of God's plagues on humanity and the end of "acts of God," diseases, insect invasions, darkness, scorching heat, contaminated water, meteorites, or any other type of plague. The bad news is these judgments are more horrific than any previously seen.

When the vial judgments are completed, God's wrath, which Romans 1:18 shows is always directed at the wicked, is finally appeased. They also fulfill Psalm 110:1, where God the Father directs his son to sit at his right hand until his enemies are subdued. These plagues and God's wrath strike through the kings of the earth, wound the heads (leaders) of many countries, and judge the heathen (Psalm 110:6). Consistent with the winepress of God in Revelation 14, the bodies of the heathen fill many places in the earth.

As the angels receive the golden vials, God's heavenly temple fills with the smoke of his power. In a scene reminiscent of the dedication of Solomon's temple in Jerusalem when the glory of God filled it and prevented people from entering (1 Kings 8:10-11), the heavenly temple opened after Jesus' coronation is now inaccessible while God pours out his wrath. Heaven's inhabitants cannot reenter the temple until the smoke clears on the end of the plagues and the appeasement of God's wrath.

God's Judgment Poured Out: The First Five Vials

Section reference: Revelation 16:1-11.

God commands the angels individually to pour out their vials. At the end of both the fourth and fifth vial judgment plagues, there is a pause while God checks to see if the wicked have repented. These are the last of three times God checks for people's repentance (the first was after the sixth trumpet). Both times, God finds they not only have not repented but instead have continued their blasphemies. Without their repentance, God continues to pour out vials until humanity has suffered their full force. Some may wonder whether God is at liberty to forego the remaining judgments since these prophesies are already recorded and they must be completely fulfilled to meet God's standard of prophetic accuracy. While this apparent conflict between God's foreknowledge and people's freedom of choice has perplexed scholars throughout history, a simple way of viewing this specific quandary is to treat Bible prophecies as historical records of historical facts. Had the facts been differ-ent, then the record would reflect these differences. In other words, if in the future humanity did repent, then the prophets would not have foretold the battle of Armageddon. God's fore-knowledge is so complete that people's free will cannot com-promise it.

Only those with the mark of the beast suffer the judgments of the first vial: body sores that are both ugly and painful. This incident is similar to Exodus 9:8-11, where Moses inflicted the Egyptians with a plague of boils. It is possible the sores will be the same boils inflicted on the Egyptians, though some suggest the sores may be an adverse reac-tion from the mark of the beast.

The second and third vials turn water into blood. One vial affects fresh water and the other salt water. This is at least the third time in biblical history and the second time in the seven-year tribulation that water is turned into blood. The first time was in Exodus 7:17-21 when the Egyptians were afflicted. The sec-ond time was during the trumpet judgments, when a third of the waters became blood. This time, God turns all fresh and saltwater into blood and he destroys every creature living in the waters.

The fourth vial judgment causes the sun to become so hot it scorches people, literally threatening their lives. Some have suggested this is the result of a supernova, and others have sug-gested it may be due to damage to the atmosphere's ozone layer.

The fifth vial judgment is a plague of darkness, and the angel pours it out on two places: the seat of power of the beast and his kingdom. Most likely, this darkness covers both Mystery Babylon and his basis of power, the ten-ruler confederation. This plague may be the catalyst God uses to turn the ten nations against the antichrist and, more importantly, Mystery Babylon. Somehow, the

darkness is so painful people bite their tongues; but even then, they still do not repent. This is another plague the Egyptians suffered (Exodus 10:21-23), but there was no evidence of this kind of pain associated with the Egyptian's darkness. If the source of the darkness is some form of caustic, airborne pollution, it might explain the

pain. As with so many mysteries in prophecies, the cause of this darkness remains a mystery.

The Sixth Vial: The Call to Destruction

Section reference: Revelation 16:12-16.

Only after God gives people one last chance to repent does he instruct the sixth angel to pour his vial. This vial irrevocably sets in motion a chain of events leading up to the climatic battle of Armageddon and Jesus' return. The effects

of the last two vials are so horrific and far-reaching that God checked twice to be certain they were necessary. Instead of repentance and acceptance of their new king, he finds hardened, unrepentant hearts cursing God. When the angel pours out the sixth vial, there are no more chances.

The sixth vial prepares the battlefield for the great tribulation's final climatic battle. It starts with the preparation of the earth for the deployment of the armies of the kings of the east (probably, those seen in the sixth trumpet). For these armies, the most formidable obstacle appears to be the Euphrates River, which this vial judgment dries up. When the path is clear, the unholy trinity calls

the nations to the battle's assembly area: Armageddon. Three unclean spirits coming from each member of the unholy trinity gather the armies of the world. This battle is Satan's last desperate attempt to annihilate Israel. The unholy trinity and their legions gather all nations (Revelation 16:14, Isaiah 13:4, Psalm 2:2, Isaiah 29:7, Zephaniah 3:8, Zechariah 14:2, Micah 4:11) and people of all tongues (Isaiah 66:18) of the world to fight against Israel. These nations fight against not only Israel but also God's authority and laws (Psalm 2:3). They first camp at Armageddon before they lay siege against Jerusalem and build military structures (Isaiah 29:3).

Isaiah 29:5-7 describes the armies as a multitude of invaders like fine dust, chaff, and a horde. This suggests a multitude so large that it is as hard to count as individual particles of dust. The number of troops involved makes all other wars pale in comparison (even the war of the sixth seal). To put this in perspective, Alexander's dominating armies ranged in size from twenty to sixty thousand. World War II had millions of combatants. This war has hundreds of millions, perhaps billions, of soldiers. Moving armies of this size is a formidable task. Even with modern transports, the movement of troops will be a slow, time-consuming task. In the Second World War, much of the troop movement for the Germans was by foot. It is likely that many of the troops (especially those in the 200-million-man army) in this final war will also deploy through marching. If this is the case, then the elimination of obstacles like the Euphrates River could substantially reduce both the difficulty and time needed to deploy the armies. If marching is involved, the process of assembling the armies could require a fair amount of time to complete. The final assembly of the armies sets the stage for the final vial judgment: the battle of Armageddon.

As the nations gather for war, Jesus pleads once more for people to turn to him. He reminds them that he comes as a thief in the night, unannounced, unexpected, and unwanted. This is an urgent plea since he will soon

Vial 6: The Call to Destruction

return during the battle of Armageddon, the war of the seventh vial judgment. Just as Jesus warned the churches of Sardis and Laodicea to get garments, Jesus now warns those on earth to keep their cloths so their nudity does not shame them when he returns. Just as Jesus warned the church of Sardis to watch because he returns as a thief at an unknown time, Jesus now warns those on earth to watch for the same reason. His reference to himself as a thief coming at any time, day or night, makes sense when given prior to the rapture. It is surprising to see the same reference just prior to battle of Armageddon when so many indicators can narrow his second coming to a very small window of time. However, the association of Jesus as a thief with the second coming does not appear to be in conflict with Luke 12:36-40, where the Lord returns after the wedding to get an accounting from his servants—a clear reference to Jesus' second coming. He warns he will return for this accounting as a thief. It appears Jesus referred to both the rapture and his second coming when he compared his arrival to a thief. Even with the detailed warnings and timeframes in Daniel and Revelation, Jesus' return catches many, Jew (servant) and Gentile, unaware and by surprise.

The Last Vial: It Is Done

Section reference: Revelation 16:17.

Once the armies assemble at Armageddon, God allows the last angel to pour out the last plague. When this vial runs its course, virtually all of God's punishments, curses, and plagues will end. While some curses, like mortality, will remain, no new ones will be added, and the effects of the remaining ones will be eased (e.g., lifespans increased to hundreds of years). Emphasizing the finality of this event, an unidentified voice from inside heaven's temple proclaims, "It is done." Since these are God the Father's plans, the voice is likely his. God's judgments and anger will now be satisfied and appeased. Never again will God plague or curse humanity, the earth, the beast of the fields, the fowls of the air, or the fish of the sea.

This vial judgment has many components, including the unleashing of the troops gathered by the sixth vial. The battle of Armageddon breaks out in Revelation 16:17 and does not finish until Jesus has completely vanquished his enemies upon his return in Revelation 19. The time between emptying the last vial and the end of the war is very active with several distinct scenes (each covered separately):

1. the beginning of the battle (Revelation 16:18-21)

2. the revealing of Mystery Babylon (Revelation 17)

3. the destruction of Mystery Babylon (Revelation 18)

4. the celebration in Heaven (Revelation 19:1-6)

5. the wedding feast (Revelation 19:7-10)

6. Jesus and his armies assemble for war (Revelation 19:11-16)

7. the end of the wars: Jesus' return and God's supper (Revelation 19:17-21)

The Battle of Armageddon Begins

Section reference: Revelation 16:18-21.

The seventh vial introduces a series of "acts of God" as great or greater in their scope and effect as any previously seen throughout the entire seven-year tribulation. These catastrophes may be a direct result of the armies' vengeance, "acts of God," or both. While these verses provide no direct evidence of the beginning of the battle of Armageddon, the following imply its start:

- the sixth vial's troop movements

- the seventh vial's massive destruction

- the fall of many cities in many nations (presumably by force)

- the backlash against Mystery Babylon (Revelation 18)

- the absence of any clear war descriptions prior to Jesus' return (Revelation 19)

A large portion of Old Testament prophecy deals unambiguously with this battle, and these passages form the basis for the battle's descriptions.

To fully appreciate and understand the devastation unleashed by this vial, it is first necessary to explore this part of the seven-year

The Battle of Armageddon Starts

tribulation in general terms. The Bible uses several unique terms to describe the seventh vial's time:

- day of destruction (Isaiah 13:6)
- cruel day with both wrath and fierce anger (Isaiah 13:9)
- day of distress and trouble (Zephaniah 1:15)
- day of devastation and ruin (Zephaniah 1:15)
- day of God's anger (Zephaniah 1:15)

While each of these applies to the seven-year tribulation as a whole, they are never any more valid than during the seventh vial's battle of Armageddon. It is a terrible time unlike anything before or after (Matthew 24:21; Mark 13:19). It is so bad that if left unchecked, no one would survive and over six billion people would perish. The devastation does not stop with people, as Zephaniah 1:2-3 indicates all life would die, including beast, fowl, and fish. Fortunately, motivated by God's compassion for his people (the Jews), Jesus' return interrupts (shortens) the seventh vial's effects and spares half of the earth's population. (Matthew 24:22; Mark 13:20).

By the end of the seventh vial's plague, God virtually eliminates sin and its corrupting effects. His jealousy and anger are clearly visible as he:

- subdues Jesus' spiritual and physical enemies (Hebrews 1:13)
- punishes sin:

- the world for their evil (Isaiah 13:11)
- the wicked for their iniquity (Isaiah 13:11)
- ends the arrogance of the proud (Isaiah 13:11, Isaiah 2:17)
- breaks the pride of the terrible (Isaiah 13:11)
- abolishes false gods and worship:
  - destroys hypocritical worshipers (Zephaniah 1:5)
  - removes the prophets and unclean spirits (Zechariah 13:2)
  - destroys those who worship false gods (Zephaniah 1:5)
  - abolishes idols (Isaiah 2:18, Zechariah 13:2, Zephaniah 1:3-5)
  - destroys idol worship (Zephaniah 1:3-5; 12:11)
- destroys men's confidence in the wealth of the world:
  - gold and silver will not save them (Zephaniah 1:18)
  - riches do not profit (Proverbs 11:4)
  - wealth fails (James 5:1-2)
  - wealth witnesses against its owners (James 5:3-5)
  - wealth consumes its owner (James 5:3-5)

People remaining on earth face two options: God's crushing wrath in his winepress or submission to Jesus' authority. God leaves no other options, and there is no compromising. They either learn the fear of the Lord (Proverbs 9:10) or perish because God's long-suffering patience has now ceased (2 Peter 3:9-10).

One of the key targets of God's wrath during this time is people's willful breaking of his first two commandments. The first of God's ten great commandments requires people have no other gods before him. The second demands people neither make idols or serve them. A single commandment summarizes the two: "And thou shalt love the Lord thy God with all thine heart, and with all thy soul, and with all thy might," (Deuteronomy 6:5). Despite these commandments, idol worship historically has flourished worldwide. Idols come in many shapes and sizes and are fabricated out of a variety of materials. Some of these idols are very elaborate and employ the most expensive materials, gems, and metals. Idol worship is so reprehensible to God that he sent his Old Testament prophets to tell the children of Israel to cease, desist, and repent from building and worshiping them. Even though many other aspects of Old Testament law never applied to them, Gentile Christians were commanded to avoid idols (Acts 15:19-20).

During the seventh vial judgment, God purges idols from the face of the earth. People's stubbornness makes the elimination of idols particularly painful. As shown in Revelation 9:20, even though plague after plague has afflicted the world's people, they refused to give up their idols. At this time in the seven-year tribulation, the citizens of the earth had already endured seven seal and six trumpet judgments, but clearly, these were not enough to eliminate idolatry. God's judgments will accomplish his goals (Zephaniah 2:11), and now they have run out of options. Isaiah 2:20-21 shows people flee to the rocks for the second time in the chapter. The first time they fled was during the sixth seal's war. Now they return as the battle of Armageddon rages. This time, they finally reject their idols and disperse them to places where they are lost forever. The fear of God is now so great that their financial loss is irrelevant and no attempt will be made to retrieve or recover the idols or even recycle their precious materials.

Reliance on money, another form of idol worship, is another key target of God's wrath. This disease is so prevalent in the last days it choked the life out the Laodicean church, and its allure is so strong Jesus warned his disciples against seeking and serving it (Matthew 6:24). Further, God declares this avarice (love of money) is the root of all evil (1 Timothy 6:10). God's hatred of avarice is seen in his condemnation of false balances, moved boundary markers, deceitful trading, and the cheating of widows and orphans (Micah 6:11, Isaiah 9:17). The bondage of sin cannot be completely broken until this love is shattered.

As people threw away their idols, the wealthy also throw away their riches because it does not protect them from God, satisfy their souls, or fill their bellies (Zephaniah 1:18, Ezekiel 7:19). As Abel's blood testified against Cain, their wealth testifies against them. It is the stumbling block of their iniquity, and it fuels the fire of God's jealousy. Only the wrath of God can drive people to rid themselves of all vestiges of their wealth.

What is so horrific about these judgments that people throw idols and wealth away like detestable garbage? The seventh vial's judgments give the first clues:

- the greatest, most devastating earthquake ever
- tremendous storms: voices, and thunders, and lightning
- huge hail

In particular, the earthquake is so devastating it divides Jerusalem into three parts, eradicates islands, and levels mountains. During the sixth seal's judgment, devastating earthquakes moved mountains and islands, but the seventh vial's judgments now destroys many of these same mountains and islands. Isaiah adds many details to the description of this earthquake: the earth shakes violently (Isaiah 24:19-20), it moves out of its place (Isaiah 13:13), and it shakes so violently it reels to and fro like a drunkard or as a hut blown in violent windstorms. These descriptions suggest God has knocked the earth out of its orbit and the earth rocks uncontrollably back and forth along its axis. The devastation caused by this is unimaginable, and Psalm 18:15 suggests the waters of the oceans and seas come crashing out of their banks, revealing the depths of the oceans. The earthquake utterly empties, wastes, turns upside down, spoils, mourns, languishes, and fades away the earth (devastates, ruins, mars, ransacks, dries up, shrivels, and withers) (Isaiah 24:1-5). The devastation is horrific and on a wider scale than any previously experienced.

Tremendous storms produce hailstones of unfathomable size: 75 to 100 pounds each (a Roman talent is generally accepted as 125 Roman pounds, each consisting of only 12 ounces). These storms are so great they shake the heavens (Isaiah 13:13) and darken the earth. It is so dark, no moonlight and very little sunlight reaches the earth (Isaiah 13:10). There are dark, thick clouds hanging over everything, creating dark and gloomy days (Zephaniah 1:15).

The battle of Armageddon's widespread impacts are every bit as devastating as these "acts of God." In Israel, the battle is primarily fought in the valley of Megiddo (Zechariah 12:11), which is the place of defeat of the last of the kings of David. It spreads to the point where the antichrist and the kings make war with the Lamb, Jesus Christ, as he returns (Revelation 17:14). Jerusalem is the focus of the war, as the antichrist apparently attempts a last act of defiance when he builds his palace on the glorious mountain where the temple of God and Jesus' rightful throne should be (Daniel 11:45). Here, the antichrist comes to his end, and no one will be willing or able to save him. God proves his preeminence as Jesus uses his brass feet of judgment to crush each member of the unholy trinity and all their armies (Revelation 1:15). God's anger and wrath is not limited to the antichrist but extends to all who help him. God destroys all nations gathering against Jerusalem, cuts them into pieces, and destroys their cities. The ringleading city, Mystery Babylon, will end up suffering the full brunt of God's wrath (Revelation 16:19). Other effects of the war include (see Jesus' return for additional details):

- the mighty ships and the ships of Tarshish are destroyed (Isaiah 2:16)

- the attacking army's horses are smitten with astonishment, madness, and blindness (Zechariah 12:3-9)

- people are scattered (Isaiah 24:1)

- people faint and their hearts melt away for fear (Isaiah 13:7-9)

- people's faces reflect pain and fear as sinners fall (Isaiah 13:7-9)

- hands will be feeble and knees as weak as water (Ezekiel 7:17)

- people burn and few are left (Zephaniah 1:18)

- happiness and joy ends (Isaiah 24:4-7)

- warriors cry out bitterly (Zephaniah 1:14)

- merchants are cut off and prominent people fade away (Zephaniah 1:11, Isaiah 24:4)

- new wine dries up (Isaiah 24:4-7)

- people's blood pours out as dust and their flesh as dung (Zephaniah 1:7-17)

- no one is left in the former seacoast of the Philistines, including Gaza (which will be forsaken) (Zephaniah 2:4-5), Ashkelon (which will be desolate), Ashdod (shall be driven out at noonday), and Ekron (which shall be rooted out) [possible birth-pang fulfillment]

- Moab and Ammon become as Sodom and Gomorrah with salt pits and a perpetual desolation (Zephaniah 2:6-10) [possible birth pang fulfillment]

- Ethiopians die by the sword (Zephaniah 2:12)) [possible sixth seal fulfillment]

The impact on Israel is equally devastating, as the war destroys the whole land of Israel (Isaiah 13:5). The ravages of war cause her to be drunk and stagger, but not due to the effects of alcohol (Isaiah 29:4-9). The men of Israel fall by the sword, and her proud women are humbled (Isaiah 3:16-25). Two-thirds of Israel's Jews perish before the seven-year tribulation ends (presumably mostly in this war), and the surviving third are refined and purified in the full tribulation's trials (Zechariah 13:8-9). Bread and water supplies fail (Isaiah 3:1-15). Thunder, earthquakes, great noise, storm, tempest, and fire consume her (Isaiah 29:4-9).

Israel's leaders who made the covenant with death come under God's wrath for leading the nation astray and stealing from the poor (Isaiah 3:1-15). God seeks out and destroys those who have turned their backs on him and those who have not sought him or his guidance (Zephaniah 1:6). He finds and punishes those who say in their hearts that God will neither reward nor punish. Some of their punishments include the theft of their wealth, the ruining of their houses, and the removal of their ability to enjoy the fruit of their labors (Zephaniah 1:12-13). Religious and secular leaders die, and this forces the Jews to turn to children and others equally unqualified for leadership (Isaiah 3:1-15). These unqualified leaders steer Israel astray, into confusion, and even further into God's wrath (Isaiah 3:1-15).

Israel experiences a time of spiritual blindness that impedes their efforts to escape God's judgments. They also suffer the effects of oppressive famine for God's Word that leaves no one in Israel who understands it (Amos 8:11-13).[8] The land intended to be the world's spiritual breadbasket with no shortage of scriptural knowledge instead suffers the ravages brought about by spiritual famine. Those entrusted with studying and understanding the Word of God are spiritually blind hypocrites who only pretend to love God (Isaiah 29:14-15). People search for understanding but find no one can expound God's Word to them (Isaiah 29:10-12). This spiritual darkness causes people to search everywhere for insights. Jesus warned them to be careful where they searched. He told them not to search for him in the desert or a secret place (Matthew 24:23-26, Mark 13:21-23, Luke 17:22-23). These warnings are primarily against the antichrist but also apply to all false prophets, false messiahs, and false teachers.

The war continues devastating humanity until it ends with Jesus' return. The next scene in this climatic act is the unveiling and destruction of Mystery Babylon.

Figure 21: Valley of Megiddo

Mystery Babylon Revealed

Earlier in the seventh vial's judgment, God promised "to give unto her [sic. Mystery Babylon] the cup of the wine of the fierceness of his wrath." The phrasing and images are curious. In Revelation 14, God uses his winepress of wrath on an unbelieving world to produce juices flowing several feet deep for hundreds of miles. This press extracts, filters, and concentrates this juice into a potent brew of God's wrath. Now, Mystery Babylon is forced to consume this dreadful concoction.

Mystery Babylon proclaims herself not only God's equal but also his superior when she says, "I am and none else beside me." She lives carelessly, fulfills all her desires, and lives in pleasure. She believes she will live and prosper forever because she places her trust in sorceries, enchantments, astrologers, multitudes of counselors, and prognosticators (Isaiah 47:7-13, Zephaniah 2:15). She leads other nations to follow in her ways, and she entices them into the intoxication caused by her cup's beverage, the cup of the wrath of God. God uses her wicked influence to destroy nations, kingdoms, armies, people, and rulers. While leading other nations astray, she shows the Jewish people no mercy and lays heavy burdens on them (Jeremiah 51:7-23, Isaiah 47:6). She hates the righteous and righteousness. Consequently, these people suffer greatly at her hands, but her day of reckoning has now come.

Mystery Babylon Destroyed

Section reference: Revelation 18:1-24.

Mystery Babylon's destruction starts with an unknown powerful angel (probably the Holy Spirit) lighting the earth with his glory and twice declaring God's judgment: Babylon's fall. Some believe the judgment's repetition emphasizes the certainty and completeness of the judgment. Others suggest the repetition declares judgments on both the religious and secular natures of Mystery Babylon. As already discussed, it most likely links the fall of Mystery Babylon to ancient Babylon.

As Mystery Babylon's fall recalls ancient Babylon's fall, ancient Babylon's fall forebode this moment. In Daniel 5:25-31, God judges the king of ancient Babylon for failing to measure up to God's standards. Twice the judgment of "MENE" is pronounced. These judgments declared the fall of his kingdom while foreshadowing Mystery Babylon's fall. This repetition not only unites both falls but also God's destruction of the golden head through the feet of clay in Nebuchadnezzar's vision (Daniel 2).

Prior to Mystery Babylon's destruction, God again calls his people out of danger (Revelation 18:4) as he did prior to destroying Sodom (Genesis 19:15-  16) and flooding the earth (Genesis 7). Here, the evacuation orders come from a voice emanating in heaven and is yet another in a sequence of supernaturally delivered messages: Revelation 14's three angels, Revelation 12's coronation proclamation, Revelation 10's mighty angel, and Revelation 16's "It is done" declaration. People have proposed various technology systems as the delivery vehicles for these messages. These ideas may prove correct, but the simple readings suggest God and the angels speak directly to people on earth. God's interaction with people during Jesus' first coming reinforces this possibility, as angels proclaimed Jesus' birth directly to shepherds (Luke 2:8-20) and God spoke from heaven at Jesus' baptism (Matthew 3:16-17).

Once the righteous are safely out of harm's way, God's judgment engulfs Mystery Babylon. As God punished Israel double for her sins (Isaiah 40:2), now God inflicts a double punishment on Mystery Babylon. This punishment will be dreadful because her sins have been boundless. As a golden cup in God's hand, she has actively led nations astray and driven them mad (Jeremiah 51:7). Her corrupting influence has extended to the farthest parts of the earth, but now God forever breaks her control over her enemies, particularly Israel, and removes the burdens she forced on them (Isaiah 14:25). Jerusalem's cup of trembling is now transferred to Mystery Babylon (Isaiah 51:22-23).

Mystery Babylon believes herself to be a queen who will never be a widow, but now her destruction comes suddenly, in one day. Revelation 18:10 and 18:17 narrow this window of time from one day down to one hour. The plagues she suffers in this hour include: death, mourning, famine, and being utterly burned with fire (also Matthew 22:7, Jeremiah 51:25). God uses the ten kings behind the beast's power to punish Mystery Babylon, including making her desolate, making her naked, eating her flesh, burning her with fire (Revelation 17:16), leaving her childless (Isaiah 47:9), making her a widow (Isaiah 47:9), sweeping her with destruction (Isaiah 14:23, Jeremiah 51:26), and breaking her into a heap of ruins (Jeremiah 51:37).

God adds to Mystery Babylon's woes by causing the seas to swell and inundate her (Jeremiah 51:42). It is difficult to comprehend the thoroughness of God's vengeance on her until one understands both its devastating quickness and long-term fallout. The reactions of Mystery Babylon's lovers give insights into both (Revelation 18:9-19). This passage shows three groups of mourners: kings, merchants, and shipmasters (those in ships, sailors, traders). Table 23 shows the reactions of each group to her demise. All have enjoyed her wealth and lascivious living but observe and mourn from a distance. Their delay in rendering aid suggests either crippling fear or physical restraints. Their cries attest to both the speed and thoroughness of her destruction, as each testifies that God completed this work in the astoundingly short time of a single hour.

Table 23: Reactions to Mystery Babylon's Demise

Kings	Merchants	Shipmasters
Stand far off	Stand far off	Stand far off
Bewail her	Weep	Cried, Weep, and Wail
Lament for her	Mourn	Cast dust on their heads
		Cries out "What city is like unto this great city!"
Cry out "Alas, alas that great city Babylon, that mighty city! For in one hour is thy judgment come."	Cry out "Alas, alas, that great city, that was clothed in fine linen, and purple, and scarlet, and decked with gold, and precious stones, and pearls! For in one hour so great riches is come to nought."	Cries out "Alas, alas, that great city, wherein were made rich all that had ships in the sea by reason of her costliness! For in one hour is she made desolate."
	No longer buy her merchandise	
	Fear for her torment	

Among the reactions in Table 23 is the archaic English phrase of "alas, alas," which is an exclamation of sorrow, pity, regret, or worry. These phrases come from the same Greek word, ouai (Strong's G3759), that woe came from in the great woe judgments of the fifth, sixth, and seventh trumpets. In other words, all three cry out, "Woe! Woe!" With these statements, they not only confirm Babylon has fallen by God's judgment but also that this is Babylon's second fall.

These verses show the diversity of Mystery Babylon's merchandise, including everything from the necessities of life (food and clothing) to expensive luxuries. Mystery Babylon's list of merchandise combined with the history of the ancient city of Rome provides additional clues to Mystery Babylon's character. At Rome's height of power and glory, her harbor continually overflowed with ships unloading their cargo: merchandise and slaves. The ships came in full but generally left empty. Rome consumed the world's wealth and confiscated the best its empire had to offer. By contrast, Jesus' royal city, Jerusalem, will produce and export wealth to all nations of the earth throughout his earthly reign. Rome took from people, and Jesus' Jerusalem gives to people. Rome enslaved people, and, from Jerusalem, Jesus frees people. The contrast is striking, and it demonstrates the difference between Satan's governmental systems and God's perfect government.

Revelation 18 concludes by listing long-term results of Mystery Babylon's destruction and commanding all who have suffered at her hands to rejoice because he has (now past tense) avenged their suffering, including the deaths of prophets and saints. The lingering effects of her punishment include:

- the voice of harpers, musicians, pipers, and trumpeters shall not be heard in her

- no craftsman shall be found in her

- the sound of a millstone (the miller) shall not be heard in her

- the light of a candle shall not shine in her

- the voice of the bridegroom and of the bride shall not be heard in her (dual reference to people getting married in the city and Jesus and his bride, the church)

- she becomes a habitation of devils and every foul spirit (Revelation 18:2)

- she becomes a dwelling place of dragons (Jeremiah 51:37)

- she becomes home to unclean and hateful birds (Revelation 18:2, Isaiah 13:21, Zephaniah 2:14)

- wild beasts will perpetually live in her
  (Isaiah 13:21, Zephaniah 2:14)

- she will never be inhabited again
  (Isaiah 13:20; Isaiah 14:21-22)

- nomads will not live in her (tents, etc.)
  (Isaiah 13:20, Jeremiah 51:29)

- no one will even pass by her (Jeremiah 51:43)

- she remains desolate forever (Jeremiah 51:26)

- she shall be as Sodom and Gomorrah (Isaiah 13:19)

- she becomes a dry land, a wilderness (Jeremiah 51:43)

- pools of stagnant water cover her land (Isaiah 14:23)

- smoke rises up forever from her (Revelation 19:3)

In short, Mystery Babylon is totally wasted, with nothing left. The land is abandoned and will lay waste forever as no one—not even nomads—will ever live there. Only the wildest animals will ever be found there. Even during Jesus' reign, when Jesus heals the rest of the earth (except Edom) from the ravages of sin, Mystery Babylon continues to lie in this state of ruin. One of the more surprising aspects of the desolation of Babylon is that it becomes the home of devils. Their leader, Satan, spends the next millennium in the bottomless pit, but the Bible is silent about the fate of his legions. It appears that, without their leader guiding their actions, they spend the time of Jesus' reign wandering aimlessly among Mystery Babylon's ruins.

The Celebration in Heaven

Section reference: Revelation 19:1-6.

Mystery Babylon's fall is cause for heavenly celebration. Again, the twenty-four elders and four beasts lead great multitudes in worshiping God. The worship reaches a crescendo not seen in the New Testament as Alleluia, which means praise God or praise Jehovah, is proclaimed at least four times. The praises start with a tremendous multitude lifting their voices in unison as though uttered by a single person. To the elder's threefold blessing of Revelation 4:11, they add Alleluia and salvation. Salvation appears only three times in the book of Revelation: after the tribulation saints victory over death (Revelation 7:10), after the victory over Satan (Revelation 12:10), and now after the victory over the whore.

Next, the twenty-four elders and four beasts praise God for the fourth and last time in Revelation. Later, they will be spectators when the 144,000 sealed Jews sing a new song in heaven. Their praises this time are simply, "Amen. Alleluia." The last worship scene involves great multitudes who are called to worship by a voice from the throne, likely the Holy Spirit, calling the hosts of heaven to praise God. The great multitude speaks in unison, again sounding like a single majestic voice that gives thanks that God still reigns and then calls all to celebrate because the wedding feast has finally arrived. They call all to honor the father of the groom, God, and proclaim the bride has made herself ready. They make no mention of the groom's preparedness because he had to be prepared before her arrival.

The Wedding and Marriage Supper

Section reference: Revelation 19:7-10.

The Lamb's marriage has finally arrived! It and the subsequent marriage supper are the last remaining timeline events in Revelation prior to Jesus' return. Revelation 19:7 announces the Lamb's formal marriage ceremony. Revelation 19:8 shows his bride prepared for the wedding. Revelation 19:9 shows the marriage supper's festivities, indicating the marriage ceremony is now past.

Prior to the wedding, Jesus' bride had to prepare herself. Esther 2:9-12 hints at some of these preparations by the ritual purification she passed through before her royal marriage. Likewise, the bride of Christ needs purifying before her marriage to be cleansed from all her impuri-

The Lamb's Wedding

ties (Ephesians 5:26-27, 1 John 1:7, Revelation 1:5). Once cleansed, she needs the proper wedding attire, which she received at the crown and raiment judgments (Revelation 3:5, Revelation 3:18, Revelation 4:4). Her white linen garments speak of her righteousness and purity[9] and are reminiscent of the Old Testament's priestly garments (suggesting the church's priesthood). Now the bride is ready, and heaven celebrates the most spectacular wedding in history. The contrast between heaven and earth is stunning, as the dreadful battle of Armageddon rages on earth while in heaven people are celebrating the Lamb's marriage and enjoying the greatest marriage festivities of all time.

Likely lasting several days, God stages a terrific celebratory marriage supper immediately following the wedding. As an Old Testament example, Leah's wedding festivities lasted a week (Genesis 29:27). Many believe the marriage supper occurs on earth after Jesus' return, but the marriage supper can only occur on earth if the wedding and marriage supper occur in two different places, separated by days, weeks, months, or even years. Not only is it difficult to find precedence for this in either the ancient or modern worlds but it also stands in direct contradiction to Leah's wedding and Jesus' teaching that the wedding occurs before his return (Luke 12:36).

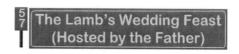

The Lamb's Wedding Feast (Hosted by the Father)

Additionally, when Jesus and his saints return to earth, the transition of power will require so much of the new rulers' time and effort that it seems unlikely that festivities of this sort are possible for several months. The guests of the marriage supper and their blessings offer additional difficulties to the idea that God holds the marriage supper on earth. Matthew 22:1-14 shows the king (God) prepares a grand feast (supper) for both the wedding parties and the wedding guests. Prepared in the location of the wedding (the king's land), it is ready at the guest's expected arrival. Since the food is ready to serve, extended delays in the guests' arrival could ruin the meal. This shows the king prepared the food in his land prior to the wedding and shows the marriage supper immediately follows the wedding. This is consistent with Revelation 19:7-9, where both the Lamb's wedding and the subsequent feast occur in heaven.

When the feast is ready (implying the readiness of both the bride and groom), the king sends for the wedding's guests. His servants go out several times to fetch them. At first, the invitees ignore the servants, but later, they ridicule them while going back to their moneymaking activities (demonstrating the love of money so prevalent in end-time prophecies). Finally, the invitees physically abuse and kill the servants. The king's unbridled anger provokes him to send his armies to destroy the murderers and burn their city to the ground prior to the wedding. Next, the king sends his servants to search the highways and byways for replacement guests, delaying the wedding pending their arrival. Likewise for the Lamb's wedding, God delays Jesus' wedding, as he sends his armies to destroy Mystery Babylon and her inhabitants. Further delays occur while his servants seek replacement guests worthy to attend the wedding: the tribulation and great tribulation saints.

As the wedding guests arrive, the king furnishes them with the proper wedding attire. In a tremendous display of disrespect, one of the guests refuses to wear the garments provided by the king, and the king has him thrown out of the wedding hall. Likewise, in heaven, God the Father furnishes each full-tribulation saint wedding guest with appropriate wedding attire as they arrive. These heavenly garments are particularly precious because Jesus' blood has cleansed and prepared them. However, one of the wedding guests for Jesus' wedding is not wearing the furnished wedding garment. When God the Father sees him, he demands an explanation, but when the guest fails to respond, God expels him to hell. This particularly troubling portion of Scripture has perplexed Christians throughout the church age. How can a guest be worthy enough to be in heaven yet still go to hell? The messages of Revelation 14's three angels contain some clues. Their messages were very simple: turn to God and reject the unholy trinity. There is no mention of Jesus or his blood. It is conceivable someone could follow the angel's admonitions and die without having first accepted Jesus as Lord and Savior. Since they rejected the antichrist, his image, and his mark according to the angel's preaching, their souls would probably go to heaven, where God would offer them their wedding garments (Jesus' salvation). While most guests gratefully accept these precious garments, at least one refuses it. Why would he refuse to wear them? Perhaps he objects to Jesus' blood washing his garments clean, he believes Jesus is just a man or a false prophet, or he feels it is sacrilege to wear anything associated with Jesus. Regardless, his refusal guarantees his expulsion from heaven.

What a tragic picture! This guest was able to see, touch, feel, and enjoy the blessings of heaven but winds up spending eternity in the lake of fire. These rejected guests are unique among the lake of fire's residents since the rest of its human occupants never spend any time in heaven but instead go directly to hell, where they await their final judgments. Imagine spending eternity in the lake of fire after first spending some time in heaven. Imagine the thoughts of regret these condemned people harbor as they suffer day after day without hope or relief. Their regrets could only magnify their agony as they get to spend eternity contemplating their rejection of Jesus.

This leaves the question of the identity of God's servants. Are they Revelation 14's three angels? No. These angels are not beaten or killed. Can they be the 144,000? No. God's seal protects and keeps them alive until Jesus' return. Probably, they are the unprepared virgins of Matthew 25:1-13. Ten virgins comprise this wedding party (normally comprised of only relatives and close friends of the bride and groom): five anxiously anticipating the wedding who made sure they were prepared and five who were indifferent and unprepared. When the groom's call came, the five prepared virgins met him and entered the marriage hall while the unprepared five scrambled to find lamp oil to burn for light. These delays cost them the opportunity to meet the groom and enter the marriage hall. The lamp's oil is symbolic of the

Holy Spirit while the lamp's light is Jesus, the light of the world. The prepared five virgins are born-again, filled with the Spirit of God, and Jesus illuminates their paths. The unprepared five virgins are not born-again, do not have their lamps filled with the Spirit of God, and do not have Jesus lighting their paths. The rapture happens so quickly that the unprepared five virgins do not have time to fill their lamps. Recognizing that the groom will not leave without his bride, the virgins cannot represent the bride and must, therefore, be the wedding party. The Jews are a natural fit for the virgins since, as the wife of God, they would be close relatives who would be part of the bridal party. They are also partly saved and partly unsaved and therefore partly ready for the rapture. When the rapture occurs, some Jews will be taken to heaven while others will be locked out and forced to face the seven-year tribulation unprotected on earth.

The millennial reign chapter shows God leaves his servants (the Jews) in charge of his estate. Likely, these Jews are God's great tribulation servants who invite the replacement guests. During the seven-year tribulation, God's servants invite guests to the wedding. Just for extending the invitation, the rest of the world hates, beats, and kills many of them.

Summarizing, the Lamb's marriage and its subsequent marriage supper both occur in heaven after the destruction of Mystery Babylon but prior to Jesus' return. In the rapture, Jesus gets his bride (the Gentile church) and the wedding party (the Jewish church). He invites multitudes, but many prove themselves unworthy, and God destroys both them and their city, Mystery Babylon. God sends his servants (the Jews left on earth) out to find and invite new guests (martyred full-tribulation saints). The Father gives them proper wedding apparel, but some refuse to wear it, and the Father casts them into hell. With the arrival of the guests, the wedding proceeds, and all heaven celebrates its completion by enjoying a spectacular wedding feast.

This section of Revelation ends with something very curious. Overcome by the sights of the vision, John, Jesus' beloved disciple, tries to worship a fellow servant. The servant rebukes John because he should worship God alone. Even after this rebuke,

John will attempt to worship his fellow servant again (Revelation 22). It is not clear why John feels compelled to worship, but this should serve as a warning to all Christians. If John, the beloved disciple, can slip into this error, then everyone is vulnerable.

Jesus Prepares for War

Section reference: Revelation 19:11-16

The scene in heaven quickly moves from the marriage celebration to preparation for war. Now, John sees the leader of the heavenly armies and identifies him as:

- Faithful
- True
- a name written that no man knew but he himself
- the Word of God
- King of kings
- Lord of lords

There can be no doubt that this is Jesus Christ. Revelation 17:14 also calls him Faithful, King of kings, and Lord of lords. Likewise, John 1 calls him the Word of God, and in Revelation 3:7, he calls himself True. In Revelation 1, his names (Alpha and Omega, First and Last) reflected his divinity. Now his names reflect his lordship. The reign of humanity is finally ending!

The details of Jesus' descriptions in Revelation 1 and Revelation 19 are very similar. Most details appear in both descriptions, but there are four notable exceptions. Missing in Revelation 19 is any mention of his feet, his voice, the stars in his right hand, or his countenance. His eyes remain a flame of fire, and the two-edged sword still comes out of his mouth, but now it is a sharp sword for smiting the nations. The two-edged sword of Revelation 1 is used to fight spiritual battles (Hebrews 4:12) while the sword of Revelation 19 strikes down and rules the nations. The swords in both places use the same Greek word (rhomphaia, Strong's G4501), suggesting they are the same swords. Some suggest Revelation 19's sword is a physical sword while Revelation 1's is spiritual, the Word of God (Ephesians 6:17). The lack of differentiation in the Greek makes this interpretation difficult. More likely, the difference in the swords is mainly how they are used. In Revelation 1, Jesus is calling people to repentance while in Revelation 19 he is ending their rebellion. In both cases, he completes his task with the words of his mouth and the power of the Spirit of God. As he prepares to rule with a rod of iron, he uses his sword to crush sin.

Jesus' white head and hair now hold many crowns, representing the many nations of Jesus' sovereignty. These are diadem crowns previously surreptitiously held by the dragon and the beast. He claims his rightful property and forcibly takes his dominions from the interlopers. In Revelation 1, Jesus wears a golden girdle identifying him as a prophet of the order of Elijah. Revelation 19 replaces this with writing on his clothing proclaiming him as "King of kings, and Lord of lords." Jesus, no longer a prophet, takes his rightful place as king. He prepares to take possession of his earthly throne, which he received after the seventh trumpet.

Revelation 1 showed Jesus among the seven candlesticks: the church. Revelation 19 shows him preparing for war with his bride. Where is the bride? They are on their horses as part of his army, and they are clothed in the garments of the righteous, which the Jesus gave them (Jude 1:14). This army also includes the angels of God and the saints of all ages (Matthew 25:31). Jesus takes his army with him as he completes the treading of the winepress of God's wrath, which began in Revelation 14.

John sees Jesus' clothing dipped in blood. Some suggest this represents the redemptive blood of Christ, but John does not tell how he knows Jesus' clothing was dipped in blood. If dipped in Jesus' blood, then the white garment remains white and no evidence of the dipping would exist. Additionally, Jesus and his clothing have no need of purification or cleansing from sin, so it is unlikely he would waste his own precious blood on himself. It is more likely this is the blood from the winepress of God's wrath. Isaiah 63:1-3 shows Jesus in red clothing after treading the winepress of God's wrath. Then, he is wearing the same garments, but they have become stained red by the blood of those crushed in the winepress. In heaven, Jesus' garments are only dipped with this blood. Soon, this blood saturates them as Jesus immerses himself in treading God's winepress.

The titles on Jesus' garments remove any questions about his authority. In Luke 12:13-14, people wanted Jesus to act as judge, but Jesus' response cut to the fundamental questions of authority. There were properly appointed judges for such matters, and Jesus was not one of them. In his first coming, Jesus came as a servant; even though he was the rightful heir to the throne of his earthly father, he had not yet received this kingdom (been coronated). What throne is that? It is the throne of David. As shown in Matthew 1, Jesus is the rightful king of Judah; having descended from the royal lineage and without offspring, the lineage ended with Jesus. Now Jesus returns with the full and complete authority of his heavenly Father's throne. As the rightful heir to the earth and the duly crowned king of all, Jesus now has final authority over everything and is judge over all.

The End of Wars and Jesus' Return

Section reference: Revelation 19:17-21.

The seven-year tribulation now comes to a climatic end with Jesus' return at the height of the battle of Armageddon. He brings the war to a swift and brutal conclusion, subjugates the rebellious armies, and rescues those locked away in the wilderness. The following sections liberally season Revelation's sparse descriptions of Jesus' return with other scriptural references to build as comprehensive a picture as possible. There are several scenes to the great tribulation's final act, including:

- the call to the supper of God (Revelation 19:17-18)
- Jesus' return
- the beast, the kings, and their armies fighting against Jesus (Revelation 19:19)
- the beast and the false prophet cast into the lake of fire (Revelation 19:20)

- Jesus defeats the world's armies by the sword of his mouth (Revelation 19:21)
- Satan thrown into the bottomless pit (Revelation 20:1-3)
- the Jews rescued from the wilderness[10]

Revelation 20 contains several transitional items (e.g., the judgment of nations and the division of the millennial government) that must occur before Jesus' reign is completely established. Except for Satan's entombment into the bottomless pit, these other scenes appear in the millennial reign chapter as part of the transition phase into Jesus' reign.

The Call to God's Supper

In heaven, the saints have just finished enjoying the Lamb's marriage feast prepared just for them by God the Father. On earth, God's supper is about to be served. He has also specially prepared it for his guests: all of the earth's birds. An angel standing in the sun invites these guests while God compels the source of their feast (the world's armies) to come to their slaughter. People from every ethnic group and every walk of life (great or small, bond [slave] or free) are served at this supper. God's supper is a vengeful feast where birds eat the meat of men and horses of the rebellious armies. Table 24 summarizes the striking contrast between the Lamb's marriage supper and God's supper.

Ezekiel expands on several aspects of God's supper, as every beast of the field also joins the birds in enjoying the feast and God apparently sends invitations to all wild creatures except those living in water (Ezekiel 39:17-20). These guests thoroughly enjoy themselves as the supper's pleasures overcome them. Beasts suffer from gluttony and the intoxicating effects of the juices coming from the winepress of God's wrath. It is probably good that these beasts enjoy themselves since it may be the last time any of them will ever taste meat or blood. During Jesus' reign, their diets are changed and they no longer kill each other, and this supper may end the carnivorous diets of most birds and beasts. Ezekiel also expands Revelation's list of animals served by

God. Where Revelation lists only horses, Ezekiel adds rams, lambs, goats, and bullocks.

God's Supper
(Host: Mighty Angel)

Table 24: Comparison: Lamb's Marriage Supper versus God's Supper

Lamb's Marriage Supper	God's Supper
everyone invited: great or small, bond (slave) or free	everyone invited: great or small, bond (slave) or free
Attendees receive blessings and eternal life	Attendees receive curses and eternal damnation
servants call the guests	an angel standing in the sun calls the guests
joyous celebration	vengeful feast
the guests are righteous people	the guests are birds
people ate the meat of animals	animals eat the meat of the wicked
many refused to attend	many attend under duress

As has been the case so often, the angel calling the guests to God's supper is unidentified. Many have suggested he is the same angel as the mighty angel in Revelation 5, 10, and 18 (verse 21). This is a possibility but seems unlikely since an adjective like mighty is missing. Possibly, it is simply one of God's legions of angels.[11]

In anticipation of God's supper, observers of end-time prophecies often scour headlines looking for evidence of increased bird populations or changes in migration patterns around Israel to show God has started calling the guests to this supper. If God calls the birds prior to the call in Revelation 19, the prophecies do not record it. It certainly is reasonable to assume God gathers the birds into the general vicinity prior to the call to the supper; but the first and only time the Bible shows God calling the birds is after the Lamb's marriage supper. Possibly, this call marks the onset of fighting in the valley of Jezreel, the start of the battle of Armageddon.

Jesus' Return

As Jesus returns, conditions on earth are miserable. The battle of Armageddon rages, and Mystery Babylon is a simmering ash heap. The Jews in Israel are suffering unmercifully, and the birds and beasts are flocking to God's supper. One last thing remains before Jesus can set foot on earth: the Jews on earth must call on him (Luke 13:35). Only the tremendous persecution of the battle of Armageddon causes this to occur. How bad will it have to be for the Jews to finally cry out to Jesus for deliverance? Clearly, it will have to be extremely desperate. The invaders will have captured Jerusalem and exiled half of the Jews throughout all nations of the world (Zechariah 14:2, Luke 21:24). They will be plundering the homes in Jerusalem, raping the Jewish women (Zechariah 14:2), and forcing their children into prostitution (Joel 3:3). Jewish military strongholds and cities will have fallen (Micah 5:10-11). Jerusalem will have depleted her food reserves, as her grain will have spoiled (shriveled and dried up), her storehouses will lay decimated, and her granaries will be demolished. Jerusalem's animals will groan, her cattle will have no pasture, and her flocks will be suffering (Joel 1:17-18). Nations, notably Israel, will be in distress and trembling (Isaiah 64:2).

Under this pressure, the Jews finally call out to God for their deliverance and the return of their Messiah (though they may not understand their Messiah is Jesus). From his temple, God hears the cries of the Jews and responds by shaking the earth at its foundations (Psalm 18:6-7, Habakkuk 3:6). Whether this is the earthquake of Revelation 18's seventh

Jesus' Return

vial judgment is not clear. While they are most likely the same, it is easy to argue to the contrary. Many references to this earthquake are scattered throughout the Bible. The most graphic describe the hills melting like wax at the presence of God (Psalm 97:5), the earth rising and falling like the Nile river (Amos 8:8), and the mountains flowing as molten wax/water down a slope (Micah 1:4). Other references to this earthquake include Joel 3:16, Haggai 2:6-7, Isaiah 64:1-3, Psalm 46:3, and Psalm 77:18.

© Pat Marvenko Smith - www.revelationillustrated.com

Several of these references also mention the heavens shaking as though being torn apart (Haggai 2:6-7, Isaiah 64:1). While this is probably Jesus' shaking of the powers of heaven (Luke

21:25-26, Matthew 24:29, Mark 13:24-25), some believe the shaking of the powers of heaven is a reference to God subduing of Satan and his demons. This interpretation seems unlikely since these references immediately precede descriptions of Jesus returning in all his glory and the dragon's defeat occurred at the beginning of the great tribulation. While the meanings of these passages may be unclear, they still convey the tremendous wonders taking place in the heavens just before Jesus' return. The stars falling from heaven is an especially confusing sign. It may refer to the light of the stars not making it to the earth or the stars appearing to move in the sky because the earth's axis is moving (the earth is wobbling like a drunkard). Regardless, the signs are so horrible that men's hearts are failing out of fear.

Darkness is a consistent theme in many references. Amos talks about the sun going down at noon and it being dark at midday on a clear day (Amos 8:9). He also describes it as very dark with no brightness (Amos 5:18-20). Isaiah describes it as a day of darkness and sorrow (Isaiah 5:30). Joel describes it as a day of gloominess, clouds, thick darkness (Joel 2:2), the sun and moon are darkened, and the stars withdraw their shining (Joel 2:10, Joel 3:15). Zephaniah repeats this description, calling it a day of wrath, a day of trouble and distress, a day of waste and desolation, a day of darkness and gloominess, and a day of clouds and thick darkness (Zephaniah 1:15). Psalm 18:9-11 and Psalm 97:2 portray similar pictures of darkness and gloominess. Psalm 77:17 adds the clouds pouring out water and the lightning creating a fierce show.

This is the backdrop for Jesus' return, a dark, gloomy day full of catastrophes on the earth, in the heavens, and on the sea. It is the day the bridegroom and his bride leave their private place (heaven) to return to the earth (Joel 2:16, Luke 12:36). While the bride accompanies her husband, the focus is on the groom. Jesus comes in a cloud with great power and glory (Matthew 24:30, Mark 13:26, Luke 21:27). He returns as lightning cometh from the east to the west (Matthew 24:27, Luke 17:24). His brightness (lightning) lights up the world, and his presence makes the earth tremble (Psalm 97:4, Psalm 77:18). Lightning originates from Jesus, attacking and striking terror into all of Jesus' enemies. He is bright as lightning, with lightning coming out of his hand (Habakkuk 3:4). The contrast of Jesus' brightness against the day's gloominess is overwhelming. His brightness causes the moon and sun to be ashamed (Isaiah 24:23). His glory fills the heavens, and his praise fills the earth (Habakkuk 3:3). This is the day where all see Jesus' glory, and on this day, the heavens declare Jesus' glory (Psalm 97:6).

Jesus comes with smoke coming out of his nostrils and fire out of his mouth (Psalm 18:8) to consume his enemies. In Revelation, Jesus has a sword coming out of his mouth; in Psalms, he has fire. Both are symbols for the Holy Spirit. Just as David went to battle Goliath without a sword, Jesus enters the battle without a sword in his hand; the only sword he carries is the Holy Spirit. For three and a half years (since his coronation), he has been restrained from returning and rescuing Israel (Daniel 10:12-13). Now he will no longer be restrained as he returns in great glory on the worst day in the history of the world to rescue the remaining Jews and subdue his enemies. As he returns, those on earth see him and have ample opportunity to prepare to welcome their new king. Instead, they choose to engage in a hopeless battle to the death—theirs.

The combination of Jesus' physical appearance, his actions, the various judgments hitting the earth, and the signs and wonders in the heavens strike abject terror into earth's rebellious citizens. Isaiah shows Zion's sinners are afraid (Isaiah 33:14), and Joel states people's faces are in pain before the armies of the Lord (Joel 2:6). His majestic arrival demonstrates his divinity and Lordship. No one on earth can doubt who he is as he steps onto the earth.

Jesus arrives on earth as he left, at Mount Olivet, just east of Jerusalem (Acts 1:11-12). As soon as he touches the mount, it splits in the middle to the east and to the west, creating a new valley. This valley is a place of refuge created to protect Jerusalem's remaining Jews. Instead of running from the earthquake,

Jerusalem's Jews run into the valley (Zechariah 14:4-5). While it is a day of God's vengeance (Isaiah 63:4), Jesus is careful to protect the righteous (Psalm 91:2-12). He delivers his people from their enemies (Habakkuk 3:13), who are cut off and beaten in pieces (Micah 4:13, 5:9). The battle in Israel occurs in the valley Megiddo. It is the valley of decision, and many are in it (Joel 3:14). The valley that saw the last king of Judah defeated and the reign of David's royal lineage end (2 Kings 23:30, 2 Chronicles 35:20-27) now sees the resumption of the reign of David's lineage and the long-awaited return of the Messiah.

The Beast, the Kings, and Their Armies Fight against Jesus

The approach of Jesus and his countless armies causes the antichrist, earth's kings and leaders, and all their armies to immediately break off their current engagements to marshal their forces against Jesus and his armies. Never have the fortunes of war changed so dramatically or quickly. The armies arrayed against Israel held an overwhelming, insurmountable advantage. Victory was certain but without warning, unanticipated and unknown allies of Israel have arrived and turned the tables. Israel's enemies are now hopelessly outnumbered and outgunned. One of the great ironies of this situation is great tribulation saints fill the ranks of Jesus' armies and the antichrist now faces people he recently beheaded.

 Rather than recognize the impossibility of their situation and retreating, the armies turn and fight against Jesus and his armies. Their judgment is certain, and their fate is sealed.

The Beast and the False Prophet Cast into the Lake of Fire

Jesus starts destroying his enemies by first striking their leaders—the one who is trying to steal Jesus' throne (the antichrist) and his enabler (the false prophet). Where the defeat of the enemy's leaders generally occurs last in human wars, this is where Jesus starts. In this case, Isaiah seems to suggest Jesus kills the antichrist (Isaiah 14:9), leaves his body to be trampled on the battlefield (Isaiah 14:19), and then resurrects him (Revelation 19:20) before casting him along with the false prophet into the lake of fire. The lake of fire is their permanent residence, and it is their distinction of infamy that they are its first and probably only occupants for a thousand years. This is their reward for their deceptions of humanity, their arrogant demand for worship, their attempt to usurp Jesus' throne, and their rebellion against God. Eventually, those who followed them will also join them in the lake of fire. For now, these members of the unholy trinity have to wait alone until the final judgments send Satan, the fallen angels, those who followed them during the seven-year tribulation, and all the wicked throughout the ages into the lake of fire.[12] Soon, Jesus will deal with the last member of the unholy trinity: Satan. His fate lies down a different path than that of the beast and the false prophet.

The Armies Defeated by Jesus and His Sword

With the leaders of the rebellion out of the way, Jesus now focuses on destroying the

remaining armies by the sword of his mouth. Jesus fights the battle, deploys his weapons, overturns kingdoms, and directs the operations of his forces. In great anger, he comes with chariots and uses fire to destroy them: "For by fire and by his sword will the Lord plead with all flesh: and the slain of the Lord shall be many." (Isaiah 66:16. See also Psalm 97:3, Isaiah 33:11.) Before he is done, wicked people burn like stubble (Malachi 4:1). The fire and the armies of God turn land that was like the garden of Eden into desolate wilderness (Joel 2:3). In addition to the fire, Psalm 18:12-14 shows Jesus using hailstones, coals of fire, arrows, and lightning bolts against the rebels. Jesus directs his armies with his voice (Joel 2:11, 3:16) and as Jeremiah describes, there is obviously great power in Jesus' utterances, for his voice sounds like a mighty roar and a shout (Jeremiah 25:30-31). Everyone on the entire earth hears his voice, as it discomforts and terrifies his enemies.

During this battle, Jesus repeats one of the miracles seen in Joshua's battles, as he commands the sun and moon to stand still until he concludes the battle (Joshua versus the Amorites in Joshua 10:11-14, Habakkuk 3:11). Zechariah describes a similar phenomenon:

6 2 Jesus Destroys World's Armies

> And it shall come to pass in that day, that the light shall not be clear, nor dark: But it shall be one day which shall be known to the Lord, not day, nor night: but it shall come to pass, that at evening time it shall be light.
>
> Zechariah 14:6-7

These verses are puzzling. Are they indicating the current day and night cycles end? Are they indicating that during this battle there is light everywhere in the world, without any demarcation of night and day? In light of the example of Joshua and the clear testimony of Habakkuk, these verses are probably giving additional insights into the day standing still while Jesus finishes treading the winepress of God's wrath.

The battle's results during this long day are devastating to Jesus' enemies:

- all nations coming against Jerusalem are destroyed (Zechariah 12:9, Zephaniah 3:6, Haggai 2:22)
- his enemies' national defenses are laid waste (Zephaniah 3:6)
- a great calamity goes forth from nation to nation (Jeremiah 25:32)
- a great whirlwind comes up from the coasts of the earth (Jeremiah 25:32)

- there is great confusion on the battlefield, and the warriors destroy each other (Haggai 2:22, Zechariah 14:13)
- people in the valley flee from the noise of tumult (Isaiah 33:3)
- the nations scatter as Jesus is lifted up (Isaiah 33:3)
- his enemies literally flee for their lives, returning to their own people and to their own lands (Isaiah 13:13-16)
- his enemies are destroyed by the sword (Isaiah 13:15, Jeremiah 25:31)
- plague goes before Jesus (Habakkuk 3:5)
- plague consumes his enemies: their flesh shall consume away while they stand upon their feet, and their eyes shall consume away in their holes, and their tongues shall consume away in their mouths (Zechariah 14:12)
- plague consumes all animals of his enemies (Zechariah 14:15)
- everyone found on the battlefield will be thrust through, and those seized are killed (Isaiah 13:13-16, Haggai 2:22)
- horse, rider, and chariot—none are spared (Psalm 76:6)
- his enemies are tread down under the feet like ashes (Malachi 4:3)
- the slain are found from one end of the earth to the other (Jeremiah 25:33)
- no one laments, gathers, or buries the dead; they are left as dung on the ground (Jeremiah 25:33)
- the children of his enemies are killed in front of them (Isaiah 13:13-16)
- the houses of his enemies are looted (Isaiah 13:13-16)
- the wives of his enemies are raped (Isaiah 13:13-16)
- all who live on the earth mourn (Amos 8:8)
- the cities and streets of his enemies lie in ruins (Zephaniah 3:6)
- the highways of his enemies are laid waste (Isaiah 33:8)

- fire consumes pastures and trees (Joel 1:19-20)
- riverbeds are dried up (Joel 1:20)

The earth is now God's threshing floor (Isaiah 21:10), where Jesus threshes the heathen in his anger (Habakkuk 3:12). It is also the winepress of God's wrath (Revelation 19:15, Jeremiah 25:30, Joel 3:13), where the juices of the winepress of Revelation 14:17-20 overflow, coming up to the bridle of a horse and extending for over 200 miles. Jesus treads this winepress in great anger by himself and wonders why there are none to help him (Isaiah 63:3-6). The blood of the winepress of God's wrath now completely stains Jesus' pure, white clothing (Isaiah 63:1-3). At this time, the kings of the world are captured and put into a pit until they are punished (Isaiah 14:18, 24:21-22).

Notice that, other than their presence, virtually nothing has been said about Jesus' armies. There is a good reason for this. From a historical perspective, nations use armies to fight wars and occupy territory. On his return, Jesus alone fights his war. Even though his armies are quite capable of fighting, this is not their purpose; they are only here to occupy. His armies are great and strong. They are powerful, righteous, glorious, and unlike any army ever seen (Joel 2:2). The number of their chariots is in the tens of thousands (Psalm 68:17), and the earth shakes before them (Joel 2:10). They climb walls like men of war, climb upon the houses, and enter windows like thieves. Each soldier maintains his path, not breaking ranks for any reason. Running like mighty men, they go wherever they want, back and forth throughout the city and on its walls. Nothing stops them or slows them down. The weapons of man do not affect them, and no one is able to hurt, resist, or hide from them (Joel 2:3-9).

Jesus has single-handedly subdued God's enemies, and the fighting is virtually over. The birds and beasts are in the middle of enjoying the delights of God's supper. Only one more enemy needs Jesus' immediate attention: Satan.

Satan Cast into the Bottomless Pit
Section reference: Revelation 20:1-3.

The battle is over, and the transition to Jesus' government is about to begin, but before that happens, an angel comes from heaven to capture and incarcerate Satan. He brings chains and the key to the pit to bind Satan. He captures him, binds him, throws him into the pit, and locks him up for a thousand years until God has use of him again.

The angel possessing the key of the bottomless pit presents something of a quandary. In Revelation 9, a fallen star, presumably Satan, received this key. If Satan had the key, when did God reclaim it from him? Did Michael take it during the war in heaven in Revelation 12? Could the fallen star of Revelation 9 have a different meaning? Could the Revelation 9 fallen angel and the Revelation 19 angel be the same? For now, it seems reasonable to assume Michael reclaimed the key sometime between Revelation 9 and Revelation 19, probably during the war in heaven of Revelation 12.

This is the second of three steps God uses to humble and punish Satan (Lucifer), fulfilling the prophecies of Isaiah 14:12-15. The first  occurred in Revelation 12's war in heaven, when Satan was permanently barred from heaven and the throne of God. The second now occurs, as Satan is bound and incarcerated for a thousand years. The last will be Satan's permanent internment in the lake of fire.

The Jews Rescued from the Wilderness

The last action of Jesus' long, long day is the rescue of the Jews in the wilderness. As seen in Isaiah 63:1-5, he does  not even pause long enough after the fighting to change clothing before getting them. He returns from Edom still wearing his winepress-stained garments. The Jews in Edom have remained in protective custody since Revelation 12, and they are probably desperate to leave their confinement. Jesus refuses to make them wait any longer than absolutely necessary. Once he releases the Jews from their wilderness stronghold, Jesus brings them back to Jerusalem. Sometime after this, he meets with the 144,000 sealed Jews on the temple mount. As they meet, God calls these Jews to heaven, where they sing their new song before his throne (Revelation 14:1-5).

The Immediate Fallout of Jesus' Return

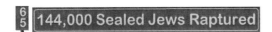

Jesus' reign affects the world in many substantial ways. Some changes happen immediately and others only as he establishes his kingdom and it matures. Changes becoming readily apparent within a short time of the conclusion of the battle of Armageddon include:

- war ceases (Psalm 46:9, 76:3)

- Jesus makes a covenant of peace with humanity (Ezekiel 37:26)

- the Lord alone is exalted (Isaiah 2:17); there is no idol worship or witchcraft (Micah 5:12-14)

- all nations worship the Lord in their own lands (Zephaniah 2:11)

- Jesus sets up a new, everlasting kingdom (Daniel 2:44)

- Jews gather the wealth of the heathen in great abundance (Zechariah 14:14)

- seven women take hold of one man to "take away their reproach," asking for nothing in return for their needs or those of their children (Isaiah 4:1)

- everyone becomes more precious than a wedge of gold of Ophir (more than $750,000) (Isaiah 13:12)
- the redeemed are gathered out of the lands of the east, west, north, and south (Psalm 107:2-3, Matthew 24:31, Mark 13:27)
- the saints rule (Revelation 20:4, Psalm 37:11)

Many additional exciting changes are coming as Jesus' reign unfolds.

Full Tribulation Recap

The seven-year tribulation has produced many dramatic and permanent changes on the earth. These events were shown in three groups: the tribulation (first three and a half years), the midtribulation (the transition from the first half of the seven-year tribulation to the second half), and the great tribulation (last three and a half years). Before looking at Jesus' millennial reign, it is useful to look at the events of the three periods as a whole. The first half of the seven-year tribulation (the tribulation) produced the following events:

- the seven seal judgments
- the revelation of the son of perdition, the antichrist
- the start of the antichrist's convoluted rise to power
- the ministry work of the two witnesses
- the revealing of the four horsemen of the apocalypse, including their work: imitation, war, famine, and death (25 percent of mankind)
- the full-tribulation saints introduced, including their persecution, deaths, prayers, and rewards
- Magog's catastrophic invasion of Israel
- the stoppage of the daily sacrifice
- God's seal placed on 144,000 Jews
- the golden censer judgment
- seven trumpet judgments

- the four minor trumpet judgments with the death of a third of the plant life, one-third of the sea becoming blood, a third of the fresh waters becoming unusable, and a third of the sunlight and the moonlight blocked
- the first great woe of the fifth trumpet released satanic forces locked in the bottomless pit
- the second great woe of the sixth trumpet released a great 200-million-man army, which destroyed a third of mankind (bringing the cumulative total to 50 percent)
- people's refusal to repent
- the seven mysterious thunder judgments
- the mighty angel's proclaiming there will be no delay in crowning Jesus as King of kings

The midtribulation produced the following events:

- the outer courtyards of the temple trodden by the Gentiles
- the death of the two witnesses
- the resurrection of the two witnesses
- judgment on Israel for the two witnesses
- seventh trumpet sounds
- Jesus Christ crowned King of kings
- angry nations
- the righteous' reward judgments
- judgments poured out on the earth for rejecting the new king
- the Jews fleeing to the wilderness
- Michael and his angels fighting a war in heaven with Satan and his angels
- the third woe judgment: Satan and his angels exiled to the earth
- Satan persecutes Israel
- the Jews intensifying their efforts to flee to the wilderness

- Satan failing in his attacks on the place in the wilderness
- Satan turning his wrath on Israel and all mankind

The great tribulation (last three and a half years) produced the following events:

- the rise to power of a worldwide dictator, the antichrist, who usurped Jesus' throne
- the revealing and working of a false prophet appearing to have the powers of Elijah
- the revealing of the unholy trinity and their power sharing
- the antichrist's invasion of Egypt and the great wealth he acquires from it
- the creation of an image of the beast, also known as the abomination of desolation
- the establishment of a new worldwide monetary system requiring people to receive the mark of the beast, a demonic counterfeit of the seal of God
- three angels preaching God's Word throughout the world, pronouncing doom on Mystery Babylon and demanding people worship God, reject the image of the beast, the beast, and the mark of the beast
- the harvest of wheat and tares, including the harvesting of the great tribulation saints
- the winepress of God's wrath with blood running several feet deep for 200 miles
- the seven vial judgments
- the first five vials judgments of body lesions, water changed to blood worldwide, scorching heat, and bitter darkness
- people's refusal to repent (twice)
- the sixth vial gathered the armies of the world to Armageddon for the last war
- the seventh vial unleashed great earthquakes, causing mountains and islands to disappear, hailstones weighing seventy-five pounds, and the battle of Armageddon

- Mystery Babylon was revealed and destroyed
- people in heaven celebrated Mystery Babylon's destruction while people on earth mourned
- the Lamb's wedding followed by his marriage supper
- Jesus and his armies prepared for war
- the hopelessness of Israel during the battle of Armageddon
- the invitation to God's supper
- Jesus' majestic return to Mount Olivet
- the unholy trinity's war against Jesus
- the beast's and false prophet's punishment in the lake of fire
- Jesus' defeat of the armies of the world and God's supper
- Satan cast into the bottomless pit
- Jesus released the Jews in the wilderness
- the 144,000 were caught up to heaven to God's throne, where they sang their new song
- many improvements on earth, including the elimination of war

The Millennial Reign (Dominion)

The tribulation in general and the battle of Armageddon specifically leaves governments in chaos and all critical infrastructure in dysfunctional ruins. Into this power vacuum, Jesus immediately starts installing his new government. As suggested by Daniel 12:11-12 and Daniel 7:12, this process requires approximately one year (see the last entry of Table 20, blessings for those waiting to the end). During this hectic transition, Jesus squashes any remaining resistance to his government, judges people and nations, brings all Jews back to Israel, divides and partitions the land of Israel, and establishes new governments for every nation on earth. Historically, transitional periods have lasted many years (e.g., in Germany and Japan after World War II) but the situation is desperate, and mercifully, Jesus acts quickly.

After this transition, Jesus and his saints govern the earth, bringing about a time of unparalleled prosperity. During this time, Jesus establishes the capital of the world in Jerusalem, where, at first, he rules from a throne in the tabernacle of David (Isaiah 16:5) but later moves it to Jerusalem's final temple. For the next thousand years, the world experiences nothing but peace and prosperity until God opens the bottomless pit and releases

Satan to once again stir up dissent and one final rebellion. This serves to once again separate the righteous and wicked.

The Transition to Jesus' Kingdom

With the world in the chaotic aftermath of the greatest war ever, Jesus and his saints initiate war recovery and new government creation. Who are the people left on earth after the seven-year tribulation? The simple answer is it appears to be a mixed group of both righteous and wicked, but this question finally forces the confrontation of a dilemma conveniently passed over during the seven-year tribulation discussions. During the great tribulation, the antichrist actively sought out and eliminated the righteous. Starting in Revelation 13, anyone refusing to worship the beast was killed and those refusing to receive the mark of the beast were prohibited from buying or selling. At the same time, God killed the wicked in Revelation 14's winepress of God's wrath. If the antichrist is killing the righteous and God is killing the unrighteous, then who survives the full tribulation to live under Jesus' reign? If God allows the purging of both the righteous and wicked to continue to their natural conclusions, then no one survives the full tribulation. This is probably what Jesus meant when he said, "And except those days should be shortened, there should no flesh be saved: but for the elect's sake those days shall be shortened," (Matthew 24:22). Indeed, if these events continued unchecked, no flesh would survive. Jesus' return stops the killings before all life ends. However, this still does not tell who survives.

Easily lost in the simple description of Revelation 13 are the obstacles in implementing the death sentences for failing to worship the image of the beast. To develop an appreciation of the enormous challenges involved in the massacre of the righteous, one only needs to look at Hitler's attempted genocide of the Jews in the holocaust. To this end, he dedicated significant amounts of German resources. This was such a high priority that even at the height of the war, death camp logistics often delayed supplies destined for the eastern front. After many years of dedicated, high-priority efforts, he had managed to slaughter six million Jews but still failed to accomplish his desired goal: genocide. Logistics were his greatest obstacle. The costs and time associated with identifying, collecting, killing, and clearing the land of the Jews proved to be far more challenging than ever anticipated. Bullets were too costly, and the act of shooting the victims was too emotionally draining for the executioners. Over time, the Germans tried and employed many methods of execution. Body disposal proved equally challenging, starting with individual graves, then mass graves, and finally, mass crematoriums. The antichrist faces the same obstacles but with far less time, far more people, and a far greater area (worldwide versus Europe). Whereas Hitler tried to kill millions, the antichrist will try to kill billions. Like Hitler, the antichrist fails in his efforts to destroy God's people, and many righteous, both Jew and Gentile, survive the seven-year tribulation to enter Jesus' millennial reign.

The question of whether any wicked survive the seven-year tribulation to enter Jesus' millennial reign is trickier. Based on Jesus' kingdom of heaven teachings, many believe the answer is no. The confirmation or refutation of this position requires a detailed investigation of the mysteries of the kingdom of heaven. Fortunately, this investigation in the next section also yields important insights into the transition period.

The Kingdom of Heaven

The New Testament contains over a hundred references to either the kingdom of God or the kingdom of heaven (used interchangeably in this section). They are heavily concentrated in Jesus' words in the four Gospels and categorized in three groups: the preaching of the gospel of the kingdom of heaven, details of the kingdom of heaven, and the kingdom parables. This section covers each group separately.

Matthew 3:1-2, 4:17, 10:7, and Mark 1:14-15 show the preaching of the gospel of the kingdom of heaven always accompanied with a call for repentance. Until Revelation 12:10, people preach the kingdom is either at hand or near. Only after Jesus' coronation does the Bible proclaim its arrival (Revelation 12:10). After Jesus' coronation, the kingdom of heaven is no longer near; it is! The gospel of the kingdom was a focal point of Jesus' preaching and was preached by John the Baptist, Jesus, and his disciples (Matthew 3:1-2, 4:17, 10:7; Mark 1:14-15; Luke 4:43, 8:1, 9:2, 9:11, 9:60-62, 10:9-11; Acts 1:3). Jesus started his ministry preaching the kingdom of heaven and continued to do so even after his crucifixion until the moment of his ascension. His disciples picked up Jesus' burden and continued to preach the kingdom of heaven after his ascension. Though mysterious, the kingdom of heaven's preaching was and is an important component of the gospel of Christ.

The kingdom of heaven is spiritual not carnal and those who inherit it leave behind their works of flesh (Romans 14:17): adultery, fornication, lasciviousness, idolatry, witchcraft, hatred, wrath, strife, seditions, heresies, envyings, murders, drunkenness, rioting (revelings), and covetousness (Galatians 5:19-21, Ephesians 5:1-5). This standard was often too high for even the greatest Bible heroes, but those inheriting the kingdom never again succumb to the works of the flesh. The kingdom of heaven standards are so high that the lowest person in the kingdom is greater than the greatest person on earth (Luke 7:28).

If carnal people cannot enter the kingdom of heaven, how can anyone enter? The answer is found in John 3:1-7. Twice in this passage, Jesus speaks of the kingdom of God and both times he precedes his comments with the phrase, "Verily, verily." The root word for verily is also root for the word amen (Strong's G281). When preceding a statement, it is rendered as verily and when it follows a statement, it is rendered as amen. Either way, it affirms what follows or precedes it is absolutely reliable. When Jesus repeated it prior to a statement, he elevated it to even greater importance, perhaps even bestowing the statement with God's full authority. Interestingly, only John's Gospel contains this repetition.

Both times, Jesus speaks of the kingdom of God in John 3:1-7, he clearly declares people have to be born-again to either see or enter into the kingdom of God. He differentiates the spiritual birth from the physical birth of the flesh, and it is the second spiritual birth that is required for one to enter the kingdom of heaven. This does not mean they immediately enter the kingdom of heaven when they are born-again but rather, they will be able to see and enter the kingdom of heaven at a future time when they receive their incorruptible bodies. Consistent with 1 Corinthians 15:50, it declares only those in resurrected, incorruptible bodies inherit the kingdom.

Jesus' declaration that one cannot see the kingdom of God unless they are born-again is sometimes the basis for concluding that only the saved will enter into the millennial reign. In this interpretation, Jesus' reign and the kingdom of heaven represent the same thing. Those who are not born-again cannot even see it and therefore must be removed from the earth (i.e., die) before its start. This position is weakened somewhat if see is translated not in a physical sense (i.e., eyesight) but in a spiritual sense (knowledge or understanding).

Other references providing insights about entering the kingdom of heaven include:

- it is a kingdom of power (1 Corinthians 4:20)
- those entering the kingdom of heaven must do the will of the Father (Matthew 7:21)
- sinners, such as harlots, and publicans, go into the kingdom of God before the leaders of Israel, chief priests, and elders (Matthew 21:31)
- Israel's religious leaders, scribes, and Pharisees are hypocrites who not only refuse to enter into the kingdom of heaven but also stop others from entering. They diligently search everywhere for people to lead astray (Matthew 23:13-15).
- many Gentiles enter the kingdom of heaven while many Jews are left out (Matthew 8:10-12)
- people only enter the kingdom of heaven if their righteousness exceeds that of the scribes and Pharisees (Matthew 5:20)

- the kingdom of heaven is made up of children Matthew 19:13-14, Matthew 18:3-4, Mark 10:14-15, and Luke 18:16-17)

- it is easier for a camel to go through the eye of a needle than for the rich to enter the kingdom of God (Matthew 19:23-24, Mark 10:23-25, Luke 18:24-25)

- people enter the kingdom of God through much tribulation (Acts 14:22)

- the kingdom of God does not come by observation. It is a spiritual kingdom and is within people (Luke 17:20-21).

References providing other details of the kingdom of God include:

- Christians are given the keys of heaven, whatever they bind or loose on earth will also be bound or loosed in heaven (Matthew 16:19).

- Christians are rewarded much more than they sacrifice for the kingdom of God (Luke 18:29-30).

- Blessed are the poor in spirit because they receive the kingdom of heaven (Matthew 5:3; Luke 6:20).

- Blessed are they which are persecuted for righteousness' sake because they receive the kingdom of heaven (Matthew 5:10).

- There can be no excuses for not entering the kingdom of God. If an eye prevents one from entering the kingdom of God, it should be plucked out so a person enters the kingdom of God maimed rather than go to hell (Mark 9:47).

- There are some who are now first who will be last and some who are now last who will be first (Luke 13:29-30).

- Seeking the kingdom of God should be the first priority in a Christian's life. The necessities and blessings of life naturally come when a person's priorities are correct (Matthew 6:33, Luke 12:31).

- At the mount of transfiguration, Peter, James, and John tasted the kingdom of God (Mark 9:1-2, Luke 9:27-28).

So far, these passages have revealed the kingdom of heaven is a spiritual kingdom whose entry is through spiritual rebirth in immortal, incorruptible bodies. Everyone living in it is incapable of sin and greater than any mortal human who ever lived. Both Jew and Gentile occupy it, and one's progenitors do not guarantee entry. It is a powerful kingdom affecting the physical lives of people possessing mortal bodies and rewarding those faithfully serving it.

Twelve "kingdom of heaven" parables enigmatically reveal the kingdom's secrets:

- fig tree and kingdom at hand (Luke 21:29-32)
- harvest of wheat and tares (Matthew 13:24-30, Matthew 13:36-43)
- net full of good and bad fish (Matthew 13:47-50)
- treasure in the field (Matthew 13:44)
- pearl of great price (Matthew 13:45-46)
- mustard seed (Matthew 13:31-32, Mark 4:30-32, Luke 13:18-19)
- leaven in the loaves (Matthew 13:33, Luke 13:20-21)
- king and unforgiving servant (Matthew 18:23-35)
- man and the day laborers (Matthew 20:1-16)
- king, the marriage feast, and the guests (Matthew 22:2-14, Luke 14:15-24)
- the ten virgins (Matthew 25:1-13)
- the nobleman and the three servants (Matthew 25:14-30, Luke 19:11-27)

Each parable is an allegory of the kingdom of heaven. There are three additional parables closely related to the first twelve, but they do not contain phrases identifying them as kingdom allegories:

- the judgment of the sheep and goats (Matthew 25:31-46) (not explicitly a parable but since it is closely related to the two other kingdom parables in Matthew 25 and seems to be a natural extension of them)
- householder bringing out treasures (Matthew 13:52)

- the sower and the seed (Matthew 13:3-8, Matthew 3:11-23, Mark 4:3-8, Mark 4:11-20, Luke 8:5-8, Luke 8:10-18)

As a caveat, virtually none of these fifteen parables has achieved universally accepted interpretations. As with any commentary, the reader should perform their own research and reach their own conclusions based on scriptural interpretations employing strong rules of hermeneutics. Brief overviews of twelve of these parables follow. Then, detailed discussions focus on the three with the most direct bearing on millennial reign admittance: the ten virgins, the nobleman and the three servants, and the sheep and goats judgment.

The parable of the fig tree speaks of the fall and rise of the nation of Israel. It links Jesus' return to Israel's rise (budding) and possibly puts bounds on when Jesus' return can occur with respect to Israel's rise. Both the harvest of the wheat and tares and the net full of good and bad fish parables refer to Revelation 14's harvest, where everyone must choose between Satan and God, thereby identifying themselves as either righteous or wicked. A common interpretation of the parables of the treasure in the field and the pearl of great price is they tell of the great value people have in God's eyes. The field is probably the world, the man would be God, and the treasure is the righteous. The merchant is God, and the pearl is most likely the church but could also reference the righteous in general.

The mustard seed parable tells of the ability of God's Word to grow and nurture. The leaven in the loaves parable is probably an allusion to the rapid spread and growth of small amounts of sin throughout the world. The parable of the king and the unforgiving servant shows the massive amount of sin debt God forgives whenever people ask and the pitifully small sin debts people owe each other. It also shows God's impatience with people unwilling to forgive another's inconsequential sin debts after he has already wiped their slates clean of far greater.

The parable of the householder bringing forth treasures new and old speaks of the value of spiritual blessings of the kingdom of God. These blessings, both new and old, retain their value despite the passage of time. The parable of the sower and the seed represents the results of the Word of God's preaching to people throughout the world. The parable of the man and the day laborers teaches that all who work in the field receive the same reward—a penny (a day's wages in ancient times)—regardless of how long each worked in the fields. The penny represents eternal life, the reward of all believers. The parable of the guests to the king's marriage feast provided important insights into the Lamb's marriage supper (Revelation 19) toward the end of the great tribulation.

Since none of these parables seems to shed any light on who enters Jesus' millennial reign or the transition to it, they will be set aside in favor of Matthew 25's parables. The parable of a nobleman and his three servants starts with a nobleman entrusting his estate to his servants prior to traveling to a far country (Matthew 25:14-15). The slow means of ancient transportation forced people to put others in charge of their possessions while they were gone since trips to distant lands took extended periods ranging from several months to many years and it was possible the master might never return. Consequently, before going away, he made his servants responsible for managing his possessions. This master gave each just as much as he could properly manage. Matthew gives no reason for the trip, but a parallel passage in Luke calls the master a noble who goes away to receive his kingdom (Luke 19:11-14). In this version, the citizens hate the master and after his departure send word that he will never reign over them. It is extraordinary for any nobleman to leave his kingdom to become king,[1] as kings are usually enthroned in the realm of their power; but this king goes to another land for his coronation before returning. Matthew 25:16-18 shows the two servants entrusted with the most doubled their master's money whereas the servant entrusted with the least proved the master's lack of confidence in him was well founded.

After receiving his throne, the master returns to start reigning and demands an accounting from the servants (Luke 19:15).

He judges the first servant (entrusted with the most) as worthy, makes him a ruler of many things, and invites him to enter into the joy of his master (Matthew 25:20-21). In Luke, the king also makes the servant a ruler of cities. Likewise, the second servant is found faithful and rewarded. Finally, he judges the last servant (entrusted with the least), but this servant's actions provoke a far different response, as the king calls him unworthy and casts him into outer darkness where there shall be weeping and gnashing of teeth, a clear reference to hell (Matthew 25:24-30). The king even takes the goods entrusted to this unfaithful servant and gives them to one of the faithful servants.

The parable's last judgment is found only in Luke's version and is against the rebellious citizens who refuse to allow the king to reign over them (Luke 19:27). Unlike the servant judgments, which produced either rewards or punishments based on their actions, there are no rewards for the citizens. There is only the death penalty for those refusing the new king's rule. The servant and citizen judgments have different standards and different results. Since the king entrusts far more to the servants care, he naturally holds his servants to higher standards. Consequently, the king judges the servants against far stricter standards, but their rewards are also commensurately greater than those of the citizens.

Jesus is the noble who went to a distinct land (heaven) to receive his kingdom (earth), and as shown, he received it in the middle of the seven-year tribulation, just after the seventh trumpet judgment. Following his return during the battle of Armageddon, he collects his servants on earth for their judgments. Traditionally, most Christian scholars have taught that the servants and the church are synonymous. However, the church has been in heaven with Jesus and has already received its judgments; therefore, the servants cannot represent the church. On the other hand, unsaved Jews remained on the earth throughout the full tribulation, and their perpetual marriage covenant obligates them to meet this judgment's higher standards.

If the servants are the church, then the master's sentencing of the last servant to hell invalidates the doctrine of eternal security (e.g., see Romans 8:38-39). However, this issue is resolved if the servants are unsaved Jews still bound by the Old Testament covenant. The servants' judgments are consistent with Ezekiel 18:26-28's standard of judgment for Old Testament Jews. God judges people living under the Old Testament covenant on their present righteousness. Eternal security does not apply and consequently, unsaved Jews do not present any challenges to this parable's interpretation. Since Jesus removes all Christians (Jew and Gentile) through the rapture prior to the tribulation, the surviving Jews are all unsaved and could have no expectation of eternal security. These "left behind" Jews are probably the noble's servants, and the Gentiles surviving the seven-year tribulation's are probably the citizens.

When Jesus left earth (his future kingdom) to go to heaven to become king, he left his servants (Jews) in charge but the Gentiles on earth sent him the unmistakable message: they did not want him to be king. While in heaven, Jesus is crowned king, and when he returns to the earth, he judges earth's Jewish survivors. The faithful Jews are handsomely rewarded while the unfaithful are killed and thrown into hell. Next, Jesus kills earth's rebellious Gentile citizens who refuse to accept him as king. The only reward the citizens can receive is the privilege of continuing to live and enjoying life under Jesus' reign. This last judgment breaks all remaining opposition and means there will be no repeat of the terror attacks following other wars such as plagued the allied victors in Germany following World War II and in Iraq following the second Gulf War.

Significantly, the parable preceding this one in Matthew 25 shows the wedding party's ten virgins (the Jews) waiting for the bridegroom. Half have their lamps filled with the Holy Spirit's oil of salvation and are prepared to meet the groom. The other half does not have oil and are unprepared to meet him. When the groom arrives, the rapture removes the prepared Jews and leaves the unprepared Jews behind on earth to face the full tribulation. The unprepared half misses both the rapture and the wedding in heaven. The next parable of the three servants foretells Jesus' coronation, Jesus' return, the judgment of the Jews (the servants), and the judgment of the Gentiles (the citizens). Matthew 25 then concludes with the sheep and goat judgment of the nations.

Just as Revelation gives the overall prophetic road map, Matthew 25 gives the millennial reign transition road map. It starts with the rapture of the church, which takes some servants and leaves others on earth. After Jesus is crowned king while in heaven, he returns at the end of the seven-year tribulation and brings the following judgments:

1. judgment of the Jews on earth (servants)
2. judgment of the Gentiles (citizens)
3. judgment of the Gentile nations (sheep and goat nations)

In the last judgment, Jesus judges the Gentile nations on how they have treated the Jews, and he destroys those nations possessing perpetual hatred for the Jews. These nations will not enjoy the blessings of this time of peace and prosperity.

Jesus' millennial reign consists of three groups of people: the immortal rulers of the kingdom of God, the mortal citizens of the world, and the mortal servants. The citizens and servants enter Jesus' millennial reign in their earthly, fleshly bodies. With these bodies, they are not part of the kingdom of God but are subject to it. For Gentiles, nothing precludes the unsaved from entering Jesus' reign other than a stubborn refusal to accept Jesus' authority. This means it is likely unsaved Gentiles live during the millennial reign. The Jewish servants are more problematic since Jesus holds them to a much higher standard: they must be faithful and productive. These parables leave the question of the Jew's salvation open but the Jews' failure to recognize Jesus and his wounds strengthens arguments that at least some the Jews entering the millennium are unsaved (Zechariah 13:6).

The Gathering and Judgment of the Jews

The first step on Matthew 25's transition timeline is Jesus' judgment of the Jews, but before this can happen, they must be gathered from wherever they have been driven throughout the world back to Israel. Jesus gathers the Jews from throughout the entire earth, brings the children of Israel back under the bond of God's covenant, and purges out any who refuse to be faithful (Ezekiel 20:33-38). He gathers Jews who did not return to Israel prior to or during the full tribulation, Jews who fled during the seven-year tribulation (including those in Edom and those in the mountains), and Jews exiled during the battle of Armageddon. After he gathers them back to Israel, Jesus takes them to the same place God purged their parents' sin after their liberation from Egypt: the wilderness (Sinai Peninsula). Here Jesus pleads with them to turn away from serving idols and return to serving their God.

Then Jesus judges (pass under the rod) the Jews and purges the nation of all rebels and transgressors (idol worshippers). Similar to the servants' judgments in the parable of

the nobleman and his three servants, this judgment focuses on works (actions) of those under judgment. Unlike the parable, Ezekiel focuses strictly on the punishment of wicked Jews without giving any insights into the rewards of the righteous remnant. At first glance, Ezekiel's punishments (shall not enter the land) do not seem as severe as those in the parable; but Jesus has not gathered all the Jews from the four corners of the earth to allow them to live elsewhere. They can only live in the Holy Land, and if Jesus prohibits them from entering the land of Israel, then they forfeit their lives. Since they are rebels, they can only suffer the unfaithful servant's plight: hell.

Based on passages like Matthew 5:20, many believe all Jews entering the land of Israel after Jesus' return must accept Jesus as Lord and Savior. Since neither the parable of the nobleman and the three servants nor Ezekiel is clear on this point, viable arguments can be offered for both positions and is the source of passionate debate. Regardless, the reprobates failing this judgment lose their lives, and neither inherit nor possess their portion of land in Israel. Those surviving this judgment submit themselves to the terms and conditions of the covenant. Presumably, this is Deuteronomy's marriage covenant, but some have proposed it is a version of this covenant modified by the Messiah while others believe it is Jeremiah 31:31's new covenant.

If salvation is not required, what standard will Jesus use for his judgments of the Jews? At a bare minimum, they will have to meet the standard that will be applied in the future judgment against the Gentiles: they must submit to Jesus' authority or  lose their lives. However, as God's wife, they undoubtedly have to meet higher standards. Most likely, Jesus uses the following:

> Behold, all souls are mine; as the soul of the father, so also the soul of the son is mine: the soul that sinneth, it shall die. But if a man be just, and do that which is lawful and right, And hath not eaten upon the mountains, neither hath lifted up his eyes to the idols of the house of Israel, neither hath defiled his neighbour's wife, neither hath come near to a menstruous woman, And hath not oppressed any, but hath restored to the debtor his pledge, hath spoiled none by violence, hath given his bread to the hungry, and hath covered the naked with a garment; He that hath not given forth upon usury, neither hath taken any increase, that hath withdrawn his hand from iniquity, hath executed true judgment between man and man, Hath walked in my statutes, and hath kept my judgments, to deal truly; he is just, he shall surely live, saith the Lord God.
>
> Ezekiel 18:4-9

Fundamentally, Jews living according to God's laws at the time of the judgment receive Jesus' rewards while the Jews currently rejecting his covenant are immediately thrown into hell.

Ezekiel 20:40-44 shows the surviving Jews serve Jesus, bring their sacrifices, and give their praises. Their remembrance of what they and their ancestors have done causes them great shame to the point they despise themselves for their sins against Jesus.

The Judgment of Gentiles

The Gentiles' judgments follow the Jews' judgments. These judgments occur in two stages: individual and national. This section covers the first of these, while the next section covers the later. The judgment of individuals is very simple since there are no rewards, just punishments. Anyone refusing to submit to Jesus' authority is condemned to death. Psalm 110:1-6 provides clues of this judgment, as they show God the Father telling Jesus to sit at his right hand until his enemies have been subdued, which occurred in the great tribulation. Now, Jesus fulfills the rest of this passage as he rules with a rod of iron out of Jerusalem, completes the judgment of the Jews, and judges the Gentiles.

In this judgment, Jesus strikes down the unrighteous kings (similar to battlefield wound), presumably fatally. He kills the heathen (Gentiles) in great numbers. He fills unspecified places with their dead bodies. He wounds and  probably kills the leaders of many countries. Recalling Jesus' admonition in Luke 12:48 (to whom much is given, much is required), it is reasonable to expect Jesus to hold the kings and leaders to a higher standard than ordinary Gentiles. Psalm 110 shows Jesus judging all Gentiles, great and small, on a day when many Gentiles die. All the condemned have rebelled against Jesus' authority, and all pay the same price: their lives.

The Judgment of the Nations

Matthew 25:31-46 provides virtually all known details of the Gentile nations' judgments. It follows the individual judgments of Matthew 25:31-46 (the servants' judgments). At this time, Jesus calls the nations together for their judgment. The Bible does not specify how the nations present themselves before his throne, though it seems reasonable that representatives present themselves since travel issues make it unlikely all citizens appear as groups before Jesus' judgment seat.

Jesus sorts the nations into those entering his millennial reign (the sheep) and those ceasing to exist (the goats) based on how they have treated Jesus' brethren. Have they met the needs and eased the suffering of these brethren; or have they turned a deaf ear; or even worse, have they piled on in their hours of need? A natural question is "Who are these brethren?"

6 9 Judgment of the Nations

They could be the church, the Jews, or both. Considering the judgment occurs immediately after the seven-year tribulation and Jesus is related to the Jews by birth, the Jews are the more likely choice.

The nations surviving this judgment (the sheep) enter Jesus' millennial reign and inherit the kingdom prepared for them. Since these people are still in their mortal bodies, they do not inherit the kingdom of God but instead enter earthly millennial kingdoms. The nations condemned in this judgment (the goats) are either thrown into the lake of fire or, most likely, hell. Since Jesus throws the nation's entire population into hell, one must assume any righteous in these nations died in the seven-year tribulation or were caught away with the church's rapture. There is no reason to believe God will ever throw any righteous person into hell for any reason.

Jeremiah 49:17-20 shows a possible goat nation (Edom) while Ezekiel 29:14-15 shows an example of a sheep nation (Egypt). Though Egypt appears to survive this judgment, it is not unscathed. For the first forty years of Jesus' reign, it is uninhabitable. After that, they become a minor nation and remain insignificant throughout Jesus' reign. Interestingly, after Egypt passes the judgment, they remain rebellious and are later disciplined by Jesus (Zechariah 14:18). With Egypt's long history of opposition and persecution of the Jews, their survival suggests Jesus is compassionate and eliminates few nations.

The Partitioning of Israel

Sometime during the transition to Jesus' reign, Jesus divides the land of Israel among the tribes of Israel and their survivors. It is unlikely the division of the land occurs before the judgment of the Jews since Jesus would have to redistribute the inheritance of anyone purged in the judgments. Since some Gentiles receive an inheritance in Israel, it is also equally unlikely that Jesus partitions the land before their judgment. The division of the land probably occurs after the national judgments because the elimination of the goat nations might affect Israel's borders and, consequently, the amount of land available for division. Israel's permanent borders for Jesus' millennial reign are likely those given in Genesis 15:18-21. These borders extend much farther east, south, and probably north than those held by modern Israel. As with all references to ancient nations, the exact boundaries are difficult to determine, but it is safe to assume land currently controlled by Iraq, Saudi Arabia, Jordon, Syria, Lebanon, and Egypt will fall inside Israel's new borders.

Ezekiel 47:20-23 describes how the land is partitioned among the survivors. This process is very similar to Joshua's division of the land of Israel. This time, Jesus divides the land among the Jews sur-  viving both the seven-year tribulation and the servant judgments. He divides it by lot so it is beyond people's influences. Like Joshua's division, Joseph receives two portions (Ephraim and Manasseh) and Levi receives none. As the tribe of priests, they receive their portion from the other tribes' shares. Ezekiel 48 gives the resulting inheritance of the land. A quick comparison of Joshua's boundaries and Jesus' millennial reign boundaries reveals many differences. The significance of these changes is not clear, but they are noteworthy.

Also noteworthy is the allocation of land to families of Gentiles who have children born in the land of Israel. Ezekiel makes it clear that both Jew and Gentile, not just Jew, inhabit the land of Israel for Jesus' entire reign. When the Jews receive their inheritance, they receive specific parcels of land based on tribal membership for themselves and their families. This allocation along tribal lines will probably force many Jews to relocate to other regions of the country. By contrast, the Gentiles receive their inheritance in the same region they currently occupy; however, they may still have to move but within the same tribal region. Figure 22 shows the approximate divisions of the Holy Land during Jesus' millennial reign. In stark contrast to the list of tribes in Revelation 7, the tribes of Dan and Ephraim are both included. Clearly, God has forgiven both for their roles in betraying their brothers and assisting the antichrist's activities.

Jesus carves out an area of almost 70 [2500]^2 square miles out of Judah for himself. This land lays just south of a very high mountain. Many have tried to map the area's descriptions to specific points in modern Israel. This exercise is probably pointless since the earthquakes and the shaking of the earth during the seven-year tribulation period have dramatically altered the topology of not only Israel but also the entire earth. In the seventh vial judgment, many mountains and islands disappeared while it is likely that many others, including Jesus' royal mountain, probably came into existence. Ezekiel 48:8 provides the basic allotment of Jesus' land. The land given to Jesus is a square with each side being 25,000 cubits [reeds] long (approximately 8.25 [50] miles). The land consists of three parts:

- the oblation unto the Lord: 25,000 cubits [reeds] long by 10,000 cubits [reeds] wide (40 percent)

- the inheritance of the Levites: 25,000 cubits [reeds] long by 10,000 cubits [reeds] wide (40 percent)

- the profane place: 25,000 cubits [reeds] long by 5,000 cubits [reeds] wide (20 percent)

The three slices run east and west, with the long sides facing north and south. Ezekiel 48:9-12 describes the oblation of the Lord, which is the northern section of Jesus' land. It contains the millennial temple and the land of the children of the priest Zadok, the only priests allowed into the inner sanctuary. The rest of the temple's Levites live in the other section of land set aside for them. Ezekiel 48:13-14 describes this section. It sits on the southern border of the Lord's oblation. Ezekiel 48:15-19 describes the last section, the smallest. It consists of three equal pieces. The middle piece contains an unnamed city, presumably Jerusalem. It is a square of 4500 cubits [reeds] per side. A band of 250 cubits [reeds] surrounds the city on all sides for the suburbs. The other two pieces of this section, each 10,000 cubits [reeds] by 5,000 cubits [reeds] in size, are set aside for the city's food production. People from all the tribes of Israel serve this city.

Figure 22: Future Division of Israel's
Land and the Millennial Temple[3]

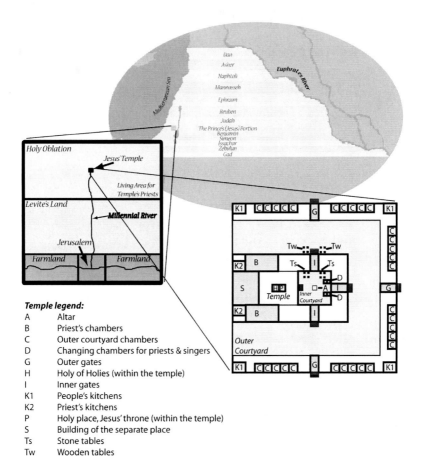

Temple legend:

A	Altar
B	Priest's chambers
C	Outer courtyard chambers
D	Changing chambers for priests & singers
G	Outer gates
H	Holy of Holies (within the temple)
I	Inner gates
K1	People's kitchens
K2	Priest's kitchens
P	Holy place, Jesus' throne (within the temple)
S	Building of the separate place
Ts	Stone tables
Tw	Wooden tables

The Millennial Rulers Appointed

Section reference: Revelation 20:4-6.

The final piece of the transition involves the appointment of millennial rulers. Jesus probably appoints these rulers just after he establishes national dominions and boundaries through the judgment of nations. Among the rulers are the last martyrs, the great tribulation saints (as evidenced by John's description of their martyrdom and their refusal to take the mark of the beast or worship the beast or his image). These martyrs are included in the first resurrection, which extends throughout the seven-year tribulation and occurs over multiple stages:

- Revelation 4's pretribulation resurrection and rapture
- the fifth seal's continuous resurrection of full-tribulation saints
- Revelation 11's resurrection and rapture of the two witnesses
- Revelation 15's harvest of the great tribulation saints
- Revelation 14's posttribulation rapture of the 144,000 sealed Jews

Though it can be debated as to when the full-tribulation saints of Revelation 6 and Revelation 15 are resurrected, it is clear they now have their new, immortal bodies. Their resurrection may occur on their deaths or collectively just prior to the wedding though the fifth seal's descriptions point to the former.

Yet another stage of the first resurrection may have occurred immediately after Jesus' crucifixion. The details are sketchy but suggest God resurrected the Old Testament saints at Jesus' death (Matthew 27:52-53). Regardless of when their resurrection occurred, all righteous dead from mankind's first six millennia now take their thrones alongside Jesus. God's love for them protected them from both hell and the lake of fire (the second death) while promoting them to positions of kings and priests.

The wicked remain in the grave and stay there until God resurrects them for their judgments and final dispositions at the great white throne judgments following Jesus' millennial reign.

Jesus' Thousand-year Reign

Section reference: Revelation 20:6.

The transition period ends with Jesus giving a grand feast (the king's feast) on his mountain for all people. Unlike the marriage supper, which was prepared and served by the groom's Father, this feast is prepared and served by the groom (Isaiah 25:6). Consisting of the very best the earth has to offer, including fat-ted animals and the finest wines, it is probably similar to one held by Solomon at the first temple's dedication (1 Kings 8:65-66). Perhaps this feast is also tied to a temple's dedication—the millennial temple. It is fair to say anyone surviving until now is truly one of Daniel's blessed ones (Daniel 12:12). Now unparalleled peace and prosperity spread throughout the earth. The Bible disperses so many descriptions about this time throughout its pages that it is surprising Revelation gives so few details. These other passages describe:

- the distinctive characteristics of Jesus' reign

- the earth during the thousand years

- the blessings on Jerusalem

- Israel's behavior and blessings

- the Gentile nation's behavior and relationship to Israel

Jesus now has total dominion over the earth, including all people, nations, lands, and animals. Breaking the grip of sin along with its corrosive effects, he ushers in a time of total peace through judging  nations and people (Isaiah 2:4, Micah 4:3, Jeremiah 3:17). Psalm 72 is a key passage to understanding this aspect of his reign, and his righteous judgments are its central theme. He protects the poor, the needy, and the meek from the deceitful and violent. No more will there be reports of scam artists taking every penny from the elderly. The abuse of poor immigrants ends. Bullies no longer extort by force from the helpless. Any who take advantage of the widow, the fatherless, the poor, the helpless, or the needy will suffer sure and swift punishment. Jesus and his rulers do not tolerate these actions, and consequently, these crimes virtually disappear. (See also Isaiah 11:4.)

Jesus is now exalted and sanctified above all else (Ezekiel 36:23). His enemies lick the dust of the earth (perhaps an indication of their death or them lying down prostrate on the earth giving homage to Jesus), and nomads in the wilderness bow down in worship. Most importantly, God's promised end of striving with humanity comes to fruition (Genesis 6:3). Kings bring offerings and tributes while people give him the praises and respect fitting the greatest king ever. All nations, including Tarshish, the nations of the isles, Sheba, and Seba bring him gifts. He changes bad things into good: ashes into beauty, mourning into the oil of joy, and the spirit of heaviness into the garment of praise (Isaiah 61:3).

Jesus also removes the veil that has so long hidden the truth from people (Isaiah 25:7). In a manner similar to Nehemiah opening the Word of God to the children of Israel after the Babylonian captivity (Nehemiah 8:1-12), Jesus teaches the citizens of the world the secrets of God and the blessings of obeying the whole law. Among the laws finally obeyed are the sabbatical years (for both rest and release of slaves), the year of jubilee, and the annual feast of tabernacles. The law is now revered and read every seven years during the feast of tabernacles (Deuteronomy 31:9-13). It is so zealously obeyed that even parents judge and execute their own children if they claim to prophesy (Zechariah 13:3). (By definition, they are false prophets since those days are done.) There are no prophets, and no one, including parents, tolerates any corruption or compromise of the Word of God.

7 3 Jesus' Thousand Year Reign

Jesus brings wonderful changes throughout the earth. Famine vanishes as God pours out showers of blessings (Ezekiel 34:26), rain is sent throughout the earth, and the harvest is fat (Isaiah 30:23). The desert blooms like a rose (Isaiah 35:1) and trees such as fir, pine, and box grow there (Isaiah 41:19). Cedar, shittah, myrtle, and olive trees grow in the wilderness (Isaiah 41:19). Lebanon becomes a fruitful field (Isaiah 29:17). Jesus feeds people (Matthew 12:1-13) and removes curses off the earth so trees of the field freely yield their fruits and the earth bountifully yields her increase (Ezekiel 34:27). The sun shines seven times brighter than it does today, yet the earth and its inhabitants seem to suffer no ill effects (Isaiah 30:26).

Today, the lack of abundant fresh water and its timely delivery are both major detriments to crop growth and the cultivation of dry lands. These problems disappear during Jesus' reign. Ezekiel 34:26 shows showers coming in due season, exactly when needed. Zechariah 8:12 says the heaven will give her dew. Isaiah describes fresh water lakes and streams appearing everywhere. In Isaiah 35:6-7, fresh water breaks out in the wilderness and streams form in the desert, parched ground becomes a pool, and springs of water form on thirsty lands. Isaiah 41:18 shows open rivers in high places, fountains in the valleys, pools of water in the wilderness, and springs of water on formerly dry land. Overnight, the precious and scarce resource of fresh water becomes free and readily available to everyone everywhere. Water conservation, flood control, waterless land, and manmade fresh water lakes all become obsolete, fading into the pages of history.

On several occasions (Mark 3:1-6, Luke 13:10-17, Luke 14:1-6, John 9:13-16), the religious rulers of Israel criticized Jesus for healing people on the Sabbath. They failed to understand the prophetic application of these activities. The Sabbatical millennial will be a time of healing of nations and people. During this time, disease will virtually disappear, with the blind seeing, the deaf hearing, the lame leaping, the dumb singing (Isaiah 35:5-6, Isaiah 32:3, Isaiah 29:18), and the stammerers speaking plainly (Isaiah 32:4). In short, Jesus eliminates the medical problems so familiar today. The extent of the change in the medical condition of humanity is best understood in light of Isaiah 65:20, where the elimination of disease and changes in physiology are so great that one hundred years is no longer considered old age. Apparently, Jesus changes people's lifespans back to the pre-flood levels, where people lived as long 969 years (Genesis 5:27). With infirmities eliminated, people are like children when one hundred years old. Even at hundreds of years of age, they will still be young and spry. Death at the early age of one hundred will be so rare that people naturally assume those dying then were condemned because of their wickedness.

The Bible is silent on whether the thousand-year barrier for a person's life span continues during Jesus' reign. This barrier was the result of man's fall in the garden of Eden, when God told Adam the day they ate of the tree of the knowledge of good and evil that they would surely die (Genesis 2:17). Theologians have long believed Adam and Eve immediately died a spiritual death. While sound teaching, this ignores the physical death. God intended for people to live forever, but their fall in the garden of Eden limited their lives to less than a thousand years, one millennial day (Psalm 90:4). God gave Adam and Eve the tree of life to ensure their eternal life, but instead they chose death by eating the fruit of the tree of knowledge of good and evil. When Adam and Eve made their choice, angels were sent to guard the tree of life so people could not be like God, living forever (Genesis 3:22-24). Starting from Adam to this day, no one has lived more than a day in God's eyes except Enoch (Genesis 5:24) and Elijah (2 Kings 2:11), who were both taken to heaven. Assuming this barrier continues in the millennial reign, then no carnal person alive at its onset live to see its conclusion.

Another key change Jesus introduces is found in Isaiah 2:4 and Micah 4:4, where war is abolished. People will convert weapons into other uses; will not create any new weapons; and will not spend money on armies, military intelligence, weapons, or training. With war eliminated, the ravages of war fade away, along with all of its human and material toils such as famine, disease, poverty, broken families, and disabled veterans.

All of these changes naturally lead to a population explosion like none ever seen. Like today, the people of the millennial reign will marry and have children. However, these children will live hundreds of years, and many may not die prior to the earth's destruction. Unlike today, a woman's years of fertility will probably last hundreds of years (as implied by Adam's descendents in Genesis 5). Under these conditions, the population of the earth increases boundlessly. By the end of the thousand years, the population will have reached unimaginable numbers and population levels considered unsustainable by modern scientists. Yet there are no dire consequences such as hunger, famine, or thirst. Obviously, the earth is capable of supporting far more people than most think because the fundamental issue is not the number of people but the amount of sin (Jeremiah 16:18, 2 Chronicles 7:14), and its absence permits God's unbounded blessings to finally flow unabated.

Isaiah 11:6-9 shows millennial changes even flowing to the animal kingdom, as natural enemies now live peacefully together. Children, even young infants, play with animals of all types safely. The most deadly poisonous snakes no longer hurt people of any age. The evil beasts (wild beasts) of the earth cease out of the land. Men dwell safely in the wilderness and sleep in the woods without fear (Ezekiel 34:25). The lion now eats straw instead of meat, and dust becomes the serpent's meat (Isaiah 65:25). Isaiah even mentions the beasts of Daniel: the bear, the lion, and the leopard. Now, all live together peacefully. This not only speaks of the various members of the animal kingdom but also suggests the end-time nations they represent.

Even people's behavior changes radically, as the knowledge of the Lord fills the earth. It restrains people from hurting or destroying anything or anyone. Now no longer feared, people become havens and places of protection (Isaiah 32:2). The knowledge of the Lord causes the rash and those erring in spirit to understand wisdom (Isaiah 32:4), vile people to no longer be called liberal (Isaiah 32:5-8), and murmurers to learn doctrine and end their complaining (Isaiah 29:24).

The changes in Israel's and Jerusalem's relationship to the nations of the world are equally dramatic. Today, Israel is a minor nation that most nations consider an irritant, a nuisance, and perhaps even a curse. The United Nations and other countries treat them with a double standard not applied to any other nation. The capital of Israel is truly the trembling cup of Zechariah 12:2, but during Jesus' millennial reign, all blessings flow from Jerusalem to Israel and finally to the Gentile nations. It is the seat of all power on earth, God's throne, and the center of all affairs: political, spiritual, and financial.

Jesus' purification of Jerusalem inaugurates the city's conversion to the world's premier metropolis. He washes away the filth of the daughter of Zion (Ezekiel 36:24-26) and purges the blood of Jerusalem through judgment and burning (Isaiah 4:4). The characteristics of the remnant living in Jerusalem during the millennial kingdom include:

- they weep no more (Isaiah 30:19, Isaiah 65:19)
- they tell the truth (Psalm 15:1-5)
- they do not backbite (Psalm 15:1-5)
- they do no evil to their neighbors (Psalm 15:1-5)
- they do not reproach their neighbors (Psalm 15:1-5)
- they walk uprightly (Psalm 15:1-5)
- they perform works of righteousness (Psalm 15:1-5)
- they condemn vile people (Psalm 15:1-5)
- they honor those who fear the Lord (Psalm 15:1-5)
- they are called holy (Isaiah 4:3)

From this point on, Jerusalem is never again forsaken or desolate. God opens a fountain to the house of David and the inhabitants of Jerusalem for sin and for uncleanness (Zechariah 13:1). Streams of living waters flow out of Jerusalem toward the seas in two directions (Zechariah 14:8) and a tabernacle is built for shade, refuge, and protection from storms (Isaiah 4:6). Jesus gives Jerusalem a new name, and people call her Hephzibah (my delight is in her) and Beulah (married) (Isaiah 62:2-4). Strangers rebuild her walls, and her gates never close, remaining open forever (Isaiah 60:10-11). People call her walls salvation and her gates praise (Isaiah 60:18). Gentile kings minister unto Jerusalem (Isaiah 60:10), and the nation not serving Israel is utterly wasted (Isaiah 60:12). All will acknowledge the Jews are the blessed seed of the Lord (Isaiah 61:9), and the children of those who afflicted Jerusalem will bow down before her (Isaiah 60:14).

Jerusalem becomes the most prosperous city this world has ever seen. King Solomon's reign of Israel hints at its future prosperity (1 Kings 10:22-29). Key aspects of King Solomon's reign include:

- the king exceeds all other kings in both his wealth and wisdom
- the king's teachings are highly sought after
- the citizens of the earth bring yearly presents and offerings
- the king makes gold and silver in Jerusalem as common as stones (see also 2 Chronicles 1:15-17)
- the king makes the wood of cedar and sycamore trees abundantly available

Jesus' reign sees these aspects of Solomon's reign repeat themselves, not for just forty years but for a thousand. It also sees Sheba bring gold and incense (Isaiah 60:6, Psalm 72:15); people from the isles and ships of Tarshish bring their sons, gold, and silver (Isaiah 60:9); and Lebanon brings its best fir, pine, and box trees for the sanctuary (Isaiah 60:13). Prosperity causes people to upgrade their building materials, as gold replaces brass, silver replaces iron, brass replaces wood, and iron replaces stones (Isaiah 60:17).

God blesses Israel in every possible way. As they received double punishment for their sins, they now receive a double reward of everlasting joy and all of Deuteronomy 28:1-14's blessings (Isaiah 61:7):

- established as a holy people (Deuteronomy 28:9)

- Israel's national relationships:
    - set above all nations (Deuteronomy 28:1)
    - they are lenders and not borrowers (Deuteronomy 28:12)
    - they are the head and not the tail (Deuteronomy 28:13)
    - people are afraid of Israel (Deuteronomy 28:10)
- Israel's general blessings:
    - blessings overtake them (Deuteronomy 28:2)
    - they are blessed wherever they go (Deuteronomy 28:3, 6)
    - their children are blessed (Deuteronomy 28:4, 11)
    - they are blessed in all they do (Deuteronomy 28:8)
    - they are blessed in their land (Deuteronomy 28:8)
    - their land, the increase of their cattle, and the flocks of their sheep are blessed (Deuteronomy 28:4, 11)
    - their savings are blessed (thy basket, thy storehouses, and thy store) (Deuteronomy 28:5, 8)
    - they have plenty of goods (Deuteronomy 28:11)
    - the rain comes at the right times (Deuteronomy 28:12)

As conquering soldiers who pursue and capture defeated troops fleeing for their lives from the battlefield, so are God's blessings on Israel. Wherever they go and whatever they do, the Jews will not even be able to flee from God's blessings. The blessings will always pursue and overtake them.

Not only does Israel receive God's blessings, but they also are a conduit through which God's blessings flow to the Gentiles (Zechariah 8:13). Ten men of all languages will latch onto the skirt of a Jew to pray with him for the blessings of God (Zechariah 8:23). Competition between Gentile and Jew virtually disappears, and Jews take great pleasure in seeing Gentile prosperity (Isaiah 61:6) because the more they prosper the greater the glory of the Jews. The Gentiles seek favor from Jews to receive more blessings from God, but both Jew and Gentile receive blessings far beyond anything imaginable today.

Throughout Jesus' reign, Israel does not fear or suffer terror (Isaiah 54:14). Violence and the threat of violence are completely gone (Ezekiel 34:27). There are no more car bombings, shootings, murders, or threats. Finally, the streets of Israel will be full of boys and girls playing while old men and women dwell safely (Zechariah 8:4-5). There are no more internal conflicts, as Israel and Judah walk together as a united nation (Jeremiah 3:18). The nation of Israel enjoys many peace dividends as the nation returns to life, the Jews rebuild it, and people plow its desolate lands. Her people fill the cities (Ezekiel 36:33), including those in desolate places, which are rebuilt from ruins (Isaiah 61:4, Ezekiel 36:38). There will be no wasting or destruction in Jerusalem (Isaiah 60:18). The Jews enjoy the fruits of their labors without fear of theft. No longer will the Jews build and another inhabit or plant and another eat (Isaiah 65:21-22). They build a highway, a holy road, called the way of holiness. It is so holy that the unclean do not pass over, the fool does not err thereon, and no lion or ravenous beast dares to set foot thereon. Only the redeemed people walk on this highway (Isaiah 35:8-9), and they use it to come to Zion with songs and everlasting joy (Isaiah 35:10).

Finally, Israel's land enjoys its jubilees and it blossoms, buds, and fills the earth with its fruit (Isaiah 27:6). Soon, people compare Israel to the garden of Eden (Ezekiel 36:34-35). God sends moderate rains to feed the crops and causes the harvest in Israel to be great (Joel 2:23-24). There is no more famine in Israel, and she overflows with wheat, oil, and wine (Ezekiel 36:30, Joel 2:24). The harvest is so great that strangers work the fields and tend the flocks (Isaiah 61:5). Additionally, Jesus creates a plant of renown that keeps people from suffering hunger (Ezekiel 34:29). This last passage is puzzling, as no other details of the plant are provided; however, Jesus promises food will always be abundantly available during his reign.

As incredible as it sounds, Israel's spiritual blessings may exceed their physical blessings. They receive a new heart and spirit to direct their paths (Ezekiel 36:26-27). Their sin and iniquities are virtually eliminated. They do not lie, deceive, or worship idols (Zephaniah 3:13, Isaiah 30:22, Zechariah 13:2). Sin now repulses them, and they loathe themselves for their prior evil ways (Ezekiel 36:31, Zephaniah 3:11). They are now the priests of the Lord and ministers of God speaking a pure language and whose paths are guided by God (Isaiah 61:6, Zephaniah 3:9, Isaiah 30:21). They no longer attempt to pray through brazen heavens because now God is so close to them that he hears and answers them before they call, even while they are still speaking (Isaiah 65:24). God is foremost on their minds as illustrated by the fact that even horse's bells in Jerusalem are engraved with "Holiness unto the Lord," (Zechariah 14:20). The Jews now joyfully observe annual feasts in the fourth, fifth, seventh, and tenth months. These four feasts are times of gladness and cheer to Judah (Zechariah 8:19).

The changes in the observed feasts, along with the Jews' new hearts and spirits, leads people to speculate about possible changes Jesus introduces to the Mosaic marriage covenant. Some suggest that not only will there be a great spiritual awakening on Jesus' return but also this continues throughout the millennial reign, where all Jews are born-again. While this is a possibility, this conclusion apparently contradicts many passages where God holds people individually accountable for their actions. Another possibility is just as God in the past judged the nation of Israel for her wickedness despite the presence of a faithful remnant (e.g., the seven thousand who had not bowed to idols in the days of Elijah, 1 Kings 19), in the future God blesses the nation of Israel for her righteousness despite the possible existence of a small, unrighteous minority.

During this time, Jesus builds his house at the top of his mountain, which is exalted above all hills and mountains. Clouds and smoke cover this mount by day, and fire covers the mount by night (Isaiah 4:5). All nations and people of the world go to Jesus' temple for his teaching (Isaiah 2:2-3, Micah 4:1-2, Zechariah 8:21-22). All kings and nations serve Jesus and every nation goes to Jerusalem during the feast of tabernacles to worship him (Psalm 72:11). Nations, including Egypt, refusing to go up during the feast of tabernacles receive no rain until they repent (Zechariah 14:16-19).

The millennial reign details discussed so far in this section are explicitly articulated in Scripture. Other details can be implicitly derived from general information. For example, throughout the seven-year tribulation, God controlled the elements to punish humanity. Earthquakes were commonplace, and the waters of the world raged, but now they and other "acts of God" are eliminated. Jesus' reign eases people's burdens by eliminating:

- famine through abundant harvests brought about by ample fresh water, fertile ground, and the elimination of blight and insect plagues

- the disabling effects of illness and the costs of battling diseases

- heavy taxation of all types and immense infrastructure required to support it

- bureaucratic red tape

- welfare programs

- the destructive effects of war and the costs associated with its preparation

- "acts of God" (earthquakes, tornados...)

- crime and the costs associated with fighting it

- false religions and the costs of religious persecutions

- border patrols

A simple way of looking at today's economy is to classify the goods and services produced by people into three broad categories based on whether a person creates wealth, consumes wealth, or is wealth neutral. Wealth producers are a nation's lifeblood. They generate the goods and services that keep its economic engine humming, and in one-way or another, their productivity not only provides for themselves but also supports the wealth consumers and wealth-neutral workers. These people produce the food, manufacture products, research and develop new products, provide essential services, furnish transportation and shipping services, deliver utilities, teach, and provide many other goods and services. Wealth consumers not only fail to produce wealth but their activities place a further drain on a community's wealth directly through its theft or destruction. They force the community to employ others to deal with their immoral behavior. Wealth consumers include criminals, terrorists, and external aggressive military regimes. Wealth-neutral work is the hardest to characterize. This work is often necessary, even vital, for the nation's good, but it does not generate any new wealth because it is usually required in response to the consequences of sin or God's curses. In an ideal, sin-free, and curse-free world, very few, if any, of these professions would be required. Many of these positions can be inferred from the prior list of burdens, including occupations in criminal justice system, national defense, health care, and many branches of the government.

Individual's prosperity is in no small measure tied to a country's wealth creation. Greater wealth production eventually translates to greater individual prosperity, and higher percentages of wealth producers translates to higher levels of wealth production. Jesus' reign virtually eliminates wealth consumers while the eradication of sin and the removal of God's curses dramatically reduces the number of wealth neutral workers. Not only does this free up the money spent on them, but also, their production now adds to the nation's overall wealth creation, and this new wealth creation sparks tremendous individual prosperity. This is one of the more subtle but powerful aspects of Jesus' reign.

A simple measure of the burden of the non-wealth-producing activities is the overall individual and corporate tax burdens. In the United States, tax studies often conclude the average American pays 50 percent or more in all taxes including direct (e.g., income taxes, property taxes, sales taxes) and hidden (e.g., usage fees, corporate income taxes) taxes. Compare these tax rates to those paid by Egyptian slaves as the result of Genesis 41-47's great seven-year famine. Joseph instituted this tax after the Egyptians had sold all their possessions, their live-stock, their lands (all possessions), and themselves (as slaves) for food (Genesis 47:13-22). The Egyptian slaves paid a paltry twenty percent tax on their income and had free use of land and property. If Americans, as free people, pay close to 50 percent in taxes and the Egyptian slaves paid 20 percent, what does this say about America's freedoms? God warned the Jews about these heavy burdens when they desired a king (1 Samuel 8:10-17), and even today, oppressive taxes are a disease that eventually afflicts every government.

Yet another subtle but very powerful effect of the millennial reign is the value of time. This is one of the most critical components of wealth creation. Investors use the rule of seventy-two to approximate the amount of time required for an investment to double in value at a constant rate of return. According to this rule, at 10 percent, an investment doubles about once every seven years. At 20 percent, it doubles in half that time, and at 5 percent, it takes twice that time. Even a humble thousand dollars grows into a million dollars by doubling ten times. At 10 percent, this takes seventy years. At 20 percent, this takes thirty-five years, and at 5 percent, this takes 140 years. With people living and working hundreds of years, even low rates of return enable small amounts of money to blossom into large amounts of wealth.

The combination of all of the effects of Jesus' reign produces seemingly boundless prosperity and means great afflu-ence is easily within everyone's reach, as all have the opportu-nity to become multimillionaires. This leads to an interesting question: if everyone is wealthy, what will be truly valuable? Isaiah 13:12 provides the answer: people become more valuable than possessions. One's relationship to God and families, wis-dom, knowledge of truth, salvation, friends, and strangers are all more valuable than money or possessions. Ironically, at the time, when wealth is finally easily attainable, people's desire and focus on acquiring it effectively evaporates because it is subor-dinated to their love for God and others (i.e., they finally obey the two great commandments).

In short, the millennial reign is a glorious time to be alive. For a thousand years, people enjoy long life, prosperity, peace, abundant joy, and health. The knowledge of God fills the earth, and God's blessings flow freely from Jesus' throne on Mount Zion to Jerusalem, to Israel, and throughout the earth. Sin is almost nonexistent, and its ravages no longer plague humanity. Before continuing to the end of the age, the next section explores one more aspect of the millennial reign: the building of the last earthly temple.

The Millennial Temple

As discussed earlier, the Bible records the construction of two prior temples: Solomon's and Ezra's. The glory of God (also known as the Shekinah glory) filled the former but was apparently absent from the later. Both temples suffered through periods of neglect that necessitated substantial repairs and reconstruction. None of these cycles of neglect was so deep that the existing structure disappeared, and, consequently, none of the reconstruction efforts was sufficiently comprehensive to qualify as a new temple. Babylon destroyed Solomon's temple, and the Romans destroyed Ezra's temple (as remodeled by Herod) in the AD 72 dispersion of the Jews.

Jeremiah suggests there are three temples (Jeremiah 7:4), which leaves only Jesus' millennial temple (Zechariah 6:12-13). This last temple is Jesus' throne on earth, which he utilizes to serve as both High Priest and King of kings. As Solomon used the best available labor and material from many countries to construct the first temple, Jesus does the same for his temple (Zechariah 6:15). This temple is by far the most glorious of the three. Jesus' presence fills this temple with the glory of God. His glory overflows from the temple to fill the whole earth (Ezekiel 43:1-5, 44:4). This temple never suffers neglect or requires rebuilding, and it stands until the earth's destruction at the end of Jesus' reign. People from all over the earth flock to it and bring their offerings (Isaiah 66:20-21). They come to worship on the Sabbath, new moons, and feasts (Ezekiel 45:21-25, Ezekiel 46:1).

Ezekiel provides extensive descriptions of Jesus' temple in Ezekiel 40-48. These word pictures provide many insights into  the temple, but like any word pictures, they are often confusing and may contain apparent contradictions. The following discussions provide an introductory, high-level overview only.

The temple sits in the middle of Jesus' oblation, meaning it is at least four [25] miles from the edge of Jesus' land to the temple. The temple contains at least two courts. The inner court contains Jesus' throne, and access to the inner court is restricted to the sons of Zadok and the singers (Ezekiel 44:15-16). This is where priests minister to Jesus and offer blood sacrifices. The outer court surrounds the inner court and is open to everyone. Possibly a third court surrounds the outer court, setting it off from everything else. The total area of the third court would be approximately one square mile, with the temple in its center.

Both the inner and outer courts have three gateways each, all apparently identical. The three gates face north, south, and east. The temple faces east so there are no western entrances in either court. The prince, the chief ruler of Israel,[4] enters and exits through the inner and outer court's eastern gates. Everyone else enters and leaves through the side gates on the north and south. Those entering the outer court through the south gateway must exit through the northern gates (and vice versa). Only those allowed into the inner court may use the northern and southern gates of the inner court. Figure 22 shows a graphical interpretation of Ezekiel's temple descriptions.

The temple's inner court contains:

- the most holy place (elevated)
- the sanctuary (elevated)
- a vestibule (elevated)
- the altar

- a building of unknown purpose on the west
- two chambers for singers and priests (place for priests entering the inner court to change clothes because the priestly garments are not to be worn when the priests are in the outer courts with the worshippers)
- ninety side chamber rooms organized in three levels, with ten rooms on the west, ten rooms on the south, and ten rooms on the north on each level surrounding the holy places. The rooms get larger in each higher level.

The ark of the covenant, so prominent for the first temple, is missing from this temple. During Jesus' reign, it will be abandoned and ultimately forgotten (Jeremiah 3:16). The temple's outer court contains:

- the outer courtyard
- thirty chambers along the walls of the outer court on a paved area surrounding the outer courtyard, with ten chambers on the west, on the south, and on the north
- four kitchens, one at each corner of the outer court walls
- tables for killing and preparing sacrifices
- two priest's chambers with adjoining cooking places for the priests, located on the north and south walls surrounding the inner court

An amazing feature of Jesus' temple is its river of blessings (Ezekiel 47:1-12). Its waters flow from the temple to the Dead Sea and possibly the Mediterranean Sea. It starts out at the temple ankle deep and increases in depth as it flows into the sea. As the waters of this river flow into the sea, they heal it, changing saltwater into fresh. Trees of all types line its banks, and these trees never lose their leaves. The leaves are for healing, and the trees produce crops monthly. This river and the trees lining it are a picture of the water of life and the tree of life that will be found in the future in new Jerusalem. As long as there are rebellious, wicked humans (as demonstrated in the upcoming final rebellion), God keeps people from accessing the actual tree and water of life.

The Final Rebellion

Section reference: Revelation 20:7-9.

Perhaps the most remarkable part of Jesus' reign is how terribly uneventful it is. Prior to his reign, the world was riddled with wars, national instability, economic chaos, diseases, famines, and natural disasters of every kind. Now, glorious blessings have replaced these curses, and they have faded into the pages of history. It seems every type of event used to mark history has for a thousand years disappeared from existence.

In short, humanity has enjoyed unparalleled prosperity and blessings. The differences between Satan's dominion and God's could not be more stark or pronounced. Against this backdrop, God releases Satan from the bottomless pit for one more opportunity to deceive humanity. What happens next is beyond comprehension. Satan not only succeeds in deceiving humanity into rebelling against Jesus Christ, he convinces them they can win! He even gets his old friends, Gog and Magog, who led the invasion of Israel in Ezekiel 38 (see the sixth seal) to lead the rebellion. Satan is able to gather countless numbers of people from every country and every place on earth to Jerusalem in a final desperate rebellion.

The stage is now set for another battle of Armageddon. For the prior thousand years, men have not learned of war, fought  wars, or built weapons of war. Jesus destroyed all weapons of war on his return. Now, without weapons and plans, they attempt to attack and destroy Jesus. A thousand years earlier, with the most advanced weapons people ever devised, they could not even mount an effective defense. Now they fight without much more than sticks and stones. How they can think they have any chance to win is incomprehensible. Why they would want to attack Jesus, who has only served and protected them, is unimaginable. In addition, this is not just a handful of dissidents but literally millions, perhaps even billions, rebelling. Unbelievable! God's response to this challenge against his authority is swift and direct. Fire comes from heaven, consuming every rebel.

In the darkest days of human history (e.g., preflood, Sodom and Gomorrah, and the battle of Armageddon), God still found righteous people. Conversely, now in the brightest day of human history, God finds wicked people. This last defiant act eliminates one of the defenses the wicked might have used at their final judgment: that of environment. One might try to argue they would have made righteous decisions if only they had lived in a good environment. Others might argue adversity makes people understand their need of God. God has now clearly demonstrated that people are more than a product of their environment. People are either righteous or wicked, regardless of their environment. It also demonstrates people have overcome all possible obstacles in their determination to live the life they choose—either for or against God.

This rebellion ends Jesus' reign, which started with a transition period lasting approximately one year. During the transition, Jesus gathered all Jews to Israel, where he individually judged them. The worthy servants received rewards while he threw the others into hell. He followed this with the Gentile judgment, where he killed all

76 Humanity's Last Rebellion

Gentiles refusing to accept his authority. He then judged the nations and destroyed those failing to have blessed Israel. The transition period ended with the partitioning of the land of Israel, the division of governments, and assignment of government leaders. With the transition period over, an unbridled period of peace and prosperity began under Jesus' caring oversight. Early during his reign, Jesus built the third and final temple. This is his throne for the duration of his reign, and people flock to it from throughout the world to worship him and seek his wisdom. At the end of the thousand years, God releases Satan to tempt humanity one more time. Many choose to follow him and gather once more outside Jerusalem to prepare for war against Jesus before fire descended and destroyed them.

The Final Judgments

Now that God has suppressed Satan and humanity's last challenge to his authority and Jerusalem's invading armies have come to an unceremonious end, God permanently purges all remnants of sin. He starts by judging Satan, followed by the judgment of the righteous and unrighteous dead at the great white throne.

Judgment of Satan

Section reference: Revelation 20:10.

Satan now joins the beast and the false prophet in the lake of fire. This third and last part of Satan's post-rapture punishment ensures he will never approach or tempt the righteous again and completes the punishments of Isaiah 14:12-15. From this time on, the creation that proclaimed himself greater than the creator suffers side by side with the people he deceived and the legions he led astray. None, including Satan, ever leave or escape this lake.

At some point, righteous people judge the angels, but precious few clues are available in either Revelation or elsewhere in Scripture to indicate when this judgment occurs (1 Corinthians 6:3). Revelation 18:2 suggested Baby-

77 | Satan Cast into Lake of Fire

lon became the habitation of devils throughout Jesus' reign, implying that fallen angels continued to reside on earth during this time. If they do, then their judgments, which must occur before God creates the new heaven and new earth, probably occurs in conjunction with or just after Satan's condemnation.

The End of Heaven and Earth

Section reference: Revelation 20:11.

A great white throne, the scene of mankind's final judgments, replaces the present earth and heavens when they flee away. The implication of the phrase "fled away" is unclear until other verses are considered. Psalm 46:2 suggests there will be an end to the earth. Isaiah goes further by saying the earth will burn up and is replaced by new heaven, a new earth, and new Jerusalem (Isaiah 51:6, 65:17-18). Peter went further in explicitly declaring fire destroys the current earth and heavens during the Day of the Lord (2 Peter 3:5-10). Since Jesus rules the earth throughout the Day of the Lord, the earth's destruction can only occur at its conclusion, precisely when Revelation shows the earth and heaven fleeing away. Therefore, "fled away" must refer to the fire's consumption of the present creations.

What happens to the billions of people on earth when fire destroys it? The presence of only the dead at the coming great white throne judgments implies the entire population of the earth perishes at this time and people will never again possess mortal, corruptible bodies. If true, only those taken by the rapture, Revelation 7's 144,000, and Enoch appear to avoid the first death.[1]

The great white throne is located somewhere other than heaven or earth since neither now exist and it occurs in a pause of unspecified duration prior to the creation of the new heaven and earth. The only recorded holdovers from the old creation are hell and the lake of fire. Hell exhausts its usefulness when it finally yields all its inhabitants during the second of the great white throne judgments. There is no evidence it exists (or is destroyed either) after these judgments, but unfortunately, the lake of fire is never exhausted, as it continuously burns forever. While it is already occupied by the unholy trinity and Satan's legions, it will but soon overflow with the wicked of all generations.

© Pat Marvenko Smith - www.revelationillustrated.com

The Judgment of the Righteous Dead

Section reference: Revelation 20:12.

The day appointed for people's judgments has arrived, and Jesus is presiding (Acts 17:31, 2 Corinthians 5:10, John 5:26-30). By the time Jesus completes his work, everyone who has ever lived will have been judged. This is the first of two great white judgments. At this judgment, Jesus judges the righteous dead as demonstrated by:

- the absence of hell with death
- the presence of the Book of Life without an indication of failed searches
- no mention of the lake of fire

Since the righteous were already resurrected during the seven-year tribulation, who are these righteous dead? Certainly all the righteous who died before the wedding feast were resurrected then, but many righteous people have died since including those perishing when God destroyed the earth. This last group of saints now stand before Jesus' throne and watch as court officials open the books of judgment, including the Book of Life, which redeems them from the judgment books' condemnations. Even at this time, Jesus will be ashamed of anyone who was ashamed of him even though their sins are forgiven (Mark 8:34-38).

What are the judgment books? First, there is the judgment's standard, which contains the law and its punishments, the Bible. Next comes evidence to ascertain guilt or innocence. In a court of law, there are witnesses and physical evidence, but for this judgment, it is contained in books of works. Some believe the book of works is not one book but multiple books consisting of the book of conscience (Romans 2:15), book of words (Matthew 12:36), book of secret words (Romans 2:16, Ecclesiastes 12:14), and the book of public works (2 Corinthians 11:15, Matthew 16:27). Since all have fallen short of God's standard, the only possible finding is a guilty verdict with an accompanying death sentence (Romans 3:23).

The book of life gives the defendant hope, as it allows someone else to pay the penalties for their sins. According to the terms of the kins-

79 Great White Throne Judgment: Righteous

man redeemer (Leviticus 26:47-55), a defendant's substitute for their sentence must be a legal relative who has the wherewithal to pay the penalty. All facing the death sentences (the wages of sin) at these last judgments must pay the penalty themselves or find a substitute. Fortunately, one has already been provided: God's sacrificial Lamb, Jesus. The defendants at these first judgments have this substitute while those at the next do not. Prior to their deaths, these first defendants repented, asked for forgiveness, and acknowledged that God raised Jesus from the grave. Jesus then agreed to pay their judgment and permanently recorded this fact in the book of life, the judgment's only redemptive book (John 10:25-29). Note that this is the only book that spares a person's life and preserves them from the lake of fire's second death. For each defendant, court officials diligently search the book of life for their name in hope of sparing them. Fortunately, all at this first judgment are found, and Jesus proceeds to reward their works.[2]

The Judgment of the Unrighteous Dead

Section reference: Revelation 20:13-15.

This second white throne judgment is the great and dreadful one most commonly referenced when people speak of this event. For this judgment, sea, death, and hell all give up their dead. Each is a holding place for the wicked, with death holding the body and hell holding the soul. Two primary theories exist for the sea: first, it holds the bodies of the wicked dying at sea, and second, it holds those destroyed in Noah's flood. The phrasing here suggests the later. Regardless, no righteous person now stands before Jesus' judgment seat. Like the first great white throne judgment, Jesus judges and rewards these dead according to their works but now, instead of rewards, Jesus condemns them with punishments in the lake of fire. Though the outcome of the judgment is not in doubt, the book of life is checked one last time to make sure no mistakes are made.

Before they can go into eternal damnation, they finally have to give Jesus the honor due the king but their confession will be too late to save them from everlasting punishment (see also Isaiah 45:23, Romans 14:10-12). Since they are already in the lake of fire, the beast and false prophet are the only wicked who do not bow to Jesus at this time. (Perhaps this happened in Revelation 19 before the angel threw them into the lake of fire.)

Matthew 7:21-23 shows a person's words and deeds will not save them in this day. Jesus sentences many who falsely claimed to be Christians or pretended to do great deeds in Jesus' name to the lake of fire. One must confess Jesus to other people so Jesus will confess them (write people's names in his book of life for example) in open court before God's angels (John 14:6, Luke 12:8-12). How could people have cast out devils and prophesied without confessing Jesus? Perhaps they used his name for their personal benefit without ever having met the terms and conditions of Romans 10:9-10: believed in their hearts and confessed with their mouth that God has raised Jesus from the dead.

© Pat Marvenko Smith - www.revelationillustrated.com

People cannot go to heaven by works because then they could boast they earned their way there and would be filled by the pride of life (Ephesians 2:9). This pride will force them to spend eternity in the lake of fire (2 Thessalonians 1:8-9). This is the place where the worm does not die and the fire never runs out of fuel. Even though the fire burns continuously, it produces no light, leaving this place in total darkness (Jude 1). Luke 16:19-31 gives insights to the punishments of hell, which, if anything, are not as horrific as those in the lake of fire. Here, the rich man had full use of his senses: seeing, hearing, tasting, and feeling. It is likely he could also smell, but this was not stated. His torment is so horrific that even a single drop of water would provide some welcome relief. The primary difference between hell and the lake of fire is the presence of the resurrected eternal body. In hell, people only have their soul, whereas in the lake of fire, they have fully functioning, eternal bodies that continuously heal themselves. Therefore, when the worm eats the body, their bodies replenish themselves so the worm can repeatedly consume their bodies. Likewise, when the body burns, it heals itself so the same flesh burns again and again. This torture continues forever without any relief. What a horrible way to exist: in eternal torture, forever separated from God, in darkness, and without hope. No wonder the Bible calls this the second death.

In the saints' judgments during the seven-year tribulation, Jesus provided for all their necessities. For food, he gave

Great White Throne Judgment: Wicked

them the bread of life and the water of life. For clothing, he gave them white raiment and, if worthy, crowns. At the great white throne judgment, the wicked receive none of these things and, consequently, face eternity without any of their needs being met now or in the future.

If Jesus already knows these people's names are not in the book of life, why does he go through the formality of a judgment? The most obvious answer is to make certain there are no mistakes and no one wrongly spends eternity in the lake of fire. A second reason is for all people to finally give Jesus the honor due to him as not only king but also as Creator. The presence of the book of works may suggest another and perhaps more important reason. Since the proof of any sin is enough to sentence someone to eternity in the lake of fire, why does the trial use records of every sin? Likely, the judgments cover not only a person's destination but also the degree of their punishments in the lake of fire. Many believe people like Nero, Hitler, and the beast receive greater punishments than people who attempted to lead good lives but never received Jesus' gift of life. If this is the case, those under judgment still have a lot at stake, and their answers to Jesus have permanent consequences.

With the completion of these great white throne judgments, Jesus has vanquished the last enemy: death. When destroyed, 1 Corinthians 15:20-28 shows Jesus returns the throne to God the Father and places himself back under the Father's reign. Now, the old heavens and earth are destroyed, the wicked are suffering in the second  death, all righteous people have their eternal incorruptible bodies, there are no more humans in mortal bodies, death is vanquished, and Jesus has again subjugated himself to God the Father.

Eternity (Perfection)

With sin purged and the wicked forever locked away in the lake of fire, God is now finally free to create his ultimate masterpiece safe in the knowledge it will never be spoiled by sin. Consisting of the new heaven, the new earth, and the new Jerusalem, these new creations are scarcely mentioned elsewhere but now take center stage in Revelation 21-22.

New Heaven and New Earth

Section reference: Revelation 21:1-8.

This description shows John has mastered the art of understatement as he casually discusses the indescribable destruction of heaven and earth and the creation of their replacement as though these were common, everyday occurrences. Though not specified, this description suggests this whole process occurs extremely quickly, as no descriptions are provided concerning how the existing creations were destroyed and the new ones created. The descriptions throughout Revelation 21-22 are the primary basis for understanding the new creations, but even these focus primarily on new Jerusalem and provide few details of the new heaven and earth.

New Creation: Eternity

Isaiah 66:22-23 provides several key insights to the new creations. First, the new heaven and new earth still have days, nights, weeks, and months (assuming the moon still rises on a monthly cycle). Second, unlike the millennial reign where only appointed representatives appeared annually in Jerusalem, now everyone worships God in his tabernacle in new Jerusalem at least once a week. Next, the omission of any mention of annual feasts suggests the only holy day observed during this time is the Sabbath, the Lord's day. Finally, people's relationship with God has changed dramatically. To understand how much, consider that when Moses requested to see God's face, God only permitted him to on gaze on his back because otherwise Moses would have died. Likewise, only once a year, the high priest and only the high priest could breach the veil and enter the holy of holies. Now people not only see God the Father but worship him face to face. Now perfected, people not only survive the sight of God but now thrive in his presence as he lovingly protects and comforts them. Now they live in a place of new beginnings, free from pain, crying, sorrow, or death where God himself wipes away their tears.

In the same way the book of Revelation opened, it now concludes with John commanded to record all he sees and hears. In so doing, God emphasizes he is giving this prophetic vision to the church, not just for John's personal benefit. The one sitting on the throne identifies himself as: I Am; Alpha and Omega, Beginning and the End; and the one who gives access to the fountain of life. The first three titles can apply to each member of the Trinity, but the last suggests the speaker is Jesus.

In this proclamation, Jesus makes several declarations:

- All things are made new.
- It is done.
- Righteous people drink the water of life freely.
- The righteous inherit all things.
- The wicked burn in the lake of fire.

The declaration that all things are made new affirms both the end of the current heavens and earth and the creation of the new heaven and new earth. In the second declaration, Jesus declares for the second time in Revelation that "it is done." This declaration is very significant since it only occurs at critical changes in the God's relationship to humanity and is only seen here and at the pouring of the seventh vial, which marked the start of the battle of Armageddon, Jesus' return, the end of God's plagues, the end of the time of the Gentiles, and the beginning of Jesus' earthly reign (Ezekiel 39:8, Revelation 16:17)

In the third declaration, Jesus returns the gift of life taken from people when Adam chose the tree of the knowledge of good and evil over the tree of life (Genesis 2-3). Ever since then, people have searched for the fountain of youth or some other magical potion to stop the aging process and prolong life. Now the righteous can freely drink of the water of life Jesus promised (John 4:7-30).

The fourth declaration, inheritance, gives the righteous ownership of all God has created, including the new heaven, new earth, new Jerusalem, the water of life, and the tree of life. God's generosity clearly demonstrates he takes great pleasure in blessing his children. Additionally, those who enjoy these blessings do so in the perfect eternal bodies promised by Isaiah: "But they that wait upon the Lord shall renew their strength; they shall mount up with wings as eagles; they shall run, and not be weary; and they shall walk, and not faint," (Isaiah 40:31).

The last declaration introduces an odd paradox as even in the midst of utopia, there is suffering: the wicked serving their sentences in the lake of fire. They do not partake of the joys and blessings of God but instead suffer the wrath of God. Where the righteous live in the full, perfect light of God, the wicked live in absolute total darkness (spiritually and physically). The lake of fire is a carryover from the old heavens and earth (probably the only one), and as Abraham and Lazarus could see the rich man in hell (Luke 16:15-31), those living in the new creation will see the wicked suffering in the lake of fire (Isaiah 66:24). While this may seem strange, it serves as a constant reminder of the horrific cost of sin. However, it is not clear how those in the lake of fire are visible if they are in utter darkness; but without a doubt, if it were possible for a person in a perfect body to fall, this serves as a constant warning. The Bible lists the wicked imprisoned in the lake of fire:

- the fearful (except the fear of God) (Revelation 21:8)
- the unbelieving (Revelation 21:8)
- the abominable (Revelation 21:8, 27)
- murderers (Revelation 21:8, Galatians 5:21)
- whoremongers (Revelation 21:8)
- sorcerers (Revelation 21:8, Galatians 5:20)
- idolaters (Revelation 21:8, 1 Corinthians 6:9, Galatians 5:20)
- all liars (Revelation 21:8, 27)
- defilers (Revelation 21:27)
- fornicators (sexually immoral) (1 Corinthians 6:9, Galatians 5:19)
- adulterers (1 Corinthians 6:9 Galatians 5:19)
- homosexuals (1 Corinthians 6:9)
- thieves (1 Corinthians 6:10)
- the covetous or envious (1 Corinthians 6:10)
- drunkards (1 Corinthians 6:10, Galatians 5:21)
- the verbally abusive (1 Corinthians 6:10)
- swindlers/extortionists (1 Corinthians 6:10)
- those who hate or cause dissentions or factions (Galatians 5:20)
- the impure and depraved (Galatians 5:19)
- those who commit acts of hostility, strife, or outbursts of anger (Galatians 5:20)
- revilers (Galatians 5:21)

New Jerusalem

Section reference: Revelation 21:9-22:5.

Like the millennial Jerusalem, new Jerusalem is near a great and high mountain. It descends from heaven as a gift from God.

© Pat Marvenko Smith - www.revelationillustrated.com

Starting with its size, everything about this city is incomprehensible. Its dimensions form a cube of approximately 1400 miles per side. The base of this city exceeds the boundaries of the United States. For example, placing one corner at Jacksonville, Florida, the city would extend west almost to El Paso, Texas and north over 500 miles into Canada. Its height is amazing, as it stands 1400 miles from base to top, dwarfing anything ever created by man. Key features of new Jerusalem include:

- adorned as a bride for her husband (Revelation 21:2)
- is the tabernacle of God (Revelation 21:3)
- near a great and high mountain (Revelation 21:10)

- a great city (Revelation 21:10)

- a holy city (Revelation 21:10)

- descended from heaven (Revelation 21:10)

- has the glory of God, its chief resident (Revelation 21:11)

- has the glorious light of God (Revelation 21:11, 23, 22:5)

- has a great, high (~216 feet) wall made of jasper (Revelation 21:12, 17, 18)

- four sides with one facing each compass point (Revelation 21:13)

- has twelve gates, one for each of the twelve tribes (see Revelation 7):
  - the name of a tribe of Israel on each gate (Revelation 21:12), without mentioning which tribe is omitted
  - an angel at each gate (Revelation 21:12)
  - four sets of three gates (Revelation 21:13)
  - three gates on each wall (Revelation 21:13)
  - gates made of pearls (Revelation 21:21)
  - never to be shut (Revelation 21:25)

- has twelve foundations (Revelation 21:14):
  - an apostle's name on each foundation (Revelation 21:14)
  - decorated with different stones: jasper, sapphire, chalcedony (agate), emerald, sardonyx (onyx), sardius (carnelian), chrysolyte, beryl, topaz, chrysoprasus, jacinth, and amethyst (Revelation 21:19-20)

- the wall and city are made of pure gold like glass (Revelation 21:18)

- streets of pure gold like glass (Revelation 21:21)

- has no temple: God the Father and the Lamb are its temple (Revelation 21:22)

- has no need of the sun or moon (Revelation 21:23)

- the nations are made up of those who have been saved through the ages, and they will walk in its light (Revelation 21:24)
- kings of the earth bring the honor and glory of their nations into new Jerusalem (Revelation 21:24, 26)

This city's gold has two properties not commonly associated with gold today: transparency and strength. Gold, as we know it, softens and weakens, as it is more highly refined. Only through the introduction of other metals does gold gain strength, but this reduces its purity. Today's most highly refined gold still contains many impurities and does not exhibit either the strength or transparency found in new Jerusalem's gold. What gives new Jerusalem's gold its transparency and at the same time enough strength to create a massive structure encompassing over three billion cubic miles designed to literally last forever? Some have suggested changes to the gold's structure (e.g., nanotube technology or some advanced variant). Perhaps there is a simpler reason suggested by the text. This gold is perfectly pure, not highly refined. It may be possible that without all its impurities gold would exhibit both transparency and great strength. If this is the case, what does this say about even the smallest impurities in people's lives? These impurities (sin) weaken people and prevent them from being the transparent, powerful beacons of light God intended.

Another key feature of the city, its gates, are at the same time amazing and incomprehensible. Each comes from a single pearl, but pearls are only produced through the suffering of oysters, and John provides no insights how such massive pearls were created. On the other hand, they constantly remind those entering the city's gates of the sacrifices and suffering Jesus went through on their behalf. Interestingly, Jews have traditionally considered pearls inferior stones, so it had to astonish them when Jesus gave them the parable of the pearl of great price, but this parable conveyed God's love for Gentiles in general and the church specifically (Matthew 13:45-46). So these gates also represent the church while at the same time honor Israel with the name of one tribe on each gate. Through their composition and names, these gates stand as eternal symbols of the new unity between Jews and Christians. The fact these gates never close emphasizes the eternal state of peace and rest pervading this time. Never will these gates close to ward off enemies and protect the city's inhabitants (as was so common in the Old Testament).

The city's light source is another striking feature of this city. Without the aid of the sun or moon, light radiating from God fills the city's every room, corner, and crevice. How is this possible? It may be a special characteristic of God's light or it may be a special property of new Jerusalem's gold. Perhaps the gold's transparency channels God's light everywhere throughout the city. Regardless, since God is the city's light and he does not change, this is a city without darkness and nights (though the new earth appears to continue to have nighttime). Since the light never goes out, this is truly a twenty-four hour city that never shuts down. Today, this is characteristic of "sin" cities (e.g., Las Vegas); however, in eternity, it is a defining characteristic of this perfect, righteous city.

Its inhabitants and visitors include not only the righteous of all ages but also God in all his glory. In contrast to Jesus' millennial reign, God the Father is no longer separated from his people but lives and reigns with them in new Jerusalem. Also in contrast to Jesus' millennial reign, there are two thrones and two monarchs (God the Father and God the Son) instead of a single throne, and neither resides in a temple because they are the temples for this city. Unlike old Jerusalem, new Jerusalem is for the Lamb's bride, not the Jews. Presumably, the Jews are part of the city's regular guests, which includes all the nations and kings on the new earth. While the Bible gives no details nor insights into the represented nations, their selection process, their rulers, or land allocation, it is probably safe to assume they include all other believers throughout the ages, including those living in the four millennia preceding Jesus' birth and the millennia of Jesus' reign.

While these passages have given many insights into new

Jerusalem, they provide few clues into the new earth. They do indicate that the new earth has nations with rulers and both a sun and moon. No further descriptions of it, including size, are provided, but if a single city is the size and splendor of new Jerusalem, what must the rest of creation be like? First Corinthians 2:9 sums up the answers to these questions best: God's new creation will be glorious beyond comprehension or imagination. Since it is free from thieves and vandals, God creates priceless, beautiful structures without concerns of defacement. The righteous probably never run out things to discover and learn about God's creation even though they explore it for all eternity.

The description of new Jerusalem ends the same way the Bible started, with the gift only God can give: the gift of life. Now eternal life flows freely, directly from God's throne as a river of life. This river is pure, clear as crystal, undefiled, uncontaminated, unpolluted, and flows down the middle of the main street leading to the throne of God.

The river's crystal nature speaks of its purity and tranquility. As it flows, it feeds the tree of life, which grows on both of its banks. As multiple trees lined the millennial river, it is probable many trees of life line the banks of the river of life. The tree of life produces twelve kinds of fruit and produces its fruit monthly, not annually. If it produces a different type of fruit each month, then the tree marks the passage of both months and years. (Both of these measures of time appear to remain in use into eternity.) Its leaves are medicinal, providing healing of nations. It is ironic that the fruit of the tree of life, the water of life, and the leaves of the tree of life are readily available at a time when there is no apparent need.

Twice in Revelation 22, John sees the throne as a dual throne for both God the Father and the Lamb. Jesus has brought all things into God's subjugation and now shares the throne with God the Father. God's servants, identified by God's name on their foreheads, now serve him at his throne without veils, either a cloth veil (as in the Old Testament tabernacle and temple) or the veil of distance and space separating heaven and earth.

In new Jerusalem, there are no more curses of any kind, including the original curse of death in Genesis 3:16-19. During the millennial reign, the original curse of death was still present but in the new creations, even it is removed. Before God removes it, humanity will have suffered its effects for seven thousand years.

The Bible's prophecies end here, with the righteous contently living on the new earth and in new Jerusalem with the Father and the Son (and, by implication, the Holy Spirit). They spend eternity fellowshipping with and worshipping God while many serve forever as kings. The Bible provides few details of the new earth, but the unfathomable, incomprehensible descriptions of new Jerusalem suggest the new earth will be equally magnificent. New Jerusalem's construction is from materials and techniques unmatchable by people. Just outside the city, the wicked suffer in total darkness for all eternity in full sight of those entering and leaving the city.

Epilogue

Section reference: Revelation 22:6-21.

After concluding its brief description of eternity, Revelation now reaches its concluding remarks. John has taken his readers through an amazing journey showing the early church age; the rapture; God's redemption of the earth; Jesus' coronation; the valley of decision; the subjugation judgments; the Lamb's wedding and marriage feast; Jesus' return; the establishment of the millennial kingdom; the final rebellion; the destruction of the current creation; the final judgments; and finally, eternity. Along the way, God poured out numerous judgments on the earth while many people foolishly chose the leadership of Satan's unholy trinity. Even after the millennial reign, many people again foolishly chose to blindly follow Satan. Revelation now ends this journey with its final instructions and blessings.

Several speakers participate in this passage, starting with one of the angels who held one of the seven vials. The other speakers include John, Jesus, the Spirit of God, and the church. Transitions between speakers often occur without warning, forcing the speaker's identities to be ascertained solely on the message's content. This dilemma becomes obvious as one compares various commentaries and notices how often they disagree, concerning which speaker makes each statement. Some statements are affected by which speaker utters them, so careful analysis is important.

The epilogue starts with the angel who previously held one of the vial judgments finishing his testimony, explaining he was sent by God to show his servants the future ("things which must shortly be done"). God gives these true and faithful "sayings" to eliminate doubts whether God orchestrated these events (Amos 3:7).

Three times in the letters to the churches and three times in the epilogue, Jesus speaks of his imminent return. These promises have caused much confusion from the days of John until now because imminent means different things to people and God. James 4:14 demonstrates these disparities as a human lifetime is but an instant for God. Something imminent for God may still be several generations away for people on earth. This does not compromise the promises of the prophets, nor does it change God's chosen times for the fulfillment of his prophecies.

God again promises special blessings to those keeping the sayings of the prophecy of this book. John's fellow servants and prophets are among those Revelation lists as blessed. How have they kept them? These sayings teach of rewards for the righteous and punishments for the wicked. The wicked view the judgments and punishments as foolishness; they ignore the warnings of the book. The righteous believe Jesus' testimonies, fear God, and turn away from sin and, by so doing, keep Revelation's sayings.

For the third time, John falls down at someone's feet (Revelation 1:17, 19:10). The first time, he fell down in fear at Jesus' feet. The next two times, he mistakenly tries to worship a fellow servant, who he describes as an angel. Perhaps, this description provides a glimmer of insight to the glory of the righteous' immortal bodies.

John receives instructions to leave Revelation unsealed because the time is close. This contrasts with the book of Daniel, where Daniel was to leave his book sealed. The book of Daniel remained a mystery for several millennia after its completion and was the last Bible book to have commentaries covering it. In comparison, the book of Revelation has been an open book. From the time of its completion, it has warned and encouraged Christians.

Here, Jesus identifies himself with several titles, including two new ones:

- I Am
- Alpha and Omega
- the Beginning and the End
- the First and the Last
- the Root and the Offspring of David (new)
- the Bright and Morning Star (new)

In the first of the two new titles, he shows his qualification to sit on the throne because he descends from the lineage of David. At the same time, he is the root (the beginning) and the offspring (the end). The next new title, the Bright and Morning Star, draws primarily from two passages. The first is the blessing Balaam pronounced on Israel in Numbers 24:17, where he foretells a star coming out of Jacob (a Jew) and ruling the entire land of Israel. Second Peter 1:19 shows the Daystar, Jesus, rising in people's hearts. In Revelation 3:20, he is shown knocking on the doors of peoples' hearts, hoping to join them in an intimate dinner. As the Daystar, he is the ruler who has risen in people's hearts.

The Spirit of God and the bride call out to people, "Come. And let him that heareth say, 'Come.' And let him that is athirst come. And whosoever will, let him take the water of life freely," (Revelation 22:17). This is the salvation invitation for people to receive the water of life and its eternal life. Today, it is the Spirit of God and the church pleading with people to receive the gift of life. Until the rapture, it is their responsibility to plead with the unsaved of the world to repent as they preach a message of salvation by grace. This message is summarized in the well-known "Roman's road":

As it is written, There is none righteous, no, not one.

Romans 3:10

For all have sinned, and come short of the glory of God.

Romans 3:23

Wherefore, as by one man sin entered into the world, and death by sin; and so death passed upon all men, for that all have sinned.

Romans 5:12

For the wages of sin is death; but the gift of God is eternal life through Jesus Christ our Lord.

Romans 6:23

But God commendeth his love toward us, in that, while we were yet sinners, Christ died for us.

Romans 5:8

That if thou shalt confess with thy mouth the Lord Jesus, and shalt believe in thine heart that God hath raised him from the dead, thou shalt be saved.

Romans 10:9

For whosoever shall call upon the name of the Lord shall be saved.

Romans 10:13

These verses teach that salvation is a freely accepted gift while death and damnation are payments already earned. People receive this gift by believing in their heart and confessing with their mouth that God raised Jesus from the dead. People must confess Jesus before others for Jesus to confess them before his Father in heaven, and everyone denying Jesus will likewise be denied by him (Matthew 10:32-33). Everyone ashamed of Jesus will likewise find him ashamed of them (Mark 8:38). Only through the acceptance of this gift can people get eternal life and stand unashamed and unafraid before Jesus' judgment seat.

Revelation concludes with a warning against adding to, modifying, or subtracting from its contents. Anyone adding to it will have the plagues, the lake of fire, added to them. Anyone taking away from it will have their name removed from the book of life and consequently, will receive the lake of fire.

In Revelation's last, concluding section, God emphasizes several key points, including:

- the testimony of the prophets has been sent by God
- the testimony is faithful and true
- the prophecies will occur shortly
- Jesus will return soon
- blessings are promised for those who observe the sayings of the prophecies of the book
- worship God and no one else
- Revelation will remain an open, understandable book
- Jesus brings rewards, both for the righteous and wicked
- Jesus is God
- the tree of life and access to new Jerusalem will be given to the righteous
- the lake of fire is promised to the wicked
- the call to salvation is extended throughout the world

The conclusion of the book of Revelation brings down the curtain on the prophetic timeline. It is an amazing story containing seven distinct phases: preparation, redemption, coronation, decision, subjugation, dominion, and perfection. The preparation phase brought the church age, Israel's second fall, and Israel's rebirth. The church age started with the church of the apostles: Ephesus. The following two thousand years saw the church develop through several different stages: the persecuted church of Smyrna, the faithful but tolerant church of Pergamos, the loving but doctrinally unsound church of Thyatira, the dead church of Sardis, the loving and effective church of Philadelphia, and concluded with the lukewarm church of Laodicea. Throughout the church age, God's judgment fell heavily on Israel as he dispersed the Jews to all parts of the earth and allowed people to persecute them wherever they went. The church age also saw the beginnings of God's mercy toward Israel as he restored the valley of dry bones and created a great army in preparation for the start of Daniel's seventieth week. The preparation phase concluded with the rapture, the crown and raiment judgments, a magnificent worship scene in heaven, a search for one worthy to open the sealed title deed to earth, and heavenly worship.

The next four phases all occurred within Daniel's seventieth week. The first half of this week brought the redemption and coronation phases while the second half brought the decision and subjugation phases. The first of these phases, redemption, saw Jesus' redemption of the earth as he reclaimed his rightful property, the earth, by breaking the title deed's seals. The breaking of the first four seals brought the four horsemen of the apocalypse: imitation, war, famine, and Death. The imitation horseman was the son of perdition, also known as the antichrist, the little horn, and the dangerous beast that rises out of the sea of humanity. At the same time, God's two witnesses prophesied against the antichrist and testified of God's plan of redemption (judgment) and Jesus' approaching coronation. Death harvested the work of all four horsemen. Through his efforts, a quarter of the world's population perished, but his work only affected the wicked. The fifth seal introduced the first fruits of the harvest of the tribulation's righteous. Unlike the church age saints, these saints cried for vengeance and set the tone for the remainder of the seven-year tribulation. God resurrected the full-tribulation saints and gave them their garment rewards. The sixth seal brought a devastating invasion of Israel by a broad coalition of countries attempting to seize her wealth. The war ended quickly in Israel's favor, but its aftereffects lingered throughout the remainder of the seven-year tribulation. These included Israel's cleansing of the battlefields (seven months); the burning of the weapons for fuel (seven years); the oilfields of Edom set ablaze (forever); the acquisition of the invader's wealth; and the crippling of many of the war's participants, both friend and foe alike. Before Jesus broke the last seal, angels put God's seal on 144,000 specially selected men from twelve tribes of Israel. The last seal introduced the next prophetic phase: coronation.

The coronation phase consisted of seven trumpet judgments divided into two groups: the "minor" first four and the three great woes. The first four trumpets brought rains of hail and fire mingled with blood that destroyed a third of all vegetation, a great mountain that destroyed a third of the ships and turned a third of the seas into blood, a great star turned a third of the fresh waters into wormwood and killed many, and sunlight and moonlight darkened by a third. The fifth trumpet, the first woe, released angry legions of fallen angels incarcerated in the bottomless pit for untold millennia. Except for the 144,000 possessing God's seal, they unmercifully tormented people for five months to the point people sought the relief of death, but even this God denied them. The sixth trumpet, the second woe, released four bound angels who led a 200-million-man army to destroy a third of the world's population (a quarter of the population preceding the tribulation's onset). The time between the last two trumpets was very active, as God checked for the first of three times to see if the punishments must continue, and then God's mighty angel came to earth and vowed to quickly coronate Jesus.

The coronation phase continued into the midtribulation, as the Gentiles started trampling Jerusalem and the temple's courtyard. This continued for the duration of the great tribulation. Next, the antichrist killed the two witnesses who he left lying in the streets for three and a half days while people celebrated and gave each other gifts. Then, God resurrected and called the two witnesses to heaven as people watched in shock and horror. Immediately after, an earthquake struck Jerusalem and destroyed 10 percent of the city and killed seven thousand of its inhabitants. When the seventh trumpet sounded, the mighty angel fulfilled his oath and crowned Jesus king in heaven while heaven's occupants rejoiced uncontrollably. After the saints received their riches reward, wise Jews fled to a wilderness place prepared for them. While they fled, Satan and his legions attacked God's hosts in heaven to prevent Jesus' assumption of power. Michael and his angels defeated and exiled them to earth, where they remained for the rest of the great tribulation. This started the last trumpet's woe, marked the start of the great tribulation, and began the decision phase of the timeline. Satan's arrival on earth increased the urgency of the Jew's fleeing. In his anger, Satan attempted to destroy the Jews in the wilderness, but God responded by sealing the place and dissipating the floodwaters.

The great tribulation opened with the antichrist's ascension to power and the introduction of the last member of the unholy trinity: the false prophet. Each member of this alliance shared all power and single-mindedly led people in rebellion against God. One of the antichrist's first actions upon assuming power was the invasion of Egypt for its wealth. Later, members of his ruling alliance stopped him in his second Egyptian invasion. During this time, the false prophet started his work. He called fire from heaven, erected an image of the beast (antichrist), gave life to the image, enacted laws requiring its worship, and created an oppressive monetary system (the mark of the beast) to control people's financial transactions. The erection of the image of the beast was Daniel's abomination of desolation, and wise Jews living outside the sealed place fled to the mountains. The image of the beast, its worship, and the beast's mark formed the basis of the decision phase of the timeline. Two of three angels declared to everyone on earth their options: serve God or Satan (the dragon and beast). The second angel declared God's judgment on Babylon and her final fall. While people's decisions continued throughout the great tribulation, the decision phase of the narrative ended with the wheat and tare harvest followed by an angel tossing the tares into God's winepress of wrath. People's moment of truth had come; no longer could they defer their decisions concerning God. Rejection of Satan and the beast carried an almost certain death sentence while rejection of God carried the certainty of the lake of fire's second death.

The subjugation phase opened with the great tribulation saints praising God in heaven and the introduction of the seven vials containing God's final judgments. These vials toppled the vast majority of opposition to Jesus' assumption of power. The first five vial judgments brought horrendous sores on those possessing the mark of the beast, all fresh and saltwater turned into blood, scorching sunlight, and painful darkness over the antichrist's seat (throne) and kingdom (power base). After angels poured the fourth and fifth vials, God checked for two last times to determine whether people had repented and thus could avoid the rest of the judgments. When the angel poured the sixth vial, the world's fate was sealed and the remaining judgments would run their course. Three demonic spirits now assembled all armies of the world against Jerusalem. Again, wise Jews living outside the protective confines of the sealed place fled to the mountains. The last vial (God's last judgment) brought the greatest earthquake ever, huge hail, and the battle of Armageddon. As the battle of Armageddon raged, God turned his attention to Mystery Babylon by first introducing and then destroying her. Her destruction came at the hands of her former lovers, and they completed it in a single hour. As she smoldered, people on earth mourned while heaven's occupants rejoiced and prepared for Jesus' wedding and its subsequent grand supper. When the celebrations wound down, Jesus and his armies prepared for war. It was finally time to see Jesus as King of kings and for him to assert his authority as the earth's rightful king. As Jesus returned, an angel called the wild beasts of the earth to God's supper. The beast, the kings of the earth, and their armies turned to fight Jesus and his armies. Jesus returned to Mount Olivet, and as he touched down, an earthquake formed a new valley used by God to protect the remaining unprotected Jews. Jesus threw the beast and the false prophet into the bottomless pit before defeating the world's armies in God's winepress, the valley of Jehoshaphat (Megiddo). Next, an angel threw Satan into the bottomless pit and Jesus rescued the Jews from the wilderness.

The dominion phase, the time of Jesus' millennial reign, started with a transition phase, which included the final gathering of the Jews, their judgments, the Gentile's judgments, the nation's judgments, and the division of governmental duties (the last of the church's rewards). Jesus' reign marked a thousand rather uneventful but boundlessly prosperous years, as God had almost eliminated sin along with most of its rotting effects. During this time, Jesus built the final temple from which he ruled. After the thousand years, God released Satan from the bottomless pit and Satan tempted people to rebel against God. Unbelievably, people listened to him and rebelled under the leadership of Gog and Magog. Fire from heaven destroyed the rebels as they camped outside Jerusalem, preparing to attack.

The dominion phase ended with the final judgments, which purged and eliminated all sin and its burdens, God's curses. The judgments started with God putting Satan and his fallen angels into the lake of fire. Next came the destruction of the existing heavens and earth through the purifying effects of fire followed by the great white throne judgments. First, Jesus resurrected and judged righteous people who died after the close of the first resurrection. Next, the wicked of all ages were resurrected, judged, and cast into the lake of fire. When the judgments were complete, God gave the saints the gifts of the new creations: new earth, new heaven, and new Jerusalem. These gifts, completely unaffected by sin, were glorious beyond description. New Jerusalem contained the tree of life and the water of life and appropriately, the Bible ends with the restoration of the gift of life, which was lost in the garden of Eden.

The analysis and description of the prophetic timeline proffered in this book contained many new insights, theories, and interpretations of prophetic passages. Each was driven not by the desire for change but by the need for scriptural consistency, the discovery process, and the push to resolve open issues in existing theories. The theories were carefully evaluated, tested, modified, and retested. Through this process, more theories were rejected than accepted, and even the accepted theories were regularly refined. Over time, this refinement process will continue as new theories are added and existing theories are modified or rejected. In short, the interpretation of prophecy is a living process that continually witnesses change. This flies in the face of the study of basic Biblical doctrines, which are generally considered immutable. Changes to basic tenants of the faith are usually a sign of the improper application of hermeneutics. Over time, new, richer insights into basic doctrine may appear, but these insights should not contradict fundamental doctrines.

This sound rule of interpretation for fundamental doctrine often creates a lot of inertia against new interpretational ideas of any sort. While good for basic doctrinal studies, this rule creates unnecessary resistance to prophetic studies. By failing to properly recognize the sealed nature of the book of Daniel and, by extension, all prophecy, this rule tends to limit free and honest discourse in the search for prophecies' truths. As an example, both the pretribulation rapture and Jesus' physical millennial reign on earth are resisted by some based on their assertions that historically numerous scholars and theologians of prior generations have held contrary positions. They view both the pretribulation rapture and Jesus' physical millennial reign on earth as new and therefore suspect and invalid. By placing disproportionate credence on prior opinions, they discount what should be basis of prophetic interpretations: the proper application of the rules of hermeneutics.

The prophecies surrounding Jesus' first coming further illustrate the challenges facing the student of prophecy. Prior to their fulfillment, scholars only partially understood the numerous prophecies of Jesus' first coming. They understood the place of his birth but expected him to immediately overthrow Rome and establish his throne (Matthew 2:5). When he did not, they rejected him. Today, studies of the numerous prophecies of Jesus' first coming fill many books. Even so, many Jews still do not understand Jesus' fulfillments of these prophecies or the mysteries of his two appearances on earth. This should not be surprising considering the prophecies baffled Jesus' disciples, even with his patient tutelage.

It seems very likely that the closer Jesus' return comes, the more rapidly the Bible will yield its end-time secrets. The next several years promise to be very exciting for prophetic studies, with new theories constantly proposed and debated. It is my sincere hope and prayer that you have been blessed by the results of this labor of love. Hopefully, this book will encourage your love for God's Word and its prophecies in this exciting prophetic period. May God bless you as you study his Word.

Bibliography

Barnes, Albert. *Barnes' Notes On The New Testament.* Cedar Rapids, Iowa: Parsons Technology, Inc., 1999.

Bullinger, E. W., D.D. *Number in Scripture.* Grand Rapids, Michigan: Kregel Publications, 1981.

Butler, Trent C., Ph.D, Marsha A. Ellis Smith, Ph.D., Forrest W. Jackson, D. Min., Phil Logan, Ph.D., and Chris Church, Ph.D. eds. *Holman Bible Dictionary.* Holman Bible Publishers, 1991.

Combs, Jim. *Rainbows from Revelation.* Springfield, Missouri: Tribune Publishers, 1994.

Clarke, Adam, LL.D., F.S.A., etc. *Adam Clarke's Commentary On The Old Testament.* Cedar Rapids, Iowa: Parsons Technology, Inc., 1999.

Dockery, David S., general editor. *Holman Bible Handbook.* Nashville, Tennessee: Holman Bible Publishers, 1992.

Duck, Daymond R. *Revelation: God's Word for the Biblical-inept.* Ed. Larry Richards. Lancaster, Pennsylvania: Starburst, Inc., 1998.

Edersheim, Alfred, D.D., Ph.D. *Sketches of Jewish Social Life.* Grand Rapids, Michigan: Wm. B. Eerdmans Publishing Company, 1980.

Fox, Robin Lane. *The Search for Alexander.* Little, Brown and Company, 1980.

Fruchtenbaum, Arnold G. *The Footsteps of the Messiah.* Tustin, California: Ariel Ministries, 2004.

Henry, Matthew. *Matthew Henry's Commentary On the Old Testament.* Omaha, Nebraska: Quickverse, a Division Of Findex.Com, Inc., 2000.

Hindson, Ed and Lee Fredrickson. *Future Wave.* Eugene, Oregon: Harvest House Publishers, 2001.

Jeremiah, David and C.C. Carlson. *Escape the Coming Night.* Word Publishing, 1997.

Jeremiah, David and C.C. Carlson. *The Handwriting on the Wall.* Word Publishing, 1992.

Josephus, Flavius. *The Works Of Josephus.* Hiawatha, Iowa: Parsons Technology, Inc., 1998.

LaHaye, Tim and Ed Hinson, eds. *The Popular Encyclopedia of Bible Prophecy.* Eugene, Oregon: Harvest House Publishers, 2004.

Nave's Topical Bible. Cedar Rapids, Iowa: Parsons Technology, Inc., 1998.

Roth, Cecil. *A History of the Jews.* New York: Schocken Books, 1989.

Strong, James. *Strong's Hebrew And Greek Dictionaries.* Omaha, Nebraska: Quickverse, a Division Of Findex.Com, Inc., 2003.

Van Impe, Jack. *Revelation Revealed.* Troy, Michigan: Jack Van Impe Ministries, 1996.

Wood, Leon. *A Survey of Israel's History.* Grand Rapids, Michigan. Academie Books, Zondervan Publishing House, 1970.

Parsons Bible Dictionary. Cedar Rapids, Iowa: Parsons Technology, Inc., 1998.

Endnotes

Preface

1   This rule sometimes fractures Christians along translation lines. As with any translated literature, heavier weighting must be given the original language and earliest authoritative texts.

2   The number of days equals the number of times one is to forgive his brother (Mathew 18:22). Perhaps, this shows God's forgiveness of humanity.

Time Line Overview

1   The use of the same name to describe both the full seven-year period and only the first three and a half years does cause confusion. This book uses full tribulation, or seven-year tribulation, to refer the full seven years and tribulation to refer to only the first half.

2   The "gap theory" holds this occurred between Genesis 1:1 and Genesis 1:2.

The Church Age (Preparation)

1   Isaiah 11:2 includes the spirit of: the Lord; wisdom, understanding, counsel, might, knowledge, and the fear of the Lord.

2   As quoted in "Revelation: God's Word for the Biblical-Inept."

Israel during the Church Age (Preparation)

1 See "Charting the End Times" and "The Footsteps of the Messiah."

2 The Old Testament predominantly uses mishkan (Strong's H4908) and ohel (Strong's H168). Cukkah (Strong's H5521), cok (Strong's H5520), sok (Strong's H7900), and cikkuth (Strong's H5522) are also used but far less frequently than the first two.

The Rapture

1 This passage's book is biblion (Strong's G975) which means a roll, bill, book, scroll, or writing.

The Tribulation (Redemption and Coronation)

1 See "The Footsteps of the Messiah" for an argument in favor of a Gentile antichrist.

2 See "The Footsteps of the Messiah" for an alternate view that this is a demonic army.

3 Other Revelation words for book are biblion (Strong's G975) and biblos (Strong's G976).

The Midtribulation (Coronation)

1 See "The Footsteps of the Messiah."

The Great Tribulation (Decision and Subjugation)

1 This passage touches on a confusing point of end-time prophecy. Daniel 7:13-14 and other passages, such as Psalm 110:1, imply Jesus passively watches throughout the tribulation while other passages, most notably Revelation 19 and Isaiah 63, show Jesus claiming the throne himself. These

apparently contradictory accounts probably speak of the Father's actions during the full tribulation until the earth is sufficiently subdued that resistance can be broken in a single battle fought by Jesus.

2　The beast's sea is thalassa, Strong's G2281, and Mystery Babylon's waters is hudor, Strong's G5204.

3　Egypt is a type of the non-Jewish/non-Spiritual world, so these prophecies could extend to the world in general.

4　This story also gives insights into God's protection of Israel over the millennia. Three times (three Jews) Israel has been a nation over the course of seven millennia (fire seven times hotter). Despite the nation's sin, God has protected her through (not from) the world's fiery judgments.

5　This same nuance has created confusion about where the nails went into Jesus.

6　This must occur after Jesus' return since he does not set foot on the earth again until his return (Revelation 19).

7　Diadema crown is used in the New Testament and suggests the dragon steals it, gives it to the beast, and God seizes it for Jesus.

8　These verses are confusing in light of the presence of the 144,000. They probably speak of Israel's condition in total.

9　Wool, produced by sheep (righteous people), was specifically excluded from the garments of priests. This demonstrates their good works are still tainted by sin.

10　See "The Footsteps of the Messiah" for an alternative view.

11　If this is the angel of the Lord, then each personage of the Holy Trinity hosts a different feast during this period: the marriage supper (the Father), God's supper (the Holy Spirit), and the King's feast (Jesus).

12 It is possible some or all of the fallen angels might be put into the lake of fire at this time, but the stronger argument seems to have them entering with Satan after Jesus' millennial reign.

The Millennial Reign (Dominion)

1 Josephus recorded a similar situation when Archelaus was crowned king over Israel in Rome. A key difference is Archelaus was under Rome's authority.

2 There is no consensus whether these measurements are in cubits or reeds. Reeds are approximately seven times larger (around 10 ½ feet) and their distances are shown bracketed after the cubits measurements.

3 See "The Footsteps of the Messiah."

4 Based on Ezekiel 34:24 and 37:25, many believe this to be David. However, Ezekiel 44-48 suggest this is a nonresurrected man as he makes sacrifices for his sin and has specific rules governing the rights of succession.

The Final Judgements

1 This assumes Elijah is one of Revelation 11's two witnesses and ignores the debate over whether John died (John 21:22-23).

2 Revelation 21:27 and Revelation 13:8 both refer to the Lamb's book of life. Some believe this is different from the book of life in Revelation 20.

listen|imagine|view|experience

AUDIO BOOK DOWNLOAD INCLUDED WITH THIS BOOK!

In your hands you hold a complete digital entertainment package. In addition to the paper version, you receive a free download of the audio version of this book. Simply use the code listed below when visiting our website. Once downloaded to your computer, you can listen to the book through your computer's speakers, burn it to an audio CD or save the file to your portable music device (such as Apple's popular iPod) and listen on the go!

How to get your free audio book digital download:

1. Visit www.tatepublishing.com and click on the e|LIVE logo on the home page.
2. Enter the following coupon code:
   fd54-7f0e-37e4-1e5c-99be-b9a8-563e-d5f2
3. Download the audio book from your e|LIVE digital locker and begin enjoying your new digital entertainment package today!